Companions
for the
Soul

❧ ❧

*For Abigail Townsend Hudson,
our littlest companion on the journey—
may you always stay close
to the heart of
God*

Companions for the Soul

A yearlong journey of miracles,
prayers, and epiphanies

366 classic Christian readings
compiled by

Robert R. Hudson
Shelley Townsend-Hudson

ZondervanPublishingHouse
Grand Rapids, Michigan

A Division of HarperCollins*Publishers*

Companions for the Soul
Copyright © 1995 by Bob Hudson and Shelley Townsend-Hudson

Requests for information should be addressed to:

Zondervan Publishing House
Grand Rapids, Michigan 49530

Library of Congress Cataloging-in-Publication Data

Hudson, Bob, 1953 –
     Companions for the soul : A yearlong journey of miracles, prayers, and epiphanies /
Robert R. Hudson and Shelley Townsend-Hudson.
          p.   cm.
     Includes index.
     ISBN: 0-310-49791-4 (alk. paper)
     1. Meditations.   2. Devotional calendars.   I. Townsend-Hudson, Shelley, 1954–
II. Title.
     BV4810.H74   1995
     242'.2—dc20   95-7661
                                                                                                          CIP

This edition is printed on acid-free paper and meets the American National Standards Institute Z39.48 standard.

To make reading easier, grammar, spelling, punctuation, syntax, and word choice have been modernized without annotation in many of these readings. Where the modernization is extensive or where a passage was largely rewritten for clarity, the reading is referred to as *adapted*. Except in poetry and quotations from the Bible, *thee, thou, thine,* etc., have been rendered as *you* and *your, yours,* etc., and gender-specific language has generally been replaced with non-gender-specific. All unattributed translations are by the compilers. Scripture references, unless otherwise noted, are from the King James Version or paraphrased by the authors or translators. A full list of permissions for the copyrighted material can be found at the end of the book.

Interior design by Sherri L. Hoffman
Edited by Lori J. Walburg

Printed in the United States of America

---

95 96 97 98 99 00 / ❖ DC / 10 9 8 7 6 5 4 3 2 1

Preface

≈§ §≈

Saints come in all stripes. Some saw visions where others saw nothing but darkness. Some heard angels singing; others only silence. While some journeyed to distant lands, others meditated in lonely desert huts. While some prayed on the rooftops, others prayed in the kitchens below. As a result, the variety of their written expression—in story, song, prayer, poem, meditation—is greater than any individual or group or nation; it transcends doctrine and dogma; it may be as vast, in fact, as all humankind. To sample that breathtaking variety of spiritual literary expression is the purpose of this book.

Historically, many of these writers were at odds with each other. That is one reason this book links a literary event with each day of the year: because it arbitrarily forces writers to stand shoulder to shoulder who, in life, would probably have refused such proximity. But Jesus made no such refusals. He stood shoulder to shoulder with each of them—which is precisely what these writers have in common. Each one of them found it wondrous beyond words that the "wild God of the universe," in Gary Wills' phrase, would confine himself to time and space, become human, die, and live again for their sakes—and for ours.

The fact that Christ should appear differently to different eyes only testifies to the limits of our vision—like the elephant in the fable of the three blind men. The one who held the tail thought the elephant was a rope. Another, touching the leg, claimed the elephant was a tree. The third, as he stroked the elephant's side, declared it to be a wall. In 1 Corinthians, Paul says, "Now we see but a poor reflection as in a mirror." Like the blind men, we know only in part. But by gathering all the pieces together, we might catch a glimpse of the larger reality of which they are a part.

In reading this book, expect to encounter the comfortable and the uncomfortable alike. Contemplate your own experience of Christ as you read, and keep a pen and paper at hand to jot down your own miracles and prayers and epiphanies. Have a Bible nearby to look up any stray references. Most of all, pray that God might use these companions for the soul to heighten your own awareness of his love and presence surrounding you, and to deepen your own experience of him day by day.

A mighty host surrounds me in my library. . . . They speak to me; they kindle the fires of my imagination; they quicken my faith, humble my pride, rebuke my wrong-doing and wrong-thinking, warn me against sin, and point my soul to the living Christ. I find tombs with angels, deserts with fountains, gardens with Saviors, prisons with praise, and crosses with crowns. Above the roar of the tempest, the flap of the split sails, the creak of the breaking timbers, and the cry of the endangered men, I hear Jesus say, "Peace, be still."

—W. W. Staley (see entry for July 21)

January

A stylite perched on his pillar, praying for the
sins of the world and his own (see January 5).
Illustration from Hone's *Every Day Book*.

1624—German Lutheran mystic Jacob Boehme (1575–1624) was a largely uneducated shoemaker whose writings, though scorned by church authorities of the time, had a profound influence on such diverse people as John Milton, William Law, Isaac Newton, William Blake, and the early Quakers. On this day, against Boehme's wishes, a group of admirers published a collection of his treatises, The Way to Christ, *from which the following ecstatic prayer is taken,* "For Divine Action, Protection, and Providence"*—an appropriate prayer with which to begin the New Year. (See also February 9.)*

———————— ❧ ❧ ————————

To You, O living Fountain, do I raise my soul's desire, and through my Savior Jesus Christ's life within me do I call with my desire to You....

Bloom within me through the Vitality of Jesus Christ, and never allow my heart and desire to depart from You, so that I may produce praise as the proper fruit of Your Kingdom.

But since in this vale of tears, in this external earthly flesh and blood I swim in vanity; ... since with my external life I swim in the stars and in the four elements where my enemies both within and without wait for me—as well as temporal death, the destroyer of this vain life; therefore do I fly to You, O holy Vitality of God, because You have revealed yourself with gracious Love within our human nature through the holy name of Jesus and given Him as an internal Companion to us. Therefore do I implore You, permit His holy angels, who minister to Him, to minister also to our souls and to encamp themselves about us to protect us....

O great, incomprehensible God! You who are omnipotent! Be my Heaven, in which I may live with my new birth in Christ! Let my spirit be the lyre, harmony, and joy of the Holy Spirit; strike the chord of Your newborn image within me. Lead my harmony into Your divine Kingdom of Joy, into the great praise of God, into the wonders of Your glory and majesty, and into the communion of the holy angelic harmony. Build within me the Holy City of Zion, in which we, as Christ's children, shall live in one community—Christ within us! I yield myself completely to You! Do with me as You will! Amen!

—adapted from the translation of John Joseph Stoudt (1947)

1699—Thomas Traherne (c. 1636–74) was an English divine and poet, one of the so-called "metaphysical" poets, along with such notable writers as John Donne and George Herbert. On this day George Hickes (1642–1715), an English clergyman and editor of Traherne's posthumous volume of meditations, Thanksgivings, ordered twenty copies of that book from the publisher, explaining: "I have received great delight and benefit in reading of it: So I shall recommend it to persons of parts and pious inclinations, as I shall find opportunities. I wish all booksellers would employ the press so much for God's honor and the public good as you do."

⋅⋅⋅

The earth is the Lord's and the fullness thereof;
   the world and they that dwell therein (Psalm 24:1).
The heavens are the Lord's, but the earth has he given
   to the children of men. . . .
The woods and trees and fields and valleys you have subjected
   to the government and work of our hands; . . .
Oil and wine, perfumes and spices,
Wheat and rye, fruits and flowers,
You have given to us to delight our senses.
Apples, citrons, lemons, dates, and pomegranates,
   Figs, raisins, grapes, and melons,
   Plums, cherries, filberts, peaches,
Are all your riches; for which we praise and bless your name.
   Clouds and vapors glorify you by serving us.
   Springs and rivers praise your name,
   Being far more precious than gold and silver.
The day is yours, the night also is yours;
   you have prepared the light and the sun.
You have set all the borders of the earth:
   you have made summer and winter.
You appointed the moon for seasons;
   the sun knows his going down.
O Lord, how manifold are your works! In wisdom
   have you made them all; the earth is full of your riches. . . .
So glorious are your works that skies full of pearl,
   globes of gold, spheres of silver larger than the earth
   are dross and poverty in comparison to your treasures,
All of which you offer me to partake of.

—"Thanksgivings for the Glory of God's Works" from *Thanksgivings* (1699)

1309—On this day, the day before her death, Italian mystic Angela of Foligno (c. 1248–1309) told her friends, "It is impossible in death to lose that which has been impressed upon your heart in life." Angela was one of the earliest and most important Franciscan women, famous for her piety and for the beauty of her mystical experiences. The peace she experienced on her deathbed was due, in part, to a visionary assurance in which God showed her what it means for a believer to be the Bride of Christ—that we are deeply beloved by God. (See also August 15.)

━━━━━━━━━━ ⋖⧚ ⧛⋗ ━━━━━━━━━━

Christ Jesus, the Son of God, has now presented me to the Father, and these words have been spoken to me: "Oh, bride and fair one, oh, you who are beloved by Me with perfect love, truly I do not desire that you should come to Me with these exceeding great sufferings, but I desire that you should come with the utmost rejoicing and with joy unspeakable, even as it is seemly that the King should lead home the bride whom He has loved so long and clothed with the royal robe."

And He showed me the robe, just as a bridegroom shows it to the bride whom he has loved a long time. It was neither of purple nor of scarlet, nor of silk, nor of woven gold, but it was a certain marvelous light that clothed the soul. And then He showed to me the Bridegroom, the Eternal Word, so that now I do understand what thing the Word is and what it means—that is to say, this Word that for my sake was made Flesh. And the Word entered into me and touched me throughout and embraced me, saying, "Come, My love, My bride, beloved by Me with true delight—come, for all the saints await you with exceedingly great joy." And He said again to me, "I will not commit you into the charge of the blessed angels or other saints, so that they might lead you to Me, but I will come personally and fetch you and will raise you to Myself, for you have made yourself acceptable to Me and pleasing to My Majesty."

—from *The Book of Divine Consolation*,
adapted from Mary G. Steegman's translation

1758—Scholars believe that on or about this date, English poet Christopher Smart (1722–71) began the writing of his ecstatic, fragmentary free-verse poem Jubilate Agno *("Rejoice in the Lamb"), which has been called by some "the strangest poem in the English language." Left among his papers at the time of his death, it was not published until 1939. Smart was a poet, hymn writer, and writer of children's verse. Poverty and emotional instability caused him much hardship, and at the time of writing* Jubilate Agno, *he was confined to a private mental institution. The following whimsical excerpt, about his cat, Jeoffry, is probably the most often quoted passage from that mystifying but beautiful devotional work. (See also April 6.)*

————— ⋗⋖ —————

For I will consider my cat Jeoffry.
For he is the servant of the Living God duly and daily serving him.
For at the first glance of the glory of God in the east he worships him.
For is this done by wreathing his body seven times round with elegant
    quickness....
For having considered God and himself he will consider his neighbor.
For if he meets another cat he will kiss her in kindness.
For when he takes his prey he plays with it to give it chance.
For one mouse in seven escapes by his dallying.
For when his day's work is done his business more properly begins.
For he keeps the Lord's watch in the night against the adversary.
For he counteracts the powers of darkness by his electrical skin and
    glaring eyes.
For he counteracts the Devil, who is death, by brisking about the life.
For in his morning orisons he loves the sun and the sun loves him.
For he is of the tribe of Tiger....
For he has the subtlety and hissing of a serpent, which in goodness he
    suppresses.
For he will not do destruction, if he is well-fed, neither will he spit
    without provocation.
For he purrs in thankfulness when God tells him he's a good Cat.
For he is an instrument for the children to learn benevolence upon.
For every house is incomplete without him and a blessing is lacking in
    the spirit....
For he knows that God is his Savior.

Fifth century—The church has traditionally honored one of its most unusual saints on this day, Simeon the Stylite (c. 390–459). Stylites were hermits who lived atop high pillars, where they would pray for their own sins and the sins of the world; Simeon is said to have perched on his pillar for thirty-seven years. The following legend is about another early stylite named Basil. After spending many years on his pillar and thinking he was more devoted to God than any man living, he was told by an angel to learn yet one more thing from a common gooseherd. Basil met the man and found him ordinary except for the fact that he had adopted and raised a poor orphan girl.

———————— ✢ ————————

"Why did you do all this?" asked the hermit. "For what reward do you look?"

The gooseherd looked at him blankly for a moment; then his face brightened. "Surely," he said, "to see her as she goes on her way, a bright, brown little thing, with her clear hair and glad eyes, is a goodly reward. And a goodly reward is it to think of her growth and to remind me of the days when she could not walk and I bore her wherever I went; and of the days when she could but take faltering steps and was soon fain to climb into my arms and sit upon my neck; and of the days when we first fared together with the geese to market and I cut her first hazel stick; and in truth of all the days that she has been with me since I found her."

As the gooseherd spoke the tears in the hermit's eyes rolled slowly down his cheeks; and when the young man ceased, he said, "O son, now I know why you are so pleasing in the eyes of God. Early have you learned the love which gives all and asks nothing, which suffers long and is ever kind, and this I have not learned. A small thing and too common it seemed to me, but now I see that it is holier than austerities and avails more than fasting and is the prayer of prayers. Late have I sought you, you ancient truth; late have I found you, you ancient beauty; yet even in the gloaming of my days may there still be light enough to win my way home. Farewell, good brother; and may God be tender and pitiful to you as you have been tender and pitiful to the little child."

"Farewell, holy man!" replied the gooseherd, regarding him with a perplexed look.

—from William Canton's *A Child's Book of Saints* (1898)

1850—Charles Haddon Spurgeon (1834–92) was perhaps the most renowned Baptist preacher in England in the late nineteenth century, credited with delivering over two thousand sermons. Many years before attaining such fame, however, a sixteen-year-old Spurgeon stepped into a church during a blizzard on this day. Intending only to find warmth from the cold in that small, unfamiliar chapel, Spurgeon, instead, had a life-changing experience. Later, after becoming a world-famous evangelist, he described the scene in his Autobiography. *(See also September 8.)*

————————————

The minister did not come that morning; he was snowed up, I suppose. At last a very thin-looking man, a shoemaker or tailor or something of that sort, went up into the pulpit to preach. Now it is well that preachers should be instructed, but this man was really stupid. He was obliged to stick to his text for the simple reason that he had little else to say. The text was: "Look unto Me, and be ye saved, all the ends of the earth" [Isaiah 45:22]. . . .

When he had . . . managed to spin out ten minutes or so, he was at the end of his tether. Then he looked at me under the gallery, and I dare say, with so few present, he knew me to be a stranger. Just fixing his eyes on me, as if he knew all my heart, he said, "Young man, you look very miserable." Well, I did, but I had not been accustomed to have remarks made from the pulpit on my personal appearance before. However, it was a good blow, struck right home. He continued, "And you always will be miserable—miserable in life and miserable in death—if you don't obey my text; but if you obey now, this moment, you will be saved." Then lifting up his hands, he shouted . . . , "Young man, look to Jesus Christ. Look! Look! Look! You have nothin' to do but to look and live." I saw at once the way of salvation. . . . There and then the cloud was gone, the darkness had rolled away, and that moment I saw the sun; and I could have risen that instant and sung with the most enthusiastic of them, of the precious blood of Christ and the simple faith which looks alone to Him.

1913—American musician James Milton Black (1856–1938) was a singing-school teacher, a hymnbook editor, and, most notably, the composer of the popular hymn "When the Roll Is Called Up Yonder" (1892). On this day Black wrote to a man who had requested permission to reprint the hymn that the fee of $20.00 was justified: "It is the common consent of people everywhere," Black immodestly wrote, "that [it] is the greatest song that has been written for the last twenty-five years. I am of that opinion myself. It goes into more books than any other one gospel song in the English language. That tells the story. Hereafter the price of that song shall be $25.00. Do you blame me?"

—

When the trumpet of the Lord shall sound, and time shall be no more,
    And the morning breaks, eternal, bright and fair;
When the saved of earth shall gather over on the other shore,
    And the roll is called up yonder, I'll be there.

On that bright and cloudless morning when the dead in Christ shall rise,
    And the glory of His resurrection share;
When His chosen ones shall gather to their home beyond the skies,
    And the roll is called up yonder, I'll be there.

Let us labor for the Master from the dawn till setting sun,
    Let us talk of all His wondrous love and care;
Then when all of life is over, and our work on earth is done,
    And the roll is called up yonder, I'll be there.

1860—The preface of an unusual book, 595 Pulpit Pungencies, *bears this date. Written by an anonymous American preacher, the book contains his favorite anecdotes and witticisms—from his own sermons. In the preface the author states: "I regard all this superstitious, unsmiling Christianity as a relic of the old Vandal times." Here is a sampling of thoughts from the book.*

———— ❧ ❧ ————

- A person may so tell the truth as to tell a lie at the same time; as when a man, offering to sell a mockingbird and being asked whether it would sing, replied, "Oh, it will delight you to hear it sing," on the strength of which reply it was purchased. There is no question but that the man who purchased it would have been exceedingly delighted to hear it sing, but he never did. . . .

- When a church was about to be built in a certain town, the people were divided with reference to where it should stand, and the minister had to preach a very strong sermon on the subject. This sermon had the desired effect. It even brought tears to the eyes of the deacons—and it is a good sign when deacons cry. The next morning one deacon called on another and said to him, "Our minister is right, and we are imperiling the cause of Christ by our dissension, and I have come to tell you that we must compromise; and now, you must give up, for I can't." . . .

- When Sunday comes round [many] a preacher says to himself, "What under the sun shall I preach about?" and the people, after they have heard him, say, "What under the sun did he preach about?" . . .

- It is a pity to see a great dwelling in which everything appears to dwarf the occupant—in which the occupant is the least circumstance. I have seen men who were only the punctuation of their wealth. . . .

- God's union with men is not a shadow, is not a figure, is not a dream; it is the statement of a fact as literal as any law in nature. The union of sunlight with vegetables is not more real. . . .

1880—On this day Lewis Wallace (1827–1905), a former Civil War offi-cer and now governor of the Virginia Territory, wrote to his wife that he needed to "manage a legislature, . . . take care of an Indian war, . . . [and] finish a book." The book was published later that year and became the most celebrated biblical novel of all time: Ben-Hur: A Tale of the Christ. In the following scene near the end of the book, Ben-Hur, a former slave and glad-iator, stands watching as Jesus "the Nazarene" is marched to the place of his execution. Ben-Hur is tempted to intervene violently. . . .

⋅≼⧽ ⧽≽⋅

The appearance of the part of the procession then passing, its bru-tality and hunger for life, were reminding him of the Nazarene—his gentleness and the many charities he had seen him do for suffering men. Suggestions beget suggestions; so he remembered suddenly his own great indebtedness to the man; the time he himself was in the hands of a Roman guard going, as was supposed, to a death as certain and almost as terrible as this one of the cross; the cooling drink he had at the well by Nazareth and the divine expression on the face of him who gave it; the later goodness, the miracle of Palm Sunday; and with these recol-lections, the thought of his present powerlessness to give back help for help or make return in kind stung him keenly, and he accused himself. He had not done all he might; he could have watched with the Galileans and kept them true and ready; and this—ah! this was the moment to strike! A blow well given now would not merely disperse the mob and set the Nazarene free; it would be a trumpet call to Israel and precipitate the long-dreamt-of war for freedom. The opportunity was going; the minutes were bearing it away; and if lost! God of Abraham! Was there nothing to be done—nothing? . . .

The sovereign moment of his life was upon Ben-Hur. Could he have taken the offer and said the word, history might have been other than it is; but then it would have been history ordered by men, not God—something that never was and never will be. A confusion fell upon him; he knew not how, though afterward he attributed it to the Nazarene; for when the Nazarene was risen, he understood the death was necessary to faith in the resurrection, without which Christianity would be an empty husk. The confusion, as has been said, left him with-out the faculty of decision; he stood helpless—wordless even.

1889—Thérèse of Lisieux (1873–97), a French Carmelite nun, sometimes called "The Little Flower," is one of the most popular modern saints of the Catholic Church. (See also July 12.) Her sublimely beautiful autobiography, The Story of a Soul, appeals to readers because of its deep conviction that even the most ordinary people can attain unusual sanctity and nearness to God. On this day, at the age of fifteen, she was officially received into the convent (in what is called her "clothing ceremony") and was blessed with a "little miracle": snow. (See January 23 for another miraculous snowfall.)

The Bishop fixed the ceremony for January 10. The time of waiting had been long, but the beautiful feast came at last. Nothing was missing, not even snow.

Have I ever told you how fond I am of snow? Even when I was quite small, its whiteness entranced me. Why this strange fancy, I wonder? Perhaps, because I was a little winter flower myself, my eyes first saw the earth clad in its beautiful mantle. It was therefore natural that on the occasion of my clothing ceremony, I should wish to see it arrayed like myself in spotless white. The weather, however, was so mild on the preceding day that it might have been spring, and I no longer dared hope for a fall of snow. The morning of the tenth bringing no change, I gave up my childish desire as impossible of realization and so went out of the convent for the ceremony.

Papa met me at the enclosure door, his eyes full of tears, and pressing me to his heart he exclaimed: "Ah! here is my little queen!" Then he gave me his arm, and we made our solemn entry into the public chapel. . . .

The moment I again set foot in the enclosure my eyes fell on the pretty statue of the Holy Child smiling at me amid flowers and lights; then, turning toward the quadrangle, I saw that everything was covered with snow! What a delicate attention on the part of Jesus! . . . Where is the creature with power enough to make even one flake fall to please his beloved? Owing to the warm temperature everyone was filled with amazement, but hearing of my desire, many have since described this even as "the little miracle" of my clothing day.

—from *The Story of a Soul*, translated by Rev. Thomas N. Taylor (1930)

1866—On this day the British steamship London *sank in gale-force winds in the Bay of Biscay, off the coast of France. Among the 240 people lost was the Rev. Daniel James Draper, an eminent Methodist minister from England who was known for his pioneering missionary work in Australia. Having just completed a year's leave in England, Draper was returning to Australia when the ship went down. A survivor of the disaster tells of Reverend Draper's "final prayer meeting."*

————— ⤞ ⤟ —————

Thursday, 11th, dawned; but it brought no ray of hope to the perishing ones. Hope there had been none before; but now the captain, "in answer to a universal appeal," calmly told them that all hope was over. There was no wild outburst of grief at this confirmation of their worst fears; but amid the solemn silence which reigned—silence the more solemn and impressive because of the rage and fury of the tempest around—Mr. Draper stood up, the tears streaming down his face, but with a firm, clear voice, said, "The captain tells us there is no hope, that we must all perish. But I tell you there is hope, hope for *all*. Although we must all die and shall never again see land, we may all make the port of heaven." We know not all the words of warning and entreaty which our brother used during those last four hours, but the testimony of the survivors is unanimous, that from the prayer meeting at midnight [the night before] till the [life]boat left, he was incessant in his prayers, warnings, and invitations. Of the former it is remembered that he often exclaimed: "O God! May those that are not converted be converted now; hundreds of them!" That among his last-heard words were: "In a few moments we must all appear before our Great Judge. Let us prepare to meet Him."

A few moments before the ship went down, one who was saved saw Mr. Draper, "his eyes filled with tears, which streamed down his face, and heard him with the clear, distinct voice of a man calm and collected, exhorting all to come to Christ."

The last man who left the ship was asked, "What was the last you heard or saw them doing on board?" His reply was: "The last I heard was this: they were singing, 'Rock of ages, cleft for me. . . .'"

—from John C. Symons' *Life of Daniel J. Draper* (1870)

1803—The Rev. Richard Cecil (1748–1810) was a prominent minister in Georgian England. On this wintry day, while he was riding through London's side streets and trying to avoid icy paving stones, his horse slipped, causing Cecil to fall into the path of an onrushing cart. The cart wheel missed Cecil's head by inches, crushing his hat, which he thereafter kept in his office as a reminder of his own mortality. In a biography of his father, The Remains of Rev. Richard Cecil, *Cecil's son recounts the spiritual significance his father drew from the experience.*

He said that he had learnt three lessons from this providence:

First, that, while we are called on to use all proper means and precautions of safety, God will sometimes show us our absolute and immediate dependence on Him by making the very means which we employ the occasion of bringing us to the very borders of the grave. He thought it his duty to avoid the stones as much as possible, and yet here danger met him.

A second lesson gathered from this event was the comparative triflingness of the cases that occupy and harass the mind. He had been much overwrought and depressed by some circumstances of domestic trial. They had almost wholly occupied his thoughts and appeared of deep interest and importance. But he compared them now with that far heavier trial that his family was so near encountering, of seeing him brought home a corpse, and he then felt them to be comparatively trifles and to be treated as trifles.

A third lesson, he said, was very obvious, but it was now brought home with peculiar force to him, and that was: to be always ready. "I went out yesterday, and I came in again with safety. I am going out today, and I shall return when my business is finished"—"No!" the Lord may say concerning me, "you shall return no more. Your time is come. My messenger waits for you with a summons!"

He attended divine service on the following Sunday, though he did not think it prudent to preach. Thanks were publicly returned by him in the congregation, and the psalms sung in the course of the service bore such an allusion to his deliverance and were so admirably selected for this purpose that the congregation was evidently much affected by the service.

Fourth century—The church has traditionally honored the memory of St. Hilary of Poitiers on this day. Hilary (c. 315–67) was a highly regarded bishop and theologian who was particularly outspoken in his opposition to the heresies of his time; because of that opposition, he was exiled from his home in Gaul for many years. He is the author of several important treatises defending Christian orthodoxy, most important of which is his treatise On the Trinity. In the following passage from that work, he movingly describes the meaning of Christ's incarnation.

———————————

The virgin, the birth, the body, then the Cross, the death, the visit to the lower world—these things are our salvation. For the sake of humankind the Son of God was born of the virgin and of the Holy Ghost. . . . He did it so that by His incarnation He might take to Himself from the virgin the fleshly nature and that through this commingling there might come into being a hallowed body of all humanity; so that through that body, which He was pleased to assume, all humanity might be hid in Him and He in return, through His unseen existence, be reproduced in all. Thus the invisible image of God scorned not the shame that marks the beginnings of human life. He passed through every stage: through conception, birth, wailing, cradle, and each successive humiliation.

The one, only begotten God, ineffably born of God, entered the virgin's womb and grew and took the frame of poor humanity. He who upholds the universe, with whom and through whom are all things, was brought forth by common childbirth. He at whose voice archangels and angels tremble, and heaven and earth and all the elements of this world are melted, was heard in childish wailing. The invisible and incomprehensible, whom sight and feeling and touch cannot gauge, was wrapped in a cradle. . . . He by whom humanity was made had nothing to gain by becoming human; it was our gain that God was incarnate and dwelt among us, making all flesh His home by taking upon Him the flesh of one. We were raised because He was lowered; shame to Him was glory to us. He, being God, made flesh His residence, and we in return are lifted anew from the flesh to God.

—adapted from the translation of E. W. Watson and L. Pullen (1898)

1529—On this day was published The Dialogue on Christian Doctrine *by Juan de Valdés (c. 1500–41), one of the earliest Spanish theologians to be influenced by the German Reformation. The* Dialogue, *which often takes the question-and-answer form of a catechism, records the edifying, though imaginary, conversation of three men: a layman named Eusebio; a priest, Antronio; and Don Fray Pedro de Alba, the learned Archbishop of Grenada. In the following passage the conversation turns to the subject of contemplation.*

EUSEBIO: [Let us pause] so the Reverend Archbishop can talk about a subject which interests me, about how one conducts himself in his contemplation.

ARCHBISHOP: Like the prophet David conducted himself and as St. Paul tells us to conduct ourselves.

EUSEBIO: Explain it to me more clearly.

ARCHBISHOP: Read the psalm of David that begins: "Blessed are the undefiled in the way . . ." [Psalm 119], and you'll see there how all the contemplation and practice of the most holy prophet was to think on the Commandments and the Law of God. You'll find the same in many other psalms. Then, if you read some of St. Paul's epistles, that is the only form of contemplation you'll find in them. Consider as certain, then, that this is the true contemplation, because from here the soul receives knowledge of the infinite goodness, greatness, and mercy of God; from here it comes to knowledge of its own smallness and wretchedness. Here one learns what one's duty is toward God, toward one's neighbor, and toward one's own self. There is, in short, no good that can't be achieved by means of this continual contemplation. I don't know what those other imaginations are (nor their art) that some people use for contemplation, nor what fruit they receive from them other than the dry satisfaction of seeming to have used that time well. I call it dry, because the soul which should enjoy these imaginations remains very cold and dry.

EUSEBIO: What book taught you that?

ARCHBISHOP: Experience.

—translated by William B. and Carol D. Jones

1650—Richard Baxter (1615–91) was a renowned Puritan divine and one of England's most prolific religious authors, writing more than a hundred books. Due to spending much time at home because of ill-health, he became a largely self-taught scholar and preacher. During one particularly severe illness, he wrote his most famous and influential work, The Saints' Everlasting Rest, *which, on this day, was officially licensed by the government for publication. In this lengthy and profound treatise, from which a sample follows, Baxter ponders the nature of life after death.*

————— ✑ ✑ —————

It is a question with some whether or not we shall know each other in heaven. Surely, no knowledge shall cease that we now have, but only that which implies our imperfection; and what imperfection can this imply? Nay, our present knowledge shall be increased beyond belief. It shall indeed be done away, but only as the light of candles and stars is done away by the rising of the sun; which is more properly a doing away of our ignorance than of our knowledge.

Indeed, we shall not know each other after the flesh, not by stature, voice, color, complexion, visage, or outward shape. If we had so known Christ, we should know him no more; not by parts and gifts of learning, nor titles of honor or worldly dignity; nor by terms of affinity and consanguinity, nor benefits, nor such relations; nor by youth or age; nor, I think, by sex; but by the image of Christ and spiritual relation and former faithfulness in improving our talents, beyond doubt, we shall know and be known.

Nor is it only our old acquaintance, but all the saints of all the ages, whose faces in the flesh we never saw, whom we shall there both know and comfortably enjoy. . . . Those who now are willingly ministering spirits for our good will willingly then be our companions in joy for the perfecting of our good; and they who had such joy in heaven for our conversion will gladly rejoice with us in our glorification. I think, Christian, this will be a more honorable assembly than ever you beheld and a more happy society than you were ever in before. . . .

What a day will it be when we shall join with them in praises to our Lord in and for that kingdom! So then I conclude, this is one singular excellency of the Rest of heaven, that we are "fellow-citizens with the saints and of the household of God."

1604—On this day at a conference at Hampton Court, King James I of Eng-land (1566–1625) considered a proposal for a book that eventually became the most influential ever published in English. One writer present recorded the events of this day as follows: "His highness wished that some especial pains should be taken . . . for one uniform translation, professing that he could never yet see a Bible well translated in English. . . . This [should] be done by the best learned in both [Oxford and Cambridge], after them to be reviewed by the bishops, and the chief learned of the church." That Bible, published in 1611, is now known as the Authorized Version, or King James Bible, from which the following beautiful passage is taken: Psalm 139:1–18.

———————— ·ঙ্গ ঞ·————————

O Lord, thou hast searched me, and known me. Thou knowest my downsitting and mine uprising, thou understandest my thought afar off. Thou compassest my path and my lying down, and art acquainted with all my ways. For there is not a word in my tongue, but, lo, O Lord, thou knowest it altogether. Thou hast beset me behind and before, and laid thine hand upon me. Such knowledge is too wonderful for me; it is high, I cannot attain unto it. Whither shall I go from thy spirit? Or whither shall I flee from thy presence? If I ascend up into heaven, thou art there. If I make my bed in hell, behold, thou art there. If I take the wings of the morning and dwell in the uttermost parts of the sea—even there shall thy hand lead me and thy right hand shall hold me. If I say, "Surely the darkness shall cover me," even the night shall be light about me. Yea, the darkness hideth not from thee, but the night shineth as the day; the darkness and the light are both alike to thee. For thou hast pos-sessed my reins; thou has covered me in my mother's womb. I will praise thee, for I am fearfully and wonderfully made; marvelous are thy works; and that my soul knoweth right well. My substance was not hid from thee, when I was made in secret and curiously wrought in the lowest parts of the earth. Thine eyes did see my substance, yet being unperfect; and in thy book all my members were written, which in continuance were fashioned, when as yet there was none of them. How precious also are thy thoughts unto me, O God! How great is the sum of them! If I should count them, they are more in number than the sand. When I awake, I am still with thee.

1941—On this day died American Quaker missionary Thomas R. Kelly (1893–1941), whose Testament of Devotion *is one of the most beloved devotional books of our time. (See also September 9.) A friend of his, Douglas V. Steere, compiled the book from Kelly's articles about the deeper life and published it three months after Kelly's death. In the following excerpt, Kelly describes in the most sublime terms the fellowship of true believers—those who live "at the Center."*

⋯

In the Fellowship, cultural and educational and national and racial differences are leveled. Unlettered men are at ease with the truly humble scholar . . . , and the scholar listens with joy and openness to the precious experiences of God's dealing with the workingman. We find men with chilly theologies but with glowing hearts. We overleap the boundaries of church membership and find Lutherans and Roman Catholics, Jews and Christians, within the Fellowship. We reread the poets and the saints, and the Fellowship is enlarged. With urgent hunger we read the Scriptures, with no thought of pious exercise, but in order to find more friends for the soul. We brush past our historical learning in the Scriptures, to seize upon those writers who lived in the Center, in the Life and in the Power. Particularly does devotional literature become illuminated, for *The Imitation of Christ,* and Augustine's *Confessions,* and Brother Lawrence's *Practice of the Presence of God* speak the language of the souls who live at the Center. Time telescopes and vanishes, centuries and creeds are overleaped. The incident of death puts no boundaries to the Blessed Community, wherein men and women live and love and work and pray in that Life and Power which gave forth the Scriptures. And we wonder and grieve at the overwhelmingly heady preoccupation of religious people with problems, problems, unless they have first come into the Fellowship of the Light.

The final grounds of holy Fellowship are in God. Lives immersed and drowned in God are drowned in love, and know one another in Him, and know one another in love. God is the medium, the matrix, the focus, the solvent. As Meister Eckhart suggests, he who is wholly surrounded by God, enveloped by God, clothed with God, glowing in selfless love toward Him—such a man no one can touch except he touch God also.

1548—Englishman Hugh Latimer (1485–1555) was a Protestant theologian and popular preacher. As one of the English Reformation's leading figures, he was actively involved in the political and religious turmoils of his day, and he was eventually burned at the stake for his views. His sermons were startling for their unexpectedness and originality; for instance, he preached two sermons "On Cards," showing how salvation could be won by "playing trumps." The following excerpt from perhaps his most famous sermon, "The Sermon on the Plow," which was preached on this day, is another example of his unexpected turn of mind in the pulpit.

———————— ᪥ ————————

And now I would ask a strange question: who is the most diligent bishop and prelate in all England, who surpasses all the rest in doing his office? I can tell you, for I know who it is; I know him well. But now I think I see you listening and hearkening that I should name him. There is one that surpasses all the others and is the most diligent prelate and preacher in all England. And will you know who it is? I will tell you— it is the devil. He is the most diligent preacher of all; he is never out of his diocese; he is never from his cure; you shall never find him unoccupied; he is ever in his parish; he keeps residence at all times; you shall never find him out of the way; call for him when you will, and he is ever at home; the most diligent preacher in all the realm; he is ever at his plow; no lording nor loitering can hinder him; he is ever applying his business; you shall never find him idle, I warrant you. . . .

Oh that our prelates would be as diligent to sow the corn of good doctrine as Satan is to sow cockle and darnel! . . . But here some man will say to me, "What, sir, are you so privy of the devil's counsel that you know all this to be true?" Truly, I know him too well and have obeyed him a little too much in condescending to some follies; and I know him as other men do, yea, that he is ever occupied and ever busy in following the plow. I know by St. Peter, who says of him, "He goes about like a roaring lion, seeking whom he may devour."

1563—The famous Heidelberg Catechism was published on this day. It was compiled by a group of Protestant theologians in Heidelberg, Germany, at the suggestion of their ruler, Frederick III, Elector of the Palatinate (1515–76). Catechisms have both a devotional and an educational purpose, following, as they do, a question-and-answer format in order to teach the basic tenets of the Christian faith. The Heidelberg Catechism, the memorable opening portion of which is given below, became a doctrinal touchstone for many Calvinists and is still taught today. (See September 15 for another famous catechism.)

QUESTION 1: What is your only comfort in life and in death?

ANSWER: That I, with body and soul, both in life and in death, am not my own but belong to my faithful Savior Jesus Christ, who with His precious blood has fully satisfied for all my sins and redeemed me from all the power of the Devil; and so preserves me, that without the will of my Father in heaven not a hair can fall from my head; yea, that all things must work together for my salvation. Wherefore, by His Holy Spirit, He also assures me of eternal life and makes me heartily willing and ready henceforth to live unto Him.

QUESTION 2: How many things are necessary for you to know, that you, in this comfort, may live and die happily?

ANSWER: Three things: First, the greatness of my sin and misery. Second, how I am redeemed from all my sins and misery. Third, how I am to be thankful to God for such redemption.

QUESTION 3: Whence do you know your misery?

ANSWER: From the Law of God.

QUESTION 4: What does the Law of God require of us?

ANSWER: This Christ teaches us in sum, Matthew 22: You shall love the Lord your God with all your heart and with all your soul and with all your mind and with all your strength. This is the first and great commandment; and the second is like it: You shall love your neighbor as yourself. On these two commandments hang all the law and the prophets.

—translation commissioned by the
German Reformed Church of the United States (1863)

1861—French Catholic missionary Théophane Vénard (1829–61) was twenty-three years old when he sailed for China. After serving in Hong Kong for several years, he went to Western Tonkin to minister to a group of ten thousand Chinese Christians who were suffering severe persecution. He was respected, even among many of his persecutors, for his patient love and gentility. After five years, Vénard was arrested and imprisoned in a cage. On this day, during his captivity, he wrote a moving letter to his family, with special greetings to his sister, Melanie. An extract follows. He was executed two weeks later.

———————— ·≈§ §≈· ————————

I do not regret this world; my soul thirsts for the waters of eternal life. My exile is over. I am approaching the soil of my true country; earth vanishes, heaven opens, I go to God. Adieu, dearest father, sister, brothers, do not mourn, do not shed tears over me, live the years that lie ahead in unity and love. . . .

Melanie, my dearest sister and friend, I want to send you a special word of love and farewell. . . . It is midnight. Round my wooden cage I can see nothing but banners and swords. In the corner of the hall where my cage stands, a group of soldiers is playing at cards; another group at draughts. From time to time the sentries strike the hour of the night on their drums. About two feet from my cage, a feeble oil lamp throws a wavering glimmer on this sheet of Chinese paper and enables me to trace these few lines. From day to day I expect my sentence—perhaps tomorrow. . . . Within a few short hours my soul shall quit this earth, exile over and battle won. I shall mount upward and enter into our true home. There, among God's elect, I shall gaze upon what the eye of man cannot imagine, hear undreamed-of harmonies, enjoy a happiness the heart cannot remotely comprehend. But first of all the grain of wheat must be ground, the bunch of grapes trodden in the winepress. May I become pure bread and wine perfectly fit to serve the Master! I trust it may be so through the mercies of my Savior and Redeemer. . . . That is why even as I stand in the arena in the thick of the fight, I dare to intone the hymn of triumph as if assured of victory. And I leave you, my dearest sister, to till the field of virtue and good works. Reap an abundant harvest for the everlasting life that awaits us both. Gather up faith, hope, charity, patience, gentleness, sweetness, perseverance, and a holy death, and so we shall go hand-in-hand now and forevermore. Goodbye, Melanie. Good-bye, beloved sister of mine. Adieu!

—translator unknown

1323—Heinrich Suso (c. 1295–1366), a German monk and mystic of the fourteenth century, was highly valued for his preaching, spiritual counsel, and writing, his most famous book being The Little Book of Eternal Wisdom. *On this day, as a young man, he had a life-changing experience, which he describes (quite humbly in the third person) in his classic spiritual autobiography,* The Exemplar.

———— ✑ ✒ ————

One day when he was feeling more wretched than usual he made his way to the choir after the midday meal and settled himself in one of the lower stalls on the right-hand side. It was January 21, the feast of Saint Agnes. As he stood there alone, a perfect specimen of melancholia, his soul was mysteriously transported, either in the body or out of the body. Human words fail when it comes to describing what he saw and heard in this ecstasy; it was a vision without form or mode but containing in itself the form and mode of every pleasurable sensation. His heart was simultaneously hungry and appeased; his wishes were stilled and every desire found its fulfillment. He did nothing but stare into the brilliant reflection, oblivious of himself and all creatures, forgetful of the passage of time. It was a sweet foretaste of heaven's unending bliss.

After about an hour he returned to his senses and said to himself: "If that was not a foretaste of heaven, then I do not know what heaven is. Now I am fully convinced that every suffering that can possibly come my way is a cheap price to pay for such a gain. Alas, dear God, where was I and where am I now? Oh, that the memory of this hour may always stay fresh in my mind."

Leaving the choir he made his way into the cloister, looking the same as before in outward appearance, but inwardly like a man returned from another world. The memory of the vision he had seen caused him anguish of body and desolation of spirit; how he longed for, not the companionship of creatures, but the heavenly joys he had tasted so briefly. He went about his duties silent and unnoticed, his soul reliving the bliss of God's touch, experiencing time and again the brightness of heavenly visions, and it seemed to him as if he were floating on air.

—translated by Sister M. Ann Edward

1904—Mary Grace Banfield (1859–1905) was a remarkable Englishwoman who, after spending several years in mental hospitals, was miraculously healed and went on to minister to other people suffering from emotional problems. On this day, late in her life, she wrote a letter to a close friend named Ben, describing the process by which she was freed from her psychological disorder, which today would probably be called severe schizophrenia.

————————•⧾§ §⧽•————————

One day, in a state of almost desperation, I took up the Bible and opened it, and the first words I read were, "She arose and ministered unto them." Instantly there sprang up in my heart such love to the Lord Jesus and to His people that, closing the book and bursting into tears, I said almost aloud, "Lord, if You would appear to me and deliver me, that is just what I would like to do directly—try to help and comfort Your dear afflicted people." But this was immediately followed by the suggestion that such a thing was not only utterly impossible, but that I had added sin to sin by entertaining such a thought, and I sank as low as before. The little ray of light which had shone for a few moments only made the darkness seem more unbearable. . . .

After about two years, while still shut up in the asylum, I was one day mourning over my desolate condition, feeling, as the Psalmist expresses it, "forgotten like a dead man out of mind." This word came to me: "The Lord has need of him." I remembered the words were spoken in reference to the colt, for which there did not appear to be any use; and, on reading the account as recorded in Mark, I was struck to see that it was "tied up at a place where two ways meet," that it could not possibly get free of itself, that the Lord had reserved it for His own special use, and that He had but to speak and then no cords or chains could bind it any longer. A little faith was raised up in my heart to believe that He was able to do the same for me—that if He would but speak, affliction and all my inward enemies and captors would have to obey His voice and let me go. And about this time that word in Psalm 105 about Joseph was very good and helpful: "The king sent and loosed him, and let him go free." I felt all I wanted was for King Jesus to appear, to heal both my soul and body. And so, dear Ben, as you have seen at length it came to pass. The Lord delivered me "out of the horrible pit and miry clay."

—from Mary Grace Banfield's *From Death Unto Life: Diaries and Letters* (1906)

1421—Margery Kempe (c. 1373–c. 1433) was a courageous and outspoken mystic of fourteenth-century England. She and her husband went on several pilgrimages, including one to Jerusalem in 1413. She was also the mother of fourteen children. Her dictated autobiography, The Book of Margery Kempe *(in which she refers to herself in the third person), was not published in its entirety until the 1940s and is a classic of medieval religious autobiography. On this day, as she describes in that book, a fire broke out in her hometown of King's Lynn, Norfolk, England, and she prayed for divine intervention.*

————— ⋅ঙ৯ ৡ৯⋅ —————

As soon as she beheld the hideous flames of the fire, she immediately cried out with a loud voice and great weeping, "Good Lord, make it well!"

These words came to her mind because our Lord had said to her before that he would make it well, and therefore she cried, "Good Lord, make it well, and send down some rain or stormy weather that may, through your mercy, quench this fire and ease my heart."

Then she went back to the church, and then she beheld how the sparks came into the choir through the tower window of the church. Then she had a new sorrow and again cried very loudly for grace and mercy, with a great abundance of tears. Soon after that, there came to her three worshipful men with white snow on their clothing, saying to her, "Lo, Margery, God has wrought a great grace for us and sent us a fair snow with which to quench the fire. Be now of good cheer, and thank God for it."

And with great cry she gave praise and thanks to God for his great mercy and his goodness, and especially because he had said to her before that all would be well when it seemed most unlikely to be well, unless a miracle and special grace were sent. And now that she saw that all was well indeed, she thought she had great cause to thank our Lord.

1345—On this day Richard de Bury (1281–1345) completed the writing of his classic treatise called the Philobiblon *("The Love of Books"). De Bury was a well-known bishop and statesman in fourteenth-century England and was once tutor for the young Prince Edward, who later became King Edward III. De Bury is now chiefly remembered as an avid collector of books and founder of some of England's greatest libraries. The following admonition from the* Philobiblon *may seem whimsical, but de Bury lived in a time that often saw little respect paid to books, which at that time were wholly hand-lettered and hand-bound.*

We are not only rendering service to God in preparing volumes of new books, but also exercising an office of sacred piety when we treat books carefully and again when we restore them to their proper places and commend them to inviolable custody; that they may rejoice in purity while we have them in our hands and rest securely when they are put back in their repositories. And surely, next to the vestments and vessels dedicated to the Lord's body, holy books deserve to be rightly treated by the clergy, to which great injury is done so often as they are touched by unclean hands. Wherefore we deem it expedient to warn our students of various negligences, which might always be easily avoided and do wonderful harm to books. . . .

Moses, the gentlest of men, teaches us to make bookcases most neatly, wherein they may be protected from any injury: "Take," he says, "this book of the law and put it in the side of the ark of the covenant of the Lord your God." O fitting place and appropriate for a library, which was made of imperishable shittim-wood and was all covered within and without with gold! But the Savior also has warned us by his example against all unbecoming carelessness in the handling of books, as we read in St. Luke. For when he had read the scriptural prophecy of himself in the book that was delivered to him, he did not give it again to the minister until he had closed it with his own most sacred hands. By which students are most clearly taught that in the care of books the merest trifles ought not to be neglected.

—from Richard de Bury's *Philobiblon*,
translated by E. C. Thomas

c. 40—The church has traditionally commemorated the conversion of the apostle Paul on this day. His life-changing experience on the road to Damascus has been the model for nearly two millennia of other believers' conversions—from St. Augustine to C. S. Lewis. Paul himself described his experience in detail to King Agrippa, at a time when Paul was defending himself against charges of heresy. Paul's powerful account is recorded in Acts 26.

I myself was convinced that I ought to do many things in opposing the name of Jesus of Nazareth. And I did so in Jerusalem; I not only shut up many of the saints in prison, by authority from the chief priests, but when they were put to death I cast my vote against them. And I punished them often in all the synagogues and tried to make them blaspheme; and in raging fury against them, I persecuted them even to foreign cities.

Thus I journeyed to Damascus with the authority and commission of the chief priests. At midday, O king, I saw on the way a light from heaven, brighter than the sun, shining round me and those who journeyed with me. And when we had all fallen to the ground, I heard a voice saying to me in the Hebrew language, "Saul, Saul, why do you persecute me? It hurts you to kick against the goads." And I said, "Who are you, Lord?" And the Lord said, "I am Jesus whom you are persecuting. But rise and stand upon your feet; for I have appeared to you for this purpose, to appoint you to serve and bear witness to the things in which you have seen me and to those in which I will appear to you, delivering you from the people and from the Gentiles—to whom I send you to open their eyes, that they may turn from darkness to light and from the power of Satan to God, that they may receive forgiveness of sins and a place among those who are sanctified by faith in me."

Wherefore, O King Agrippa, I was not disobedient to the heavenly vision, but declared first to those at Damascus, then at Jerusalem and throughout all the country of Judea, and also to the Gentiles, that they should repent and turn to God and perform deeds worthy of their repentance.

—Revised Standard Version (1946)

151—Although disputed, this date is listed in many martyrologies as the day on which St. Polycarp, a disciple of John the Evangelist, was martyred (c. 69–c. 151). In any event, this day has been honored as his feast, the day on which his sacrifice is remembered. The circumstances are as follows: In spite of Polycarp's advanced age (eighty-six), the proconsul of Smyrna ordered that he should be burned at the stake for refusing to renounce Christ and "swear by the genius of Caesar." Polycarp replied, "Fourscore and six years have I been His servant, and He has done me no wrong. How then can I blaspheme my King who saved me?" Just before the fire was ignited, Polycarp is reported to have spoken the following prayer.

O Lord God Almighty, the Father of Your beloved and blessed Son Jesus Christ, through whom we have received the knowledge of You, the God of angels and powers and of all creation and of the whole race of the righteous, who live in Your presence; I bless You because You have granted me this day and hour, that I might receive a portion amongst the number of martyrs in the cup of Christ unto resurrection of eternal life both of soul and of body, in the incorruptibility of the Holy Spirit. May I be received among these in Your presence this day, as a rich and acceptable sacrifice, as You did prepare and reveal it beforehand, and have accomplished it, You who are the faithful and true God. For this cause, yea, and for all things, I praise You, I bless You, I glorify You, through the eternal and heavenly High-priest Jesus Christ, Your beloved Son, through whom with Him and the Holy Spirit be glory to You both now and for the ages to come. Amen.

—from the "Letter of the Smyrnaeans"
in J. B. Lightfoot's *Apostolic Fathers* (1889)

1612—On this day, an anonymous English Jesuit, known only by the initials A. H., dedicated his translation from the Italian of Achilles Galliardi's book The Abridgment of Christian Perfection *to "the religious men and women of our nation . . . who desire to attain to the eminent state of Christian perfection: health in our Lord." Galliardi, an Italian Jesuit theologian of the time, outlines a method for achieving unity with God. In the following adapted passage, he offers six beautiful metaphors for better understanding true unity with the Lord.*

The first is of a *red hot iron*; considering how the fire wholly penetrates and possesses the iron, not changing the substance but only the appearance, as rustiness, coldness, and hardness, but making it bright, hot, and soft, you may make this aspiration in your heart: "O Lord, that I might be worthy to be so penetrated and informed by you! Oh, how bright, how inflamed would my soul be! How soft and tractable! How well disposed to keep your commandments!" And staying here a little in an ardent desire of union with God, you shall soon taste of the desired fruit.

The second is of *wine* when it is mingled with water; to consider how this mixture or union beautifies the water with its color and other qualities.

The third is of a *carnation flower* of some *fair rose*; considering how the color is united to the quantity and substance of the flower, making it so delightful to behold: oh, how much more beautiful would that soul remain to which the Creator of those colors should come and unite himself!

The fourth is of the *light united with the air*, making it so clear and transparent: how much more if the true Sun of justice should unite himself with the soul!

The fifth is of a *white or ruddy cloud*, such as sometimes appears out of the reflection of the sunbeams.

The sixth is of the *morning*, when as arising by little and little it goes changing and investing the horizon with the light of the sun: so does the love of God change the just who persevere therein, giving them every day more and more light, until they are wholly transformed.

1897—Scotsman Alexander MacLaren (1826–1910) became a full-time Baptist preacher when he was only nineteen years old. He eventually earned renown as a scholar and is still considered one of the most insightful Bible expositors of the nineteenth century. In 1897 an American minister, the Rev. George Coates, edited a daily devotional called Music for the Soul, *made up of selected readings from the works of Rev. MacLaren. In the January 28 reading from that book, MacLaren reflects on Exodus 10:26: "We know not with what we must serve the Lord."*

———————— ❧ ❦ ————————

The weakest and the lowest, the roughest and the hardest, the most selfishly absorbed man and woman among us has lying in him and her dormant capacities for flaming up into such a splendor of devotion and magnificence of heroic self-forgetfulness and self-sacrifice as is represented in many words in the Bible. A mother will do it for her child and never think that she has done anything extraordinary. Husbands will do such things for wives; wives for husbands; friends and lovers for one another. All who love the sweetness and power of the bond of affection know that there is nothing more gladsome than to fling one's self away for the sake of those whom we love. . . .

Astronomers tell us that sometimes a star that has shone inconspicuous, way down in their catalogues at fifth or sixth magnitude, will all at once flame out, having kindled and caught fire somehow, and will blaze in the heavens, outshining Jupiter and Venus. And so some poor vulgar, narrow nature, touched by this Promethean fire of pure love that leads to perfect sacrifice, will "flame in the forehead of the morning sky" and become an undying splendor and a light forevermore. All have this capacity in them, and all are responsible for the use of it. What have you done with it? Is there any person or thing in this world that has ever been able to lift you up out of yourselves? Is there any magnet that has proved strong enough to raise you from the low levels along which your life creeps? Have you ever known the thrill of resolving to become the bond servant and the slave of some great cause not your own? Or are you, as so many are, like spiders living in the midst of your web, mainly intent upon what it can catch for you? Have you ever set a light to that inert mass of enthusiasm that lies in you? Have you ever woke up the sleeper? Learn the lesson that there is nothing that so ennobles and dignifies a common nature as enthusiasm for a great cause, self-sacrificing love for a worthy heart.

1626—Famed English poet John Donne (1572–1631) was, in his youth, a fashionable courtier who was known for his wittily elegant verses. (See also May 31.) In 1615 he became a priest of the Anglican Church and, in 1621, dean of St. Paul's, London. As a priest, he continued to write stunningly beautiful poetry, though he was even more beloved in his own time as one of England's greatest preachers. His poetic nature is manifest in his sermons, which can be seen in the following extract. On this day in St. Paul's Cathedral, Donne preached on the subject of joy and took Psalm 63:7 as his text: "Because you have been my help, therefore in the shadow of your wings will I rejoice."

I return often to this endeavor of raising your hearts, dilating your hearts with a holy joy, joy in the Holy Ghost, for *under the shadow of his wings*, you may—you should—*rejoice*.

If you look upon this world in a map, you find two hemispheres, two half-worlds. If you crush heaven into a map, you may find two hemispheres too, two half-heavens. Half will be joy and half will be glory, for in these two—the joy of heaven and the glory of heaven—is all heaven represented to us. And as of those two hemispheres of the world, the first has been known long before, but the other (that of America, which is the richer in treasure) God reserved for later discoveries. So, though He reserve that hemisphere of heaven which is glory until the Resurrection, yet the other hemisphere, the joy of heaven, God opens to our discovery and delivers for our habitation even while we dwell in this world. . . . Be content that He produce joy in your heart here. . . . Since God gives you the shadow of his wings—that is, consolation, respiration, refreshment, though not always a present and complete deliverance from your afflictions—not to thank God is murmuring, and not to rejoice in God's ways is an unthankfulness. Howling is the noise of hell, singing the voice of heaven. Sadness is the miasma of hell, rejoicing the serenity of heaven. And the person who has no joy here lacks one of the best pieces of evidence of the joys of heaven and has neglected or refused that down-payment which God uses to bind his bargain: that true joy in this world shall flow into the joy of heaven, as a river flows into the sea. This joy shall not be put out in death, but a new joy kindled in me in heaven. . . . I shall have a joy that shall no more evaporate than my soul shall evaporate—a joy that shall pass upward and put on a more glorious garment above and be a joy super-invested in glory. Amen.

1877—Dwight L. Moody (1837–99) was the preeminent American evangelist of his time. (See also October 8.) Among his many accomplishments was the founding of the Chicago Bible Institute, now called Moody Bible Institute. On this day, a man named J. B. McClure wrote the preface to a volume called Anecdotes and Illustrations of D. L. Moody, *in which McClure collects his favorite passages from Moody's revival sermons. In the following selection from that book, Moody recalls a sermon he once heard that became something of a model for his own preaching. The text is Proverbs 30:24–28: "There be four things which are little upon the earth, but they are exceeding wise: the ants, . . . the conies, . . . the locust, . . . the spider."*

The speaker said the children of God were like four things. The first thing was: "The ants are a people not strong," and he went on to compare the children of God to ants. . . . They pay no attention to the things of the present, but go on steadily preparing for the future. The next thing he compared them to was the coney bird. "The conies are but a feeble folk." It is a very weak little thing. "Well," said I, "I wouldn't like to be as a coney." But he went on to say that it built upon a rock. The children of God were very weak, but they laid their foundation upon a rock. "Well," said I, "I will be like a coney and build my hopes upon a rock." . . . The next thing the speaker compared them to was a locust. I didn't think much of locusts, and I thought I wouldn't care about being like one. But he went on to read, "They have no king, yet they go forth all of them by bands." There were the Congregationalist, the Presbyterian, the Methodist bands going forth without a king, but by and by our King will come back again, and these bands will fly to Him. "Well, I will be like the locust; my King is away," I thought. The next comparison was a spider. I didn't like this at all, but he said if we went into a gilded palace filled with luxury, we might see a spider holding on to something, oblivious to all the luxury below. It was laying hold of the things above. "Well," said I, "I would like to be a spider." I heard this a good many years ago, . . . and it makes a sermon.

Eighth century—*This was the Celtic church's feast day in honor of Irish St. Maedoc of Ferns, who died in 726. Maedoc founded many monasteries, became an influential bishop, and was known for his severe austerities; for instance, he is said to have recited five hundred psalms a day and fasted on barley and water for seven years. The following legend (which has also been attached to other Celtic saints) concerns a crate of soil, drenched in the blood of the early Christian martyrs, that Maedoc is said to have brought back to Ireland from Rome.*

In the little graveyard about the fair church of his brotherhood, he spread the earth which had drunk the blood of the martyrs, so that the bodies of those who died in the Lord might await His coming in a blessed peace.

Now it happened that but a few days after his return the friend of his boyhood, a holy brother who had long shared with him the companionship of the cloister, migrated from this light; and when the last requiem had been sung and the sacred earth had covered the dead, the saint wept bitterly for the sake of the lost love and the unforgotten years.

And at night he fell asleep, still weeping for sorrow. And in his sleep he saw, as in a dream, the gray stone church with its round tower and the graveyard sheltered by the woody hills—but behold! In the graveyard tall trees sprang in lofty spires from the earth of Rome and reached into the highest heavens; and these trees were like trees of green and golden and ruddy fire, for they were red with the blossoms of life, and every green leaf quivered with bliss, like a green flame. And among the trees, on a grassy sod at their feet, sat a white lark, singing clear and loud, and he knew that the lark was the soul of the friend of his boyhood.

As he listened to its song, he understood its unearthly music; and these were the words of its singing: "Do not weep anymore for me; it is pity for your sorrow that keeps me here on the grass. If you were not so unhappy, I should fly."

And when the saint awoke, his grief had fallen from him, and he wept no more for the dead man whom he loved.

—from William Canton's *A Child's Book of Saints* (1898)

February

VERA EFFIGIES.

Italian mystic Catherine of Siena contemplates
the Cross of Christ (see February 14).
From an engraving by Francesco Vanni.

Sixth century—The Celtic church commemorated St. Brigid (c. 453–523) on this day. Though her life is clouded by legend, she is said to have been the beautiful daughter of an Irish chieftain; because of her extraordinary piety and compassion for the poor, she was allowed to leave her noble pagan family and become a nun. She founded four monasteries and became the Abbess of Kildare. Her traditional symbols are the dandelion, the lamb, and the sea bird, and she is the patron of poets, blacksmiths, and all who practice the healing arts. After St. Patrick, she is probably Ireland's most beloved saint. The following anonymous poem, "Brigid's Feast," is a traditional Celtic evocation of her generous spirit.

————— ⋅≈§ ⁊⋙⋅ —————

I should like a great lake of the finest ale
For the King of Kings.
I should like a table of the choicest food
For the family of heaven.
Let the ale be made from the fruits of faith,
And the food be forgiving love.

I should welcome the poor to my feast,
For they are God's children.
I should welcome the sick to my feast,
For they are God's joy.
Let the poor sit with Jesus at the highest place,
And the sick dance with the angels.

God bless the poor,
God bless the sick;
And bless our human race.
God bless our food,
God bless our drink,
All homes, O God, embrace.

First century—Traditionally, on this day, churches worldwide celebrate Jesus'
"presentation" in the temple as described in Luke 2:26–35. The celebration
is often called "Candlemas" because of a custom, begun in fifth-century
Jerusalem, of lighting candles in the church on this day. Jesus' presentation
was the fulfillment of Old Testament law, which requires that every firstborn
should be offered to God. Here the scene is dramatized in the words of Scot-
tish minister and Bible scholar William Hanna (1808–82) in his Life of
Christ *(1863).*

———————— ✧❧ ————————

So ardent as his years ran on had Simeon's faith and hope become
that this one thing had he desired of the Lord, that before his eyes
closed in death they might rest upon his Savior. . . . It was revealed to
him that the desire of his heart should be granted, but how and when
he knew not. That forenoon, however, a strong desire to go up to the
temple seizes him. He was not accustomed to go there at that hour, but
he obeyed that inward impulse, which perhaps he recognized as the
work of the Divine Spirit by whom the gracious revelation had been
made to him. He enters the temple courts; he notices a little family
group approach; he sees an infant dedicated to the Lord. That infant,
an inward voice proclaims to him, is the Messiah he has been waiting
for, the Consolation of Israel come at last in the flesh. Then comes into
his heart a joy beyond all bounds. It kindles in his radiant looks; it beats
in his swelling veins; the strength of youth is back again in his feeble
limbs. He hastens up to Mary, takes from the wondering yet consenting
mother's hands the consecrated babe, and clasping it to his beating
bosom, with eyes uplifted to heaven, he says, "Lord, now let your servant depart in peace, according to your word; for my eyes have seen
your salvation, which you have prepared before the face of all people, a
light to lighten the Gentiles, and the glory of your people Israel." Joseph
and Mary stand lost in wonder. How has this stranger come to see anything uncommon in this child? How came he to see in him the salvation of Israel? Have some stray tidings of his birth come into the holy
city from the hill country of Judea, or has the wondrous tale the shepherds of Bethlehem "made known abroad" been repeated in this old
man's hearing? What he says is in curious harmony with all the angel
had announced to Mary and to the shepherds about the child.

1919—On this day William Lyon Phelps (1865–1943), noted American literary critic and Yale University professor, delivered a lecture called "Reading the Bible" at the Princeton Theological Seminary. In this selection from that talk, he discusses the sublime nature of the Bible's poetry.

--------------- ⋖⋗ ---------------

The poetry of the Old Testament—especially in the books of Solomon's Song, Job, Psalms, Isaiah—excels in every variety of poetical expression, ranging from pure lyrical singing to majestic epic harmonies. The most conventional subject for a poem is Spring, and among the millions of tributes to the mild air and the awakening earth, none is more beautiful than the passage in the Song of Songs: "My beloved spake and said unto me, 'Rise up, my love, my fair one, and come away. For lo, the winter is past; the rain is over and gone; the flowers appear on the earth; the time of the singing of birds is come; and the voice of the turtle is heard in our land. The fig tree putteth forth her green figs, and the vines with the tender grape give a good smell. Arise, my love, my fair one, and come away. . . .'"

If one reads the book of Psalms straight through, no matter how familiar many passages may be, the glory and splendor of the majestic poetry will come like a fresh revelation; and if one will read the last three psalms aloud, one will feel how all the hymns of sorrow, delight, repentance, and adoration unite in one grand universal chorus of praise: "Praise the Lord from the earth, ye dragons, and all deeps; fire and hail; snow and vapors; stormy wind fulfilling his word; mountains and all hills; fruitful trees and all cedars; beasts and all cattle; creeping things and flying fowl; Kings of the earth and all people; princes and all judges of the earth; both young men and maidens; old men and children. . . . Praise ye the Lord. Praise God in his sanctuary; praise him in the firmament of his power. . . . Let everything that hath breath praise the Lord. Praise ye the Lord."

The poetry of the Bible is not only the highest poetry to be found anywhere in literature, it contains the essence of all religion. . . . Job, the Psalms, and Isaiah contain an eternal element of truth that no advance in the world's thought can make obsolete. Through such poetry, rather than through any formal creed, man is lifted into a communion with the Divine.

1874—Frances Ridley Havergal (1836–79) was an English woman who wrote many remarkable religious poems and hymns. Her most enduring collection is called Ministry of Song, *published in 1870. One of her most famous hymns, "Take My Life and Let It Be," was written on this day. Here she describes the circumstances. (See also July 17 and October 13.)*

———————⋖⋗———————

I went for a little visit of five days. There were ten persons in the house, some unconverted and long prayed for, some converted but not rejoicing Christians. He gave me the prayer, "Lord, give me *all* in this house!" And He just *did!* Before I left the house every one had got a blessing. The last night of my visit I was too happy to sleep and passed most of the night in praise and renewal of my own consecration, and these little couplets formed themselves and chimed in my heart one after another, till they finished with, "Ever, only, all for Thee!"

> Take my life and let it be
> Consecrated, Lord, to Thee.
> Take my moments and my days
> Let them flow in endless praise.
>
> Take my hands and let them move
> At the impulse of Thy love.
> Take my feet and let them be
> Swift and beautiful for Thee.
>
> Take my voice and let me sing
> Always, only, for my King.
> Take my lips and let them be
> Filled with messages from Thee. . . .
>
> Take my love, my God, I pour
> At Thy feet its treasure store;
> Take myself, and I will be
> Ever, only, all for Thee.

—from *Memorials of Frances Ridley Havergal*
by her sister, Maria Havergal (1880)

1863—Mrs. Frances Jane Crosby van Alstyne, better known as Fanny Crosby (1820–1915), was one of the finest American hymn writers of her generation, beloved for such hymns as "Blessed Assurance," "Redeemed, How I Love to Proclaim It," and "To God Be the Glory." For a time she wrote hymns with Ira D. Sankey (1840–1908) and assisted Dwight L. Moody (1837–99) in his evangelistic campaigns. She was blind, as was her husband, organist Alexander van Alstyne. In her autobiography, Memories of Eighty Years, *she commemorates February 5, 1863, as the day on which she first presented one of her hymns to a composer to set to music. Though she had written verses since childhood, she had never attempted to compose words for musical performance.*

—————— ✥❦✥ ——————

I presented myself at the office of William B. Bradley, 425 Broome Street. To my surprise, Mr. Bradley said, "Fanny, I thank God that we have at last met; for I think you can write hymns; and I have wished for a long time to have a talk with you." At the end of a brief interview I promised to bring him something before the week drew to a close, and three days later I returned with some verses that were soon set to music and published as my first hymn:

> We are going, we are going
> To a home beyond the skies,
> Where the fields are robed in beauty,
> And the sunlight never dies;
>
> Where the fount of joy is flowing
> In the valley green and fair.
> We shall dwell in love together;
> There shall be no parting there.
>
> We are going, we are going,
> And the music we have heard,
> Like the echo of the woodland,
> Or the carol of the bird.

Early fourth century—The church has traditionally ascribed this day as the feast day of St. Dorothea, who was martyred during the persecutions of the Roman emperor Diocletian. According to legend, she told the Roman governor, who ordered her execution, that she had remained a virgin because her heart belonged only to Jesus. A young pagan lawyer named Theophilus approached her on the way to the place of execution.

Now as she was being led away from the judgment seat, the young advocate Theophilus said to her jestingly, "Farewell, sweet Dorothea. When you have joined your lover, will you not send me some of the fruit and roses of his Paradise?"

Looking gravely and gently at him, Dorothea answered, "I will send some."

Whereupon Theophilus laughed merrily and went his way homeward.

At the place of execution, Dorothea begged the doomsman to tarry a little, and kneeling by the block, she raised her hands to heaven and prayed earnestly. At that moment a fair child stood beside her, holding in his hand a basket containing three golden apples and three red roses. "Take these to Theophilus, I pray," she said to the child, "and tell him Dorothea awaits him in the Paradise from which they came." Then she bowed her head and the sword of the doomsman fell.

Mark now what follows. Theophilus, who had reached home, was still telling of what had happened and merrily repeating his jest about the fruit and flowers of Paradise, when suddenly, while he was speaking, the child appeared before him with the apples and the roses. "Dorothea," he said, "has sent me to you with these, and she awaits you in the garden." And straightway the child vanished.

The fragrance of those heavenly roses filled Theophilus with a strange pity and gladness; and, eating of the fruit of the Angels, he felt his heart made new within him, so that he also became a servant of the Lord Jesus and suffered death for His name and thus attained to the celestial garden.

—from William Canton's *A Child's Book of Saints* (1898)

1941—On this day a Rev. J. W. Welch first contacted Oxford professor and author C. S. Lewis (1989–1963) to propose that Lewis present a series of broadcast talks over BBC Radio about the Christian faith. Lewis accepted. He later compiled these talks into a book that has since become one of the landmarks of Christian literature in this century: Mere Christianity. *Lewis was a writer of both academic studies and popular books, including the novels in his* Chronicles of Narnia, *which have become children's classics. The following excerpt is one of the best-known passages from* Mere Christianity. *(See also September 20.)*

———————— ⊷⊱ ————————

What should we make of a man, himself unrobbed and untrodden on, who announced that he forgave you for treading on other men's toes and stealing other men's money? Asinine fatuity is the kindest description we should give of his conduct. Yet this is what Jesus did. He told people that their sins were forgiven, and never waited to consult all the other people whom their sins had undoubtedly injured. He unhesitatingly behaved as if He was the party chiefly concerned, the person chiefly offended in all offenses. This makes sense only if He really was the God whose laws are broken and whose love is wounded in every sin. In the mouth of any speaker who is not God, these words would imply what I can only regard as a silliness and conceit unrivaled by any other character in history. . . .

I am trying here to prevent anyone saying the really foolish thing that people often say about Him: "I'm ready to accept Jesus as a great moral teacher, but I don't accept His claim to be God." That is the one thing we must not say. A man who was merely a man and said the sort of things Jesus said would not be a great moral teacher. He would either be a lunatic—on a level with the man who says he is a poached egg— or else he would be the Devil of Hell. You must make your choice. Either this man was, and is, the Son of God: or else a madman or something worse. You can shut Him up for a fool, you can spit at Him and kill Him as a demon; or you can fall at His feet and call Him Lord and God. But let us not come with any patronizing nonsense about His being a great human teacher. He has not left that open to us. He did not intend to.

356—Greek theologian and priest Athanasius (c. 293–373), called "the Father of Orthodoxy," spent much of his adult life debating the heretical Arians, who denied the divinity of Christ. On this day, while Athanasius was preparing to lead a communion service, his church was attacked by soldiers under the control of his enemies. Miraculously, Athanasius escaped. He spent the next six years in exile in the desert, during which time he wrote many of his greatest works. The Arians called his flight cowardly and said he should have faced martyrdom like a true saint. A portion of Athanasius' famous reply, "Apology for My Flight," is given here. (See also March 6.)

———————————— ·ᴇᴈ ᴇ·ᴈ ————————————

The flight of the Saints was neither blamable nor unprofitable. If they had not avoided their persecutors, who would have preached the glad tiding of the Word of Truth? It was for this that the persecutors sought after the Saints—that there might be no one to teach [the Word]. For this cause the Saints endured all things, that the Gospel might be preached. Behold, while they were thus engaged in conflict with their enemies, they passed not the time of their flight unprofitably; nor while they were persecuted, did they forget the welfare of others. But as ministers of the Good Word, they grudged not to communicate it to all men; so that even while they fled, they preached the Gospel and gave warning of the wickedness of those who conspired against them and confirmed the faithful by their exhortations. Thus, the blessed Paul, having found it so by experience, declared, "All that will live godly in Christ shall suffer persecution" (2 Timothy 3:12). And straightway he prepared those who fled for the trial, saying, "Let us run with patience the race that is set before us" (Hebrews 12:1); for although there be continual tribulations, yet "tribulation worketh patience, and patience experience, and experience hope, and hope maketh not ashamed" (Romans 5:4)....

Thus the Saints were abundantly preserved in their flight by the Providence of God, as physicians for the sake of them that had need.... This rule the blessed Martyrs observed in their persecutions: When persecuted they fled; while concealing themselves they showed fortitude; and when discovered they submitted to martyrdom.

—adapted from the translation of Rev. M. Atkinson (1891)

1623—German mystic theologian Jacob Boehme (1575–1624) wrote on this day a short essay on repentance and conversion, outlining steps he felt essential to a knowledge of God in Christ. The essay was published the next year, the year of Boehme's death, as part of a longer work, The Way to Christ. *An excerpt follows. Although Boehme was a humble shoemaker, his sublime and inspiring books influenced many later writers and thinkers. (See also January 1.)*

Today when you hear the Lord's voice do not plug up your ears and hearts. For the desire for future conversion is God's voice in man, which the Devil, by his imported images, covers up and hinders so that it is postponed from one day to the next, until the soul finally becomes a thistle and can no longer reach Grace.

Let such a person merely do this thing in his perceptive apprehension and look to his whole life-course and measure it with God's Ten Commandments and with the Gospel's Love, which bids him love his neighbor as he loves himself, so that in Christ's Love he will be a child of Grace. Let him see how far he has wandered away from this and what his daily practice and desire is. Then the Father's compulsion in God's Righteousness will be directed into him, revealing the self-fabricated images in this heart which he loves in place of God and which he held—and still holds—as his best treasure. . . .

But he is not to despair of God's Grace, only of his own self and of his own powers and capabilities. He should humble his soul before God with all his might, even though his heart says nothing but, "No, wait! This is not the day for it!" or "Your sins are too great, you cannot come to God's graciousness." . . . But he shall stand fast and hold God's prophesies as certain and unfailing truth, sighing to God with depressed heart and surrendering himself to Him in all his unworthiness. . . . For soon Christ will come to him again in His promised Word which He presses into him and with which He envelops him, assuming the life-form. He will begin to work within him by which his prayers will increase and become invigorated more and more in the Spirit of Grace.

—from *The Way to Christ*, translated by John Joseph Stoudt (1947)

1614—On this day an official of the Catholic Church approved for publication John Genninges's Life and Death of Mr. Edmund Genninges. It was John's biography of his brother, the English priest Edmund Genninges (1567–91), who was cruelly martyred during the reign of Queen Elizabeth I. One of the most moving passages of the book is found in a letter by Swithune Welles, a priest who was imprisoned with and executed at the same time as Father Genninges. In this letter Swithune Welles discusses the "uses" of imprisonment for the edification of the Christian. This passage echoes the sentiments of other Christian prisoners of all ages—from St. Paul to John Bunyan to Alexander Solzhenitsyn.

The comforts that captivity brings are so manifold that I have rather cause to thank God highly for his Fatherly correction than to complain of any worldly misery whatsoever. . . . These and the like cannot but comfort a good Christian and cause him to esteem his captivity to be a principal freedom, his prison a heavenly harbor, and his irons an ornament and comely badge of Christ himself. These will plead for him, and the prison will protect him. . . . When I pray, I talk with God; when I read, he talks with me, so that I am never alone. He is my chief companion and only comfort.

I have no cause to complain of the hardness of prison, considering the effects thereof, . . . because I fasten not my affection upon worldly vanities, of which I have had my fill, to my great grief and sorrow. I renounced the world before I ever tasted imprisonment, even in my baptism. This being so, how little does it matter in what place I am in the world since, by my promise, I vowed never to be of the world, which promise and profession, how slenderly soever I have kept heretofore, I purpose for the time to come, God assisting me with his grace in my commenced enterprise, to continue to my life's end. I utterly refuse all commodities, pleasures, pastimes, and delights, saving only the sweet service of God, in whom is the perfection of all true pleasures. Bound I am and charged with fetters, yet am I loose and unbound toward God. And far better I account it to have the body bound than the soul to be in bondage.

Seventh century—This day is the traditional feast day in honor of Caedmon (died c. 680), considered the first Christian poet to write in (Old) English. Caedmon was a simple herdsman in medieval England, near the town of Whitby. Being shy by nature, he often felt embarrassed at local celebrations by his inability to improvise songs and poetic verses on the harp, which was a popular custom of the time. One evening, to avoid having to entertain, Caedmon crept out to the stables, where he fell asleep. This story may seem to have the trappings of legend, but the following account was written in 731 by the English historian Bede (673–735) at a time when many people who had known Caedmon were still living.

———————— ⋙⋘ ————————

A person appeared to him in his sleep and said, "Caedmon, sing some song to me." He answered, "I cannot sing; for that was the reason why I left the entertainment and retired to this place because I could not sing." The other who talked to him replied, "However, you shall sing."—"What shall I sing?" rejoined he. "Sing the beginning of created beings," said the other. Hereupon he presently began to sing verses to the praise of God, which he had never heard, the purport whereof was thus:

> We are now to praise the Maker of the heavenly kingdom,
> The power of the Creator and his counsel, the deeds of the Father of
>   glory.
> How He, being the eternal God, became the author of all miracles,
> Who first, as almighty preserver of the human race,
> Created heaven for the sons of men as the roof of the house,
> And next the earth. . . .

Awaking from his sleep, he remembered all that he had sung in his dream, and soon added much more to the same effect. . . . In the morning he came to the steward, his superior, and having acquainted him with the gift he had received, was conducted to the abbess, by whom he was ordered, in the presence of many learned men, to tell his dream. . . . They all concluded that heavenly grace had been conferred on him by our Lord.

—adapted from Bede's *Ecclesiastical History*,
translated by J. Stevens (1723)

1880—Charlotte Mary Yonge (1823–1901), author of The Heir of Red-clyffe, *was one of Victorian England's most popular religious writers. On this day she wrote the preface to an English edition of* Paillettes d'Or *("Gold Dust"), an anonymous volume of meditations, long the most popular devotional book in France. The following reflection is from that edition.*

———— ✦ ————

I saw her from afar, poor child. She looked dreamy as she leaned against the window and held in her hand a daisy, which she was questioning by gradually pulling it to pieces. What she wanted to ascertain I cannot tell; I only heard in a low murmur, falling from her pale lips, these words, "A little, a lot, passionately, or not," as each petal her fingers pulled away fell fluttering at her feet. . . . Finally, when the daisy was all but gone, when her fingers stopped at the last petal and her lips murmured the word *little*, she dropped her head upon her arms, discouraged, and, poor child, she wept. Why weep, my child? Is it because this word does not please you? Let me, in the name of the simple daisy you have just destroyed, give you the experience of my old age.

Oh! If you only knew what it costs to have *much* of anything! A great deal of wit often results in spitefulness, which makes us cruel and unjust, in jealousy that torments, in deception that sullies all our triumphs, and pride, which is never satisfied. . . . A great deal of attractiveness often means a consuming vanity, overwhelming deception, an insatiable desire to please, a fear of being unappreciated, a loss of peace, domestic life much neglected. A great deal of wealth and success is the cause of luxury that enfeebles, loss of calm, quiet happiness, loss of love, leaving only the flattery that captivates. . . .

God may deprive a face of beauty, a character of amiability, a mind of brilliancy, but He will never take away a heart of love; to love He adds the power of prayer and the promise to always listen to and answer it. As long as we can love and pray, life has charms for us. . . . Do you see, my child, how much may lie beneath those simple words *a little* that the daisy gave you and that you seem so much to despise! Never scorn anything that seems wanting in brilliancy and remember: to be really happy we must have more virtue than knowledge, more love than tenderness, more guidance than cleverness, more health than riches, more repose than profit.

1601—On this day died Doctor Alexander Nowel (1507–1602), Dean of the Cathedral Church of St. Paul's in London. In his time, he was known for his piety and as the author of three popular catechisms. If he is remembered today, however, it is as the humble clergyman and fisherman briefly portrayed in Izaak Walton's whimsical treatise on the art of fishing, The Compleat Angler. *For Walton (1593–1683), Nowel was a reminder to all Christians to keep a sense of balance in their spiritual lives by pursuing restful and edifying pastimes. Walton himself was an early biographer of John Donne and other eminent English churchman. In the following passage from* The Compleat Angler, *Walton draws a picture of Nowel as an example of the charity, simplicity, and humility he so admired in religious people.*

The good old man (though he was very learned, yet knew that God leads us not to Heaven by many nor by hard questions), like an honest angler, made that good, plain, unperplexed catechism, which is printed with our good old service-book. I say, this good old man was as dear a lover and constant practicer of angling as any age can produce; and his custom was to spend, besides his fixed hours of prayer, . . . a tenth part of his time in angling; and also (for I have conversed with those who have conversed with him) to bestow a tenth part of his revenue—and usually all his fish—amongst the poor that inhabited near to those rivers in which it was caught; saying often "that charity gave life to religion"; and, at his return to his house, would praise God he had spent that day free from worldly trouble, both harmlessly and in recreation that became a churchman. And this good man was well content, if not desirous, that posterity should know he was an angler, as may appear by his portrait, . . . in which . . . he was drawn leaning on a desk, with his Bible before him, and on one hand of him his lines, hooks, and other tackling lying in a round; and on his other hand are his angle-rods of several sorts. . . . 'Tis said that angling and temperance were great causes of these blessings, and I wish the like to all that imitate him and love the memory of so good a man.

1379—Catherine of Siena (1347–1380) was an important figure in the fourteenth-century Italian church. Her piety, visions, humility, and spiritual wisdom attracted a large following. She was the author of an important mystical work The Dialogue, *as well as many letters and prayers. On this day, in Rome, she wrote the following lovely prayer.*

———— ⋅⊰ ⊱⋅ ————

You, eternal Godhead,
are life
and I am death.
You are wisdom
and I am ignorance.
You are light
and I am darkness.
You are infinite
and I am finite.
You are absolute directness
and I am terrible twistedness.
You are the doctor
and I am sick.
And who could ever reach up to you,
supreme exaltedness,
eternal Godhead,
to thank you for such infinite blessings
as you have given us?
You yourself will reach up to you
with the light you will pour out
into all who are willing to receive it,
and with your own cord
you will bind all who will let themselves be bound
by not resisting your will.

Do not be slow,
most kind Father,
to turn the eye of your mercy on the world.

—translated by Suzanne Noffke

1524—Popular astrologers caused panic in Germany by predicting that the world would end in a second flood, which was to occur on this day. The following poem, credited to a German reformer named Heinrich Pastoris, responds to those astrologers and all doomsayers who make such predictions. It is from a pamphlet published at the time called Casting a German Horoscope.

—⋅≪⋅≫⋅—

The stargazers of our time predict
That in this year, 1524,
A host of stars will converge in Pisces,
One of the twelve signs of the zodiac,
Which means, they all agree,
That a flood will soon transform
The world far and near.
In response, I offer this little treatise
And say: May God protect the house
That he built in the very beginning,
So that everyone might enter it.
Because for His sake were all things made
That dwell on the sphere of the earth,
Made by His word, His will, and His wisdom.
For Jesus Christ, His Son,
Who alone is the door to Heaven,
Was prefigured in the book of Moses,
Exodus chapter twelve:
For He was the doorpost streaked with blood,
While God struck down the Egyptians in the night
And displayed his power over Pharaoh
And led His children from the land—
True Israelites were they called,
And now they profess Christ everywhere.
Ultimately Christ defeated the Devil
With his own bright-colored blood,
As the holy Scriptures teach—
And nothing, nothing will be changed
No matter how fiercely Satan tries.

1867—*English author, minister, and folklorist Sabine Baring-Gould (1834–1924) is probably best remembered in our time as the author of the words to the hymn "Onward, Christian Soldiers." On this day his children's hymn "Now the Day Is Over" was published in the* Church Times. *The children for whom he wrote this moving hymn were mostly impoverished woolen-mill workers who could only attend his mission-school class at night, after their long days of hard labor.*

Now the day is over,
  Night is drawing nigh,
Shadows of the evening
  Steal across the sky.

Now the darkness gathers,
  Stars begin to peep,
Birds and beasts and flowers
  Soon will be asleep.

Jesu, give the weary
  Calm and sweet repose;
With thy tenderest blessing
  May our eyelids close.

Grant to little children
  Visions bright of thee;
Guard the sailors tossing
  On the deep blue sea.

Comfort every sufferer
  Watching late in pain;
Those who plan some evil
  From their sin restrain.

Through the long night-watches
  May thine angels spread
Their white wings above me,
  Watching round my bed.

When the morning wakens,
  Then may I arise
Pure and fresh and sinless
  In thy holy eyes.

Glory to the Father,
  Glory to the Son,
And to thee, blest Spirit,
  Whilst all ages run.

1687—Thomas Ken (1637–1711), bishop of Bath and Wells, was a well-known English prelate and hymn writer of the seventeenth century. In our time he is best remembered as the author of the "Doxology": "Praise God, from whom all blessings flow; / Praise Him, all creatures here below; / Praise Him above, ye heavenly host; / Praise Father, Son, and Holy Ghost." On this day he wrote "A Pastoral Letter to His Clergy Concerning Their Behavior During Lent" to the clergymen under his authority. In it Ken outlines what attitudes they should adopt during the Lenten season.

———————— ❧ ❧ ————————

No one can read God's Holy Word but he will see that the greatest saints have been the greatest mourners. David "wept whole rivers"; Jeremiah "wept sore, and his eyes ran down in secret places day and night like a fountain"; Daniel "mourned three full weeks and ate no pleasant bread and sought God by prayer and supplications with fasting and sackcloth and ashes"; St. Paul was humbled, and bewailed and wept for the sins of others; and our Lord himself when he "beheld the city wept over it." Learn then of these great saints, learn of our most compassionate Savior to weep for the public and, weeping, to pray that "we may know in this our day the things that belong to our peace, lest they be hid from our eyes." To mourn for national guilt, in which all share, is a duty incumbent on all, but especially on priests, who are particularly commanded "to weep and to say, 'Spare your people, O Lord, and give not your heritage to reproach,' that God may repent of the evil and become jealous for his land and pity his people." Be assured that none are more tenderly regarded by God than such mourners as these; there is "a mark" set by him on "all that sigh and cry for the abominations of the land"; the destroying angel is forbid to "hurt any of them"; they are all God's peculiar care and shall all have either present deliverance or such supports and consolations as shall abundantly endear their calamity.

1678—Pilgrim's Progress has been second only to the Bible in the hearts of Christian readers over the past three centuries, and it remains one of the timeless classics of world literature. Its author, John Bunyan (1628–88; see also August 18 and December 15), was an English preacher and writer, who was twice imprisoned for preaching without a license. During his second confinement, in 1675, he wrote much of Pilgrim's Progress, and three years later, on this day, the first part of the book was published. It is the allegorical account of a pilgrim's journey to heaven through the temptations and hardships of life. In the following passage, the pilgrim, named Christian, hears a description of what awaits him in the heavenly city at his journey's end.

———— ⋘ ⋙ ————

You must there receive the comforts of all your toil and have joy for all your sorrow; you must reap what you have sown, even the fruit of all your prayers and tears and sufferings for the King by the way. In that place you must wear crowns of gold and enjoy the perpetual sight and vision of the Holy One, for "there you shall see him as he is." There also you shall serve him continually with praise, with shouting and thanksgiving, whom you desired to serve in the world, though with much difficulty because of the infirmity of your flesh. There your eyes shall be delighted with seeing and your ears with hearing the pleasant voice of the Mighty One. There you shall enjoy your friends again that are gone thither before you; and there you shall with joy receive, even every one that follows into the holy place after you. There also shall you be clothed with glory and majesty, and put into an equipage fit to ride out with the King of Glory. When he shall come with sound of trumpet in the clouds, as upon the wings of the wind, you shall come with him; and when he shall sit upon the throne of judgment, you shall sit by him; yea, and when he shall pass sentence upon all the workers of iniquity, let them be angels or men, you also shall have a voice in that judgment, because they were his and your enemies. Also, when he shall again return to the city, you shall go too, with sound of trumpet, and be ever with him.

1701—French priest and writer François Fénelon (1651–1715) served as tutor for the grandson of France's most renowned king, Louis XIV, and also wrote what was in its time a best-seller, The Maxims of the Saints. *He was especially beloved for his personal letters, which were wise and filled with a warm spirituality, as can be seen in the following, written on this day. (See also May 25.)*

People who love themselves rightly, even as they ought to love their neighbor, bear charitably, though without flattery, with self as with another. They know what needs correction at home as well as elsewhere; they strive heartily and vigorously to correct it, but they deal with self as they would deal with someone else they wished to bring to God. They set to work patiently, . . . not being disheartened because perfection is not attainable in a day. . . . They do not heed the peevishness of pride and self-esteem, which so often mingles with that quiet resolution with which grace inspires us for the correction of our faults. That sort of irritable peevishness only discourages a man, makes him self-absorbed, repels him from God's service, wearies him in his way, makes him seek unworthy consolations, dries him up, distracts, exhausts him, fills him with disgust and despair of ever reaching his end. Nothing so hinders souls as this inward peevishness when it is encouraged; but if endured without consenting to it, it may be turned to good, like all other trials by which God purifies and perfects us. The only thing to be done is to let such troubles pass away, like a headache or a feverish attack, without doing anything to promote or prolong them.

Meanwhile, it is well to go on with your interior practices and your exterior duties as far as possible. Prayer may be less easy, the Presence of God less evident and less comforting, outward duties may be harder and less acceptable, but the faithfulness which accompanies them is greater, and that is enough for God. A boat which makes a quarter of a mile against the wind and tide requires greater power on the part of the rowers than when it makes a mile with both wind and tide favorable. The vexations of self-esteem should be treated as some men treat their nervous fancies, taking no notice of them any more than if they did not exist.

—from Fénelon's *Spiritual Letters to Women,*
translated by H. L. Sidney Lear (1902)

1865—Englishwoman Christina Rossetti (1830–94) wrote some of the finest religious poems of the nineteenth century. Her most famous poem, "Goblin Market" (1862), was written for children. She was the younger sister of poet and painter Dante Gabriel Rossetti, who was one of the founders of the Pre-Raphaelite Brotherhood, a group of Victorian artists and writers who sought to rejuvenate English arts. Christina's poems are finely honed and generally have a melancholy, contemplative tone, as in the following sonnet, called "If Only." In her thirty-fifth year, she wrote this poem on this day, and in it she ponders the fact that half her life is now passed.

--------⋙ ⋘--------

If I might only love my God and die!
   But now He bids me love Him and live on,
   Now when the bloom of all my life is gone,
The pleasant half of life has quite gone by.
My tree of hope is lopped that spread so high;
   And I forget how Summer glowed and shone,
   While autumn grips me with its fingers wan,
And frets me with its fitful windy sigh.
When Autumn passes then must Winter numb,
   And Winter may not pass a weary while,
   But when it passes Spring shall flower again;
And in that Spring who weepeth now shall smile,
   Yea, they shall wax who now are on the wane,
Yea, they shall sing for love when Christ shall come.

1804—Scottish church worker Isabella Graham (1742–1814) helped to found many charities for society's disenfranchised: the poor, orphans and widows, the homeless, and prisoners. (See also June 4.) Her journal, published posthumously under the title Devotional Exercises *(1819), is a classic of prayer and devotional thought. In her journal on this day she wrote this prayer for the renewal of God's church, a prayer that draws its inspiration from Revelation 2–3.*

————— ⋅⋅⋅ —————

"O you who are Alpha and Omega, . . ." write with power, speak with power, in the heart of the angel of this church. Have you not in former days had your dwelling among them? In days of trouble did you not work in them the fruits of labor and patience, so that for your name's sake they labored and fainted not? You blessed them and gave them peace, and they rejoiced in the light of your countenance. . . . Alas, Lord, we have . . . left our first love; we have not watched and prayed as you gave us command; . . . we have forsaken the counsel of our old men and given heed to flatterers; we have forgotten our dependence on you. . . .

We are poor and blind and miserable and naked, rich in our fancied wisdom, seeing by our own light, compassing ourselves about with our own sparks, and flaunting our rags. "We feed on ashes. . . ."

"Your covenant is well ordered in all things, and it is sure." Here, O Lord, I take my stand; here I lay my foundation, and on this your covenant I build; or rather here you yourself have laid my foundation, and on this rock you have set my soul and built my hopes, you subduing my enmity. I acquiesce. I will now "remember the years of your right hand." . . .

O Lord, ever, ever, and again did you deliver [your people] and send provision for them by your own covenant: "chose David your servant and took him from the sheepfolds, from following the ewes great with young. You brought him to feed Jacob, your people, and Israel, your inheritance. So he fed them according to the integrity of his heart and guided them by the skillfulness of his hands. . . ."

"This God is our God; we will make mention of his righteousness, and his only." By his own covenant, in his own time, and by means of his own providing, he will revive us. Amen.

—from *The Power of Faith: The Life and Writings of Mrs. Isabella Graham* (1819)

1913—On this day, his thirty-first birthday, English sculptor, engraver, and designer Eric Gill (1882–1940) and his wife were baptized. Gill's artistic legacy is great; among other things, he created the typeface that was used on most public signs in England in his day. He was also an illustrator and printer of genius. In the following passage from his Autobiography *he describes what went through his mind on this, his baptismal day.*

————— ❧ ❧ —————

I hadn't any qualms because I refused to have any. I refused to have any "difficulties" because you can't have difficulties unless you make them, and I wasn't making any. When I was "under instruction" they told me all sorts of things that seemed pretty rum, but I was past that sort of worrying. "Do you believe all that the Holy Church teaches?" That is the all-inclusive and final question; and I could unhesitatingly answer yes. But as to *what* she teaches on all the multiplication of funny subjects that we worry ourselves about, well, at the great risk, or, rather, certainty of being thought both lazy and unscrupulous, I made up my mind to confine my attention to things that seemed fundamentally important and things that intimately concerned me. As to whether or not the sun stood still over Jericho, or whether a real snake tempted Eve, . . . or whether lions would have lain down with lambs if Adam hadn't sinned, . . . well, don't you think these are awfully boring questions? And just think how stupendously learned you'd have to be to answer them with any assurance! In a kind of way they mentally "turn me up." Dear reader, you make me ashamed by your look of sad surprise. I am sorry. But let us turn our attention to more important matters. The bride is in love with her husband and his Bride is in love with Christ. I am a member of that mystical body and share her ecstasy.

So on February 22nd, my 31st birthday, 1913, we went together and were baptized.

1895—French writer Joris-Karl Huysmans (1848–1907) was in the avant garde of the French decadent movement at the end of the nineteenth century. He was so dissipated, according to one writer, that he would have to either put a bullet in his brain or kneel at the foot of the cross. Huysmans chose the latter. His autobiographical novel, En Route, was published on this day. He had become a Christian three years earlier while visiting the Trappist monastery at Igny in France. In the fictional character of Durtal in En Route, Huysmans describes his own journey from hopelessness and despair to the love of Christ.

As soon as Mass was over he quitted the chapel and escaped to the park. Then gently, without sensible effects, the Sacrament worked; Christ opened, little by little, Durtal's closed house and gave it air; light entered into Durtal in a flood. From the windows of his senses, which had looked till then into he knew not what cesspool, into what enclosure, dank and steeped in shadow; he now looked suddenly, through a burst of light, on a vista which lost itself in heaven.

His vision of nature was modified; . . . the sudden clearness of his soul was repeated in its surroundings.

He had the sensation of expansion, the almost childlike joy of a sick man who takes his first outing, of the convalescent, who having long crawled in a chamber, sets foot without; all grew young again. These alleys, this wood, through which he had wandered so much, which he began to know in all their windings, and in every corner, began to appear to him in a new aspect. . . .

Durtal looked on in transport. He desired to cry aloud his enthusiasm and his Faith to the landscape; he felt a joy in living. The horror of existence counted for nothing when there were such moments, as no earthly happiness can give. God alone had the power of thus filling a soul, of making it overflow and rush in floods of joy.

—from *En Route*, translated by C. Kegan Paul

1209—Francis of Assisi (1182–1226) epitomizes the spirit of Christianity as it was expressed in the late Middle Ages, though his example speaks powerfully to all ages. (See also May 11, August 11, and September 16.) As a poor friar and itinerant preacher, he had a remarkable influence on reforming the church of his day and converting the people to whom he preached. So great was his reputation that he was officially canonized by the church only two years after his death. On this day, as a devout young man of twenty-seven, Francis heard Matthew 10:7–13 read during a church service. So moved was he by the words that it marked the beginning of his itinerant life of poverty and preaching.

———————— ·⊱ ⊰· ————————

Now the blessed Francis . . . was wearing the habit of a hermit, carrying a staff in his hand, and walked with his feet shod with sandals, girt with a leather belt. But hearing on a day at the celebration of Mass those words that Christ spoke to His disciples when He sent them forth to preach, that they should carry on their journey neither gold nor silver, nor wallet, nor staff, nor have sandals nor two coats, and understanding these words more clearly afterward from that same priest, he was filled with joy unspeakable. "This," said he, "is that which I am fain with all my might to fulfill." Therefore, committing to memory all that he had heard, he strove joyfully to fulfill the same, casting aside without delay whatsoever he had two of, from thenceforward he used neither staff, sandals, purse, nor wallet; but, making for himself a right sorry and rough tunic, he threw aside his leather belt and took for a girdle a rope. Moreover, applying all the anxious endeavor of his heart to the work of this new grace, by what means he might persevere in that work, he began by Divine intuition to be the herald of Gospel perfection and to preach repentance in simple wise in public. Nor were his words empty, nor meet for laughter, but full of the might of the Holy Spirit, piercing unto the marrow of the heart, so that his hearers were rapt in amazement as they listened.

—from *The Legend of St. Francis* (1246),
translated by E. G. Salter

1890—Today famed Scottish novelist and poet Robert Louis Stevenson (1850–94), then living in the South Pacific, wrote his "Open Letter" to a certain Reverend Dr. Hyde of Honolulu concerning the memory of Father Damien (1840–89). After Damien's death from leprosy (resulting from his work among the lepers on Molokai), Reverend Hyde had published a letter in which he accused Damien of being "a coarse, dirty man, headstrong and bigoted." With insightful sarcasm, Robert Louis Stevenson replied:

Damien was *coarse.*

It is very possible. You make us sorry for the lepers, who had only a coarse old peasant for their friend and father. But you, who were so refined, why were you not there, to cheer them with the lights of culture? Or may I remind you that we have some reason to doubt if John the Baptist were genteel; and in the case of Peter, on whose career you doubtless dwell approvingly in the pulpit, no doubt at all that he was a "coarse, headstrong" fisherman! Yet even in our Protestant Bibles, Peter is called a saint.

Damien was *dirty.*

He was. Think of the poor lepers annoyed with this dirty comrade! But the clean Dr. Hyde was at his food in a fine house.

Damien was *headstrong.*

I believe you are right again; and I thank God for his strong head and heart.

Damien was *bigoted.*

I am not fond of bigots myself, because they are not fond of me. . . . But the point of interest in Damien . . . was that his bigotry, his intense and narrow faith, wrought potently for good and strengthened him to be one of the world's heroes and exemplars.

1838—On this day a certain Lady Barham wrote to English minister William Jay (1769–1853) to inform him that she planned to present Queen Victoria with a copy of Jay's most famous book: Morning and Evening Exercises, *from which an extract is given below. Lady Barham said she hoped the Queen would "condescend to accept of your book." Jay was a popular congregational preacher who spent more than sixty years as pastor of Argyle Chapel in Bath, England.*

———— ঙ্গ ————

Our Savior addressed his hearers and said, "Consider the lilies." There were many other flowers equally of notice with the lilies; but he selected these as specimens, and probably because they were near him and in sight, for he was sitting on the side of a hill, and he mentions not the cultured lilies but lilies "of the field."

Consider the lilies as productions of God's creating skill. All his works praise him. . . . Nothing can be added to them, nothing can be taken from them—"His work is perfect."

Consider the lilies as objects of his providential care. This was the peculiar aim of our Lord in the admonition. He would free the minds of his disciples from all undue solicitude respecting their temporal subsistence. Therefore, says he, "Take no thought for your life, what you shall eat or what you shall drink; nor yet for your body, what you shall put on. Is not life more than meat, and the body more than raiment? . . ."

Consider the lilies as emblems. First as emblems of Christ. The image indeed comes very short of his glory, but it will help our conceptions and serve to remind us a little of his purity, his meekness, his loveliness, and "the savor of his knowledge." Therefore, says he, "I am the rose of Sharon and the lily of the valley." Secondly, as emblems of Christians. In all things he must have the pre-eminence, but his people are held forth in the Scripture by the same resemblances; for there is not only a union but a conformity between them. They have the same mind which was in him. They have the image of the heavenly. And therefore to express their residence in the world, and how he values them above others, he adds, "As the lily among thorns, so is my love among the daughters."

1881—A. E. Kittredge (1834–1912) was a highly regarded American preacher of the nineteenth century, having held positions on both coasts and in between. On this day at the Third Presbyterian Church in Chicago, Kittredge delivered a sermon called "The Value of Christ to the Soul," in which he made the following interesting comparison.

⋅≈§ ξ≈⋅

Suppose a worm had the power of speech, and as you saw it creeping on the earth, it should say to you, "They tell me that the eagle has a nobler, grander life than I have, but I am perfectly satisfied. I am well enough as I am. I had rather be a worm than an eagle." Would such language change the manifest fact of the meanness of the worm-life and the grandeur of the eagle-life? But there is a vaster difference between the man of the world, however outwardly moral, and the Christian; between him who cries, "I live for wealth, for fame, for pleasure, for human love," and the humble, joyful believer who cries, "For me to live is Christ, and to die is gain." And if the former assures you, "I am well enough as I am," it is only a sign of the insanity of sin that not only makes man a slave, but makes him love his chains. . . .

Oh! I fear I cannot make you who are spiritually blind apprehend this truth of the value of Jesus as a friend, any more than I could give to one who had always had sightless eyes any idea of the beauty of a flower. But, my friends, I can only declare to you the glorious fact, praying that the Holy Spirit will touch your souls, that you may see in Jesus the One altogether lovely. What the bursting of the sunlight into a dark room is to those who have been enshrouded in the darkness, the coming of Jesus into the soul is to the heart of the believer, and there are many here this morning who can testify to the truth of my words, that He is the truest, richest friend, whose love is a rock to stand on, a pillow to lie on, an arm to rest on, a fellowship in which is found an unearthly peace and joy and strength. . . .

Oh! He is a precious friend, no words can describe His value, the language of heaven will be too poor to express it, but each of us may know that friendship by a blessed experience, and may, in that friendship, find our heaven begun below, for to know Him is to know heaven.

1899—Henry van Dyke (1852–1933) was an American minister, a writer, a university professor, and later in his career, an international diplomat. In his own time, as in ours, he was especially beloved for his tale The Story of the Other Wise Man *(see December 1) and for writing the words to the hymn "Joyful, Joyful We Adore Thee." On this day, in his office at Brick Church Manse in New York City, he wrote the preface to his book* The Gospel for a World of Sin, *a series of essays on the subject of sin and atonement. The following thoughtful passage is from that book.*

———— ✦ ————

Every "Thou shalt not" [in the Ten Commandments] is a disclosure of what men have done, and are prone to do, and would like to do again if they dared. The commandments sound like a shouting from the mountain top of the secrets of many hearts. After each divine word which says, "Thou shalt not," follows a human murmur which says, "But I will."

A Bible was once published in which, by a typographical error, the *not* was omitted from the seventh commandment ["Thou shalt commit adultery"]. It was called "the wicked Bible." The history of Israel, starting from Sinai, reads like a commentary on a wicked Bible with the printer's error multiplied by ten. Carry the commandments through the books of the Judges and the Kings, and you must acknowledge that they compel the conclusion that man is what he ought not to be and ought not to be what he is.

The one bright spot in the law given by Moses is the commandment to make a mercy-seat in the Tabernacle, where the sins of the people may be confessed before Almighty God (Exodus 25 and Leviticus 16) and where the blood of sacrifice, sprinkled upon the Ark, may symbolize an atonement between man and God. The one good hope which cheered Moses in his ministry to a disobedient and gainsaying folk was the promise that God would raise up a prophet from among his brethren unto whom the people should hearken (Deuteronomy 18:15). Blot out that prediction of Christ, and Moses stands as an embodiment of failure—a leader who emancipated the nation and condemned the race—the messenger of a divine law which was broken even while he was carrying it down from the burning mount.

Fifth century—On this day the Eastern church has traditionally honored St. John Cassian (c. 360–c. 435), an early church father. Cassian was a monk in Bethlehem, lived as a hermit with the desert fathers in Egypt, and later became a disciple of John Chrysostom (c. 347–407). In the following excerpt from Cassian's writings, he beautifully describes the soul in prayer.

———— ﻌﯽ ﻌﯽ ————

The nature of the soul is not inaptly compared to a very fine feather or very light wing, which, if it has not been damaged or affected by being spoilt by any moisture falling on it from without, is borne aloft almost naturally to the heights of heaven by the lightness of its nature and the aid of the slightest breath. But if it is weighted by any moisture falling upon it and penetrating into it, it will not only not be carried away by its natural lightness into any aerial flights, but will actually be borne down to the depths of earth by the weight of the moisture it has received. So also our soul, if it is not weighted with faults that touch it and the cares of this world, or damaged by the moisture of injurious lusts, will be raised, as it were, by the natural blessing of its own purity and borne aloft to the heights by the light breath of spiritual meditation, and leaving things low and earthly will be transported to those that are heavenly and invisible. Wherefore we are well warned by the Lord's command: "Take heed that your hearts be not weighted down by surfeiting and drunkenness and the cares of this world" (Luke 21:34). And therefore if we want our prayers to reach not only the sky, but what is beyond the sky, let us be careful to reduce our soul, purged from all earthly faults and purified from every stain, to its natural lightness, so that our prayer may rise to God unchecked by the weight of any sin. . . .

And [so] that you may see the character of true prayer, I will give you not my own opinion but that of the blessed Anthony, whom we have known sometimes to have been so persistent in prayer that often as he was praying in a transport of mind, when the sunrise began to appear, we have heard him in the fervor of his spirit declaiming: "Why do you hinder me, O sun, who are rising for this very purpose—to withdraw me from the brightness of this true light?"

—from Cassian's *Conferences*,
translated by Edgar C. S. Gibson (1898)

March

COME·NOT·
ANY·
NEARER;
TURN·THY·
FACE·
TO·THE·
FOREST·
AND·GO
DOWN

The monk Diarmait refuses to shelter the
woman in the wilderness (see March 13).
Illustration by T. H. Robinson from William
Canton's *A Child's Book of Saints*.

1827—Not only was African-American reformer and evangelist Sojourner Truth (c. 1797–1883) a controversial public figure in her day, but she remains an icon for both the civil rights and feminist movements in our time. A former slave, she boldly chided the established church for its failure to endorse the rights of African-Americans and women. On this day, as a young woman, she first encountered Christ as a living Savior. Before then, feeling too sinful to pray directly to God, she had searched for someone to pray to God in her behalf but soon discovered that everyone she knew was as sinful as she. At that point, a mysterious figure came to her in a vision.

------------ ⋅⋧ ⋦⋅ ------------

"Who *are* you?" she exclaimed as the vision brightened into a form distinct, beaming with the beauty of holiness and radiant with love. She then said, audibly addressing the mysterious visitant, "I *know* you, and I *don't* know you," meaning, "You seem perfectly familiar; I feel that you not only love me but that you always *have* loved me—yet I know you not—I cannot call you by name." When she said, "I know you," the subject of the vision remained distinct and quiet. When she said, "I don't know you," it moved restlessly about, like agitated waters. So while she repeated, without intermission, "I know you, I know you," so that the vision might remain—"Who are you?" was the cry of her heart, and her whole soul was in one deep prayer that this heavenly personage might be revealed to her and remain with her. At length, after bending both soul and body with the intensity of this desire, till breath and strength seemed failing and she could maintain her position no longer, an answer came to her, saying distinctly, "It is Jesus." "Yes," she responded, "It is *Jesus*."

Previous to these exercises of mind, she had heard Jesus mentioned in reading or speaking, but had received from what she heard no impression that he was any other than an eminent man, like a Washington or a Lafayette. Now he appeared to her delighted mental vision as so mild, so good, and so every way lovely—and he loved her so much! And how strange that he had always loved her and she had never known it! And how great a blessing he conferred in that he should stand between her and God! And God was no longer a terror and a dread to her.

—from *The Narrative of Sojourner Truth*
by Olive Gilbert and Sojourner Truth (1878)

1911—The seminal book Mysticism *by Evelyn Underhill (1875–1941) was published on this day. Underhill, herself a poet and mystic as well as a scholar, was this century's greatest authority on the mystics of the Christian faith. In the following passage from* Mysticism, *Underhill discusses the meaning the Incarnation of Christ holds for the traditional mystics of the church.*

———————— ᴥᵹ ᵹᴥ ————————

The Incarnation . . . has best been able to describe and explain the nature of the inward and personal mystic experience. The Incarnation, which is for traditional Christianity synonymous with the historical birth and earthly life of Christ, is for mystics of a certain type, not only this but also a perpetual Cosmic and personal process. It is an everlasting bringing forth, in the universe and also in the individual ascending soul, of the divine and perfect Life, the pure character of God, of which the one historical life dramatized the essential constituents. Hence the soul, like the physical embryo, resumes in its upward progress the spiritual life-history of the race. "The one secret, the greatest of all," says Patmore, is "the doctrine of the Incarnation, regarded not as an historical event that occurred two thousand years ago, but as an event that is renewed in the body of everyone who is in the way to the fulfillment of his original destiny."

We have seen that for mystical theology the Second Person of the Trinity is the Wisdom of the Father, the Word of Life. The fullness of this Word could therefore only be communicated to the human consciousness by a Life. In the Incarnation this Logos, this divine character of Reality, penetrated the illusions of the sensual world—in other words, the illusions of all the selves whose ideas compose that world—and "saved" it by this infusion of truth. A divine, suffering, self-sacrificing Personality was then shown as the sacred heart of a living, striving universe: and for once the Absolute was exhibited in the terms of finite human existence.

1642—Sir Thomas Browne (1605–82) was a talented English physician and author. Though he had a skeptical turn of mind concerning many doctrines of the church, he adhered to the basic tenets of the faith and wrote one of Christendom's great literary classics, Religio Medici *("The Religion of a Doctor"). On this day he wrote an urgent letter to a reviewer of his book to explain that the book had not yet been published and that the copy in the reviewer's hand had been published without his permission. The official edition appeared the next year. In the following passage from* Religio Medici, *Browne discusses divine revelation as seen in Nature.*

To raise so beauteous a structure as the world and the creatures thereof was but God's art.... There are two books from which I collect my Divinity; besides that written one of God, another of his servant Nature, that universal and public manuscript that lies expansed unto the eyes of all. Those that never saw Him in the one have discovered Him in the other. This was the Scripture and Theology of the heathens.... Surely the heathens knew better how to join and read these mystical letters than we Christians, who cast a more careless eye on these common hieroglyphics and disdain to suck Divinity from the flowers of Nature.... The wisdom of God has ordained the actions of His creatures, according to their several kinds. To make a revolution every day is the nature of the sun, because of that necessary course which God has ordained it, from which it cannot swerve but by a faculty from that voice which first did give it motion.... I hold there is a general beauty in the works of God, and therefore no deformity in any kind or species of creature whatsoever. I cannot tell by what logic we call a toad, a bear, or an elephant ugly; they being created in those outward shapes and figures which best express the actions of their inward forms, and having past that general visitation of God, who saw that all He had made was good, that is, conformable to His will, which abhors deformity and is the rule of order and beauty.... To speak yet more narrowly, there was never anything ugly or misshapen but the Chaos; wherein, notwithstanding, there was no deformity because [there was] no form. Now Nature is not at variance with art, nor art with Nature, they being both servants of His providence.

1844—Theodore Parker (1810–60) was an American minister who was controversial for his radical views; for instance, as a staunch abolitionist, he was on a committee that helped finance John Brown's unsuccessful slave uprising at Harpers Ferry. However, he was beloved by many, and his warm and deeply felt writings show why. In 1844 he toured Europe, and on this day he visited the famous Roman catacombs, as he describes in his diary. Note that while moved by the experience, he could not resist a little souvenir hunting on the side.

I passed along whole miles of passages, I should think, all lined with Christian graves "in the sides of the pit." The bones still lie there; perhaps they have lain there for sixteen or seventeen hundred years. The bones of the martyrs have been gathered up and removed; but the Christians who went down to the sides of the pit in peace are still here, but they all have nearly moldered to dust. Here and there were entire bones, skulls, thigh-bones, etc. I gathered up some fragments and have them still.

I know no place that fills me with deeper emotion in Rome than these Catacombs. Here the persecuted when alive found refuge; when dead found refuge too, for their ashes and bones long tortured. Here the relations of a martyr laid down his lacerated body and in the *ampullæ* [flasks] deposited the blood they had piously collected with sponges. Well, the Master died the martyr's death, the servants need not fear to do the same! I shall never forget the impression left on my mind by this visit. I should like to come and sit here all night and read the Fathers— Origen's exhortation to his young converts, urging them to be martyrs, or something of Cyprian or Tertullian or the lives of the martyrs themselves. No wonder the Catholic Church has such a hold on the hearts of the world, while she keeps in her bosom the relics of the sainted dead! Yet as I walked about here I could not but think how easy it must have seemed, and must have been too, to bear the cross of the martyrdom. The recollection of Christ, of the Apostles, the certainty of the prayers and best wishes of men on earth, the expectation of heavenly satisfaction—all would conspire to stimulate the spirit and make men court, and not shun, the martyr's death.

—from *The Prayers of Theodore Parker* (1861)

Fifth and sixth centuries—The Celtic church commemorated St. Kieran of Saighir on this day. While roughly contemporary with St. Patrick, Kieran has the distinction of being the first saint born on Irish soil (since Patrick was born in England). Saighir, a small town near the geographical center of Ireland, seems to have been an important pagan religious site; so it was here that Kieran founded his monastery, the ruins of which can still be seen. According to legend, Kieran, like St. Francis, is said to have possessed a special charm over animals. In fact, when he first founded his monastery, the legend states, there were no people in the region, and his first converts were wild animals. The following account is from William Canton's charming Child's Book of Saints *(1898).*

———— ❧ ❦ ————

The blessed Bishop Kieran of Saighir . . . was the first saint born in green Erin. For he wandered away through the land seeking the little well where he was to found his monastery. That well was in the depths of a hoary wood, and when he drew near it the holy bell that he carried rang clear and bright, as it had been foretold him. So he sat down to rest under a tree, when suddenly a wild boar rushed out of its lair against him; but the breath of God tamed it, and the savage creature became his first disciple and helped him to fell small trees and to cut reeds and willows so that he might build him a cell. After that there came from brake and copse and dingle and earth and burrow all manner of wild creatures; and a fox, a badger, a wolf, and a doe were among Kieran's first brotherhood. We read too that, for all his vows, the fox made but a crafty and gluttonous monk, and stole the saint's leather shoes and fled with them to his old earth. Therefore Kieran called the religious brotherhood together with his bell and sent the badger to bring back the fugitive, and when this was done the saint rebuked the fox for an unworthy and sinful monk and laid penance upon him. . . .

These things are not matters of faith; you may believe them or not as you will. Perhaps they did not happen in the way in which they are now told, but if they are not altogether true, they are at least images and symbols of truth.

1861—On this day, English clergyman and scholar Arthur Penrhyn Stanley (1815–81) wrote the preface to his scholarly compilation Lectures on the History of the Eastern Church. *Among other things, Stanley suggested in this work that the modern Western church could benefit by emulating certain aspects of Eastern Orthodoxy. The following touching story from this book, however, has a less serious intent and tells a legend about the childhood of Athanasius, one of the greatest and most courageous figures in early church history. (For more about Athanasius see also February 8.)*

—◆§ §◆—

[Athanasius'] first appearance is in a well-known story, which, though doubted in late times from its supposed incongruity with the dignity of the great saint, has every indication of truth. Alexander, Bishop of Alexandria, was entertaining his clergy in a tower or lofty house overlooking the expanse of sea beside the westernmost of the two Alexandrian harbors. He observed a group of children playing on the edge of the shore and was struck by the grave appearance of their game. His attendant clergy went, at his orders, to catch the boys and bring them before the Bishop, who taxed them with having played at religious ceremonies. At first, like boys caught at a mischievous game, they denied, but, at last, confessed that they had been imitating the sacrament of baptism, that one of them had been selected to perform the part of the Bishop, and that he had duly dipped them in the sea with all the proper questions and addresses. When Alexander found that these forms had been observed, he determined that the baptism was valid; he himself added the consecrating oil of confirmation and was so much struck with the knowledge and gravity of the boy-bishop that he took him under his charge. This little boy was Athanasius, already showing the union of seriousness and sport that we shall see in his after life. That childish game is an epitome of the ecclesiastical feelings of his time and of his country. The children playing on the shore, the old men looking at them with interest—these, indeed, are incidents which belong to every age of the world.

202—*According to Alfonso de Liguori (1697–1787; see also April 28), Italian priest and theologian, this is the day on which St. Perpetua (second century) and her companions were martyred for their refusal to renounce Christianity. As residents of Carthage, they were victims of an edict of the Roman emperor Severus, stating that all Christians who refused to pray to the Roman gods should be sacrificed in the arena. In his book* Triumphs of the Martyrs *(1776), Liguori quotes an earlier document,* The Passion of St. Perpetua, *which is supposed to contain writings by St. Perpetua herself; in the following passage, Perpetua relates the circumstances of her imprisonment and a vision she had just before her death.*

———————— ✥ ————————

My father used every artifice to dissuade me from the Christian faith; but I responded to him firmly, "Father, I am a Christian." Full of indignation, he flew into a rage, as if to tear out my eyes, and he threatened to do me countless injuries. A few days later, we all received the holy baptism, and then we were put into prison, where I was frightened by the darkness, the noxious smells, and the intense heat that was created by the great number of prisoners. There, I obtained the favor of having my son brought to me, which consoled me greatly. My brother came to see me and asked me to pray to the Lord to let me know whether I was destined to become a martyr. So I began to pray, and I saw in a vision a golden ladder that reached right up to heaven; but it was very narrow, and on the sides were fixed sharp knives and iron spikes. At the foot of this ladder stood a dragon who threatened to devour anyone who might attempt to climb it. The first to go up was a certain Christian named Saturnus [one of Perpetua's companions], who invited me to follow him. I climbed up and found myself in a large garden where I met a man with a kindly face who said to me: "You are welcome, my daughter." And so, this vision informed me that we were all destined to become martyrs—and I told my brother so.

My father came again to see me in prison, and with his eyes brimming with tears, he threw himself at my feet. "My daughter," he said, "have pity on me, this poor old man who is your father; have pity, at least, on your child, and do not bring ruin on our entire family with your obstinacy." I was prostrated with grief, but I remained immovable in my resolution.

1768—Augustus Montague Toplady (1740–78) was an eminent English minister and hymn writer whose most familiar hymn is "Rock of Ages, Cleft for Me." Toplady was such an energetic proponent of Calvinism in the Church of England that he was often at odds with John Wesley and the early Methodists. In his Diary *for this day, Toplady recorded the following event.*

————— ∙≼ᢀ ᢀ≽∙ —————

Mr. Harris and myself took a walk about two in the afternoon to the top of Fen-Ottery Hill. Looking round, I observed to him how plainly we could see the two churches . . . in the vale beneath us. Perceiving, however, a pillar of smoke rising into the air at a little distance from Harpford tower, I asked my companion what he thought it was. He replied, "I suppose they are burning straw." Imagining this to be the case, we continued our walk. . . . By the time I arrived at the wooden bridge, I met a man [who] saluted me with "Sir, your house is burnt to the ground." . . .

What I chiefly enter down this account in my diary for is this: Namely, as a memento of God's great goodness to me, both in a way of providence and grace. . . . Neither the report, nor the sight of this alarming visitation made me so much as change countenance or feel the least dejection. This could not proceed from nature, for my nerves are naturally so weak that, in general, the least discomposing accident oversets me quite, for a time. It was therefore owing to the supporting goodness of God who made me experience the truth of that promise: "Your shoes shall be iron and brass; and as is your day, so shall your strength be" [Deuteronomy 33:25]. Surely we can both do and endure all things through Christ enabling us. . . . But the strength of God was made perfect in my weakness, and, therefore, it was that my heart stood fast, believing in the Lord. Oh, may Your grace be ever sufficient for me! . . .

You, Lord, can make the feeble as David. Thus, the 8th of March was a day to be particularly noted, not in my book only, but in my latest remembrance, on account of that wonderful support with which I was favored, which not only made my feet as hind's feet and caused me to walk on the high places of Jacob, but which even bore me up as on eagle's wings, above the reach of grief, fear, and weakness, and, as it were, laid me at rest on the bosom of Christ and within the arms of God.

1863—Alexander Moody Stuart (1809–98), pastor of Free St. Luke's Church in Edinburgh, Scotland, was a popular preacher known for his warmth and sensitivity, which led an admiring D. L. Moody to say of him, "He has poetry in his soul." Stuart, on this day, wrote in his preface to his classic book The Three Marys: *"The author has only to add his request for the reader's prayer for a blessing on these pages; . . . for the breathing of the Spirit on whatever is of God; and for the sprinkling of the whole with that blood of the Lamb." In the following passage from that work, he considers Mary Magdalen's special role in the Resurrection account in John 20.*

--------⋅⋨ ⋩⋅--------

Mary is denied the desire of her heart in nearer approach to Jesus and closer fellowship with him; but she has more than her heart's desire, and more than had entered her mind to conceive, when Christ makes her his chosen messenger to the apostles themselves. To be Christ's herald is higher honor than to be Christ's worshiper.

Mary must not tarry with Jesus but must run for him as his messenger and must carry to the disciples the promise of his ascension to the Father and of his brotherhood to them.

"Jesus saith unto her, Touch me not, but go to my brethren" (John 20:17). A woman must go to the apostles; the finder of the King must carry his word; it is better for her to go from Christ with his message than to tarry beside him without it; and Mary has now reached the crowning transaction in her life.

A *woman* must go to the disciples; Mary must not stay with Christ as his friend, but in his own strength go forth from him as his messenger. A woman is Christ's first commissioned herald after his resurrection; a woman in whom seven devils had dwelt, his elect messenger to his followers; a woman not suffered to speak in the church, ambassador to the great apostles. It is God's chosen way; he takes the weak things of the world to confound the mighty, and the foolish to confound the wise, that no flesh may glory in his presence. "He saves the tents of Judah first, that the glory of the house of David may not magnify itself." Let therefore no woman say, "I can bear no message for Jesus." In your own place by God's strength you can; and if you can, you must, or you will displease your Lord.

1662—Jacques Bénigne Bossuet (1627–1704) was a French Catholic bishop, a tutor to the French prince, and one of the greatest preachers that France ever produced. In the following extract from a sermon called "On Providence," which was delivered on this day, Bossuet attempts to answer the criticisms of the "libertines" (free-thinkers) who attacked the idea of God because they could see no order or fairness in the distribution of good and evil.

———————— ◈ ◈ ————————

When I consider the disposition of human affairs—confused, inequitable, irregular—I often compare it to certain pictures that are sometimes hung in book shops that specialize in such curiosities—pictures that contain optical illusions. At first sight they only show us formless shapes and a confused mixture of colors, which seem to be the trial efforts of an apprentice painter or maybe even the plaything of some child, rather than the work of a master's knowing hand. But then, those who know the picture's secret can teach you how to view it from a certain perspective, and suddenly all the uneven lines seem to gather together in a certain fashion in our sight; all the confusion disentangles itself, and you see appearing before you a face with all its features in proportion, where just a moment ago you saw nothing at all. This, it seems to me, is a perfect image of our world, with its apparent confusions and its hidden perfections, which we cannot properly view unless we view it from the angle of faith that Jesus Christ has shown us. . . .

The unthinking libertine cries that there is no order . . . or that God has abandoned human life to the caprices of fate. But perhaps that which seems like confusion to you is really a hidden work of art, and if you could only find that point from which to view things properly, all inequalities would rectify themselves and you would see only wisdom where you saw only disorder before.

Open your eyes, O mortals; for it is Jesus Christ himself who exhorts you to do so in his admirable discourses in Matthew 6 and Luke 12.

Early ninth century—In the medieval Celtic church, this day was held as the feast day of St. Oengus the Culdee. He was born into a royal Irish family sometime in the eighth century, but he forsook his family and became a hermit and later a monk. He was part of the Céli Dé movement (meaning "servant of God," from which Oengus's epithet, "Culdee," is derived), which emphasized simplicity, discipline, and personal devotion. Oengus died in about 824. It is especially appropriate to remember him in this present book because he wrote what is probably the earliest "daily devotional": an anthology of the lives of the Celtic saints and martyrs, one for every day of the year. The work, written in Gaelic verse, is called The Feliré, and the following is the opening prayer—the "Invocation"—of that collection.

———— ❧ ❧ ————

Sanctify, O Christ, my words!
O Lord of the seven heavens,
Grant me the gift of wisdom;
O Sovereign of the bright sun,
The heavens with all Your holiness!
O King of the government of angels,
O Lord of the people,
O King, all righteous and good,
May I receive the full benefit
Of praising Your royal host!
Your royal host I praise
Because You are my Sovereign.
I have disposed my mind
To be constantly beseeching You.
I beseech a favor from You—
That I may be purified from my sins
Through the peaceful bright-shiny flock,
The royal host whom I celebrate.

—translated by Father Eugene O'Curry (1888)

Sixth century—Gregory the Great (c. 540–604), who is honored by the church on this day, was one of the most influential popes who ever lived. Not only is he admired for his theological writings and liturgical songs (now known as "Gregorian" chants), but also for his humility and charity. He was the first pope to call himself "the servant of the servants of God." In this tale from The Golden Legend *by Jacob de Voragine (c. 1228–98), Gregory's charity as a young abbot leads to a startling prophecy.*

—◆§ §◆—

One day when he was busy writing in a cell of the monastery over which he ruled as abbot, a shipwrecked sailor appeared at the door and asked him for alms. Gregory gave him six pieces of silver; but some hours later the mariner returned and said that he had lost much and had received too little. Again Gregory gave him six pieces of silver; and once more the mendicant returned, begging alms more insistently than before. Then the steward of the monastery told Gregory that he had nothing more to give, save only a silver porringer in which Gregory's mother was wont to send cooked vegetables to her son. At once Gregory ordered him to give the porringer to the beggar, who accepted it with joy and disappeared. . . .

Another day he had asked his chancellor to invite twelve pilgrims to his table. And during the repast, he perceived that there were thirteen in the company and remarked it to his chancellor. But he, after counting them, said, "Believe me, Father, there are only twelve!" And then Gregory became aware that one of the guests, who was seated not far from him, constantly changed his appearance, sometimes looking like a youth, sometimes like an aged man. When the meal was finished, Gregory led this guest into his chamber and implored him in the name of God to tell him who he was. And the guest answered, "Know then that I am the shipwrecked mariner to whom you once gave the silver porringer in which your mother used to send you cooked vegetables! And know also that since that day, the Lord chose you to become the head of His church. . . ." And Gregory asked, "But how is it that you know that the Lord destined me to this office?" And the stranger responded, "I knew it because I am an angel, charged now by the Lord to watch over you. . . ." And instantly he vanished

—from *The Golden Legend,*
translated by Granger Ryan and Helmut Ripperger

Seventh century—The Celtic church honored St. Kenach on this day. He was a seventh-century Irish monk, abbot, and founder of two monasteries. In one legend, Kenach and a disciple, Diarmait, received two unexpected visitations while praying and meditating in a wilderness cave.

———————— ❧ ❧ ————————

In the midst of the storm there was a space of light, as though it were moonshine, and the light streamed from an Angel, who stood near the wall of rock with outspread wings, and sheltered a blackbird's nest from the wintry blast. And the monks gazed at the shining loveliness of the Angel, till the wind fell and the snow ceased and the light faded away and the sharp stars came out and the night was still.

Now at sundown of the day that followed, when the Abbot was in the cave, the young monk, Diarmait, standing among the rocks, saw approaching a woman who carried a child in her arms; and crossing himself he cried aloud to her, "Come not any nearer; turn your face to the forest, and go away."

"Nay," replied the woman, "for we seek shelter for the night, and food and the solace of fire for the little one."

"Go away, go away," cried Diarmait; "no woman may come to this hermitage."

"How can you say that, O monk?" said the woman. "Was the Lord Christ any worse than you? Christ came to redeem woman no less than to redeem man. Not less did He suffer for the sake of woman than for the sake of man. Women gave service and attendance to Him and His apostles. A woman it was who bore Him, else had men been left forlorn. It was a man who betrayed Him with a kiss; a woman it was who washed His feet with tears. It was a man who smote Him with a reed, but a woman who broke the alabaster box of precious ointment. It was a man who thrice denied Him, a woman stood by His cross. It was a woman to whom He first spoke on Easter morn, but a man thrust his hand into His side and put his finger in the prints of the nails before he would believe. And not less than men do women enter the heavenly kingdom. Why then should you drive my little child and me from your hermitage?"

Then Kenach, who had heard what was said, came out and blessed the woman.

—adapted from William Canton's *Child's Book of Saints* (1898)

1534—In sixteenth-century England it was customary for trades people to enact religious dramas on appropriate holidays and at religious festivals. Literary scholars call them the "crafts cycles." The sheepshearers and tailors of Coventry, England, enacted a Christmas play called The Magi, Herod, and the Slaughter of the Innocents. *One imagines that they elected to do this play because of the sumptuous costumes that the shearers and tailors would be able to provide for the actors playing the exotic Magi. On this day, according to a note at the end of the play, the finishing touches were made on the script by a certain Robert Croo. This speech (which has been modernized) is spoken by the first of the Magi as he travels toward Bethlehem.*

———— ও§ ৡ৯ ————

Now blessed be God for this sweet sign,
    For yonder, a fire, a bright star I see!
Now is He come among us,
    As the prophet said it should be.

He said there should be a baby born,
    Coming out of the root of Jesse,
To save mankind that was forlorn.
    And truly, come now is He.

Reverence and worship to Him I will do,
    To God, who made us from naught.
All the prophets agreed and said even so,
    That with His precious blood all should be bought.

May He grant me grace,
    By yonder star that I see,
And into that place
    Bring me
That I may worship Him in humility
    And see His glorious face.

1794—On this day the British magazine the Cambridge Intelligencer *published an anonymous "Hymn," bearing the inscription, "Sung at a meeting of the Friends of Peace and Reform in Sheffield, held on the late Fast Day." In England at that time, days of prayer and fasting were set aside because of the wars with France. The French armies at that time were led by a youthful upstart general named Napoleon Bonaparte.*

———————— ·ఆ ୬· ————————

O God of Hosts, thine Ear incline,
Regard our prayers, our cause be thine;
When orphans cry, when babes complain,
When widows weep—can'st thou refrain?

Now red and terrible thine hand
Scourges with War our guilty land;
Europe thy flaming vengeance feels,
And from her deep foundation reels.

Her rivers bleed like mighty veins;
Her towers are ashes, graves her plains;
Slaughter her groaning valleys fills,
And reeking carnage melts her hills.

O Thou! whose awful word can bind
The raging waves, the raving wind,
Mad tyrants tame; break down the high
Whose haughty foreheads beat the sky;

Make bare thine arm, great King of kings!
That arm alone salvation brings,
That wonder-working arm which broke
From Israel's neck th' Egyptian Yoke.

1673—Lancelot Andrewes (1555–1626) was a brilliant Anglican scholar and churchman in the time of King James I of England. He was also one of the most noted preachers of his day. At the Hampton Court Conference (see January 16) he was selected as one of the translators of the King James Bible (1611), his chief responsibilities being the Pentateuch and historical books. After his death, his personal prayer book, which was written in Latin and called Preces Privatae *("Personal Devotions"), was published. On this day, the first complete edition received its imprimatur (the official seal that the book was free of doctrinal error), and it contained the following psalm-like prayer, called "Hosanna on Earth: A Prayer for Things Temporal."*

—————— ⚜ ⚜ ——————

Remember, O Lord, to crown the year with Your goodness; for the eyes of all wait upon You, and You give them their meat in due season. You open Your hand and satisfy the desire of every living thing.

On us also, O Lord, vouchsafe the precious things of heaven and the dew above and the deep that couches beneath, the fruits of the sun, the growth of the moons, the chief things of the ancient mountains, the precious things of the everlasting hills, the precious things of the earth and of its fruit, good seasons, wholesome weather, full crops, plenteous fruits, health of body, peaceful times, mild government, equal laws, wise counsels, just judgments, loyal obedience, vigorous justice, fertility, fruitfulness, ease in bearing, happiness in offspring, careful nurture, sound training; that our sons may be as plants grown up in their youth, our daughters as cornerstones, polished after the similitude of a palace; that our garners may be full, affording all manner of store; that our sheep may bring forth thousands and ten thousands in our fields; that our oxen may be strong to labor; that there be no breaking in, nor going out; that there be no complaining in our streets. Happy is that people that is in such a case; yea, happy is that people whose God is the Lord.

—translated by Alexander Whyte

1889—Gerard Manley Hopkins (1844–89) was an English Jesuit priest who taught Greek at Dublin University, Ireland. Most of his students were not aware that he was also a poet of exceptional originality, since most of his poems were published posthumously in 1918. Since that time his poetry has had a considerable influence on English literature. On this day, not long before his death, he wrote the following untitled sonnet, which has justifiably became one of his most famous. It is based on Jeremiah 12:1: "Righteous art thou, O Lord, when I plead with thee: yet let me talk with thee of thy judgments: Wherefore doth the way of the wicked prosper? Wherefore are all they happy that deal very treacherously?"

————— ❧ ❧ —————

Thou art indeed just, Lord, if I contend
With thee; but, sir, so what I plead is just.
Why do sinners' ways prosper? and why must
Disappointment all I endeavor end?

Wert thou my enemy, O thou my friend,
How wouldst thou worse, I wonder, than though dost
Defeat, thwart me? Oh, the sots and thralls of lust
Do in spare hours more thrive than I that spend,

Sir, life upon thy cause. See, banks and brakes
Now, leavèd how thick! lacèd they are again
With fretty chervil, look, and fresh wind shakes

Them; birds build—but not I build; no, but strain,
Time's eunuch, and not breed one work that wakes.
Mine, O thou lord of life, send my roots rain.

1212—Italian woman Clare of Assisi (1194–1253) was an early follower of Francis of Assisi. On this day, during a Palm Sunday ceremony in church, she received a palm branch, at Francis's suggestion, as a symbol of her renunciation of her worldly life and her willingness to be a martyr for Christ if need be. She then became the first female Franciscan, and later this same year, with Francis's assistance, she founded a Franciscan order of nuns, known as the Poor Clares. Her humility, love for the poor, and passion for serving the living Christ continue to be examples in our time. The following passage, from one of her letters, describes her ideal of the Christian life.

————————•◦§ ◦◦•————————

Dearly beloved, may you too "always rejoice in the Lord" (Philippians 4:4). And may neither bitterness nor a cloud [of sadness] overwhelm you....

Place your mind before the mirror of eternity! Place your soul in the brilliance of glory! Place your heart in the figure of the divine substance! And transform your whole being in the image of the Godhead Itself through contemplation! So that you too may feel what His friends feel as they taste the hidden sweetness which God Himself has reserved from the beginning for those who love Him.

Since you have cast aside all things which, in this deceitful and turbulent world, ensnare their blind lovers, love Him totally Who gave Himself totally for Your love. His beauty the sun and moon admire, and of His gifts there is no limit in abundance, preciousness, and magnitude....

Who would not dread the treacheries of the enemy of mankind, who, through the arrogance of momentary and deceptive glories, attempts to reduce to nothing that which is greater than heaven itself? Indeed, is it not clear that the soul of the faithful person, the most worthy of all creatures because of the grace of God, is greater than heaven itself? For the heavens with the rest of creation cannot contain their Creator. Only the faithful soul is His dwelling place and [His] throne, and this [is possible] only through the charity which the wicked do not have. [He Who is] the Truth has said, "Whoever loves me will be loved by My Father, and I too shall love him, and We shall come to him and make our dwelling place with Him" (John 14:21).

—from *Francis and Clare*,
translated by Regis J. Armstrong and Ignatius C. Brady

Ninth century—Joseph of the Studium (c. 810–86) was a Greek hymn writer who is said to have written more than a thousand hymns. He is considered one of the greatest and most prolific hymn writers of the Eastern Church. The following verses are drawn from a much longer work of his that was traditionally sung on this day, the Feast Day of Saints Chrysanthus and Darla. It is called "The Pilgrims of Jesus." This English translation of Joseph's hymn is, in turn, by one of England's greatest hymn writers, John Mason Neale, who wrote and translated many well-known hymns, such as "O Come, O Come, Emmanuel."

———————— ❧ ❧ ————————

The Cross that Jesus carried
    He carried as your due:
The Crown that Jesus weareth
    He weareth it for you. . . .

The trials that beset you,
    The sorrows ye endure,
The manifold temptations
    That Death alone can cure,—

What are they, but His jewels
    Of right celestial worth?
What are they but the ladder
    Set up to Heav'n on earth?

O happy band of pilgrims,
    Look upward to the skies;—
Where such a light affliction
    Shall win you such a prize!

—from *Hymns of the Eastern Church,*
translated and edited by John Mason Neale (1862)

687—*Cuthbert (c. 635–87) was one of the towering figures of Celtic Chris-*
tianity during the Middle Ages. Although his original intent was to be a
humble monk and hermit, his outstanding abilities led to his being named
bishop of the island monastery of Lindesfarne. Wearied by his exertions late
in life, he returned to the solitary life of a hermit in 685. Two years later, on
this day, he died, but not before giving some final instructions to the monks
who took care of him and had formerly resided under his care. Herefrith, one
of those monks, faithfully recorded the scene.

———— ❦ ❦ ————

I took my seat by his side, but he spoke very little for the weight of
his suffering prevented him from speaking much. But when I earnestly
asked him what last discourse and valedictory salutation he would
bequeath to the brethren, he began to make a few strong admonitions
respecting peace and humility, and told me to beware of those persons
who strove against these virtues and would not practice them. "Have
peace," said he, "and divine charity ever amongst you, and when you
are called upon to deliberate on your condition, see that you be unanimous in council. Let concord be mutual between you and other servants
of Christ; and do not despise others who belong to the faith and come
to you for hospitality, but admit them familiarly and kindly; and when
you have entertained them, speed them on their journey, by no means
esteeming yourselves better than the rest of those who partake of the
same faith and mode of life. . . ."

When his hour of evening service was come, he received from me
the blessed sacrament and thus strengthened himself for his departure,
which he now knew to be at hand, by partaking of the body and blood
of Christ; and when he had lifted up his eyes to heaven and stretched
out his hands above him, his soul, intent upon heavenly praises, sped
his way to the joys of the heavenly kingdom.

—from Bede's *Life of St. Cuthbert,*
translated by J. A. Giles

1748—Today John Newton (1725–1807), slave trader and sailor, found himself providentially saved from a storm at sea, an experience that led to his conversion. Sixteen years later he became an ordained minister. He eventually became a noted author as well, famous for his inspiring autobiography and especially for cowriting, with William Cowper, an influential hymnal called The Olney Hymns *(1779; see also December 9). Among Newton's well-known hymns are "Glorious Things of Thee Are Spoken" and "The Lord Will Provide." Of course, Newton is even better remembered as the author of the words to the hymn "Amazing Grace." Here is Newton's own account of his conversion.*

The twenty-first of March is a day much to be remembered by me, and I have never suffered it to pass wholly unnoticed since the year 1748. On that day the Lord sent from on high and delivered me out of deep waters. . . .

I began to think of my former religious professions; the extraordinary turns in my life; the calls, warnings, and deliverances I had met with; the licentious course of my conversation, particularly my unparalleled effrontery in making the gospel history, which I could not then be sure was false, though I was not as yet assured it was true, the constant subject of profane ridicule. I thought, allowing the Scripture premises, there never was nor could be such a sinner as myself; and then, comparing the advantages I had broken through, I concluded at first that my sins were too great to be forgiven. . . .

When I saw beyond all probability there was still a hope of respite, and heard about six in the evening that the ship was freed from water, there arose a gleam of hope; I thought I saw the hand of God displayed in our favor. I began to pray. I could not utter the prayer of faith; I could not draw near to a reconciled God and call him Father. My prayer was like the cry of the ravens, which yet the Lord does not disdain to hear.

—from *The Life of the Rev. John Newton Written by Himself* (1764)

1474—On this day, after ten years of depression, Catherine of Genoa (1447–1510) was converted. This remarkable Italian woman then became a noted mystic and a beloved spiritual counselor; she was also known for her tireless charity and for her work in the hospital of Pammatone, Italy. In the following passage, her conversion is described. The reading is from Vita e Dottrina *("Life and Doctrines"), a book compiled by her followers and published in 1551, forty years after her death.*

───────── ◦§ ࢡ◦ ─────────

At the urging of her sister, who was a nun, Catherine went to make her confession to the confessor of that nunnery; but she was not disposed to do it. Then said her sister, "At least go and recommend yourself to him, because he is a most worthy religious man"—in fact, he was a very holy man. Suddenly, as she knelt before him, she received in her heart the wound of the unmeasured Love of God, with so clear a vision of her own misery and her faults, and of the goodness of God, that she almost fell upon the ground. And by these sensations of infinite love, and of the offenses that had been done against this most sweet God, she was so greatly drawn by purifying affection away from the poor things of this world that she was almost beside herself, and for this she cried inwardly with ardent love, "No more world! no more sin!" At this point, if she had possessed a thousand worlds, she would have thrown all of them away. . . .

And she returned home, kindled and deeply wounded with so great a love of God, the which had been shown her inwardly, with the sight of her own wretchedness, that she seemed beside herself. And she shut herself in a chamber, the most secluded she could find, with burning sighs. And in this moment she was inwardly taught the whole practice of [prayer]: but her tongue could say naught but this: "O Love, can it be that you have called me with so great a love, and made me to know in one instant that which worlds cannot express?"

—translated by Evelyn Underhill (1911)

1780—St. Tikhon of Zadonsk (1724–83), one of Russia's great spiritual leaders, served as bishop of Voronezh until 1769, after which he retired to the Zadonsk monastery in central Russia to spend his remaining years in prayer and meditation. From there, he wrote many letters of encouragement to his friends and acquaintances. On this day, he wrote the following letter to a fellow monk, outlining a recommended routine of devotion.

───────── ·◦§ ◦◦· ─────────

Living in your cell, conduct yourself as follows: rising from sleep, thank God and pray. Coming back from church, read some book salutary for your soul, then undertake some manual labor. Having performed part of this work, rise and pray and, having prayed, return to your reading. If you do all these things alternately, you will experience great devotion and zest as the result of the variety in your occupations. In the same manner do men walk from place to place and take their exercise; and so also is a variety of food more palatable than if we always partake of the same fare. When dejection, ennui, or sadness troubles you excessively, leave your cell and walk about in whatever place is accessible and, while walking, sigh after Christ that He may help you. Think often of death, of Christ's judgment, and of eternity. These thoughts, like a whip, drive away all dejection, ennui, and melancholy. All that is temporal is brief and soon finished. That which occurs after death endures forever. The day passes, and with it everything that is sad or joyful. And in the same manner, all our life passes away, drawing nearer and nearer to death. And with that occupation in which a man is engaged when death overcome him shall he appear in eternity.

P.S.: Beware of going on visits, lest you disperse among men that which you have gathered in solitude. It is rare that a man returning to his cell is the same as when he left it. The desert and the cell accumulate riches, but the temptations of the world disperse them. In the cell man gathers up his whole past life in his thought, and contemplating it, turns to Christ with sighs and asks for His mercy. Nothing causes a man to sin so often as his tongue. . . .

—from A *Treasury of Russian Spirituality*,
translated by Helen Iswolsky (1948)

1955—In his twenties French-born American writer Thomas Merton (1915–68) was well on his way to a distinguished career as a scholar and poet. Rather than entering the academy, however, he became a Trappist monk, a spiritual journey that is recounted in his classic autobiography, The Seven Storey Mountain *(see December 10). Thereafter, he wrote many best-selling books, combining his political activism and his interest in world religions with his own articulate expressions of his Christian faith. One of his most popular books,* No Man Is an Island, *was an introduction to the spiritual life of the monastery, and it was published on this day. The following is an excerpt.*

The fruit of my labors is not my own: for I am preparing the way for the achievements of another. Nor are my failures my own. They may spring from the failure of another, but they are also compensated for by another's achievement. Therefore the meaning of my life is not to be looked for merely in the sum total of my own achievements. It is seen only in the complete integration of my achievements and failures with the achievements and failures of my own generation, and society, and time. It is seen, above all, in my integration in the mystery of Christ....

Every other man is a piece of myself, for I am a part and a member of mankind. Every Christian is part of my own body, because we are members of Christ. What I do is also done for them and with them and by them. What they do is done in me and by me and for me. But each one of us remains responsible for his own share in the life of the whole body. Charity cannot be what it is supposed to be as long as I do not see that my life represents my own allotment in the life of a whole supernatural organism to which I belong. Only when this truth is absolutely central do other doctrines fit into their proper context. Solitude, humility, self-denial, action and contemplation, the sacraments, the monastic life, the family, war and peace—none of these makes sense except in relation to the central reality which is God's love living and acting in those whom He has incorporated in His Christ. Nothing at all makes sense, unless we admit, with John Donne, that: "No man is an island, entire of itself; every man is a piece of the continent, a part of the main."

1890—On this day a young professional baseball player named William Ashley Sunday gave up baseball to become a Christian. Eventually, he became the most renowned American evangelist of his time—better know as Billy Sunday (1862–1935). Many years later he described the experience in a sermon (here transcribed from an account in the Boston Herald*).*

Twenty-nine years ago I walked down a street in Chicago in company with some ball players who were famous in this world (some of them are dead now), and we went into a saloon. It was Sunday afternoon and we got tanked up and then went and sat down on a corner. I never go by that street without thanking God for saving me. It was a vacant lot at that time.

We sat down on a curbing. Across the street a company of men and women were playing on instruments—horns, flutes, and slide trombones—and the others were singing the gospel hymns that I used to hear my mother sing back in the old church, where I used to go to Sunday school.

And God painted on the canvas of my recollection and memory a vivid picture of the scenes of other days and other faces. Many have long since turned to dust. I sobbed and sobbed, and a young man stepped out and said, "We are going to the Pacific Garden Mission; won't you come down to the mission? I am sure you will enjoy it. You can hear drunkards tell how they have been saved and girls tell how they have been saved from the red light district."

I arose and said to the boys, "I'm through. I am going to Jesus Christ. We've come to the parting of the ways," and I turned my back on them. Some of them laughed, and some of them mocked me; one of them gave me encouragement; others never said a word.

Twenty-nine years ago I turned and left that little group on the corner of State and Madison streets and walked to the little mission and fell on my knees and staggered out of sin and into the arms of the Savior.

I went over to the West Side of Chicago, where I was keeping company with a girl, now my wife, Nell. I married Nell. She was a Presbyterian, so I am a Presbyterian. If she had been a Catholic, I would have been a Catholic—because I was hot on the trail of Nell.

1862—On this day, a young minister named Joseph Henry Gilmore (1834–1918) was asked to preach at the First Baptist Church of Philadelphia. His prepared topic was Psalm 23, but as Gilmore wrote later, "I did not get further than the words 'He leadeth me.' Those words took hold of me as they had never done before. I saw in them a significance and beauty of which I had never dreamed." After the service, on the back of his sermon notes, he wrote the words of the hymn "He Leadeth Me! O Blessed Thought."

———— ✍ ————

He leadeth me! O blessed thought!
Oh words with heavenly comfort fraught!
Whate'er I do, where'er I be,
Still 'tis God's hand that leadeth me!

> CHORUS: He leadeth me, he leadeth me,
> By his own hand he leadeth me:
> His faithful follower I would be,
> For by his hand he leadeth me.

Sometimes 'mid scenes of deepest gloom,
Sometimes where Eden's bowers bloom,
By waters still, o'er troubled sea,
Still 'tis his hand that leadeth me.

Lord, I would clasp thy hand in mine,
Nor ever murmur nor repine,
Content, whatever lot I see,
Since 'tis thy hand that leadeth me!

And when my task on earth is done,
When by thy grace the victory's won,
E'en death's cold wave I will not flee,
Since God through Jordan leadeth me.

1228—Antony of Padua (1195–1231) was an Italian friar of the late Middle Ages and one of the most eloquent of the early Franciscan preachers. He was known not only for his miracles (see June 13), but also for his willingness to face martyrdom. On this day, he boldly confronted an Italian tyrant named Ezzelino whose armies had been ravaging Padua at the time.

Antony's heart bled for the trouble that had fallen on his beloved city, and not only did he grieve for that distress, but he saw the fruit of his labors, the work of his Master, the salvation of many souls endangered by the tumult of excited passions, the bloodshed, and rapine....

Our saint went to plead the cause of God and His people with [the tyrant]. Antony stood before Ezzelino in the simple majesty of holiness, full of zeal for the glory of God and the salvation of the poor sinner before him, and in words of fearless energy reproved him for the ambition that made him—a young man in the flower of his age—trample on every consideration of justice and compassion, shed the blood of his brethren, stir up feuds and hatred where he found peace and harmony, and add to these acts of savage cruelty the basest arts of dissimulation and bad faith. He told him that God would hold him answerable not only for his own sins, but for every act of brutality and rapine committed by his followers; that now was the time, when the voice of God's messenger was sounding in his ears, to turn back from the path of guilty ambition, to put an end to bloodshed, to give peace to the land....

For some time Ezzelino strove to resist Antony's words, and those who were present expected a burst of furious anger from him, little used as he was to words of counsel, far less of rebuke. But the outburst did not come. They saw him cast aside his sword and throw himself at the feet of the simple friar, with his belt round his neck in token of submission and humility, begging him to pray for him to the Lord....

Antony seems to have said no more to Ezzelino at the time, but to have left him to listen to the voice of conscience, whilst he himself went away to commend the matter in earnest prayer to God.

—from Henry James Coleridge's *The Chronicle of St. Antony of Padua* (1875)

1754—On the second anniversary of the death of his beloved wife, Tetty, English author and lexicographer Samuel Johnson (1709–84) recorded the following two prayers in his Diary. Dr. Johnson (as he was known) compiled the first comprehensive dictionary of the English language (published in 1755; see also September 18). Not only was he a devout Christian believer, but he was also one of the greatest wits of England. These prayers are appropriate for any Christian who has suffered the loss of a loved one.

MORNING: O God, who on this day was pleased to take from me my dear wife, sanctify to me my sorrows and reflections. Grant that I may renew and practice the resolutions that I made when your afflicting hand was upon me. Let the remembrance of your judgments by which my wife is taken away awaken me to repentance, and the sense of your mercy by which I am spared, strengthen my hope and confidence in you, that by the assistance and comfort of your holy spirit I may so pass through things temporal, as finally to gain everlasting happiness, and to pass by a holy and happy death, into the joy that you have prepared for those who love you. Grant this, O Lord, for the sake of Jesus Christ. Amen.

AT NIGHT: Almighty God, vouchsafe to sanctify unto me the reflections and resolutions of this day, let not my sorrow be unprofitable; let not my resolutions be vain. Grant that my grief may produce true repentance, so that I may live to please you, and when the time shall come that I must die like her whom you have taken from me, grant me eternal happiness in your presence, through Jesus Christ our Lord. Amen.

c. 461—St. Patrick (c. 389–c. 461), the greatest Irish saint, was sold into slavery as a boy but later gained his freedom and returned to his native England. From there he heeded a call to become a missionary to Ireland and eventually became that country's spiritual leader—as well as the greatest saint of the early Celtic church. He died on March 17, around the year 461, and for twelve days, according to legend, his followers held a funeral celebration that culminated with his burial on this day. Though the authenticity of Patrick's most famous writing, "St. Patrick's Breastplate," is in question, the excerpt below is offered in his memory.

I bind to myself this day
The strong virtue of the Invocation of the Trinity,
The Faith of the Trinity in Unity,
The Creator of the Elements. . . .
I bind to myself today
The power of Heaven,
The light of the sun,
The whiteness of snow,
The force of fire,
The flashing of lightning,
The swiftness of wind,
The depth of sea,
The stability of earth,
The hardness of rocks. . . .
I bind to myself today
The Power of God to guide me,
The Might of God to uphold me,
The Wisdom of God to teach me,
The Eye of God to watch over me,
The Ear of God to hear me,
The Word of God to give me speech,
The Hand of God to protect me,
The Way of God to lie before me,
The Shield of God to shelter me,
The Host of God to defend me. . . .

—translator unknown

1835—Stephen Grover, pastor of the Presbyterian Church in Caldwell, New Jersey, today wrote that he hoped that the Rev. Samuel Phelps "may accomplish the object he has in view, both for the public good as well as for his personal benefit." That object was the private printing of Phelps's lengthy epic poem The Triumphs of Divine Grace, *which paints a vivid picture of the New Jerusalem.*

------- ✑ ✑ -------

... This vile world of ours, cleansed, purified,
And organized anew, will be the seat
Of the redeemed and is the very place
In Scripture styled the kingdom of the saints,
Prepared before earth's cornerstone was laid.
The image of the world, as I have said
Before, being hid in God's omniscient mind,
He clearly saw his purposed end attained
In the destruction of the devil's works,
The renovation of the ruined earth
And reign of love and truth and righteousness,
Under the banners of the Prince of Peace....
The sovereign architect himself will fix
His residence with men and be their God,
And they shall be his people, nations saved,
First by his grace through his anointed son,
Then by his presence in their new abode;
From which he'll banish pain, disease, and grief,
Sorrow and death and every other ill
That can annoy, disturb, or break their peace;
And with his own soft hand wipe off the tears
From every face, and pouring streams of love,
Pure, perfect, blessed love, into their hearts,
From that eternal fountain that supplies
Ten thousand times ten thousand souls with life
And light and peace and every other good,
Make them rejoice with joy unspeakable,
And full of glory round his holy throne.

1631—On this day English poet and Anglican priest John Donne (1573–1631) died. (See also January 29.) Few people have taken as much deliberate care for their own deaths as Donne: Six weeks before his death, he preached his final and most famous sermon, "Death's Duel," though Donne was so sick that some said he was preaching his own funeral oration. He then posed for a portrait of himself dressed in his death shroud, a sculptural rendering of which still stands in St. Paul's Cathedral in London. The day after delivering his "Death's Duel" sermon, some of Donne's friends visited him, and when they asked him why he looked so sad, Donne replied:

———— ◦§ §◦ ————

I am not sad, but most of the night past I have entertained myself with many thoughts of several friends that have left me here and are gone to that place from which they shall not return, and that within a few days I also shall go hence and be no more seen. And my preparation for this change has become my nightly meditation upon my bed, which my infirmities have now made restless to me. But at this present time, I was in a serious contemplation of the providence and goodness of God to me; to me, who am less than the least of His mercies: and looking back upon my life, I now plainly see it was His hand that prevented me from all temporal employment; and that it was His will I should never settle nor thrive till I entered into the ministry; in which I have now lived almost twenty years, I hope to His glory—and by which, I most humbly thank Him, I have been enabled to requite most of those friends who showed me kindness when my fortune was very low, as God knows it was. . . . I have quieted the consciences of many that have groaned under the burden of a wounded spirit, whose prayers I hope are available for me. I cannot plead innocence of life, especially of my youth; but I am to be judged by a merciful God, who is not willing to see what I have done amiss. And though of myself I have nothing to present to Him but sins and misery, yet I know He looks not upon me now as I am of myself, but as I am in my Savior, and has given me, even at this present time, some testimonies by His Holy Spirit that I am of the number of His Elect. I am therefore full of inexpressible joy and shall die in peace.

—from Izaac Walton's *Life of Dr. John Donne*

April

English poet John Milton at age sixty-three,
only a few years after the publication of *Paradise Lost*
(see April 27). From an old engraving.

1548—On this day the Parliament of England ordered the printing of the first official liturgy to be published in the English language: The Book of Common Prayer. *This famous book was first introduced to the many churches in the Church of England the next year on Whitsunday (which in that year fell on June 9). The following responsory invocation is from that first edition.*

O all ye works of the Lord:
    Speak good of the Lord, praise him, and set him up forever.
O ye angels of the Lord:
    Speak good of the Lord, praise him, and set him up forever.
O ye heavens: . . .
O ye waters that be above the firmament: . . .
O all ye powers of the Lord: . . .
O ye sun and moon: . . .
O ye stars of heaven: . . .
O ye showers and dew: . . .
O ye winds of God: . . .
O ye fire and heat: . . .
O ye winter and summer: . . .
O ye dews and frosts: . . .
O ye frost and cold: . . .
O ye ice and snow: . . .
O ye nights and days: . . .
O ye light and darkness: . . .
O ye lightnings and clouds: . . .
O let the earth speak good of the Lord: . . .
O ye mountains and hills: . . .
O all ye green things upon the earth: . . .
O ye wells: . . .
O ye seas and floods: . . .
O ye whales and all that move in the waters: . . .
O all ye fowls of the air: . . .
O all ye beasts and cattle: . . .
O ye children of men:
    Speak good of the Lord, praise him, and set him up forever. . . .
Amen.

1933—On this day Patrick Cardinal Hayes granted the imprimatur (notice that the book was free of doctrinal error) to the book The Seven Last Words *by Fulton J. Sheen (1895–1979). This small volume contains the author's profound reflections on the words Christ spoke from the cross. Sheen was a well-known spokesman for Catholicism in the United States and is fondly remembered not only for his many excellent books but for his work in radio (on a program called "The Catholic Hour") and, later, television (on a program called "Life Is Worth Living"). In the following passage from* The Seven Last Words, *Sheen meditates on the meaning of Christ's act of forgiveness from the cross (Luke 23:34).*

———— ঙ৯ ————

The congregation anxiously awaited His first word. The executioners expected Him to cry, for every one pinned on the gibbet of the Cross had done it before Him. Seneca tells us that those who were crucified cursed the day of their birth, the executioners, their mothers, and even spat on those who looked upon them. Cicero tells us that at times it was necessary to cut out the tongues of those who were crucified to stop their terrible blasphemies. Hence the executioners expected a cry but not the kind of cry that they heard. The Scribes and Pharisees expected a cry too, and they were quite sure that He who had preached "Love your enemies," and "Do good to them that hate you," would now forget that Gospel with the piercing of feet and hands. They felt that the excruciating and agonizing pains would scatter to the winds any resolution He might have taken to keep up appearances. Every one expected a cry, but no one, with the exception of the three at the foot of the Cross, expected the cry they did hear. Like some fragrant trees which bathe in perfume the very ax which gnashes them, the great Heart on the Tree of Love poured out from its depths something less a cry than a prayer of pardon and forgiveness: "Father, forgive them for they know not what they do."

1310—On this day began the trial of French woman Marguerite Porete (1250–1310), who had already spent more than a year in prison. She was a Beguine, a member of an unofficial sisterhood that was declared heretical at the time. At her trial, Marguerite's devotional book, The Mirror for Simple Souls, *was presented as evidence against her and condemned, even though the book had twice been reviewed and approved by church authorities before this time. She was found guilty and, two months later, burned at the stake. The following passage from her book is taken from a chapter called "The Noble Virtue of Charity and How She Obeys None Other than Love" and is loosely based on 1 Corinthians 13.*

———————— ❧ ❧ ————————

Charity obeys no created thing but Love alone.

Charity owns nothing of her own, and if she should own anything, she says it does not belong to her.

Charity leaves her own needs behind and attends to the needs of others.

Charity never requires remuneration from any creature for whatever good or pleasing service she has performed.

Charity knows no shame nor fear nor uneasiness; she is so upright that she does not bend, no matter what circumstances afflict her.

Charity creates "nothing new under the sun"; yet all the world is but her leftovers and castoffs.

Charity gives to everyone the things she values most, and so she often promises those things she does not own, out of the excess of her bounty, in the hope that the more she gives away, the more abundance she will have [to give away].

Charity is such a wise merchant that she always makes a profit where others lose, and she always escapes the fetters with which others are bound, and so she has a great quantity of things that are pleasing to Love.

And note that whoever would have perfect charity must mortify his or her fondness for the spiritual life by performing works of charity.

1878—Frederic William Farrar (1831–1903) was a popular religious writer and clergyman in Victorian England, known especially for his school stories. He often preached on the subject of church history, and on this day, at St. Andrew's Church in Holborn, he delivered a sermon called "The Early Franciscans," in which he discusses the ideals of Francis's early followers.

———— ⋅§ §⋅ ————

It happened one day that St. Thomas [Aquinas], who was a Franciscan monk, was sitting in the Vatican with Pope Innocent IV, when masses of gold and silver were being carried into the Papal treasury. "You see," said the Pope with a touch of self-satisfaction, "the age of the Church is past when she could say, 'Silver and gold have I none.'" "Yes, Holy Father," replied the Angelic Doctor, "and the day is also past when she could say to the paralytic—'Take up thy bed and walk!'"...

[Bossuet says] there are three things that make up all business, which enter into all the intrigues, which inflame all the passions, which actuate all the eagerness of the world. St. Francis saw that they were illusions; he saw that riches enslave, that honors overpower, that pleasures effeminate the heart. He saw that these broad roads lead many to perdition. For himself, he sought another road. He found riches in poverty; joy in suffering; glory in self-abasement.

[The early Franciscans] possessed nothing, either for their order or for themselves; and thus making poverty their bride amid the mad desire of their age for wealth, they introduced nobler aims and holier feelings into a luxurious and ambitious Church, into an oppressive, blood-stained, cruel world. It was a grand, emphatic protest that appealed to the imagination of all men. Nothing can show more forcibly the power of this appeal than the fact that St. Francis, as the chosen bridegroom of Poverty, was celebrated alike in the paintings of Giotto and in the verse of Dante. When men saw Francis at the table of nobles and cardinals, bright and courteous, but while he went on talking, unostentatiously deluging his plate with cold water or quietly sprinkling a few ashes over the rich food, with the half apology, "Brother ash is pure," they saw at least that these men had other thoughts and other hopes than the fat monks and immoral priests and splendor-loving bishops, of whom the Church in that day was full.

1883—Henry Drummond (1851–97) was a Scottish naturalist and religious writer who is especially beloved for his inspirational sermon The Greatest Thing in the World *(see May 10). But works of serious theology and natural science were his primary labor of love. On this day was published his controversial and influential* Natural Law in the Spiritual World, *in which Drummond attempts to reconcile Darwin's theory of evolution and Christian theology. This Christian classic is still read today. Here is a thought from that book.*

And so, out of the infinite complexity there rises an infinite simplicity, the foreshadowing of a final unity, of that

> One God, one law, one element,
> And one far-off divine event,
> To which the whole creation moves.

> [—from Tennyson's "In Memoriam"]

This is the final triumph of Continuity, the heart secret of Creation, the unspoken prophecy of Christianity. To Science, defining it as a working principle, this mighty process of amelioration is simply *Evolution*. To Christianity, discerning the end through the means, it is *Redemption*. These silent and patient processes, elaborating, eliminating, developing all from the first of time, conducting the evolution from millennium to millennium with unaltering purpose and unfaltering power, are the early stages in the redemptive work—the unseen approach of that Kingdom whose strange mark is that it "cometh without observation." And these Kingdoms, rising tier above tier in ever-increasing sublimity and beauty, their foundations visibly fixed in the past, their progress and the direction of their progress being facts in Nature still, are the signs which, since the Magi saw His star in the east, have never been wanting from the firmament of truth, and which in every age with growing clearness to the wise, and with ever-gathering mystery to the uninitiated, proclaim that "the Kingdom of God is at hand."

1763—On this day was published "Song of David" by Christopher Smart (1722–71), which has been called one of the most ecstatic religious poems in the English language. Smart, an English poet, hymn writer, and writer of children's verse, suffered from mental illness for many years, and he wrote the psalm-like "Song of David" while confined to a hospital for the insane. These are the concluding stanzas of that great poem. (See also January 4.)

⋅⋅⋅⋅⋅⋅⋅⋅

Glorious the sun in mid career;
Glorious the assembled fires appear;
 Glorious the comet's train:
Glorious the trumpet and alarm;
Glorious the Almighty's stretched-out arm;
 Glorious the enraptured main:

Glorious the northern lights astream;
Glorious the song, when God's the theme;
 Glorious the thunder's roar:
Glorious hosanna from the den;
Glorious the catholic amen;
 Glorious the martyr's gore:

Glorious—more glorious is the crown
of Him, that brought salvation down
 By meekness, called Thy Son;
Thou that stupendous truth believed,
And now the matchless deed's achieved,
 Determined, dared, and done.

1541—Francis Xavier (1506–52) was a Spanish missionary and saint, dubbed "the apostle of the Indies" for his pioneering missionary voyages to India, Ceylon, and Japan. He also helped Ignatius of Loyola found the Jesuit order. On this day Xavier left Lisbon to venture on his first missionary trip. He went to India. A year later, eager that those under his charge learn the basics of the Christian faith, he wrote a short catechism, which concluded with this prayer to be said by the former Hindu believers under his care.

O my God! mighty and merciful Father, Creator of all things of the world! without the possibility of doubt, I firmly believe in you, my God and Lord, since you are my entire good. I believe that I shall be saved through the infinite merits of the sufferings and death of your Son Jesus Christ, my Lord, even though my sins from the time of my childhood, and those I have committed up to this present hour, are very great, for your mercy is greater than the malice of my sins. You, Lord, created me, and not my father or my mother; and you have given me a body and soul and all that I have. And you, my God, have made me to your likeness, and not the idols, which are the gods of the gentiles in the form of animals and wild beasts of the devil. I renounce all idols, magicians, and soothsayers, since they are the slaves and friends of the devil. . . .

O Christians, let us give praise and thanks to God, three and one, for having revealed to us the true faith and law of his Son Jesus Christ. . . .

Weigh, Lord, my sins with the merits of the passion and death of my Lord Jesus Christ and not with my few deserts. I shall thus be free from the power of my enemy and shall go to enjoy an eternal and everlasting bliss. . . .

May God unite us in paradise. Amen.

—translated by M. Joseph Costelloe

1546—The convening of the Council of Trent was one of the Catholic Church's responses to the Protestant Reformation. Among the decisions made by this body was the official proclamation, dated on this day, reaffirming the Latin translation of the Bible by St. Jerome (c. 320–420), called the "Vulgate" (c. 404), as the official Bible of the Catholic Church. Inspired by this pronouncement, a group of expatriate Catholic Englishmen living in France later translated the Vulgate into English (New Testament 1582; Old Testament 1609). Their English version of the Vulgate, called the Douai-Reims Bible, greatly influenced the translation of the King James Bible of 1611, as can be seen by the following passage from Matthew 5:1–17.

And seeing the multitudes, [Jesus] went up into a mountain; and when he was set, his Disciples came unto him. And opening his mouth, he taught them, saying, "Blessed are the poor in spirit, for theirs is the kingdom of heaven. Blessed are the meek, for they shall possess the land. Blessed are they that mourn, for they shall be comforted. Blessed are they that hunger and thirst after justice, for they shall have their fill. Blessed are the merciful, for they shall obtain mercy. Blessed are the clean of heart, for they shall see God. Blessed are the peacemakers, for they shall be called the children of God. Blessed are they that suffer persecution for justice, for theirs is the kingdom of heaven. Blessed are ye when they shall revile you and persecute you and speak all that naught is against you untruly, for my sake. Be glad and rejoice, for your reward is very great in heaven. For so they persecuted the Prophets that were before you. You are the salt of the earth. But if the salt lose its virtue, wherewith shall it be salted? It is good for nothing anymore but to be cast forth and to be trodden of men. You are the light of the world. A city cannot be hid, situated on a mountain. Neither do men light a candle and put it under a bushel, but upon a candlestick, that it may shine to all that are in the house. So let your light shine before men that they may see your good works and glorify your Father which is in heaven."

1816—The African Methodist Episcopal Church was established on this day at a conference in Philadelphia. Reverend Richard Allen (1760–1831), who was elected its first bishop two days later, was instrumental in its founding. As a Methodist minister, he and other African-American ministers had experienced severe prejudice within the white-led churches and felt that the only solution was to form their own denomination. Allen recalls the founding of the AME Church in the following excerpt from his autobiography, The Life Experience and Gospel Labors of the Rt. Rev. Richard Allen, *and he attaches an anonymous hymn for the occasion that must have had special meaning for his own congregation at Bethel Church in Philadelphia.*

—————— •◦§ ◦§ ◦§• ——————

We deemed it expedient to have a form of discipline whereby we may guide our people in the fear of God, in the unity of the Spirit, and in the bonds of peace, and preserve us from that spiritual despotism which we have so recently experienced—remembering that we are not to lord it over God's heritage, as greedy dogs that can never have enough. But with long-suffering and bowels of compassion, to bear each other's burdens and so fulfill the Law of Christ, praying that our mutual striving together for the promulgation of the Gospel may be crowned with abundant success.

> The God of Bethel heard her cries;
> He let his power be seen;
> He stopped the proud oppressor's frown,
> And proved himself a King.
>
> Thou saved them in the trying hour,
> Ministers and councils joined,
> And all stood ready to retain
> That helpless church of Thine.
>
> Bethel surrounded by her foes,
> But not yet in despair,
> Christ heard her supplicating cries;
> The God of Bethel heard.

1601—On this day Arthur Dent (who died in 1607), an English religious writer in Queen Elizabeth's England, dedicated his dialogue The Plain Man's Pathway to Heaven *to a certain Dr. Caesar. The book proved popular in its time. A century later, it was one of John Bunyan's favorite books, having been a gift to him from his father-in-law. Not only was Dent's book influential in Bunyan's writing of* Pilgrim's Progress, *but even before then it was instrumental in Bunyan's own conversion. In the following passage from* The Plain Man's Pathway, *Theologus, the theologian, discusses the nature of doubt with Philagathus, the honest man.*

———— ⋖⋗ ————

PHILAGATHUS: But are there not some doubts at some times even in the very elect and those who are grown to the greatest persuasion?

THEOLOGUS: Yes, verily. For he that never doubted, never believed; for whosoever believes in truth, feels sometimes doubtings and waverings. Even as the sound body feels many grudgings of diseases, which if he had not health, he could not feel; so the sound soul feels some doubtings, which if it were not sound, it could not so easily feel. For we feel corruption by grace, and the more grace we have, the more quick are we in the feeling of corruption. Some men of tender skins and quick feeling will easily feel the lightest feather in softest manner laid upon the ball of their hands, which others of more slow feeling and hard flesh cannot so easily discern. So then it is certain that although the children of God feel some doubtings at some times, yet the same do no whit impeach the certainty of their salvation, but rather argue a perfect soundness and health of their souls; for when such little grudgings are felt in the soul, the children of God oppose against them the certainty of God's truth and promises, and so do easily overcome them; for the Lord's people need no more to fear them than he that rides through the streets upon a lusty gelding with his sword by his side needs to fear the barking and bawling of a few little curs and whippets.

1898—On this day a popular English Victorian writer named Jesse Penn-Lewis (1861–1927) wrote the preface to her slim volume of reflections, The Message of the Cross. *Published by the Young Women's Christian Association, the volume contains much quiet wisdom about the meaning of the Cross, as can be seen in the following extract.*

"Let this mind be in you which was in Christ Jesus . . ." [Philippians 2:5].

He, as God, deliberately laid aside His position and power.

He deliberately took the form of a servant.

He deliberately took the place of weakness.

He, as a man, deliberately humbled Himself.

He deliberately carried out an obedience even unto death.

He deliberately went to the cross.

"Let this mind be in you which was in Christ Jesus." We too will count position and power not as things to be grasped. We too will take the place of a bond slave, living not to do our own will, but the will of the Father. We too will rejoice in weakness, so that the power of Christ shall tabernacle upon us. We too will not shrink from going down in deepest humiliation before the eyes, or at the feet, of others. We too will set our face as a flint and ask no better than to be crucified followers of a crucified Lord. "There are those who follow the Lamb whithersoever He goes." "Even unto death." . . .

Finally, let us see the sustaining power along this pathway of the cross. . . . Dwelling within the veil with our glorified Lord, we shall see the cross from God's standpoint and glory in it. The joy set before us, the joy unspeakable and full of glory, shall even now break forth, as with unveiled face beholding the glory of the Lord, we are changed into the same image, from glory to glory, by the Spirit of the Lord. "Wherefore we faint not!" "For our light affliction, which is for the moment works for us . . . and eternal weight of glory" (2 Corinthians 4:16–18).

1797—William Wilberforce (1759–1833) was an English statesman and philanthropist whose most renowned accomplishment was his successful leadership of the antislavery movement in England. He was also a leader in the Clapham Sect, a group of evangelical Christians who had a profound influence on English religious life. On this day Wilberforce's powerful and challenging book A Practical View of the Prevailing Religious System *was published. In it he shows the extent to which Christianity as practiced in England at the time had strayed from true faith. Here is an extract from that book in which he discusses the value of persecution.*

✍ ⧉

Persecution generally tends to quicken the vigor and extend the prevalence of the opinions which she would eradicate. . . . It has grown at length almost into an axiom that "the devilish engine back recoils upon herself." Christianity especially has always thriven under persecution. At such a season she has no lukewarm professors, no adherents concerning whom it is doubtful to what party they belong. The Christian is then reminded at every turn that his Master's kingdom is not of this world. When all on earth wear a black and threatening aspect, he looks up to heaven for consolation; he learns practically to consider himself as a pilgrim and stranger. He then cleaves to fundamentals and examines well his foundation at the hour of death. When religion is in a state of external quiet and prosperity, the contrary of all this naturally takes place. The soldiers of the church militant then forget that they are in a state of warfare. Their ardor slackens, their zeal languishes. Like a colony long settled in a strange country, they are gradually assimilated in features and demeanor and language to the native inhabitants till at length almost every vestige of peculiarity dies away.

If, in general, persecution and prosperity be respectively productive of these opposite effects, this circumstance alone might teach us what expectations to form concerning the state of Christianity in this country, where she has long been embodied in an establishment which is intimately blended with our civil institutions and is generally and justly believed to have a common interest with them all.

1742—German musician George Frideric Handel *(1685–1759) is remembered as one of the greatest Baroque composers, second only to Johann Sebastian Bach (see April 15). In his own time, however, he was largely neglected. In the hope of improving his lot, he settled in England in 1712. His most familiar work,* The Messiah, *had its premiere on this day in Dublin, Ireland—as a Lenten, rather than as an Advent, oratorio. The following excerpt from the second section of that piece, based on parts of Isaiah 52, contains the famous "Hallelujah Chorus."*

CHORUS: Lift up your heads, O ye gates, and be ye lifted up, ye everlasting doors, and the King of Glory shall come in. Who is the King of Glory? The Lord strong and mighty, the Lord mighty in battle.... Who is the King of Glory? The Lord of Hosts, he is the King of Glory.... Let all the Angels of God worship him....

SOPRANO: How beautiful are the feet of them that preach the gospel of peace and bring glad tidings of good things.

CHORUS: Their sound is gone out into all lands, and their word unto the ends of the world.

BASS: Why do the nations so furiously rage together, and why do the people imagine a vain thing? The kings of the earth rise up, and the rulers take counsel together against the Lord and against His Anointed.

CHORUS: Let us break the bond asunder and cast away their yokes from us.

TENOR: He that dwelleth in heaven shall laugh them to scorn; the Lord shall have them in derision. Thou shalt break them with a rod of iron; Thou shalt dash them in pieces like a potter's vessel.

CHORUS: Hallelujah: for the Lord God Omnipotent reigneth. The kingdom of this world is become the kingdom of our Lord and of His Christ; and he shall reign for ever and ever. King of Kings and Lord of Lords. Hallelujah!

1879—George Park Fisher (1827–1909) was an American Congregational clergyman, author, and professor of divinity at Yale University. Among his scholarly works are The Christian Religion *(1882) and* Outlines of a Universal History *(1885). On this day he wrote the preface to an earlier volume of essays called* Faith and Rationalism, *based on lectures that he had given at Princeton Theological School. It is a scholarly study of the uses and limits of reason in defining and believing the Christian faith. This excerpt, which reaffirms the rudiments of Christian belief, is from the conclusion of the book.*

———— ৯়ঌ ঌ় ————

The great argument for Christianity is Christianity itself. But for the argument to have effect, it must be no single member, no isolated feature of the system, that is held up to view. The pure morals of the Gospel, the perfect example of Christ, the humane, elevating influence of His teaching, the attractive idea presented of the character of God—not [any] of these apart, not even all of them taken together, suffice to give that argument its overpowering force. We must look at all in the light of the one comprehensive design of Christianity. We must contemplate the end which it undertakes to accomplish. It is nothing less than the redemption of mankind from sin and death. As an idea simply, how sublime it is! How infinitely does it transcend the most daring dream of philosophers, moralists, reformers! Not this or that kind of sin alone—as misrule, cruelty, impurity, fraud—is aimed at; but sin itself is to be extirpated from human nature. Not one kind of distress alone, but death, the anticipation of which keeps the guilty heart of man all his lifetime in bondage to fear, is to be stripped of its terror and made harmless, like a conquered enemy. The whole burden that weighs upon mankind is to be lifted off. The recovery of the world from the slavery of sin and from its condemnation, to the freedom of the children of God—what human mind could have even dreamed of such an achievement as within the limits of possibility? This is the Gospel, the good tidings. Regarded from this point of view, it bears on itself the stamp of its divine origin. The Deliverer Himself was a man; but He could be no mere man. It is credible that He was what He professed to be—the Son of God.

1729—On this day German Baroque composer Johann Sebastian Bach (1685–1750) conducted the premiere of his oratorio The Passion According to Saint Matthew. *It was never performed again in his lifetime. The work has since been called the greatest choral work ever written, and from it comes one of Bach's most famous hymns, "O Sacred Head Now Wounded." The words are given below not in the well-known hymn version but as they appear in an early English translation of the oratorio itself.*

O sacred head sore wounded,
Defiled and put to scorn!
O Kingly Head surrounded
With mocking crown of thorn.

What sorrow mars Thy grandeur?
Can death Thy bloom deflower?
O countenance whose splendor
The hosts of heaven adore.

Thy beauty long desired
Hath vanished from our sight.
Thy power is all expired
And quenched the Light of Light.

Ah, me! for whom thou diest,
Hide not so far Thy grace.
Show me, O Love most highest,
The brightness of Thy face.

1900—Methodist Episcopal minister Louis Albert Banks (1855–1933) was one of America's most tireless revivalists at the turn of the century. He published many collections of sermons, and he wrote the preface to one of them, David and His Friends, on this day. The following excerpt from that book is from a sermon entitled "The Tears of the Sower and the Sheaves of the Reaper."

----------- ❧❧ -----------

There is a little book called *Miss Toosey's Mission,* which tells the story of a strange little old woman, seventy years of age, who heard a sermon by a missionary bishop which wonderfully inspired her and resulted in her going to her rector and offering herself as a missionary to Africa. The rector was filled with amusement that this little, feeble woman, . . . should offer herself as a missionary; but he finally told her that her mission was to stay at home and give all she could to the cause. . . . There was a young Englishman in that village, rich and prosperous, without much religion; a generous, manly fellow, fond of his dogs and horses; and he found himself often attracted to this quaint old Miss Toosey, at whom all the village was laughing for her strange ways and missionary enthusiasm. One night this young man, John Rossiter, heard that Miss Toosey was ill, and he went to see her and found her in tears over what she called the failure of her work. She said between her sobs, "John, my money only counts up a few small shillings, and my influence is not anything, for the people laugh at me. The five barley loaves and the two small fishes that I tried to bring to the Master are all valueless." That night Miss Toosey died, and John Rossiter sat all the next day in that lonely little house with his head in his hands. There was something in that simple, noble, pure Christian life that touched him; and that night John Rossiter wrote to the missionary society of the Church of England offering himself as a missionary to Africa. Miss Toosey's loving Christian service and her tearful devotion did not fail of their sheaves. And yours will not fail; you may be so hedged in, your hands may be so tied by difficult circumstances, that you will often feel like saying, with Paul, when signing his name to a letter in prison, "Remember my bonds"; but God is not bound, and if you live faithfully in God's sight, the gracious influence of your devotion and love will be as seeds sown in the earth that shall bear fruit unto eternal life.

1534—Sir Thomas More (1478–1535), English statesman and writer, was the author of the well-known satire Utopia *(1516; see September 3). While chancellor of England, he fell from King Henry VIII's favor by refusing to take the king's side in a dispute over Henry's divorce of Catherine of Aragon (Henry's first wife). As a result, More was imprisoned in the tower of London on this day and executed in July of the following year. During his fifteen months in prison, he wrote the remarkable* Dialogue of Comfort Against Tribulation, *in which an autobiographical character, Anthony, discusses with his nephew, Vincent, the comforts found in tribulation. In this modernized passage, he compares God to a mother hen.*

------------------ ◦◦◦ ------------------

The prophet says, "My strength and my praise is our Lord, He has been my safeguarder" (Psalm 117:14) . . . "With His shoulders shall He shadow you, and under His feathers shall you trust" (Psalm 90:4). . . .

That is, for the hope you have in His help, He will take you so near Him, into His protection, that as the hen keeps her young chicks from the hawk, nestling them together under her own wings, so from the devil's claws (the ravenous hawk of this dark air) will the God of heaven gather the faithful trusting folk near to his own side and set them in surety, well and warm, under the covering of his heavenly wings. . . .

Here are, cousin Vincent, words of no little comfort for every Christian, by which we may see with how tender an affection God, in His great goodness, longs to gather us under the protection of His wings. And how often, like a loving hen, He clucks home to Himself even those chicks of His that willfully walk abroad in the hawk's danger and will not come at his clucking. But ever more He clucks for them, the farther they go from Him. And, therefore, can we not doubt, if we will follow Him and with faithful hope come running to Him, but that He shall in all matter of temptation take us near to Him and set us even under His wing. And then are we safe if we will tarry there.

For against our will no power can pull us from there, nor hurt our souls.

1521—Martin Luther (1483–1546) was a German priest, professor, and reformer who came into conflict with the church over the custom of indulgences and other theological issues. Before being excommunicated, Luther defended himself against the charge of heresy at a conference called "The Diet of Worms," at which Luther made his famous defense on this day: "Here I stand; I can do no other." Because some of these disagreements concerned Bible interpretation, a few of Luther's thoughts concerning Scripture are given below.

———————— ∙◦§ ❧∙ ————————

• The reader of the Scriptures should be a humble person, who shows reverence and fear toward the Word of God, who constantly says, "Teach me, teach me, teach me." The Spirit resists the proud, even though they are zealous and preach Christ for a time without fault. . . . Pride drove the angel from heaven, and it spoils many a preacher. Therefore it is humility that we need in the study of sacred literature.

• Genesis is a charming book and has wonderful stories! I cannot understand it at all, however. I shall need to have been dead several years before I shall thoroughly understand the meaning of creation and the omnipotence of God.

• The litany of litanies is the Lord's Prayer. The learning of the learned is the Ten Commandments. The virtue of the virtuous is the Apostles' Creed. . . . These three make a person perfect and absolute in thought, word, and deed; that is, they nourish and bring to the highest perfection the mind, tongue, and body.

• The New Testament throws light upon the Old as the day lights up the night.

• One must hold fast to the Word of God, so that if I should behold all the angels and hear them telling me not to believe some verse of Scripture, not only ought I not to be moved by them, but I ought to close my eyes and ears, for they would be unworthy of being looked upon or listened to.

• There are two things in the world that Christians ought to attend to: the word of God and the work of God.

—From Luther's *Table Talk*,
translated by Preserved Smith and H. P. Gallinger

1855—Father F.-J.-F. Fortin was a French priest and curé of the cathedral church of St. Étienne in Auxerre, France. (See also November 2.) On this day, the church authorities granted the imprimatur (notice that the book is free from doctrinal error) to Fortin's volume of collected homilies, Parish Sermons. *The following excerpt is from his sermon "On the Triumph of the Cross" and explains Christ's words "I will be raised up and draw all people to myself" (John 12:32).*

By bringing about the greatest and most difficult revolution in the history of the world, the Cross has triumphed over the religions of the people, over the wisdom of the philosophers, over the politics of the rulers of this world....

Having witnessed his death, the soldiers appointed to guard the crucified Lord beat their breasts and proclaimed, "Truly, this was the Son of God." Millions of people from all the nations under the sun have proclaimed him as the Messiah; have you not seen people from all parts of the world running to the Cross? The Greek, whose villages are embellished with masterpieces of art, comes to ask for a new wisdom that he never knew before. The Roman in his forum, in his camps, in the midst of his legions, adores the Cross and prostrates himself before it. The African, beneath his burning sky, raises temples to it. The Scythian, wandering through the deserts of Asia Minor in his chariot, trembles with joy and hope in the face of the Cross. The Gaul, in the depths of his forests, has given his heart to the Cross and become its soldier. The learned, the ignorant, the philosopher, the old, the young, the infant, the virgin—all have been known to brave death and scorn life in their love for the Cross. The Gentile, the barbarian, and the Jew alike have bowed their humble forehead to the dust in the presence of the Cross. All run to the Cross; all desire to have it. It is the hope of all the ends of the earth....

And we too, O our Redeemer, prostrate ourselves before your Cross in the transports of our love, and we will repeat before the whole world the song that the angels chant ceaselessly in heaven: "The lamb that was sacrificed is worthy to receive power and divinity and might and wisdom and honor and glory and blessing." Amen.

1913—Sir William Osler (1849–1919) was a renowned Canadian physician and teacher who served at Johns Hopkins University and completed his career as a professor of medicine at Oxford University, England. On this day, he delivered an inspirational lecture, which has since become famous, to the students of Yale University (then, an all-male institution). It is called "A Way of Life." The following is an excerpt.

—————— ❧ ❧ ——————

Do you remember that most touching of all incidents in Christ's ministry, when the anxious ruler Nicodemus came by night, worried lest the things that pertained to his everlasting peace were not a part of his busy and successful life? Christ's message to him is His message to the world—never more needed than at present: "Ye must be born of the spirit." You wish to be with the leaders—as Yale men it is your birthright—know the great souls that make up the moral radium of the world. You must be born of their spirit, initiated into their fraternity, whether of the spiritually minded followers of the Nazarene or of that larger company, elect from every nation, seen by St. John.

Begin the day with Christ and [the Lord's] prayer—you need no other. Creedless, with it you have religion; creed-stuffed, it will leaven any theological dough in which you stick. As the soul is dyed by the thoughts, let no day pass without contact with the best literature of the world. Learn to know your Bible, though not perhaps as your fathers did. In forming character and in shaping conduct, its touch has still its ancient power. Of the kindred of Ram and sons of Elihu, you should know its beauties and its strength. Fifteen or twenty minutes day by day will give you fellowship with the great minds of the race, and little by little as the years pass you extend your friendship with the immortal dead. They will give you faith in your own day. Listen while they speak to you of the fathers.... Mankind, it has been said, is always advancing, man is always the same. The love, hope, fear, and faith that make humanity, and the elemental passions of the human heart, remain unchanged, and the secret of inspiration in any literature is the capacity to touch the cord that vibrates in a sympathy that knows no time nor place....

1109—St. Anselm (1053–1109), Benedictine monk and writer, died on this day, which the church has since celebrated in his honor. Anselm was involved in many of the political and religious disputes of his time, but his integrity and heart for God were always evident and led to his being made Archbishop of Canterbury in 1093. After Thomas Becket, Anselm is probably the most famous man to hold that position. (See also December 5.) To commemorate St. Anselm's day, this passage from his Meditations *is offered: "On the Incarnation of Our Lord."*

He was made flesh that He might call you back to the things of the spirit. He was made a partaker of your changeableness that He might make you a partaker of his unchangeableness. He condescended to your lowliness that He might exalt you to His high loftiness. He was born of a pure virgin that He might heal the corruption of your sinful nature. . . . He was presented in the temple and received by the holy widow Anna (Luke 2:37) that He might admonish His faithful servants to be continually in the house of God and to endeavor by the practice of holy living to be worthy to receive Him. He was taken into the arms of the aged Simeon and glorified by him that He might show forth His love toward gravity of life and ripeness in righteousness. He was baptized that He might sanctify the sacrament of our baptism. In the river Jordan, as He bowed Himself to receive baptism at the hand of John, He heard the voice of the Father and received the Holy Ghost coming upon Him in the form of a dove, that He might teach us that we should abide in humility of mind and therein be honored by the word of the Father in heaven coming to us. . . . By day He abided with the people preaching the kingdom of God and edifying the multitudes by His wonderful works and by His words. By night he went into a mountain and gave Himself to prayer, teaching us, as the season requires, sometimes by word and deed to show forth, according to our ability, to our neighbors, among whom we live, the way of life; sometimes, entering into the stillness of our soul and ascending the mountain of virtue, to breathe the sweet air of heavenly contemplation and without fainting to direct our thoughts to things above.

—adapted from *The Devotions of St. Anselm*,
translated by Clement C. J. Webb (1903)

1892—Handley Carr Glyn Moule (1841–1920) came from an illustrious family of English ministers. He was one of the most noted preachers of his time and was a particular favorite of the British royal family, for whom he performed many Christian services. On this day, he completed the writing of the preface to his book of practical advice for novice ministers, called To My Younger Brethren. *In it he gives this simple advice for reading the Bible.*

———— ❧ ❧ ————

We are in the nineteenth century, almost in the twentieth, and perhaps we therefore need, even more than our elder brethren of the fourth [century], to renew our energies in Scripture study by prayerful, painstaking recollection of what the Book is. We need an ever fresh realization of what it is immortally, unalterably; the divinely trustworthy and therefore authoritative account of God's mind, and especially and above all of God's mind concerning Jesus Christ and our relations to Him, our life by Him, our peace and power and hope in Him.…

Take one of the holy Books, or a section of one of them; and for this purpose shorter is better. By a certain exercise of imagination suppose yourself to be reading a newly discovered fragment of the apostolic age.… Now I attempt from time to time, reverently but very simply, to treat some inspired Epistle somewhat in the same way. I place myself before it as much as possible as if it were new to me and others. I seek, with something of the curiosity which such conditions would create, to collect and arrange its theology and its ethics. And then I bring in upon the results of my study the fact that it is God's Word, the Word which I am to embrace and live upon and act upon today.…

To stimulate our consciousness of what the Epistle contains to reward the search, … let us try to place it before us as what it is not now, but once was, a newly given oracle of God. It was once read for the first time, perhaps in the house of Lydia. Let it be to us, so far as thought can make it so, what it was then. And let us remember all the while that it is really even now new, for it is immortal with the breath of the Spirit of God. It not only "abideth," but "liveth."

1667—Mary Boyle, Countess of Warwick (1624–78), was a talented, well-connected woman of seventeenth-century England. (See also September 23.) Although she was born into a noble family and accustomed to moving in elite social circles, her Diary, published long after her death, shows her to have been a remarkably humble, compassionate, and devout woman. Her entry for this day records a profound insight she had while attending the public festivities in honor of St. George, the patron saint of England.

———————— ✦ ✦ ————————

In the morning, as soon as dressed, in a short prayer I committed my soul to God; then went to Whitehall and dined at my lord chamberlain's; then went to see the celebration of St. George's feast, which was a very glorious sight. Whilst I was in the banqueting house, hearing the trumpets sounding, in the midst of all that great show, God was pleased to put very mortifying thoughts into my mind and to make me consider: What if the trump of God should now sound! Which thought did strike me with some seriousness and made me consider in what glory I had in that very place seen the late king [Charles I], and yet out of that very place he was brought to have his head cut off. And I had also many thoughts how soon all that glory might be laid in the dust; and I did in the midst of it consider how much greater glory was provided for a poor, sincere child of God. I found, blessed by God, that my heart was not at all taken with anything I saw [at the festivities for St. George], but esteemed it not worth the being taken with. At night, committed my soul to God . . .

1902—Thomas de Witt Talmage (1832–1902) was a brilliant American pastor of the Dutch Reformed Church, and he also served as the editor of the Christian Herald. *In his time, his preaching was as popular as Moody's and Spurgeon's. On this day the preface was written for a posthumous commemorative volume in his honor,* The Authentic Life and Time of T. de Witt Talmage, *from which this excerpt, from one of Talmage's sermons, is taken.*

———— •◦§ ◦§◦• ————

A widowed mother, with her little child, went West, hoping to get better wages there; she was taken sick and died. The overseer of the poor got her body and put it in a box and put it in a wagon and started down the street toward the cemetery at full trot. The little child—the only child—ran after it through the streets, bare-headed, crying: "Bring me back my mother! . . ." And it was said that as the people looked on and saw her crying after that which lay in the box in the wagon—all she loved on earth—it is said the whole village was bathed in tears. . . . Dear Lord, is there no appeasement for all this sorrow that I see about me? Yes, the thought of resurrection and reunion far beyond this scene of struggle and tears. "They shall hunger no more, neither thirst any more, . . . for the Lamb which is in the midst of the throne shall lead them to living fountains of water, and God shall wipe away all tears from their eyes." . . . It is peace. It is sweetness. It is comfort. It is infinite satisfaction, this Gospel I commend to you.

Someone could not understand why an old German Christian scholar used to be always so calm and happy and hopeful, when he had so many trials and sicknesses and ailments. A man secreted himself in the house. He said, "I mean to watch this old scholar and Christian." And he saw the old Christian man go to his room and sit down on the chair beside the stand and open the Bible and begin to read. He read on and on, chapter after chapter, hour after hour, until his face was all aglow with the tidings from heaven, and when the clock struck twelve, he arose and shut his Bible and said, "Blessed Lord, we are on the same terms yet. Good night. Good night." Oh, you sin-parched and you trouble-pounded, here is comfort, here is satisfaction. Will you come and get it? I cannot tell you what the Lord offers you hereafter so well as I can tell you now. "It doth not yet appear what we shall be."

1910—Rev. Arthur F. W. Ingram (1858–1946), the Lord Bishop of London, was a well-known English prelate. Some of his most stunning sermons are collected in the book The Mysteries of God. *On this day, an acquaintance of Ingram's named A. F. London testified in the preface to that book that the sermons so moved one clergyman that he wept, explaining to Ingram, "Forgive me, Bishop; I'm a Welshman!" In the following passage from that book, Ingram answers the question, "What do we know about our life in eternity?"*

———————— ᘒ ᘓ ————————

First of all, it must be a *human life*—that is to say, it must be a life that men and women will enjoy. Why am I so certain about that? Because Jesus was Himself truly man. He has prepared it all and got it ready. Do you not remember our text: "In My Father's house are many mansions; if it were not so, I would have told you"? . . . The person who said that came from Heaven; . . . I am perfectly certain that the reason so many are afraid of death . . . is that we have a false idea of what life is. But Christ knows what we enjoy; He knows perfectly what is in man. God knows; He made man. And if it is a human life, then I think you will find three things follow: (a) First, our old friendships and old loves, where they are pure and true, go on. . . . That is the joy of loving home ties; that is the joy of friendship between man and man, between man and woman, between woman and woman; that is the joy of children clustering round your knee—*that it goes on.* (b) The second consequence of its being a human life is that we shall know one another. . . . In Scripture it is revealed to us that those who know each other here will know each other there. (c) And, thirdly, there will be scope for all human faculties. . . . The rest that is spoken of in the other world is the rest of happy activity, with every faculty trained here used there in loving and perfect service. We are told of the angels that each one had six wings: "With twain he covered his face"—adoration; "with twain he covered his feet"—self-abasement; "with twain he did fly"—activity.

1630—English poet George Herbert (1593–1633) was known in his life-time as a priest in the Church of England. (See also May 17.) Just before his death, he entrusted his poems to Nicholas Ferrar, and their posthumous publication in a volume called The Temple *established Herbert as one of the greatest poets of England. Having been born into a noble family, Herbert was destined to become a courtier, but because of a spiritual crisis, he was drawn to the church. He was made a priest only three years before his death, and the same year, on this day, he was inducted as rector at Bemerton Church. His devout nature may be seen in the following passage from Izaak Walton's* Life of Mr. George Herbert *(1675).*

———————— ❧ ————————

When at his induction he was shut into Bemerton Church, being left there alone to toll the bell (as the law requires of him), he stayed so much longer than an ordinary time before he returned to those friends that stayed, expecting him at the church door, that his friend Mr. Woodnot looked in at the church window and saw him lie prostrate on the ground before the altar, at which time and place (as he after told Mr. Woodnot) he set some rules to himself for the future management of his life and then and there made a vow to labor and keep them.

And the same night that he had his induction, he said to Mr. Woodnot, "... I will now use all my endeavors to bring my relations and dependents to a love and reliance on him, who never fails those that trust him. But above all, I will be sure to live well, because the virtuous life of a clergyman is the most powerful eloquence to persuade all that see it to reverence and love, and at least to desire to live like him. And this I will do because I know we live in an age that has more need of good examples than precepts. And I beseech that God, who hath honored me so much as to call me to serve him at his altar that as by his special grace he hath put into my heart these good desires and resolutions, so he will by his assisting grace give me ghostly strength to bring the same to good effect; and I beseech him that my humble and charitable life may so win upon others as to bring glory to my Jesus, whom I have this day taken to be my master and governor."

1667—As a young man, John Milton (1608–74), an ardent English Puritan, could have gained renown in any number of fields: music, philosophy, politics, education, and religion. His first love, however, was poetry. On this day, he signed a copyright agreement with publisher Samuel Symmons for the publication of Paradise Lost, *which some scholars have called the most sublime poem in the English language. Milton was paid a mere 10£. The purpose of the epic, as Milton wrote, is to "justify the ways of God to men." The following lovely "morning hymn," sung by Adam and Eve in the Garden of Eden before the Fall, is from Book V of* Paradise Lost.

Ye mists and exhalations that now rise
From hill or steaming lake, dusky or grey,
Till the sun paint your fleecy skirts with gold,
In honor to the world's great author, rise,
Whether to deck with clouds the uncolored sky
Or wet the thirsty earth with falling showers,
Rising or falling still advance his praise.
His praise, ye winds that from the four quarters blow,
Breathe soft or loud; and wave your tops, ye pines,
With every plant, in sign of worship, wave.
Fountains and ye that warble as ye flow,
Melodious murmurs, warbling, tune his praise.
Join voices all ye living souls, ye birds,
That singing up to Heaven gate ascend,
Bear on your wings and in your notes his praise;
Ye that in waters glide and ye that walk
The earth and stately tread or lowly creep;
Witness if I be silent, morn or even,
To hill or valley, fountain or fresh shade
Made vocal by my songs and taught his praise.
Hail universal Lord, be bounteous still
To give us only good; and if the night
Have gathered aught of evil or concealed,
Disperse it, as now light dispels the dark.

304—This day is traditionally commemorated as the day on which St. Pollio was executed under the Roman persecutions. Pollio was a "Lector" of the church; that is, he was an educated layperson who proselytized by reading the Bible aloud to others, especially the illiterate. Italian theologian and martyrologist St. Alfonso de Liguori (1696–1787; see also March 7), in his classic book Triumphs of the Martyrs *(1776), records the following dialogue between St. Pollio and Probus, the Roman governor of the city of Cibales in ancient Illyria. After this conversation, Probus condemned Pollio to death.*

———— ❦ ————

Probus interrogated him concerning his religion. Pollio answered that he was not only a Christian, but the chief of the Lectors. Probus asked, "What Lectors?" To which the saint replied, "Those who read the Word of God to the people." Probus: "Those, perhaps, who are accustomed to convincing women to refrain from marriage and to observe a vain continency?" Pollio: "They are indeed vain who abandon their Creator and follow your superstitions; they are wise, on the contrary, who in spite of being tortured persist in observing the Commandments." Probus: "What commandments are you talking about?" Pollio: "The Commandments that teach us to honor one God only and not all those gods made of stone and wood; the commandments that help us overcome our sins and give us the power to persevere in doing good; that teach virgins to value their virginity and teach married people to remain faithful to each other; that teach subjects to obey their sovereign and rulers to make decisions with justice; finally, those Commandments that teach us that eternal life has been prepared for all who despise the kind of death that you can inflict upon us." Probus: "But what hope does a man have who, along with life, loses the enjoyment of the light and all other physical pleasures?" Pollio: "There is an eternal light that is infinitely better than this light, which after a short time, must be extinguished forever in our eyes. The good that endures eternally is incomparably more desirable than that which comes to an end. Is it not wise to prefer eternal things to those that are quickly passing away?"

1879—In this year a Scottish writer by the name of Robert MacDonald published a daily devotional called From Day to Day: Helpful Words for the Christian Life. *His thought for this day is called "The Loving Interest of Large Hearts" and discusses the apostle Paul's great love for people.*

———————— ❦ ————————

In their views and feelings, some people are so restricted and narrow that they can think and speak of family and kindred only. This is their world, and little though it be, it bounds all their vision, and they have not a thought beyond it. Others are so diffusely wide and general in their sympathies that, though professedly interested in mankind, they do nothing whatever for individual men. But the great apostle of the Gentiles fell into neither of these extremes. His vision was such that it could take in the distant and yet not miss the near. It could be wide-reaching and yet minutely centered. And it was the same with his feelings. He had so large a heart that he yearned for the eternal good of all his fellows. It was not the king only he thought of when he stood before Agrippa, but his whole audience: "I would to God," he said, "that not only you, but also all that hear me this day, were altogether such as I am, except for these bonds." Yet so minutely and lovingly mindful was he that he never forgot a single friend. Accordingly, his epistles abound in such special and kindly salutations as these: "Greet Priscilla and Aquila, my helpers in Christ Jesus. Greet Mary, who bestowed much labor on us. Salute Andronicus and Junia, my kinsmen and my fellow prisoners. Salute Rufus, chosen in the Lord, and his mother and mine. Salute my well-beloved Epenetus, who is the first fruits of Achaia unto Christ." Thus mothers, sisters, brothers, fellow laborers, and fellow sufferers were all tenderly and affectionately remembered by him.

So should it ever be with all who love the Lord. "To be in such a list as this," said Dr. Wardlaw, "is to be in the roll of true honor and lasting fame. It may be little thought of in this world, but it will be envied in eternity. The humblest name here will stand higher in the world to come than that of the mightiest monarch who lived and died without the grace of God. See, brethren, to have your names associated with those of the saints of God—among those whom an apostle would have acknowledged as Christ's and whom Christ will acknowledge as his own."

1735—Elizabeth Singer Rowe (1674–1737) was an English poet. Among other works she wrote a well-known paraphrase of the Book of Job *and metrical renderings of* Daniel *and* The Song of Solomon. *After her death, hymn writer Isaac Watts gathered her papers into a volume called* Devout Exercises *of the Heart, from which the following piece, "A Review of Divine Mercy and Faithfulness," is taken. This meditation was written on this day, two years before her death.*

------------------ ✺ ------------------

I am now setting to my seal that God is true, and leaving this as my last testimony to the Divine veracity. I can from numerous experiences assert His faithfulness and witness to the certainty of His promises. . . . [O Lord,] I know not where to begin the recital of Your numerous favors. You have hid me in the secret of Your pavilion, from the pride of man and from the strife of tongues, when by a thousand follies I have merited reproach. You have graciously protected me when the vanity of my friends or the malice of my enemies might have stained my reputation. You have covered me with Your feathers and under Your wing have I trusted. Your truth has been my shield and my buckler. To You I owe the blessing of a clear and unblemished name, and not to my own conduct, nor the partiality of my friends. Glory be to You, O Lord.

You have led me through a thousand labyrinths and enlightened my darkness. When shades and perplexity surrounded me, my light has broken forth out of obscurity and my darkness has been turned into noonday. You have been a Guide and a Father to me. When I knew not where to ask advice, You have given me unerring counsel. . . .

I have yet a thousand and ten thousand deliverances to recount, ten thousand unasked-for mercies to recall! No moment of my life has been destitute of Your care. . . . Hitherto God has helped, and here I set up a memorial to that goodness which has never abandoned me to the malice and stratagems of my infernal foes, nor left me a prey to human craft or violence. The glory of His providence has often surprised me when groping in thick darkness. With a potent voice He has said, "Let there be light, and there was light." He has made His goodness pass before me and loudly proclaimed His name, "The Lord, the Lord God, merciful and gracious." To Him be glory forever. Amen.

May

BENE DIXISTI. CONSUMMATUM EST.

The Venerable Bede writing one of his many books,
above, and on his death bed, below (see May 26).
From Sabine Baring-Gould's *Lives of the Saints*.

1734—Isaac Watts (1674–1748) was one of England's greatest hymn writers, author of more than six hundred hymns, including "O God, Our Help in Ages Past" and "When I Survey the Wondrous Cross." (See also June 18.) In 1734, at the age of sixty, he collected his earliest writings and published them as Reliques Juveniles *("Youthful Remains"), which included the following "Meditation on the First of May."*

——————— ⚜ ———————

What astonishing variety of artifices, what innumerable millions of exquisite works, is the God of Nature engaged in every moment! How gloriously are His all-pervading wisdom and power employed in this useful season of the year, this Spring of Nature! What infinite myriads of vegetable beings is He forming this very moment in their roots and branches, in their leaves and blossoms, their seeds and fruits! ... What endless armies of animals is the hand of God molding and figuring this very moment throughout His dominions! What immense flight of little birds are now fermenting in the egg, heaving and growing toward shape and life! What vast flocks of four-footed creatures, what droves of large cattle, are now framed in their early embryos, imprisoned in the dark cells of nature! ... What unknown myriads of insects in their various cradles and nesting places are now working toward vitality and motion! And thousands of them with their painted wings just beginning to unfurl, expand themselves into fluttering and daylight! ...

An exquisite world of wonders is complicated even in the body of every little insect—an ant, a gnat, a mite—that is scarce visible to the naked eye. Admirable engines! which a whole academy of philosophers could never contrive—which the nation of poets has neither art nor colors to describe—nor has a world of mechanics skill enough to frame the plainest or coarsest of them. Their nerves, their muscles, and the minute atoms which compose the fluids fit to run in the little channels of their veins, escape the notice of the most sagacious mathematician, with all his aid of glasses. The active powers and curiosity of human nature are limited in their pursuit and must be content to lie down in ignorance.

It is a sublime and constant triumph over all the intellectual powers of man which the great God maintains every moment in these inimitable works of nature—in these impenetrable recesses and mysteries of Divine art.

1882—Charles John Vaughan (1816–97), Dean of Llandaff, Wales, was a Welsh minister and scholar. He was widely recognized for the number of young men he trained for ordination, who were known as "Vaughan's Doves." On this day, Vaughan wrote the preface to his book Sermons, *comparing the language of the Revised and King James Versions of the Bible. Here is a passage from a sermon called "Garden and City—Paradise and Heaven," in which he examines Revelation 22:14: "Blessed are they that wash their robes, that they may have the right to come to the tree of life" (*RV*), which he prefers to the very different King James: "Blessed are they that do his commandments, that they may have right to the tree of life."*

How beautiful, how animating in its suggestion—"Blessed are they that wash their robes, that they may have the right to come to the tree of life." It carries us back to one of the most Evangelical of Old Testament visions, where the high priest is seen standing before the Lord, and Satan standing at his right hand to resist him. The high priest, at the beginning of the vision, is clothed with filthy garments—garments of earth and fallen nature. And it is said to the ministering spirits before the throne, "Take away from him the filthy garments." And to him it is said, "Behold, I have caused thine iniquity to pass from thee, and I will clothe thee with change of raiment." Forgiveness and cleansing—the grace of justification, and the grace of sanctification—are the two gifts typified in the figure before us. The robes were not always white—the robes are not made white by once washing. "Blessed are they that wash their robes"—there is no benediction upon the wearers of the self-white clothing—*they* are those who trust in themselves that they are righteous and need no repentance. A whole Gospel is in the saying. It is not only, "Blessed are they that have washed"—there is a recognition of the daily, the hourly, the perpetual washing: for the Greek word is "they that keep washing"—they who—to introduce a slightly different similitude of the Christian standing—having once washed the whole body in the fountain opened for sin and for uncleanness, have need constantly to wash the feet, soiled afterwards, and again and again, by contact with the dust and the miry clay of this world.

328—On this day Helena, the mother of Roman Emperor Constantine (306–337), is said to have found the cross on which Jesus was crucified. Whether the story is legend or not, this day, called Holy Cross Day, is still celebrated as a reminder of Christ's sacrifice. In honor of this day, the concluding lines of an Old English poem called "The Dream of the Rood," which dates from the Middle Ages, are given. In the poem, the narrator has a vision in which the Cross itself speaks to him. The narrator then awakens and concludes the poems with these lines.

This is my heart's desire and my hope:
To wait on the Cross. I have few noble friends
Still left in the world; all have journeyed
Far from this paltry earth, seeking the Lord of universe,
Living with their exalted Father in their heavenly home,
Living in ecstasy! Now, each day I wait
For the cross of God, of which I had a vision once
Here on earth, to take me from
This quickly passing life and carry me
To where there is great bliss and heavenly joy—
Where the people of the Lord sit at the feast.
The cross will set me down in a place where
I may always dwell in glory and live in endless rapture
Among the saints. May the Lord be a friend to me,
He who suffered on the wooden tree
For the sins of all the earth. He saved us
And gave us new life and a heavenly home.
Hope and glory and joy were restored
To those who deserved the burning fires of hell.
The Son was full of power on his journey here,
Conquering and victorious, and when
The mighty Lord of all creation brought with him
The hosts of souls to God's kingdom,
Joyfully among the angels and all the other souls
Who already live in heaven in glory,
Then God almighty himself had come—
The King had reclaimed his throne.

1415—Englishman John Wycliffe (c. 1330–84) was the first to translate large portions of the Bible into vernacular English. On this day the Council of Constance, a group opposed to his work, decreed that his body be exhumed and burned—thirty-one years after Wycliffe's death—and that the ashes be thrown into the River Swift as a symbolic means of discouraging the spread of his influence. Wycliffe wrote in what is now called Middle English. The Lord's prayer (Matthew 4:9–13) is given below in Wycliffe's original spelling, and that is followed by a modernized version of Wycliffe's rugged translation of John 8:3–11.

—◦§ ❧◦—

Oure fadir that art in hevens, halewid be thi name. Thi kyngdoom come. Be thi wille don in erthe as in hevene. Gyve to us this day oure breed, and forgyve to us oure dettis as we forgyven to oure dettouris, and lede us not into temptacioun, but delyvere us fro yvel. Amen.

———

In the gray morning, he came again into the temple, and all the people came to him, and he, sitting, taught them. And the scribes and Pharisees brought a woman taken in adultery and set her in the middle. And they said to him, "Master, this woman is now taken in adultery. Truly, in the law, Moses commanded us to stone such a woman; therefore what do you say?" Truly, they said this thing to tempt him, that they might accuse him.

But Jesus, bowing down, wrote with his finger in the earth. And when they finished asking him, he raised himself and said to them, "He of you that is without sin, cast he the first stone on her."

And after that he bowed himself down and wrote in the earth.

Then, hearing these things, they went away one after the other, beginning with the oldest, and left Jesus alone and the woman standing in the middle.

Then Jesus raised himself and said to her, "Woman where are they that accuse you? Does no man condemn you?"

She said, "No man, Lord."

Jesus said to her, "Neither shall I condemn you. Go, and never more sin."

1919–Baron Friedrich von Hügel (1852–1925) was a major Catholic theologian at the end of the nineteenth and beginning of the twentieth centuries. In his theology, he combined a practical, critical, and historical view of Christianity with the need for mystical and intuitive spiritual experience as well. On this day, in his late sixties, he wrote to his beloved niece Gwendolen Green on the subject of the Church, and that we should judge it by its best representatives, not its worst.

—◦§ ɛ◦—

The Church . . . has at its worst done various kinds of harm, introduced complications and oppressions which, but for it, would not have been in the world. I know this in a detail far beyond, my Gwen, what you will ever know. . . .

The main point to consider [is] not the harm done by churchmen at their worst, but the special function and work of the Church at its best. You see, Gwen, this is but the same principle which comes continually into everything. Take *marriage*. What a unique means of training the soul, how magnificent is its ideal! Yes, but nothing is, of course, easier than to collect volumes full of instances of infidelity, tyranny, non-suitedness, etc. A good lawyer-philanthropist friend of mine has enthusiastically put forward the example of certain American states which allow sixteen varied reasons for divorce.

Take *parenthood:* what a unique relation, what an irreplaceable means for the mind's and soul's growth. Yes, but the volumes full of misguided parental affection of folly or tyranny! So with the *State*, so with *Art*, so with *Science*, so with all that the hands of men touch at all— hands which so readily soil even what they most need, what is most sacred. But notice how Church, State, Family, Children, the Marriage Tie, these, and other right and good things, not only possess each its Ideal, unattained outside of and above it. No, no: they each possess within them more or less of that Ideal *become real*—they each and all live on at all because, at bottom, they are necessary, they are good, they come from God and lead to Him, and really in part effect what they were made for.

1541—King Henry VIII (1509–47) of England issued a royal proclamation on this day to remind every parish in the country of its responsibility to own a copy of the first complete English translation of the Bible. That translation, published in 1539 and dubbed "The Great Bible," was the work of English scholar Miles Coverdale (c. 1488–1569). The following version of Psalm 19 is from "The Great Bible," which predated the famous King James Version by more than seventy years.

———— ✧ ————

The heavens declare the glory of God, and the firmament showeth his handiwork. One day telleth another, and one night certifyeth another. There is neither speech nor language, but their voices are heard among them.

Their sound is gone out into all lands, and their words into the ends of the world. In them hath he set a tabernacle for the sun, which cometh forth as a bridegroom out of his chamber and rejoiceth as a giant to run his course. It goeth forth from the utmost part of heaven and runneth about unto the end of it again, and there is nothing hid from the heat thereof.

The law of the Lord is an undefiled law, converting the soul. The testimony of the Lord is sure and giveth wisdom unto the simple. The statutes of the Lord are right and rejoice the heart; the commandment of the Lord is pure and giveth light unto the eyes. The fear of the Lord is clean and endureth forever; the judgments of the Lord are true and righteous altogether.

More to be desired are they than gold, yea, than much fine gold; sweeter also than honey and the honeycomb. Moreover, by them is thy servant taught, and in keeping of them there is great reward. Who can tell how often he offendeth? Oh, cleanse thou me from my secret faults. Keep thy servant also from presumptuous sins, lest they get the dominion over me; so shall I be undefiled and innocent from the great offense. Let the words of my mouth and the meditation of my heart be always acceptable in thy sight, O Lord, my strength and my redeemer.

1898—Frenchman Henri Joly (1839–1925) was an eminent psychologist and the author of the book The Psychology of the Saints. *On this day, Joly's English translator, a man named G. Tyrrell, wrote in that book's preface, "All can drink in some measure of the chalice which the saints have drained." Joly felt that there were certain psychological traits that many of the great saints held in common and that these traits were not unattainable to the average believer. For instance, though a skeptic concerning miracles, Joly felt that the saints shared an interesting attitude toward such occurrences.*

———— ⋅◦§ ◦◦⋅ ————

Our Lord Himself complained of those who asked wonders of Him before believing, and that His having done so is a lesson for us. It is a lesson that the saints who asked God to work this or that miracle by their means had learned and certainly applied to themselves. Let us listen to what they themselves have to say and let us learn from them what were their maxims and traditions on the subject.

First and foremost, the saint holds that the gift of miracles is absolutely worthless, that it is either an illusion or else the greatest possible danger to its possessor, if it is not completely under the control of two virtues which are of far greater value: charity and humility. No one will be surprised, I think, that I place these two virtues side by side, for there is nothing so inimical to the love of our neighbor as self-complacency and, still more, pride.

The following story is told by the latest biographer of St. Bernard: One dark thought tormented him, and that was the recollection of the miracles he had worked. At last he spoke out to his traveling companions, "How can it be," he said, "that God should use such a man as I am to work these wonders? Generally speaking, real miracles are worked by great saints; false miracles by hypocrites. It seems to me that I am neither the one nor the other." Nobody dared give him the answer that was in the minds of all, for fear of offending his modesty. All at once the answer to the riddle seemed to strike him. "I see," he said, "miracles are not a proof of sanctity; they are a means of gaining souls. God worked them not to glorify me, but for the edification of my neighbor. Therefore, miracles and I have nothing in common with one another."

1919—Arthur Clutton-Brock (1868–1924) was a British lawyer, an art critic for the Times *of London, a scholar, and a popular writer on religious topics. The following selection is from his intriguing book* What Is the Kingdom of Heaven? *which was published on this day.*

———————————

There are things that we must see in a relation of use to ourselves, if we are to live at all. For instance, food is to us rightly and naturally that which we eat; and, if we grow cabbages, we are necessarily in a relation of use to them. But there are other things that we cannot understand at all if we see them only in the relation of use. For instance, music. If I listen to a symphony by Beethoven, expecting it to give me some information of use to myself, information that will help me to increase my income or cure my indigestion, I shall not hear the music at all, and it will be to me a mere chaos of sounds. The music does not exist to give me useful information. . . . True, to perceive it will profit me; I shall have the delight of experiencing beauty. But the paradox of the process is this, that I shall not experience the beauty if I try to experience it with an eye to my own profit. For in that case I shall have certain expectations and make certain demands of my own upon it, not perhaps that it shall increase my income or cure my indigestion, but that it shall give me just the kind of pleasure I expect of it. If I am to experience the music as it is, I must forget about myself and all my demands and expectations, and allow myself to fall in love with it, if I can; I must allow that relation, which is the music, to happen to me.

Now, according to Christ, the universe, in its nature, is not like cabbages that we grow for our own kitchens; it is like music. Its reality consists in a relation that is not a relation of use to us at all; and we must get ourselves and our own wants and demands and expectations out of the way if we are to be aware of that reality. But, further, to be aware of that reality of the music of the universe is the highest good, the highest happiness. Then we ourselves become part of the music; we are by hearing the music constrained to make ourselves part of it; for it is a real music, irresistible in its beauty, and we cannot but dance to it when we hear it. He Himself heard it and danced to it; and the beauty of His dance, of His life, of His whole state of being, has for two thousand years allured the world, even while the world would not understand the meaning of it.

1661—Jeremy Taylor (1613–67) was one of the greatest English devotional writers, whom, a century and a half later, poet Samuel Taylor Coleridge dubbed "the Shakespeare of divines." Taylor's most famous works were Rules and Exercises for Holy Living *(1650, see also November 24) and* Holy Dying *(1651). Later in his life, as Bishop of Down, he addressed the Irish Parliament, and on this day, the day after his address, the speaker of the parliament asked Taylor to print the sermon so that everyone might hear its compassionate message. This excerpt is still relevant to politicians and lawmakers in our own time.*

Mercy intercedes for the most benign interpretation of the laws. You must, indeed, be as just as the laws; but you must be as merciful as your religion; and you have no way to tie these together but to follow the pattern in the [Sermon on the] Mount. Do as God does, who "in judgment remembers mercy."

To conclude: If everyone in this honorable assembly would join together to promote Christian religion, in its true notion, that is, peace and holiness, the love of God and the love of our brother, Christianity in all its proper usefulness, and would not endure in the nation anything against the laws of the holy Jesus; if they were all zealous for the doctrines of righteousness and impatient of sin, in yourselves and in the people, it is not to be imagined what a happy nation we should be! But if you divide into parties and keep up useless differences of names or interests; if you do not join the bands of peace, . . . you can never hope to see a blessing to the end of your labors. Remember the words of Solomon: "Righteousness exalts a nation; but sin is a reproach to any people" (Proverbs 24:34). But when righteousness is advanced in the hearts and lives of the nation, who shall dare to reprove your faith? Who can find fault with your religion?

God, of his mercy, grant that in all your consultations the Word of God may be your measure, the Spirit of God may be your guide, and the glory of God may be your end. He, of his mercy, grant that moderation may be your limit, and may peace be within your walls, as long as you are there, and in all the land forever after. . . . Amen.

1887—Scottish naturalist and evangelist Henry Drummond (1851–97; see also April 5), wrote to a friend on this day: "[D. L.] Moody writes urgently about going to America for a students' gathering, and I think I must go." As it turned out, one of the addresses he delivered on that trip was not only his most famous, but also one of the most beloved pieces of inspirational literature ever written: The Greatest Thing in the World. *It is a study of the "love" passage from 1 Corinthians 13. Drummond's stirring conclusion to that work follows.*

———————— ⋅≼ ≽⋅ ————————

In the book of Matthew, where the Judgment Day is depicted for us in the imagery of One seated upon a throne and dividing the sheep from the goats, the test of a man then is not "How have I believed?" but "How have I loved?" The test of religion, the final test of religion, is not religiousness, but Love ... not what I have done, not what I have believed, not what I have achieved, but how I have discharged the common charities of life. Sins of commission in that awful indictment are not even referred to. By what we have not done by *sins of omission*, we are judged. It could not be otherwise. For the withholding of love is the negation of the spirit of Christ, the proof that we never knew Him, that for us He lived in vain. . . .

It is the Son of Man before whom the nations of the world shall be gathered. It is in the presence of Humanity that we shall be charged. And the spectacle itself, the mere sight of it, will silently judge each one. Those will be there whom we have met and helped; or there, the unpitied multitude whom we neglected or despised. No other Witness need be summoned. No other charge than lovelessness shall be preferred. Be not deceived. The words which all of us shall one Day hear sound not of theology but of life, not of churches and saints but of the hungry and the poor, not of creed and doctrines but of shelter and clothing, not of Bibles and prayer books but of cups of cold water in the name of Christ. Thank God the Christianity of today is coming nearer the world's need. Live to help that on. Thank God men know better, by a hair's breadth, what religion is, what God is, who Christ is, where Christ is. Who is Christ? He who fed the hungry, clothed the naked, visited the sick. And where is Christ? Where? "Whoso shall receive a little child in My name receiveth Me." And who are Christ's? "Everyone that loves is born of God."

1227—On this day Brother Leo, a disciple of St. Francis (1182–1226), completed the writing of his gentle and wise biography of Francis, The Mirror of Perfection. *In this book, Brother Leo includes what is no doubt Francis's most famous prayer, "The Canticle of the Sun."*

————— ◦§ §◦ —————

Most High, Omnipotent, Good Lord,
Yours is the praise, the glory, the honor, and all blessing. . . .
Be praised, my Lord, for all Your creatures, especially Brother Sun,
    for he gives us daylight and shines upon us;
    he is beautiful and radiant with great splendor;
    and in that way, Most High, he is a symbol of You.
Be praised, my Lord, for Sister Moon and all the stars;
    for you have formed them in the sky, clear and precious and beautiful.
Be praised, my Lord, for Brother Wind
    and for the air and for the cloud and for fair weather—
      for all weather—
    by which You give Your creatures sustenance.
Be praised, my Lord, for Sister Water,
    for she is useful and humble and precious and pure.
Be praised, my Lord, for Brother Fire,
    by whom You light up the night,
    for he is beautiful and joyful and robust and strong.
Be praised, my Lord, for our Sister Mother Earth,
    for she sustains us and governs us
    and produces many fruits and colored flowers and herbs.
Be praised, my Lord, for those who forgive others because of Your love
    and those who endure sickness and tribulation.
Blessed are those who endure it in peace,
    for they will be crowned by You, Most High.
Be praised, my Lord, for our Sister Bodily Death,
    from whom no one living may escape.
Woe to those who die in mortal sin!
Blessed are those who are found within Your most holy will,
    for the second death will never do them harm.
Praise and bless my Lord and give Him thanks
    and serve Him with great humility.

1792—William Carey (1761–1834) was an English shoemaker who became one of the greatest influences on the modern missionary movement. In a sermon delivered to a group of ministers in 1792, Carey first spoke the famous phrase that has become a byword for missionary service: "Expect great things from God and attempt great things for God." His enthusiasm led to the founding of the Baptist Missionary Society. On this day, in the same year as his famous sermon, Carey's treatise, The Enquiry into the Obligations of Christians to Use Means for the Conversion of the Heathen, *was first announced for publication. In the following passage he characterizes the perfect missionary. A year later Carey himself sailed for India, and nine years later he succeeded in printing the first Bible in the Bengali language.*

Missionaries must be people of great piety, prudence, courage, and forbearance, of undoubted orthodoxy in their sentiments, and must enter with all their hearts into the spirit of their mission; they must be willing to leave all the comforts of life behind them and to encounter all the hardships of a torrid or a frigid climate, an uncomfortable manner of living and every other inconvenience that can attend this undertaking. Clothing, a few knives, powder and shot, fishing tackle, and the articles of husbandry ... must be provided for them; and when arrived at the place of their destination, their first business must be to gain some acquaintance with the language of the local people ... and by all lawful means to endeavor to cultivate a friendship with them.... They must endeavor to convince them that it was their good alone which induced them to forsake their friends and all the comforts of their native country. They must be very careful not to resent injuries that may be offered them, nor to think highly of themselves so as to despise the poor unbelievers, and by those means lay a foundation for their resentment or rejection of the gospel. They must take every opportunity of doing them good, and laboring and traveling night and day, they must instruct, exhort, and rebuke with all long-suffering and anxious desire for them, and above all, must be constant in prayer for the effusion of the Holy Spirit upon the people of their charge. Let but missionaries of the above description engage in the work, and we shall see that it is not impracticable.

1895—James Russell Miller (1840–1912) was a prominent American Presbyterian minister and writer. (See also August 6.) He was particularly famous for his many devotional books, the most ambitious of which was his Devotional Hours with the Bible, *which was published in eight volumes between 1909 and 1913. It sold more than two million copies. Another of his devotional works, published in 1895, was called simply* Dr. Miller's Year Book. *The following is its reading for May 13. The text is 1 Peter 1:5: ". . . you who are kept by the power of God through faith unto salvation ready to be revealed in the last time."*

It is related of a saintly man that, by his own request, his only epitaph was: "Kept." We are all kept, if we do not fall away into the darkness of eternal death, by the power of God unto final salvation. Only those who overcome at last get home to glory. Only Christ can help us to be conquerors. And important as was his death for us, his real work in saving us is that which he does with us, one by one, in keeping us, guiding us, giving us grace for living, lifting us up when we have fallen, bringing us back when we have wandered away. Were it not for the patient, watchful, never-wearying love of Christ, not one of us would ever get home. We are kept.

This divine keeping comes to us in many ways. We believe in angel guardianship. Then there is human guardianship. The mother is her child's first keeper. Robert Browning says that even "angels are less tenderwise than God and mothers"; and the old rabbis used to say that God could not be everywhere present, and therefore he made mothers. All through life, God gives human guardians who become helpers of our faith. Then we have ever the real divine presence in which we find perfect keeping. "The Lord is your keeper."

*1373—During a severe illness Julian of Norwich (c. 1342–c. 1413), an English anchoress, received on this day the last of a series of sixteen mystical revelations. Twenty years later she recounted her experience in her book Rev-*elations of Divine Love. *Although little is known of her life, her book, which contains many beautiful passages, remains one of the enduring classics of Christian literature. In many portions of the book Julian struggles with the problem of evil and how God could allow it to have so much dominion in the world. In one of her visions, Christ came to her.*

———— ❧ ⚜ ❧ ————

One time our Lord said to me, "All things shall be well." And another time He said, "You yourself shall see that all manner of things shall be well," and my soul understood these two sayings to mean several different things.

One meaning was that His will is for us to know that He takes notice not only of great and noble things, but of little and small things as well, low and simple things, one and the other. And so this is what He meant by saying, "All manner of things shall be well." For it is His will that we know even the smallest of things will not be forgotten.

Another meaning was this: We see many evil deeds done all around us, deeds that cause great harm, and sometimes it seems impossible that they should ever result in anything good. Sometimes when we see these evils, sorrowing and mourning because of them, we find it difficult to concentrate on beholding God blissfully, which is something we should do. And the cause of this is that our reasoning capacity is now so blind, low, and simple that we cannot know His high and marvelous wisdom, the power and the goodness of the blissful Trinity. And this is what He meant when He said, "You yourself shall see that all manner of things shall be well." It was as if He had said, "Take heed faithfully and trustingly now, and at the end of all things, you will truly see them in the fullness of joy."

1926—American inspirational writer Bertha Condé wrote on this day, "Every capacity of spirit, mind, and body is needed to make vivid to the world the triumphant personality of the Christ, who freed men from sin by his death and opened untold possibilities for spiritual adventure by his resurrection." That and the following passage, which takes Luke 9:51–56 as its text, are from her book Spiritual Adventuring.

———————— ❧ ❧ ————————

There was a day in the life of Jesus when he was passing through the country for the last time before his death on the cross. It was an eventful day because of the many people who resisted the chance to enter into Jesus' way of life. The first inhospitality came from an entire village in Samaria. Jesus desired especially to get near them, and he sent certain messengers ahead to prepare for his coming. Think of the honor that came to an obscure place to have the Lord of life with them where they could talk with him about all the hopes and fears of their lives! At last he came—and they would not receive him. Why? Because he was on his way to Jerusalem, the rival center of worship. The Samaritans were like many of us who are so sure that our own point of view about religion is right that they could not rise above their own prejudices long enough to listen to Jesus. They would not let him stay in the village and actually sent the Lord himself away.

John the beloved disciple was so stirred by this discourtesy that he wanted to call down fire from heaven to consume the whole village. How Jesus towered above it all in his divine Spirit when he rebuked the resentment of his friend by saying, "Ye know not what manner of spirit ye are of." Sometimes we try to prove our love to God by being unloving to others. The two spirits cannot be in the same heart at the same time. God's love is like the sun which shines with equal warmth upon the good and evil alike. It is the evil man who cuts himself off from God by refusing to let the light of love shine in his heart. The childlike heart does not discriminate; it ever reaches out. A mother once lamented to a friend, "My little girl plays with everyone and doesn't seem to know any difference. I have such a time keeping her from undesirable playmates." We ought to thank God for that quality of heart and spend our time filling the hearts of our children with such pure and high ideals that the undesirable child will want to be like them—or will flee from them, as the people treated Jesus.

1853—Born a slave in 1811, African-American minister Daniel A. Payne (who died in 1893) became one of the most gifted leaders in the African Methodist Episcopal Church. In 1852 he became the denomination's chief bishop, and in the following year, on this day, he delivered a landmark sermon at the annual denominational conference in Philadelphia. In the final part of that sermon, after dealing with the essentials of church government and the education of ministers, he addressed the issue of revival and renewal— not outside the church, but within it. The following passage is from that inspired exhortation.

———————•◦ ◦•———————

The highest part of our glorious vocation [is] the salvation of souls in the revivals of religion. . . .

Yes, brethren, be glad, for angels have rejoiced in the conversion of penitent sinners during the past year throughout our circuits and in all our stations! But cannot something be done during the opening Conference year that will make the field still more productive?

Yes, there can be more holy living among those who bear the ark of the Lord of Hosts—more zeal and devotedness in the cause of our Redeemer—more love for the souls of perishing sinners—more tender solicitude for the reputation and usefulness of one another!

O yes! There can be found in every one of us more of the mind that was in Christ, his meekness, his gentleness, his patience, his courage, his self-denying, self-sacrificing spirit. Above all, and over all, his unspotted holiness; maintained, fortified, and rendered invulnerable by his incorruptible integrity towards God and towards man!

Then shall we be as a "shining light, yea, as a flaming fire, burning now and burning ever." Then shall the shout of the King be heard in the camp of Israel; our conquering Immanuel will lead us on from victory to victory, and the slain of the Lord be many.

1942—*Fleeing the Nazis, French writer and philosopher Simone Weil (1909–43) left France on this day, never to return. Before leaving, however, she sent her "Spiritual Autobiography" in a letter to her friend and adviser Father J.-M. Perrin. In it she described how she first encountered Christ by reading a poem by English poet and priest George Herbert (1593–1633): "It is called 'Love.'" Weil wrote. "I used to think I was merely reciting it as a beautiful poem, but without my knowing it the recitation had the virtue of a prayer. It was during one of these recitations that, as I told you, Christ himself came down and took possession of me." Here is Herbert's poem "Love," which is the concluding poem from his posthumously published collection of verse called* The Temple *(1633). (See April 26 for more about Herbert.)*

───── ◦§ ३◦ ─────

Love bade me welcome; yet my soul drew back,
    Guilty of dust and sin.
But quick-eyed Love, observing me grow slack
    From my first entrance in,
Drew nearer to me, sweetly questioning,
    If I lacked anything.

"A guest," I answered, "worthy to be here";
    Love said, "You shall be he."
"I, the unkind, ungrateful? Ah my dear,
    I cannot look on thee."
Love took my hand and, smiling, did reply,
    "Who made the eyes but I?"

"Truth Lord, but I have marred them; let my shame
    Go where it doth deserve."
"And know you not," says Love, "who bore the blame?"
    "My dear, then I will serve."
"You must sit down," says Love, "and taste my meat."
    So I did sit and eat.

1927—Englishman Oswald Chambers (1874–1917) has been described as "an evangelical mystic." He was an extremely popular lecturer and Bible study leader. His most famous book, and one of the best-selling daily devotionals of all time, is My Utmost for His Highest *(1927), which was compiled—ten years after his death—from lectures he delivered to English troops in Egypt during World War I. The following entry for May 18, entitled "Careful Unreasonableness," is based on Matthew 6:26, 28: "Behold the fowls of the air. . . . Consider the lilies of the field." It shows both his deep devotion to Christ and also his contemplative bent.*

——————— ·≈§ §≈· ———————

Consider the lilies of the field, how they grow, they simply *are!* Think of the sea, the air, the sun, the stars, and the moon—all these *are*, and what a ministration they exert. So often we mar God's designed influence through us by our self-conscious effort to be consistent and useful. Jesus says that there is only one way to develop spiritually, and that is by concentration on God. "Do not bother about being of use to others, believe on Me"—pay attention to the Source, and out of you will flow rivers of living water. We cannot get at the springs of our natural life by common sense, and Jesus is teaching that growth in spiritual life does not depend on our watching it, but on concentration on our Father in heaven. Our heavenly Father knows the circumstances we are in, and if we keep concentrated on Him we will grow spiritually as the lilies.

The people who influence us most are not those who buttonhole us and talk to us, but those who live their lives like the stars in heaven and the lilies in the field, perfectly simply and unaffectedly. Those are the lives that mold us.

If you want to be of use to God, get rightly related to Jesus Christ and He will make you of use unconsciously every minute you live.

1924—Englishman William Temple (1881–1944) was an Anglican minister and bishop, who, during World War II, became Archbishop of Canterbury. (See also August 17.) His father, Frederick Temple, had also been Archbishop of Canterbury nearly a half century before. On this day, while serving as Bishop of Manchester, William Temple delivered a sermon, "The Church, Which Is His Body," at Manchester Cathedral. It was published a year later as part of his collection of sermons Christ in His Church.

————— ⊰ ⊱ —————

[The Church] is not an association together of people who, finding that they are agreed upon certain points, think it desirable to combine in order to propagate their opinions. It is the actual and necessary product of the fact of the Incarnation.... St. Paul sees the Christian Church as the perfect fellowship in which all the divisions among men have become negligible. The deepest division based upon religious history is negligible; there is neither Jew nor Gentile. The deepest division based on culture or education is negligible; there is neither Greek nor barbarian. The deepest division based on economic difference is negligible; there is neither bond nor free. Even the very division of sex has become spiritually negligible, and there is neither male nor female. What is there? There is "one man in Christ Jesus." Now if it be true, as I should maintain, that the best principle to take as our guide to the whole conception of personality is the principle of will or purpose, then it is true, quite literally and accurately true, that if you have an assembly of persons all dominated by one will and one purpose, they are in a true sense one person. St. Paul sees the members of the Christian Church so possessed by the Spirit of Christ, and so dedicated to the fulfillment of His purpose, that they are one person in Christ; and he looks forward to the time when all races and all individuals will have brought in their own contribution to that corporate personality; then, and then only, we shall see the measure of the stature of the fullness of the Christ, when we are all come to a full-grown man, the one man in Christ Jesus grown to the fullness of His stature.

1746—Rev. James Hervey (1714–58) was an English minister and author whose books, though extremely popular in his own time, are forgotten in ours. (See also December 20.) His writings, however, contain profound insights and are of the highest quality. On this day he dedicated his book Meditations among the Tombs and Reflections on a Flower Garden *to an anonymous Mrs. R. T. In the following excerpt from that book, from the section about his reflections while walking through a garden, he meditates on the humble bee.*

———————————— ⸎ ————————————

There are [those], I perceive, who still attend the flowers and, in defiance of the sun, ply their work on every expanded blossom. The bees, I mean—that nation of chemists to whom Nature has communicated the rare and valuable secret of enriching themselves without impoverishing others, who extract the most delicious syrup from every fragrant herb without wounding its substance or diminishing its odors. I take the more notice of these ingenious operators because I would willingly make them my pattern. While the gay butterfly flutters her painted wings and sips a little fantastic delight, only for the present moment; while the gloomy spider . . . is preparing his insidious nets for destruction, or sucking venom even from the most wholesome plants—this frugal community [of bees] are wisely employed in providing for futurity and collecting a copious stock of the most balmy treasures.

And, oh, these meditations sink into my soul! Would [that] the God who suggested each heavenly thought vouchsafe to convert it into an established principle to determine all my inclinations and regulate my whole conduct! I would then gather advantages from the same blooming objects, more precious than your golden stores, you industrious artists. I also should go home laden with the richest sweets and the noblest spoils, though I crop not a leaf nor call a single flower my own. . . .

All that is rich and resplendent in the visible creation has been called in to aid our conceptions and elevate our ideas. But indeed, no tongue can utter, no pen can describe, no fancy can imagine, what God, of his unbounded munificence, has prepared for them that love him.

1857—On this day the personal library of English librarian and scholar J. O. Halliwell (1820–89) was sold. It contained a copy of a rare prayer book from 1609 entitled Four Birds of Noah's Ark *by English dramatist Thomas Dekker (c. 1572–c. 1632), a contemporary of Shakespeare's. Only two other copies are known to exist. Aside from writing the popular play* The Shoemaker's Holiday, *Thomas Dekker also wrote the well-known children's lullaby "Golden Slumbers." In all his work he delighted in portraying the lives of ordinary men and women; for instance, his* Four Birds of Noah's Ark *contains such prayers as "For a Midwife," "For a Soldier Going to a Battle," and the following, "For a Mariner Going to Sea."*

———————— ❦ ————————

O You who rides upon the cherubim and flies on the wings of the wind; You, at the brightness of whose presence the clouds move and at whose chiding the hailstones and coals of fire fall upon the world; whose arrows are swiftest lightning and whose bow, when it goes off, shoots forth thunder—be merciful to me, O my God, for I am about to venture into the horrors of the deep. There shall I see Your wonders, but let me not see Your wrath. There shall I look into hell, but let me not fall into the jaws of fear and desperation. Preserve me, O Lord, in the womb of the ship, though the waters may climb about the ribs to swallow me up, just as You saved Jonah in the belly of the whale. And when, with Your servant Peter, I cry out to Your Son, "Help, Lord, or we perish," let His hand be stretched forth to command the waters to be quiet. Fill our sails with gentle and prosperous winds. Let not the sun be covered in storms by day, nor the moon and the stars conspire with darkness by night to spoil us with shipwreck. But set an angel at our helm when we hoist sails and go forth, and charge the same angel to guide us through that wilderness of waters till we safely arrive on shore. Or, if for our sins it be Your pleasure that our bodies in this voyage shall perish, yet, O our merciful Pilot, save our souls from the great Leviathan whose jaws are ever open to devour. Upon whatsoever rocks the vessel that bears us be split, yet we, most wretched sinners, beg that our heavenly vessels, by Your hands, may arrive at the everlasting land of promise. Grant this, O Father, for the sake of Him who swam through a red sea of His precious blood on the cross to be man's redeemer.

359—On this day what has become known as the "Dated Creed" was issued—"dated" because it was one of the few early creeds of the church to have a specific date attached to it. After many decades of wrangling among orthodox and heretical theologians, an ecumenical group of scholars attempted to draw up this universal creed that would state the basic beliefs of the entire Christian church. Still, many considered the "Dated Creed" heretical because it rejected the idea that Christ was like the Father only "in essence." Instead, the "Dated Creed," a portion of which follows, asserted that Jesus was like the Father "in all things." The distinctions are lost on most of us today, but they were vital in the early centuries of the church. In any case, the creed was soon discarded in favor of the better known Nicene Creed.

———— ⋅⋖⧽⋗⋅ ————

We believe in one God, the only and true God, the Father all-sovereign, creator and artificer of all things.

And in one only-begotten Son of God, who, before all ages and before all beginnings and before conceivable time and before all comprehensible being, was begotten impassibly from God; and through him the ages were set in order and all things came into being; begotten as only-begotten, only from the only Father, God from God, in all things like to the Father that begat him, according to the Scriptures. No one knows his begetting save the Father that begat him. We know that he, the only-begotten Son of God, at the Father's bidding came from the heavens for the putting away of sin, was born of the Virgin Mary, went about with the disciples, fulfilled all his stewardship according to the Father's will, was crucified, died, and descended to the lower regions, and set in order all things there; and the gate-keepers of Hades were affrighted when they saw him (Job 38:17); and he rose from the dead the third day and had converse with the disciples, and fulfilled all his stewardship; and when thirty days were accomplished he ascended into the heavens, and sits at the right hand of the Father, and is to come at the last day in his Father's glory, giving to each according to his works. . . .

—translator unknown

1273—On this day Pope Gregory X made Franciscan professor Giovanni di Fedanza (1221–74) a cardinal. Fedanza is better known as St. Bonaventure, one of the greatest writers and philosophers of the church, who was also beloved as a preacher and mystical devotional writer. (See also October 3.) His cardinalship brought to a halt the writing of his last great work, The Collations on the Six Days of Creation, which was still incomplete when Bonaventure died a year later. In this extract from that work, Bonaventure discusses his views on Bible study.

———————— ❧ ❧ ————————

The follower of Christ must concentrate on Sacred Scripture as children first learn their ABCs and then make syllables and learn to read and finally understand the meaning of the parts of speech. Likewise, in reference to Sacred Scripture, one must study the text and have it at the tip of one's fingers and then understand "what is said by the word," and this, not as [someone] who always gives attention to the literal meaning. The whole of Scripture is like a single zither, and the lesser string does not produce harmony by itself, but only in combination with the others. Likewise, any single passage of Scripture depends upon some other, or rather, any single passage is related to a thousand others.

Note that when Christ performed the miracle of changing water into wine, he did not say from the very first, "Let there be wine." Nor did He produce it out of nothing; as Gregory comments, He asked the servants to fill the water jars. It is impossible to explain what He did in a literal sense, but a reason may be given in terms of spiritual understanding: The Holy Spirit does not provide spiritual understanding unless man provide the jar, that is, his capacity, and the water, that is, the understanding of the literal sense. Then does God change the water of literal understanding into the wine of the spiritual. Paul was great because of the fact that he was teaching the Law at the feet of Gamaliel. He, then, who possesses Scripture is powerful in his speech. . . . Blessed Bernard [twelfth-century monk and saint], for instance, knew little. Yet, because he had studied Scripture intensely, he was able to speak with elegance.

—translated by José de Vinck

1738—Although he had been an Anglican priest and missionary for ten years, English minister John Wesley (1703–91) dated the true awakening of his faith to a mysterious, unaccountable blessing he received on this day while attending a worship service in a building on Aldersgate Street in London. Wesley went on to become one of the most influential preachers and religious thinkers of his, or any, era. Although Wesley himself never left the Church of England, his followers, taking Wesley's "method" of study and sanctification as their guide, went on to found the Methodist Church. Here is Wesley's own account of his experience.

In the evening, I went very unwillingly to a society in Aldersgate Street, where one was reading Luther's preface to the Epistle to the Romans. About a quarter before nine, while he was describing the change which God works in the heart through faith in Christ, I felt my heart strangely warmed. I felt I did trust in Christ, Christ alone for salvation; and an assurance was given me that He had taken away *my* sins, even *mine*, and saved *me* from the law of sin and death.

. . . I then testified openly to all there what I now first felt in my heart. But it was not long before the enemy suggested, "This cannot be faith, for where is your joy?" Then was I taught that peace and victory over sin are essential to faith in the Captain of our salvation but that, as to the transports of joy that usually attend the beginning of it, especially in those who have mourned deeply, "God sometimes gives, sometimes withholds them, according to the counsels of His Will."

After my return home, I was much buffeted with temptations, but cried out and they fled away. They returned again and again. I as often lifted up my eyes and He "sent me help from His holy place." And herein I found [where] the difference between this and my former state chiefly consisted. I was striving, yea, fighting with all my might under the law, as well as under grace. But then I was sometimes, if not often, conquered; now, I was always conqueror.

—from John Wesley's *Journals*

1693—François Fénelon (1651–1715) was a renowned French priest and writer. (See also February 19.) Although he faithfully served France's royal family as chaplain, his personal piety and concern for the poor and spiritually immature were great. He is now chiefly remembered for his beautifully composed letters of advice and counsel, which have been published in English as Spiritual Letters to Women. *The following excerpt from that book was written on this day.*

—◦§ ε◦—

The crosses that we make for ourselves by overanxiety as to the future are not Heaven-sent crosses. We tempt God by our false wisdom, seeking to forestall His arrangements and struggling to supplement His Providence by our own provisions. The fruit of our wisdom is always bitter. God suffers it to be so that we may be discomfited when we forsake His fatherly guidance. The future is not ours; we may never have a future; or, if it come, it may be wholly different than all we foresaw. Let us shut our eyes to that which God hides from us in the hidden depths of His Wisdom. Let us worship without seeing; let us be silent and lie still.

The crosses actually laid upon us always bring their own special grace and consequent comfort with them. We see the hand of God when it is laid upon us. But the crosses wrought by anxious foreboding are altogether beyond God's dispensations; we meet them without the special grace adapted to the need—nay, rather in a faithless spirit, which precludes grace. . . . Let us throw self aside, and then God's will, unfolding hour by hour, will content us as to all he does in our circumstances around us. . . .

He turns all within and without, the sins of others, our own failings, to our sanctification. All in heaven and earth is designed to purify and make us worthy of Him. So let us be glad when our Heavenly Father tries us with sundry inward or outward temptations. When He surrounds us with external contrarities and internal sorrow, let us rejoice, for thus our faith is tried as gold in the fire. Let us rejoice to learn the hollowness and unreality of all that is not God. It is this crucial experience that snatches us from self and the world. Let us rejoice, for by such travail the new man is born in us.

—translated by H. L. Sidney Lear (1902)

735—Bede (673–735), also called "The Venerable Bede," was a medieval English monk and scholar, who earned the epithet "father of English church history" for his historical writings. His most famous work is The History of the English Church. *He taught Hebrew, Greek, Latin, and theology at the monastery in Jarrow, England. He died on this day, and according to legend, his final act in life was to sing two brief songs. The first is now called "Bede's Death Song." The second was a song in praise to God, which is now commonly known as the "Gloria Patri" ("Glory Be to the Father"). Many scholars believe that this second song does indeed date from the time of Bede and could very possibly be his composition. (See also November 1.) Bede's songs are given below.*

Bede's Death Song

In the face of the journey that lies before us all,
no one is so wise as to have no need
to ponder, before setting out from here,
how the soul will be judged after death—
whether for good or whether for evil.

Gloria Patri

Glory be to the Father,
and to the Son,
and to the Holy Ghost.
As it was in the beginning,
is now and ever shall be,
world without end.
Amen. Amen.

1696—Cotton Mather (1663–1728) was a Puritan writer, preacher, and scholar, whose book The Ecclesiastical History of New England *(1702) is a landmark of American religious history. He was the son of famed Puritan preacher Increase Mather (see December 11), but was, in his own right, renowned as an effective and compassionate preacher. On this day, he preached one of his most famous and compelling sermons, "Things for a Distressed People to Think Upon," from which the following passage, on the need for prayer, is taken.*

———————— ⋘ ⋙ ————————

Household prayer and secret prayer may be conscientiously practiced by all.... All the blessings that we can want or wish, yea, the very best of blessings, are to be obtained by supplication to the blessed God for them. Why should I launch forth into this vast ocean of assurances ... (which our God has given to His people) that "they shall not seek his face in vain"? All New England has been filled with demonstrations from its first settlement to this day that prayer is, as it has been sometimes called, "A golden key to unlock all the treasures of heaven." Many and many and many a time, it might be said, this poor land cried out to the Lord, and the Lord has heard and saved. And what is the use that we should make of all the salvations in which we have so wonderfully seen the prevalence of prayer demonstrated? What but this: that we will, with our prayer, again and always come to You, O Hearer of Prayer! We would have a supply of provision from the bounties of heaven sent to us in our scarcity. Why, supplications like those of Elijah, will [loosen] the very corks on the bottles of heaven. We would have lions that are threatening to devour us restrained from doing so. Why, supplications like those of Daniel will muzzle the most ravenous lions. All our undertakings— would they not prosper the more if by more prayer over them, like the servant of Abraham, we acknowledged the Lord in all our ways? ...

The times which we are fallen into do loudly call for our supplication to that God in whose hands are all our times. All the whole tribe of thinking [people] that have any understanding of the times, do know this: that of all the things that we ought now to do, there is nothing more seasonable than unfeigned prayer to the Lord. ... Pray, pray, pray. Never more need than now.

1663—English Puritan Joseph Alleine (1634–68) was ejected from the Church of England for his Nonconformity in 1662. A year later, on this day, he began a year-long imprisonment for refusing to stop preaching at a time when only licensed ministers of the church were allowed to preach. Other ministers, like John Bunyan, were also imprisoned during this restrictive era. Alleine's vivid and passionate preaching style can be seen in his posthumously published book, An Alarm to the Unconverted *(1672), which was drawn from his sermons. This classic greatly influenced such later preachers as George Whitefield and Charles Spurgeon.*

———— ❧ ————

Now the Lord Jesus stretches wide his arms to receive you; he beseeches you through us. How movingly, how meltingly, how compassionately he calls. The church is put into a sudden ecstasy at the sound of his voice, "the voice of my beloved." Oh, will you turn a deaf ear to his voice? Is it not the voice that breaks the cedars and makes the mountains to skip like a calf; that shakes the wilderness and divides the flames of fire? It is not Sinai's thunder, but a soft and still voice. It is not the voice of Mount Ebal, a voice of cursing and terror, but the voice of Mount Gerizim, the voice of blessing and glad tidings of good things. It is not the voice of the trumpet nor the noise of war, but a message of peace from the King of Peace. I may say to you, O sinner, as Martha to her sister, "The Master is come, and he calls for you." Now then, with Mary, arise quickly and come unto him. How sweet are his invitations! He cries at the crossroads, "If any may thirst, let him come to me and drink." How beautiful is he! He excludes no one. "Whosoever will, let him take the water of life freely." . . .

Behold, O you sons of men, the Lord Jesus has thrown open the prison and now he comes to you by his ministers and beseeches you to come out. . . . It is from your prison, from your chains, from the dungeon, from the darkness, that he calls you, and yet will you not come? He calls you to liberty, and yet will you not hearken? His yoke is easy, his laws are liberty, his service is freedom, and whatever prejudice you may have against his ways, if God may be believed, you shall find them all pleasure and peace, and shall taste sweetness and joy unutterable, and take infinite delight and felicity in them.

1545—A prayer book called simply The Primer, *one of the most influential and popular English devotional books in its time, was first published on this day. Authorized by King Henry VIII of England (1491–1547), it contains psalms, prayers, and "offices," that is, special prayers to be read in the morning ("matins") and evening ("evensong"). Drawn from earlier prayer books, many prayers in* The Primer *date back to the fourteenth century. Here is a matin and an evensong from that collection.*

A PRAYER AT YOUR UPRISING: O Lord Jesus Christ, who is the very bright sun of the world, ever rising, never falling, who, with your wholesome look, engenders, preserves, nourishes, and makes joyful all things that are in heaven and earth: shine favorably, I beseech You, on my spirit so that the night of sins and mists of errors might be driven away by Your inward light, so that I may walk all my life without stumbling and offense, comely as in the daytime, being pure from the works of darkness. Grant this, O Lord, who lives and reigns with the Father and the Holy Ghost forevermore. Amen.

A PRAYER BEFORE YOU GO TO BED: ... I beseech You in Your bountiful goodness, O Lord, to forgive me in whatever ways I have offended You this day and to receive me under Your protection this night, so that I may rest in quietness both of body and soul. Grant my eyes sleep, but let my heart watch perpetually for You so that the weakness of the flesh might not cause me to offend the Lord. Let me at all times feel Your goodness toward me, so that I may be at all times stirred to praise You; late and early and at midday may Your praise be in my mouth, and at midnight, Lord, instruct me in Your judgments so that, all the course of my life being led in holiness and purity, I may be inducted at last into the everlasting rest that You have promised by Your mercy to them that obey Your Word, O Lord, to whom be honor, praise, and glory forever. Amen.

1625—On this day a theologian named Nicholas Ferrar (1592–1637) and his mother purchased a rural English parish estate and church called Little Gidding. Thus began one of the most notable religious communes in history. Lasting for more than twenty years, the Little Gidding group was made up of Ferrar, his mother, brother, sister, and their families, about thirty people in all. They followed a strict rule of daily devotion, organized around the Psalter, and ministered to the local people. In the following passage from an early biography of Ferrar, a certain Dr. Jebb describes their Sabbath routine and the positive influence one family can have on an entire community.

Children came from neighboring parishes, to whom notice was given that such of them as would but take the pains to learn the psalms by heart and come on Sunday morning to repeat them at Gidding, should have each of them a Psalter bestowed upon them and a penny for every psalm they could say perfectly and their Sunday dinner into the bargain. This drew so many boys and girls that an honest divine who frequently visited the place assured me he had seen forty or fifty children there at a time. Their parents, who were most of them plain country folks, were extremely pleased and obliged by it, and quickly not only their parents but the adjoining ministers, when they came to Gidding, protested that a mighty change was wrought not only on the children, but on the men and women who sat hearing their children reading and repeating at home. And whereas before their tongues were exercised in singing either naughty or lewd or else vain ballads—which much estranged their young minds from the ways of virtue—now they heard the streets and doors resounding with the sacred poetry of David's harp, which drove away the evil spirit from Saul (1 Samuel 16:23). Thus, one devout family brought again into their neighborhood the golden age of the church, as it is described in St. Jerome, "when every plowman, every day laborer refreshed himself at his toil by singing the psalms and knew the hour of the day without the sun by the progress he had made in his Psalter."...

"[Sunday] is," says [Ferrar], "a day of rest, not of pleasures. It frees us from bodily labors, but it should the more intend the exercise of the mind. God blessed the day and sanctified it; they must go together. If we would have it be happy, we must make it holy."

1917—Scotsman John Henry Jowett (1864–1923) was a popular preacher and writer who served as minister in Newcastle, Birmingham, and other cities in England. In 1911 he came to the United States to assume the pulpit of the Fifth Avenue Presbyterian Church in New York City, a pastorate that lasted until 1918. He soon became one of the most colorful and popular preachers in New York at the time. During his American stay he wrote and published a daily devotional book called My Daily Meditation for the Circling Year, *from which the following reflection from May 31 is taken. It takes as its text* 1 Corinthians 12:12–13: *"For the body is one and has many members, and all the members of that one body, being many, are one body; so also is Christ. For by one Spirit are we all baptized into one body."*

It is only in the spirit that real union is born. Every other kind of union is artificial and mechanical and dead. We dovetail many pieces of wood together and make the unity of an article of furniture, but we cannot dovetail items together and make a tree. And it is the union of a tree that we require, a union born of indwelling life. We may join many people together in a fellowship by the bonds of a formal creed, but the result is only a piece of social furniture; it is not a vital communion. There is a vast difference between a connection and a concord.

Many members of a family may bear the same name, may share the same blood, may sit and eat at the same table, and yet may have no more vital union than a handful of marbles in a boy's pocket. But let the spirit of a common love dwell in all their hearts and there is a family bound together in glorious union.

And so it is in the spirit, and there alone, that vital union is to be found. And here is the secret of such spiritual union. "By one Spirit are we all baptized into one body." The Spirit of God, dwelling in all our spirits, attunes them into glorious harmony. Our lives blend with one another in the very music of the spheres.

June

Celtic saint and abbot Columba in Derry Wood with
his beloved animals (see June 2 and June 9).

1869—English minister and inspirational writer J. Baldwin Brown (1820–84), famous in his own time for his liberal theological opinions, wrote the preface to his book The Divine Mysteries *on this day. Near the end of the book, he offers this comforting meditation.*

────────── ❧ ❧ ──────────

Your citizenship *is* in Heaven. Not *shall be* in Heaven, but *is*, in virtue of that victory of your Lord. He has won your freedom and has proclaimed it. The world's chain is off you; the world's claim on your allegiance is disowned and cast out. The question is not *can* you be a citizen of the heavenly kingdom, *can* you hold high fellowship with the angels and move in the rhythm of the motion of the world of spirits; you *are* a citizen already. Christ, your King, has come to you from Heaven and has made you its citizen. The real question is, can you, having your citizenship in Heaven, turn again to the beggarly elements from which He has set you free? The truth which the angels know He has made known to you, perhaps as they can never know it. There are things which you know, into which the angels desire to look. The motives which animate them, the objects which inflame their ardor, the spirit which inspires their zeal, are all before you and within you. The Lord's overcoming of the world has been the lifting of the curtain of sense around you; the whole universe is now in sight. Life and immortality are now no more dim thoughts, haunting the verge of the invisible; they are brought out into light by the Gospel. The sunlight of God shines over all the scene of your travail and conflict; your daily marches are lit by the luster whose fountain is the light ineffable, that streams from the throne of God and of the Lamb. If Heaven can do anything to make the conquest of earth an easy victory, Heaven is yours. If the spirit within you has heard the call, "My child," has uttered the joyful response, "My Father—my Father," has set its face homeward with the cry, "Make me glad, O my Father, with the light of Thy countenance; guide me on earth by Thy counsel and afterward receive me to Thy glory"—[then] there is infinite solace in the thought that the world from which you are struggling to extricate your spirit, imposing as it seems, has been beaten and struck to the dust by your Savior, and that all Heaven's forces, all Heaven's influences, are around you and within you, to strengthen you to win the same everlasting glory.

597—One of the towering figures of Celtic Christianity is St. Columba (c. 521–97), an Irish monk, abbot, poet, and founder of monasteries in Britain and Ireland (see also June 9). The legends of him are numerous. Like St. Francis, he had a special love for animals and nature in general. It is said he built his first monastery in an Irish oak grove, but he presumably built it of stone and rushes in such a way that no tree would have to be felled, for he did not want to destroy any of God's creatures. One writer said Columba more feared the sound of an ax in Derry Wood than the fires of hell itself. Later in life he established a monastery on the desolate island of Iona, off the coast of Scotland, and it became an important center for the Celtic church. On this day, nearly a week before his death, according to a reliable source, Columba had an unusual vision during Sunday Mass at his monastery on Iona.

———————— ⋅⊰ ⊱⋅ ————————

While the solemnity of the Mass was being celebrated according to custom on the Lord's Day, suddenly, with eyes raised heavenwards, the countenance of the venerable man was seen to be suffused with a ruddy glow, for as it is written: "When the heart is glad the countenance blossoms" [Proverbs 15:13]. For in that hour he alone saw an angel of the Lord hovering above within the walls of his oratory, and because the lovely and tranquil aspect of the holy angels sheds joy and gladness in the breasts of the elect, this was the cause of that sudden joy infused into the blessed man. When those who were there present inquired what was the cause of the gladness thus inspired, the saint, gazing upward, gave them this reply: "Wonderful and incomparable is the subtlety of the angelic nature. For behold! An angel of the Lord was sent to fetch a certain deposit, dear to God, and, after looking down upon us and blessing us within the church, has returned again through the roof of the church and has left no trace of his passing out." Thus spoke the saint. But not one of the bystanders was able to understand the nature of that deposit which the angel was sent to claim. But our patron gave the name of a "holy deposit" to his own soul, which had been entrusted to him by God. And this soul, after an interval of six days from that time, on the night of the next Lord's Day passed away to the Lord.

—from Adamnan's *Life of Saint Columba* (late seventh century), translated by Wentworth Huyshe (1905)

1678—Annually, for more than a century before the American Revolution, leading colonial preachers were invited to preach to the men of the Artillery Companies of New England. Although this annual "Artillery Sermon" was usually martial in character, it provided one of the few opportunities for religious leaders to address the military authorities. On this day, Puritan preacher and statesman Samuel Nowell (1634–88), a military chaplain himself, delivered an "Artillery Sermon" entitled "Abraham in Arms," and in the following modernized selection he glosses Ephesians 6:13–14: "Take unto you the whole armor of God, that you may be able to withstand in the evil day, and having done all, to stand. Stand therefore, having your loins girt about with truth, and having on the breastplate of righteousness."

Put on the whole armor of God; that is the way to make a good soldier, to have the complete armor—armor for the inward man. Without such a guard for the inward man, there will be failure. If the conscience is wounded or unprotected, if the breastplate of righteousness is not on, if men have guilty consciences, they will find and feel the sad effects of it. Before finding yourself in danger, put on your "spiritual armor," look to the breastplate of righteousness. I commend the keeping of a good conscience. With such a breastplate a man may look death in the face. When the vital organs are protected, a man of courage and spirit will not value a scratch in the arm or leg. If a man has a good, large breastplate, sufficient to defend himself, it will make him bold. He will know that his life is secure, and he who has spirit will venture his limbs. Take care of your inward man, therefore, if you would be good soldiers. Look to your heart, that it be well guarded and defended, that you have a good breastplate for the defense of it. Abraham first taught piety: engage God with you, and that will make even a coward fight. For a man to have his conscience against him in the day of battle is a very sad thing. It frightens a man far more than the enemy.

1802—Isabella Graham (1742–1814) was a Scottish woman known for her piety and charity. (See also February 21.) In both the United States and the British Isles, she helped to establish schools for orphans, shelters for the homeless and widowed, and ministries to prostitutes and prisoners. On this day, from a relative's home in New York, she wrote the following beautiful letter to a friend in England.

———— ✑ ✑ ————

This is his majesty [King George III's] birthday. You have, no doubt, . . . been drinking his health and are at this moment, perhaps, set in some social company . . . to honor the anniversary, to repeat the wish of long life, health, and comfort to the lawful sovereign of Britain.

Here I sit in my dear little room, with a lovely landscape in view: [the] park in velvet verdure; the full-grown trees scattered thin to display the carpet, and in full foliage; the clump of willows weeping to the very ground, with a gentle wave, agitated by the zephyr; while the other trees keep their firm majestic posture; the Hudson River covered with vessels crowded with sail to catch the scanty breeze; some sweet little chirpers bring to the ear its share of pleasure. I think I never hear any little warbler in this land sing so sweet as those which now salute my ear. "These are thy glorious works, Parent of Good." Can all the philosophic ingenuity of London, this evening, produce such a scene? The gardens no doubt will be glorious, but the groundwork is also God's . . . All is His. The very notes that warble through so many throats are His creation; all the art of man cannot add to their number. Sweet bird, your notes are innocent, oh how sweet! Lovely trees! You who stand erect and you who weep and wave. I wish no brighter scene. [But] the shadows lengthen fast, so do yours and mine, my sovereign. A few, a very few anniversaries, and we must change the scene, change to where no courtiers flatter, no false meteors blaze; where shadows flee way, realities appear, and nothing but realities will stand in any stead.

Oh may we meet! For me, I have nothing; I am nothing. But One there is, who was and is all that the mind of saint or angel can conceive of glory and of happiness, and He is mine and I am most blessed. Lengthen on, you shadows, until all is shadow on these orbs of flesh. Then, oh then, "My captive soul set free from cloggish earth [will] grasp the deity."

—from *The Power of Faith: The Life and Writings of Mrs. Isabella Graham* (1819)

754—Born in medieval England, St. Boniface (675–754) is remembered as one of the earliest missionaries to Frisia and Germany. After spending many years reforming and organizing churches throughout Europe, he was martyred on this day by a band of pagans in revenge for his Christianizing influence. This day has since been commemorated in his honor. In the following letter, written many years earlier, Boniface consoles an English abbess in a time of great trial.

O my dear sister, . . . I send you a brotherly letter of cheer and consolation, and ask you not to let pass from your mind the Word of Truth, where it says, "In your patience, possess ye your souls" (Luke 21:19); and the word of Solomon the wise: "For whom the Lord loves he corrects; even as a father the son in whom he delights" (Proverbs 3:12); and the judgment of the psalmist: "Many are the afflictions of the righteous; but the Lord delivers him out of them all" (Psalm 34:19); and elsewhere: "The sacrifices of God are a broken spirit; a broken and a contrite heart, O God, you will not despise" (Psalm 51:17). Recall the words of the apostle where he said, "We must through much tribulation enter into the kingdom of God" (Acts 14:22); and elsewhere, "We glory in tribulation, knowing that tribulation works patience, and patience experience, and experience hope, and hope makes us not ashamed" (Romans 5:3–5). In that hope, my dear sister, always rejoice and be glad, because you will not be made ashamed. Despise the tribulations of this world with all the strength of your mind, because all the soldiers of Christ, men and women, have looked down upon the storms and tribulations and infirmities of this life, and held them as nothing, on the witness of Saint Paul, who says, "When I am weak, then am I strong" (2 Corinthians 12:10); and elsewhere: "Who shall separate us from the love of Christ? Shall tribulation?" (Romans 8:35). . . . Rejoice, then, beloved, in the hope of your future inheritance in your heavenly home, to all adversities that assail your heart or body, oppose the shield of faith and patience, so that with the aid of Christ, your spouse, in a happy old age you may complete for the glory of God the tower of the spirit which you began to build in the goodly days of your youth.

—adapted from the translation of Edward Kylie (c. 1900)

1768—Since the Anglican church was the official state religion in many American colonies before the Revolution, other denominations were often legally prohibited from preaching in public. This is why the framers of the Bill of Rights later included the "separation of church and state" clause: to protect minority religions. For instance, a trial was held on this day in Fredericksburg, Virginia, at which a man named John Waller, along with several other Baptists, stood accused of preaching in public. Baptist historian David Benedict (1779–1874) describes the scene in his seminal General History of the Baptist Denomination in America, *published in 1813.*

<hr>

At court they were arraigned as disturbers of the peace; at their trial they were vehemently accused by a certain lawyer who said to the court, "May it please your worships, these men are great disturbers of the peace; they cannot meet a man upon the road but they must ram a text of Scripture down his throat." Mr. Waller made his own and his brethren's defense so ingeniously that they were somewhat puzzled to know how to dispose of them. They offered to release them if they would promise to preach no more in the county for a year and a day. This they refused and, therefore, were sent to jail. As they were moving on from the courthouse to the prison through the streets of Fredericksburg, they sung the hymn "Broad Is the Road" [by Isaac Watts].

> Broad is the road that leads to death,
> And thousands walk together there;
> But wisdom shows a narrow path,
> With here and there a traveler.
>
> "Deny thyself, and take thy cross,"
> Is the Redeemer's great command;
> Nature must count her gold but dross,
> If she would gain this heavenly land.

This had an awe-inspiring appearance.... Waller and the others continued in jail forty-three days and were then discharged without any conditions. While in prison they constantly preached through the grates. The mob without used every exertion to prevent the people from hearing, but to little purpose. Many heard, indeed, to whom the word came in demonstration of the Spirit and with power.

1913—At an evangelistic meeting in Michigan on this day, the hymn "The Old Rugged Cross" had its public premiere. It was written by evangelist and hymn writer George Bennard (1873–1958), who wrote more than three hundred other hymns in his lifetime but is best known for this single hymn.

On a hill far away stood an old rugged cross,
　　The emblem of suffering and shame;
And I love that old cross where the dearest and best
　　For a world of lost sinners was slain.

CHORUS: So I'll cherish the old rugged cross,
　　Till my trophies at last I lay down;
I will cling to the old rugged cross,
　　And exchange it some day for a crown.

Oh, that old rugged cross so despised by the world,
　　Has a wondrous attraction for me;
For the dear Lamb of God left his glory above,
　　To bear it to dark Calvary.

In the old rugged cross, stained with blood so divine,
　　A wondrous beauty I see;
For 'twas on that old cross Jesus suffered and died,
　　To pardon and sanctify me.

To the old rugged cross I will ever be true,
　　Its shame and reproach gladly bear;
Then he'll call me someday to my home far away,
　　Where his glory forever I'll share.

1483—On this day renowned English printer William Caxton (c. 1422–91) published The Pilgrimage of the Soul. *This allegorical poem, written by Frenchman Guillaume de Deguileville in the fourteenth century, was translated into English in about 1420 by poet and monk John Lydgate (c. 1370– c. 1451). The poem, which later influenced John Bunyan's* Pilgrim's Progress *(see February 18), depicts a vivid dream in which the dreamer is inspired to go on a pilgrimage to heaven. The following is a modernized and adapted portion of that poem.*

Within a mirror large and bright
I thought I caught sight
Of that fair heavenly city.
It appeared to me
Full holy and dear
Within the glass, bright and clear. . . .
And truly, I could see,
It excelled in beauty
All others by comparison;
For God himself was its mason, . . .
And an angel, early and late,
Waited always at its gate,
Ever ready, there he stood,
His sword was red with the blood
Of Christ's holy passion
When he bought our Redemption
To restore mankind again.
The angel that I had seen
Left me much astonished.
But I was quickly comforted
When I beheld his sword turn
Blunt, which once did burn
like any fire bright.
For now, the sharpness of its light
Was quenched, no more avenging,
By virtue of Christ's great suffering.

597—Today is the death day and the traditional Celtic feast day of St. Columba (c. 521–97), who ranks in importance with St. Patrick and St. Brigid among the Celtic saints. (See also June 2.) One of his most renowned accomplishments was the founding of the monastery on the remote isle of Iona, off the coast of Scotland. It became one of the greatest centers of Celtic Christianity. In honor of St. Columba's Day, the following ancient poem, traditionally attributed to Columba, is given. Though scholars doubt its authenticity, it nevertheless beautifully describes the great saint's love for his island and the kind of life he lived there.

Delightful would it be to me to sit on the pinnacle of a rock,
That I might often see the face of the ocean;
That I might see its heaving waves over the wide ocean
When they chant music to their Father upon the world's course;
That I might see its level sparkling strand—it would be no cause
    of sorrow;
That I might hear the song of the wonderful birds, source of happiness;
That I might hear the thunder of the crowding waves upon the rocks;
That I might hear, by the side of the church, the roar of the
    surrounding sea;
That I might see its noble flocks over the watery ocean;
That I might see the sea monsters, the greatest of all wonders;
That I might see its ebb and flood in their career; . . .
That contrition might come upon my heart while I look upon her;
That I might bewail my evils all, though it were difficult to
    compute them;
That I might bless the Lord who conserves all heaven
With its countless bright orders, land, strand, and flood;
That I might search the books all, that would be good for any soul;
At times kneeling to Beloved Heaven; at times at psalm singing;
At times contemplating the King of Heaven, Holy the Chief;
At times at work without compulsion; this would be delightful.
At times plucking crabs from the rocks; at times fishing;
At times giving food to the poor; at times in a solitary cell.
The best advice in the presence of God to me has been vouchsafed.
The King Whose servant I am will not let anything deceive me.

—adapted from the translation of Professor O'Curry (1905)
in Adamnan's *Life of Saint Columba* (late seventh century)

1824—English essayist and journalist William Cobbett (1763–1835) was one of the most controversial and irascible writers of his time. He was a radical, a Christian social reformer, the author of an excellent and idiosyncratic English grammar, a part-time farmer, and a staunch defender of the working classes. His outspoken crankiness can be seen in the following passage, which is an excerpt from a letter he wrote on this day to a nobleman, the Earl of Roden. The Earl had recently given a speech commending the British and Foreign Bible Society for their work.

———— ◈ ————

I am of the opinion that the printing and publishing of the Bible has done a great deal of mischief in the world. No matter how good the contents of the book may be, no matter how true the history of it, no matter how excellent its precepts and examples—like most other good things, it is possible for it to be so applied as to produce mischievous effects. And what was the first effect of this printing and publishing? The splitting up of the people who had before been all of one faith into numerous sects, each having a faith different from all the rest. However, this really seems to be, by some persons, regarded as a happy circumstance. This patch and piebald work in religion is spoken of by some as affording the Almighty the pleasing spectacle of great variety!

But come, let us try this a little. What! A variety of religious creeds pleasing to God! Will anyone openly hold that God delights in lies? Yet he must delight in lies if he delights in a variety of beliefs. There can be but one true belief; all the rest must be false. Every deviation from the truth is a lie. Each must believe that all the other sects are on the high road to perdition. To think in any other way about the matter is to consider all faith and all religion as a mere farce. And yet there are men who pretend that a variety of faith is pleasing to the God of truth. . . .

What says the Word of God? . . . "One faith, one church." And again, "I will build my church upon a rock, and the gates of hell shall not prevail against it." Look at your own country then, my Lord, and say whether this promise has not then been fulfilled.

1164—John of Hildesheim (who died in 1375) was a German Carmelite monk, best remembered for his book The Three Kings of Cologne. *It purports to be the history of the three wise men ("kings") from the time of their first seeking the Christ child until their deaths. On this day, as John reports, because of political instability, the supposed bodies of the kings were transferred from a church in Milan, Italy, to Cologne, France. The following excerpt from John's book tells the folk legend of the thirty pieces of gold given to Jesus by Melchior, the king.*

Now when Mary fled to Egypt for fear of King Herod, she lost the [frankincense, myrrh, and gold] that had been offered to her Son. They were all knit together in a cloth. A shepherd, who happened to be keeping sheep in the same country, had an illness that no doctor could heal; and all his money had been given to various doctors to make him whole, but it would not be. As he led his sheep to the field one day, he found the thirty gold pieces, with the incense and myrrh bound together in a cloth, and he kept them until a short time before Christ's crucifixion. The shepherd had heard of a prophet so holy that he could heal men with a word, so the shepherd came to Him and prayed for grace. Our Lord Jesus Christ healed him with a word and instructed him in the faith. With great devotion, the shepherd offered Jesus the thirty gold coins, with the incense and myrrh, but Jesus told him to go to the temple and offer all these things on the altar instead. . . . When the priest of the temple saw these gifts, he was overjoyed, for such gifts were seldom seen in the temple, so he burned the incense on the altar and kept the coins in the common treasury. On the third day before Christ's crucifixion, Judas came to the temple and bargained with the priests to betray his master. And for this, the priests took out of the treasury the same thirty coins. When Christ had thus been betrayed and had died for all mankind according to His sweet will, Judas repented and returned to the temple and cast down the thirty gold pieces, and, as the Gospels say, he hanged himself. . . . And part of the myrrh was mixed with the vinegar and was offered to our Lord on the cross, and the other part Nicodemus mixed with aloes and other spices for His burial.

—adapted from *The Most Excellent Treatise of the Three Kings of Cologne* (c. 1499)

1509—Bishop John Fisher (1459–1535) was an outspoken Catholic leader in England in the sixteenth century, who was martyred for his opposition to King Henry VIII's marriage to Anne Boleyn. He served as a professor of divinity and chancellor at Cambridge University, and he wrote many power-ful treatises, including his Commentary on the Seven Penitential Psalms, *which was published on this day—"emprinted in the Fleet Street by Wynkyn de Worde." In the following passage from that book, Fisher uses a fascinating metaphor to describe the burden of sin referred to in Psalm 38:4: "My sins be heavy upon me like to a heavy burden."*

───── ⋞⋟ ─────

We have given so great license to this serpent sin and so easily entreated it, that now, when it is once entered, it will not go out again, but, as a tyrant, has decreed to keep in possession the habitation that he hath won, either peaceably or by strength. First or ever we committed sin, many motions of it were felt in us, but it was only in the inferior part of the soul. And now since it is suffered to have any interest, he has enhanced himself above the highest part of the soul and there is resident, commanding what he desires, thrusting down the poor soul with his grievous burden and weight, so that oftentimes it is compelled to do that thing which it would not do. Peradventure some sinner will say, "I neither perceive nor feel any weight in myself, even if I commit ever so many sins." To whom we answer that if a dog, having a great stone bound about his neck, be cast down from a high tower, he feels no weight of that stone as long as he is falling down, but when he is once fallen to the ground he is burst all to pieces by reason of that weight. So the sinner going down toward the pit of hell feels not the great burden of sin, but when he shall come into the depths of hell he shall feel more pain than he would. Also every creature who is about to take off the yoke of sin feels the great and grievous weight of it.

1231—On this day, Antony of Padua (1195–1231) died, and the day has since been honored in his memory. He was one of the most powerful of the early Franciscan preachers (see March 27), and he was famous for his miracles. The following miracle, his most renowned, was witnessed by only one man, Tiso, a friend of Antony's. Though many people now classify such miracles as either legends or superstitions, these stories often have a poetic power and devotional beauty that make them worth reading and enjoying. The following account was written by Henry James Coleridge in his Chronicle of St. Anthony of Padua, *published in 1875.*

Tiso loved and reverenced Antony greatly, and when he became an inmate of his house he closely observed everything about this one whom he saw to be a great saint. One night as Tiso was passing by the door of his room, he saw brilliant rays of light streaming under the door, and on looking through the keyhole, he saw a little child of marvelous beauty standing upon a book which lay upon the table and clinging with both arms round Antony's neck. Who was he? But as he gazed, unable to take his eyes away, and saw the flood of heavenly light with which he was surrounded and the ineffable tenderness with which he embraced Antony and in return was caressed by him, and as he felt his own soul filled with an ineffable sweetness and rapture in watching the mutual endearments of the saint and his wondrous visitor, Tiso knew with a certainty that needed no further proof that it was indeed the Divine Babe of Bethlehem who was consoling his favored servant and filling him with heavenly delights. After a time, Tiso saw the child point toward the door and whisper into Antony's ear. Then he knew that his secret was told and that his Lord, in the act of so wonderfully favoring his beloved Antony, was not unmindful of his poor servant outside the door, nor displeased with his loving boldness. So Tiso watched on with deepening joy and rapture till the beautiful child vanished. . . . Then Antony opened the door and charged his friend, for the love of him whom he had seen, to tell the vision to no man, so long as he was alive. . . .

We are far from saying that every beautiful imagination carries with it its own evidence. But we may surely [choose] between admitting its truth on the evidence of the eye-witness or giving him credit for a creative power for which the highest poets might well envy him.

Fourth century—The Eastern Church honors St. Basil (c. 330–c. 379) on this day. After spending his early adulthood as a desert eremite in Egypt, he emerged to serve as an official in the church and to actively combat the heresies of his time. He is one of the great "doctors" of the church. He wrote many letters, and among his influential treatises is The Hexaemeron, *in which Basil meditates on the six days of creation. In the following passage he reflects on why God might have created animals.*

───────── ୶ξ ξ୶ ─────────

Do we not see sheep, when winter is approaching, devouring grass with avidity as if to make provision for future scarcity? Do we not also see oxen, long confined in the winter season, recognize the return of spring by a natural sensation and look to the end of their stables toward the doors, all turning their heads there by common consent? Studious observers have remarked that the hedgehog makes an opening at the two extremities of his hole. If the wind from the north is going to blow, he shuts up the aperture that looks toward the north; if the south wind follows it, the animal passes to the northern door. What lesson do these animals teach man? They not only show us in our Creator a care that extends to all beings, but a certain presentiment of the future—even in brutes. Then we ought not to attach ourselves to this present life and ought to give all heed to that eternal life that is to come. Will you not be industrious for yourself, O man? And will you not lay up in the present age spiritual treasures for that which is to come, after having seen the example of the ant? The ant during summer collects treasures for winter. Far from giving itself up to idleness, before this season has made it feel its severity, it hastens to work with an invincible zeal until it has abundantly filled its storehouses. . . .

What language can attain to the marvels of the Creator? What ear could understand them? And what time would be sufficient to relate them? Let us say, then, with the prophet, "O Lord, how manifold are your works! In wisdom you have created them all" (Psalm 104:24). . . .

Beasts bear witness to the faith.

—adapted from the translation of Blomfield Jackson (1894)

1917—Christian history offers few characters more colorful than Irishman G. A. Studdert Kennedy (1883–1929), who served as a chaplain in the Allied trenches during World War I and earned the nickname "Woodbine Willie" for his habit of passing out woodbine cigarettes to the troops. He spoke the language of the common soldier, even in his sermons, and had the endearing knack for explaining his faith in everyday terms. On this day, just a day after surviving a major battle, Kennedy wrote the following reflection in his diary, later published as The Hardest Part.

———————— ఆర్ ————————

I know it is hard to see in Nature what God is; its many voices seem to contradict one another. Its tenderness and cruelty, its order and its chaos, its beauty and its ugliness, make discords in its song and mar the music of its message to the soul of man. There is much truth in the charge that Nature is red in tooth and claw. It is hard to see God in a cobra or a shark. . . .

That is the picture of God that Nature gives when you look square in her face and refuse to blind yourself either to her failure or her success. God was forced to limit Himself when he undertook the task of material creation. He had to bind Himself with chains and pierce Himself with nails, and take upon Himself the travail pangs of creation. The universe was made as it was because it is the only way it could be made, and this way lays upon God the burden of many failures and of eternal strain—the sorrow of God the Father which Christ revealed. . . .

When in Nature one sees God suffering and striving as a creative Father Spirit, and when one sees how much that His sorrow has produced is quite perfect, like this red dawn and that white bird upon the wing, the rose that blooms at the cottage door, and the glory of sweet spring days, and the eyes of my dog, and the neck of my horse, and a million other perfect things—and when one sees all this as the fruit not only of God's power, but also of God's pain, then the love of Nature's God begins to grow up in one's soul. One remembers the great words, "He that has seen me has seen the father," and there comes a burst of light, and one sees Nature in Christ and Christ in Nature. One sees in Christ the Revelation of suffering, striving, tortured, but triumphant Love that Nature itself would lead us to expect. . . . I have no fear of Nature's horror chambers; they are just God's Cross, and I know that the Cross is followed by an empty tomb and victory.

1752—William Law (1686–1761) was an English spiritual writer noted for his outstanding book A Serious Call to a Devout and Holy Life *(1728). That book stresses the importance of the interior aspects of faith—prayer, virtue, meditation, and ascetic exercises—holding them in higher esteem, even, than church attendance or group worship. Later in life Law was greatly influenced by mystical writer Jacob Boehme (see January 1), and as a result, Law's later writing exudes a spirit of holy mystery that have led some to call him one of the few true Protestant mystics. The following passage, written on this day, is from one of those late mystical works,* The Spirit of Love.

———— ❧ ❧ ————

You may indeed do many works of love and delight in them, especially at such times as they are not inconvenient to you or contradictory to your state or temper or circumstances in life. But the spirit of love is not in you until it is the spirit of your life, until you live freely, willingly, and universally according to it. For every spirit acts with freedom according to what it is. It needs no command to live its own life or be what it is, no more than you need bid wrath be wrathful. And therefore, when love is the spirit of your life, it will have the freedom and universality of a spirit; it will always live and work in love, not *because* of this or that, here or there, but because the spirit of love can only love, wherever it is or goes and whatever is done to it. As the sparks know no motion but that of flying upwards, whether it be in the darkness of the night or in the light of the day, so the spirit of love is always on the same course. It knows no difference of time, place, or persons, but whether it gives or forgives, bears or forbears, it is equally doing its own delightful work, equally blessed by itself—for the spirit of love, wherever it is, is its own blessing and happiness, because it is the truth and reality of God in the soul. . . .

Would you know the blessing of all blessings? It is this God of love dwelling in your soul and killing every root of bitterness that is the pain and torment of every earthly, selfish love. . . . For as love is the God that created all things, so love is the purity, the perfection, and the blessing of all created things; and nothing can live in God but as it lives in love. . . . Love alone is, and only can be, the cure of every evil; and he that lives in the purity of love has risen out of the power of evil into the freedom of the one spirit of heaven.

601—*Pope Gregory the Great (590–604) was a powerful influence in spreading Christianity across Europe (see also March 12). It is recorded that he saw fair-skinned slaves for sale in a marketplace one day. He was told they were Angles (English). Punningly, he stated that their skin was so bright they might well be called "angels." These slaves made such an impression on him that he determined to convert the nation of the Angles, so, in 597, he sent a missionary named Augustine to England. On this day, four years later, Gregory wrote to an abbot named Mellitus about the proper way to win the English to Christ. Mellitus was on his way to join Augustine at the newly founded mission in Canterbury, England.*

When, therefore, Almighty God shall bring you to the most reverend Bishop Augustine, our brother, tell him what I have, upon mature deliberation on the affair of the English, determined upon—that is, that the temples of the idols in that nation ought not to be destroyed; but let the idols that are in them be destroyed; let holy water be made and sprinkled in the said temples, let altars be erected and relics placed. For if those temples are well built, it is requisite that they be converted from the worship of devils to the service of the true God; that the nation, seeing that their temples are not destroyed, may remove error from their hearts and, knowing and adoring the true God, may the more familiarly resort to the places to which they have been accustomed . . . to the end that, while some gratifications are outwardly permitted them, they may the more easily consent to the inward consolations of the grace of God. For there is no doubt that it is impossible to efface everything at once from their obdurate minds; because he who endeavors to ascend to the highest place, rises by degrees or steps and not by leaps. . . . This it behooves your affection to communicate to our aforesaid brother, that he, being there present, may consider how he is to order all things. God preserve you in safety, most beloved son.

—from Bede's *Ecclesiastical History*, translated by J. Stevens and J. A. Giles

1715—English hymn writer and theologian Isaac Watts (1674–1748) wrote more than six hundred hymns in his lifetime, including "When I Survey the Wondrous Cross" and "O God, Our Help in Ages Past." On this day, he wrote the dedication of his Divine Songs Attempted in Easy Language for the Use of Children. *He addressed it to the family of Sir Thomas Abney, especially Abney's three daughters whom Watts tutored: "May the blessings of His right hand more enrich you daily as your capacities and your years increase." The following poem, called "For the Lord's Day Evening," is from that collection.*

Lord, how delightful 'tis to see
A whole assembly worship thee!
At once they sing, at once they pray;
They hear of heaven and learn the way.

I have been there and still would go:
'Tis like a little heaven below!
Not all my pleasure and my play
Shall tempt me to forget this day.

O write upon my memory, Lord,
The text and doctrines of thy Word;
That I may break thy laws no more,
But love thee better than before.

With thoughts of Christ and things divine
Fill up this foolish heart of mine;
That, hoping pardon through his blood,
I may lie down and wake with God.

1885—American theologian, professor, and Indian scholar Samuel Henry Kellogg (1839–99), on this day, completed the preface to his monumental study comparing Buddhism and Christianity, called The Light of Asia and the Light of the World. *Kellogg was fluent in the Indian languages, helped to translate the Old Testament into Hindi, and spent many years studying Eastern myths and religious practices. The volume is one of the first great studies in the field of comparative religions. The following excerpt is his stirring concluding paragraph to the book.*

———— ·⋲§ ⋟· ————

In their missionary spirit the early Buddhists may well put many Christians to shame. It was, as we have seen, but a very pitiful salvation that they had to proclaim, and one which ill-deserved the name—a salvation without a Savior, and that, not everlasting. Yet their earnestness and devotion in the proclamation of what they supposed to be the truth more than deserves the emulation of all Christians. Be it so that they were taught that they would thus acquire merit, make an end of what they deemed sin, and so at last reach the rest of Nirvana, the extinction of existence and pain. All the more should we be fired with zeal and missionary enthusiasm, who have a message so much grander and more blessed—one so eloquent with heavenly hope. All the more should we be inspired for this holy work, who for a motive have something so much higher, even a love which is infinite and everlasting; and who, as "the joy that is set before us," look forward—not to a Nirvana of apathy and final extinction—but to the complete and everlasting triumph of righteousness and eternal life in Christ over sin and death, throughout this curse-burdened earth; a triumph which, while it comprehends the whole race in its scope, brings in for us also as individuals the attainment of a perfect [humanness] transfigured with the glory of the incarnate Son of God, and a most holy, exalted, and never-ending fellowship with Him, who alone is the eternal Life and Light, not of Asia only, but also of the whole world.

1894—Pope Leo XIII (1810–1903) was one of the most influential popes in history. Not only was his pontifical reign one of the longest (twenty-five years), but he was also responsible for opening the Vatican Library to scholars, founding Catholic University in Washington, D.C., and participating in international diplomacy. On this day he issued an influential encyclical (that is, a letter sent to all the churches) called "The Reunion of Christendom," in which he urges both Catholics and Protestants to seek common ground. The following passage is from that document.

O Savior and Father of mankind, Christ Jesus, hasten and do not delay to bring about what You once promised to do—that when lifted up from the earth You would draw all things to Yourself.... [We can recall nothing] more pleasing or better calculated to extol the work of divine Providence than the memory of the days of yore, when the faith that had come down from heaven was looked upon as the common inheritance of one and all; when civilized nations, separated by distance, character, and habits, in spite of frequent disagreements and warfare on other points, were united by Christian faith in all that concerned religion. The recollection of that time causes us to regret all the more deeply that as the ages rolled by the waves of suspicion and hatred arose....

Let us one and all, then, for the sake of the common welfare, labor with equal assiduity to restore the ancient concord. In order to bring about this concord and spread abroad the benefits of the Christians revelation, the present is the most seasonable time; for never before have the sentiments of human brotherhood penetrated so deeply into the souls of men, and never in any age has man been seen to seek out his fellow men more eagerly in order to know them better and to help them. Immense tracts of land and sea are traversed with incredible rapidity, and thus extraordinary advantages are afforded not only for commerce and scientific investigation but also for the propagation of the word of God from the rising of the sun to the going down of the same.

We are well aware of the long labors involved in the restoration of that order of things, ... but we unhesitatingly place all our hope and confidence in the Savior of mankind, Jesus Christ, well remembering what great things have been achieved in times past by the folly of the Cross and its preaching to the astonishment and confusion of the wisdom of the world.

—translator unknown

1653—After being raised a Protestant, a young Polish nobleman named Johannes Scheffler (1624–77) was publicly confirmed a member of the Catholic Church on this day. He made this change after finding that Protestants were not comfortable with his mystical and polemical interests. On this day he also adopted the pen name Angelus Silesius, meaning "Silesian Angel," referring to his homeland of Silesia in Poland. He became one of Christianity's great mystic poets. Four years after his public confirmation, he published a collection of short epigrammatic couplets that delve into the nature of God and the believer's love for him. The book was later called The Cherubinic Wanderer, *from which the following verses are chosen.*

If Christ were reborn a thousand times Bethlehem's stall
And not in you, then still you are lost beyond recall.

Enlarge your heart, my friend, and God will enter in.
You will be His kingdom, and He will be your king.

The bird rests in the air, the stone rests on land,
The fish lives in water, my spirit in God's hand.

Here and now, the rose your outer eyes behold,
For all eternity has also bloomed in God.

How came it to pass that into such as me
Almighty God could flow—into one drop the sea?

Whoever sees in his neighbor nothing but God and Christ
Sees with the light that God Himself does cast.

Christian, it is not enough if I but be in God.
I must draw in God's sap if I would grow and bud.

Alas, that we do not do as the wild birds do,
Each uttering our note and singing together in joy!

Nothing is imperfect: gold is no better than tin,
Frogs are every bit as beautiful as the Seraphim.

—adapted from the translation of Willard Trask

1851—English minister, author, and social reformer Charles Kingsley (1819–75) was best known for his children's stories Westward Ho! *and* The Water Babies. *From the pulpit he was ferociously outspoken about the social ills of the day; as one man remarked, "Kingsley delivered sermons like a man wrestling with demons." On this day, he delivered a sermon at St. John's Church in London in which he denounced the social system that allowed the wealthy and educated to make money at the expense of the poor. It was called "A Message of the Church to Laboring Men."*

———— ⋅⊰ ⊱⋅ ————

What, my dear friends, is the message of the Lord's supper? What more distinct sign and pledge that all men are equal? Wherever in the world there may be inequality, it ceases there. One table, one reverential posture, one bread, one wine, for high and low, for wise and foolish. That sacrament proclaims that all alike are brothers of each other, because they are all alike brothers of one—and he the son of a village maiden. That sacrament proclaims that all are equally debtors—all equally in need of the pardon which he has bought for them—and that that pardon is equally ready and free to all of them. . . .

When I have been inclined to give in to that subtlest of all temptations—the notion that one Gospel is required for the man of letters and another for the laboring drudge . . . that sacrament has warned me: "Not so—one bread, one wine, for you and them. One Lord, one pardon, one fountain of life, one guiding and inspiring spirit. They have not only the same rights but the same spiritual wealth in them. If you have been put into circumstances in which you can use your gifts more freely than they can theirs, why is it but that you may share your superfluity with their need—that you may teach them, guide them, nourish up into flower and greet the heaven-given seed of nobleness which lies in them as surely as in you? For after all, as that bread and that wine proclaim to you—you have nothing of your own—wit, scholarship, utterance—what do you have that you did not receive? Fool! Instead of priding yourself on it as your own property, confess it to be that which it is, the gift of God, who has only bestowed it on you as his steward—give it freely to all, as he has given freely to you."

1626—One of the strangest incidents in all of book history took place on this day. In a fish market in Cambridge, England, a codfish was cut open, and in its stomach was discovered a small book, containing three anonymous and rare religious treatises. This unique volume was later published under the title Vox Piscis *("The Voice of the Fish"). The final treatise, a portion of which is shown below, is called* A Mirror, or Looking Glass, to Know Thyself By, *and has been attributed, probably inaccurately, to English reformer and martyr John Frith (c. 1503–33).*

————————◆§ ß◆————————

I have read of a shepherd who, keeping his sheep in the field, espied a foul toad, and when he had well marked her and compared her shape and nature unto himself and his nature, he fell a-weeping and cried out piteously. At the last came a bishop by, riding right royally, and when he saw the shepherd so sorely lamenting, he reined his horse and asked him the cause of his great wailing. Then answered the shepherd, "Verily, sir, I weep for my unkindness towards almighty God, for I have given thanks to God for many things, but yet I was never so kind since I was born as to thank him for this thing."

"What is that?" said the bishop.

"Sir," said he, "see you not this foul toad?"

"Yes," said the bishop, "what is that to the purpose?"

"Verily," said the shepherd, "it is the creature of God as well as I am, and God might have made me even such a foul and unreasonable beast as this is, if it had pleased him, and yet he hath not done so; but of his mercy and goodness he hath made me a reasonable creature after his own likeness; and yet was I never so kind as to thank him that he had not made me so vile a creature; which thing I greatly bewail, and my unkindness causes me now thus to weep."

With that the bishop departed and, I trust, learned to [thank God] thereafter. And I beseech God that we may so do and be the faithful followers of our Savior Christ Jesus, to whom be praise, honor, and glory forever. Amen.

Fourth century—The following legendary event is supposed to have taken place on this day, on which the church traditionally celebrates the birth of John the Baptist. An early abbot named Hilary and his monks were said to have encountered on this day a mysterious and beautiful woman—Lady Pelagia. Christian folk tales like this powerfully symbolize the supplanting of pagan myths by Christianity.

———— ✥ ————

Said the Lady Pelagia, "Let me have knowledge of divine things from you, most holy father, for you are wise and can answer all my questionings. First tell me which of all the small things God has made in the world is the most excellent?"

"Of all small things made by God," answered Hilary, "most excellent is the face of man and woman; for among all the faces of the children of Adam not one has ever been wholly like any other; and there, in smallest space, God has placed all the senses of the body, and it is in the face that we see, as in a glass darkly, all that can be seen of the invisible soul within."

"Let me ask again," said the lady, "what part of the earth is nearest to heaven?"

Again Hilary mused. "The body of Him who died on the tree to save us, for He was of our flesh and our flesh is earth of the earth."

"That too is well answered," said the lady, who had grown pale and gazed on the Bishop with great gloomy eyes. "Once more let me question you: What is the distance between heaven and earth?"

"Who can tell us that more certainly than Lucifer who fell from heaven?"

With a bitter cry the Lady Pelagia rose from her seat and raised her beautiful white arms above her head, and in an instant the starry eyes were darkened, and the spirit and flower of life perished in her sweet body; and the companions saw no longer the Lady Pelagia but in her stead a statue of white marble. At a glance Hilary knew it for a statue of the goddess whom men in Rome called Venus and in Greece Aphrodite. But swifter even than that thought, it seemed to them as though the statue were smitten by an invisible hand for it reeled and fell, shattered to fragments.

—adapted from William Canton's *A Child's Book of Saints* (1898)

1915—Lyman Abbot (1835–1922), like his close friend Henry Ward Beecher, was a popular American writer and Congregational preacher of the late nineteenth and early twentieth centuries. He retired in 1899 to devote himself to writing and editing. On this day he completed his Reminiscences, *in which he describes his life and formative influences. Perhaps his most important influence was his father, Jacob Abbot (1803–79), who was also a preacher and writer, particularly noted for his excellent children's books. The following extract is from Lyman Abbot's* Reminiscences.

———— ⋅◦⋅ ————

[My father] not only gave me some specific counsels which have remained with me ever since, but also, without my realizing it then, as I have realized it since, he laid for me, by his thoughts, the foundations of much of my theological thinking, and, by his personal character and influence, the foundations of much of my religious experience.

"If I were a preacher [now]," he said, "I would make my first sermon of any convenient length. The next Sunday I would make it five minutes shorter, and I would continue to take off five minutes until the people complained that my sermons were too short. Then I would take five minutes off from that, and the result should give me my standard." This counsel was emphasized by the saying of a Methodist minister to me when I was ordained in the following spring: "I have resolved not to attempt to make myself immortal by being eternal." . . .

My father's second counsel respected the method of a preacher's approach to his congregation. "It is," he said, "a principle of mechanics that, if an object is at one point and you wish to take it to another point, you must carry it through all the intermediate points. Remember that this is also a principle in morals. If your congregation is at one point and you wish to bring them to another point, you must carry them through all the intermediate points." . . .

My father's third counsel respected the cause of sectarian differences and the secret of Christian unity: "I am convinced," he said, "that nine-tenths of the controversies which have agitated the religious world have been controversies about words, and I rather think the other tenth has been also."

1902—On this day, American Catholic writer and lecturer Henry Austin Adams (1861–1931) wrote the preface to his collected Orations. *In one of these lectures, he tells the story of the Irish people and the special place they have had in church history, in part because of their humor.*

————— ❧ ❧ —————

[God] gave the Irish heart its matchless sense of humor.... It was put there by a divinely tender and gentle Heavenly Father. I venture to say that if the Irish had not been the wittiest people, they could not have possibly borne, as they have, the centuries of bitterness and wrong. An old writer declares, with good reason, that nobody can get to heaven without a sense of humor! And in the lives of Saints we frequently read that the most saintly have been those whose wit and keen enjoyment of the humorous was the greatest. It lifts a man out of the valleys. Despair dares not face one who is a wag, for it knows well that he is as likely as not to burst out into laughter straight in his face.

An Irishman sees something comical in the blackest situations, and as he stops to have his joke over it, he forgets about the bitter part. That is a very deeply significant story that they tell of one good son of Erin, and its lesson will be my excuse for repeating it now.

It seems that the poor fellow was on a journey, and, being penniless, he had had nothing to eat for a day or two. So he trudged along disconsolately enough until he saw a charitable-looking old lady standing before a farmhouse. Approaching her, our friend stated his desperate condition, and the good heart of the lady was touched with pity. Bidding the man sit upon her doorstep, she went into her kitchen and presently returned with a plate, on which Pat saw a fine, large piece of beef. The lady laid the meat before the starving man, delighted at the gladness that her act had evidently brought to the poor devil's heart. Pious man that he was, he closed his eyes for a moment to say a grace before eating, when, in that instant, a dog came and ran away with the meat!—Wait! That accident has nothing peculiarly Irish about it! This is the Hibernian touch in the story: When the man saw that the food was gone, he said, "Well, thanks be to God! I've me appetite left, anyhow!" *That* is Irish.

1925—Lettie B. Cowman (1870–1960), better known as "Mrs. Cowman," was one of the best-selling devotional writers and compilers of the twentieth century, second only to Oswald Chambers. She drew largely on other sources to compile her devotionals, the most famous of which is her Streams in the Desert, *which contains this entry for June 27. Its source is an anonymous work called* The Silver Lining *and takes Psalm 68:28 as its text: "Thy Lord has sent strength for you."*

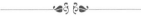

The Lord imparts to us that primary strength of character that makes everything in life work with intensity and decision. We are "strengthened with might by his Spirit in the inner man." And the strength is continuous; reserves of power come to us that we cannot exhaust.

"As your days, so shall your strength be"—strength of will, strength of affection, strength of judgment, strength of ideals and achievement.

"The Lord is my strength" to go on. He gives us power to tread the dead level, to walk the long lane that seems never to have a turning, to go through those long reaches of life that afford no pleasant surprise, and that depress the spirits in the sameness of a terrible drudgery.

"The Lord is my strength" to go up. He is to me the power by which I can climb the Hill of Difficulty and not be afraid.

"The Lord is my strength" to go down. It is when we leave the bracing heights, where the wind and the sun have been about us, and when we begin to come down the hill into closer and more sultry spheres, that the heart is apt to grow faint.

I heard a man say the other day concerning his growing physical frailty, "It is the coming down that tires me!"

"The Lord is my strength" to sit still. And how difficult is the attainment! Do we not often say to one another, in seasons when we are compelled to be quiet, "If only I could do something!"

When the child is ill, and the mother stands by in comparative impotence, how severe is the test! But to do nothing, just to sit still and wait, requires tremendous strength. "The Lord is my strength!" "Our sufficiency is of God."

1848—In the Shaker community of Alfred, Maine, scholars believe, a man known as Elder Joseph Brackett wrote on this day one of the most familiar of all American folk hymns, ."Simple Gifts." The beloved tune was later borrowed by American composer Aaron Copeland (1900–90) as the theme to his Appalachian Spring, and contemporary songwriter Sydney Carter used the tune for his well-known song "Lord of the Dance." *The original song was sung as a "quick dance" during the Shaker worship services, which included energetic choral dancing and singing, and is valued for its emphasis on humility. Although controversial and considered a cult by many, the celibate, pacifist Shakers contributed enormously to the culture of the United States, not only with their beautiful hymns and primitive "spirit-given" artwork, but also with their many practical innovations. They invented, for instance, such things as the flat broom, cut nails, the spring-loaded clothespin, the circular saw, and, of course, their famous furniture. Their motto was: "Hands to work; hearts to God." Here, then, are the original words to Elder Brackett's "Simple Gifts."*

—————— ≈§ ¿≈ ——————

'Tis the gift to be simple, 'tis the gift to be free,
'Tis the gift to come down where we ought to be,
And when we find ourselves in the place just right,
'Twill be in the valley of love and delight.

When true simplicity is gained,
To bow and to bend we shan't be ashamed,
To turn, turn will be our delight
'Til by turning, turning we come 'round right.

Sixth century—St. Brendan (c. 486–c. 575) was one of the most influential Irish monks of his time. He founded several monasteries and influenced many Irish religious leaders. According to legend he was a relentless explorer, said to have sailed as far as Iceland and the New World—exploits that earned him the name "Brendan the Navigator." These stories are recounted in a biography, called The Voyage of St. Brendan, *written in the ninth or tenth century. In one legend he was said to have anchored his ship on a remote island only to discover it was a whale. In another legend, Brendan celebrated Mass on this day, St. Peter's Day, at sea with his sailors.*

———— ·•§ §•· ————

St. Peter's Day was celebrated by St. Brendan at sea, and the water was so clear that the monks could see every movement of life beneath the boat; so clear, indeed, that the animals on the ocean bed seemed near enough to touch. If the monks looked down into the deep, they could see many different kinds of creatures lying on the sandy bottom like flocks at pasture, so numerous that, lying head to tail, and moving gently with the swell, they looked like a city on the march.

The monks urged their master to say Mass silently lest the fish, hearing his voice, might rise up and attack them. Brendan chaffed them: "I am surprised at your foolishness. What—are you afraid of these creatures? Have you not several times landed on the monarch of the deep, the beast who eats all other sea creatures? Why, you have sat down on his back and sung psalms, have even gathered sticks, lighted a fire and cooked food—and all this without showing fear. Then how can you be afraid of these? Is not our Lord Jesus Christ the Lord of Creation? Can he not make all creatures docile?" Brendan sang at the top of his voice, causing the brethren to cast an anxious eye in the direction of the fish, but at the sound of singing the fish rose up from the sea bed and swam round and round the coracle. There was nothing to be seen but crowds of swimming forms. They did not come close but, keeping their distance, swam back and forth till Mass was over. Then they scurried away on their own tracks over the paths of the ocean, out of sight of the servants of God. St. Brendan journeyed on. . . .

—from *The Voyage of St. Brendan*,
translated by J. E. Webb and D. H. Farmer

1558—Although disputed, many authorities give this as the day on which Teresa of Ávila (1515–82; see also November 29) first experienced one of her remarkable "raptures." Teresa was a Spanish Carmelite nun, who did much to reform her own religious order. She wrote many beautiful books describing her ecstasies and visions, and she is still considered one of the most influential mystics in the history of Christianity. In the following passage from her autobiography, The Life of Teresa of Jesus, she poetically describes the effects of the intensely prayerful state—rapture—that she experienced.

───────── ◆§ §◆ ─────────

The soul is like water in a glass; which, unless the sun shines on it, appears to be quite clear; but when the sun does shine on it, it is shown to be full of motes and dirt. This comparison is actually quite literal. Before the soul experiences this ecstasy, it thinks it has been cautious about not offending God and that it has done everything that is in its power to do; but once the Sun of justice bestows on the soul this state of prayer and opens its eyes, it sees so many bits of dirt that it wishes only to turn its gaze away. It is not yet enough of a child of this powerful eagle that it can stare into this sun; and yet, for a little while, it does hold its eyes steady and sees that they are filled with mud. It reminds one of the verse that says, "Who will be just in Your presence?" (Psalm 143:2).

When the soul beholds this divine Sun, it is dazzled by its brilliance; when it looks at itself, the mud covers its eyes; this little dove is blind. So quite often it is left completely blind, absorbed, terrified, fainting from seeing so many grandeurs. And thus the soul attains a state of humility in which it does not care about saying good things about itself, nor that others say them. The Lord, not the soul, distributes the fruit of the garden and so nothing sticks to the soul's hands. All the good it has is directed to God; if it does say something about itself, it does so only for God's glory. It knows that it owns nothing in the garden and that even if it should want to ignore this truth, it doesn't have the power to do so. It sees with its own eyes, whether it wishes to or not, that the Lord brings it closer to all the things in the world, so that there it may keep them open for the perceiving of truths.

July

French nobleman and priest Francis of Sales,
patron saint of writers (see July 22). From Sabine
Baring-Gould's *Lives of the Saints*.

1655—Bishop Joseph Hall (1574–1656) was an influential and highly respected English prelate who was deeply embroiled in the religious and political controversies of his time. He even spent time in the Tower of London for his views. In Higham, England, on this day—his eightieth birthday—he delivered one of his most beloved sermons, which has come to be called "The Octogenarian's Sermon," a portion of which follows. Bishop Hall died the following year.

———————— ✧ ————————

It has pleased the providence of my God so to contrive it that this day, fourscore years ago, I was born into the world. "A great time since," you are ready to say, and so, indeed, it seems to you who look at it forward. But to me, who look at it as past, it seems so short that it is gone like a tale that is told or a dream by night, and looks like but yesterday.

It can be no offense for me to say that many of you who hear me this day are not like to see so many suns walk over your heads as I have done. Yea, why speak I of this? There is not one of us that can assure himself of his continuance here one day. We are all tenants at will, and, for all we know, may be turned out of these clay cottages at an hour's warning. Oh, then what should we do but as wise farmers, who know the time of the lease is expiring and cannot be renewed, carefully and seasonably provide ourselves of a surer and more enduring tenure?

I remember our witty countryman Bromiard tells us of a lord in his time that had a fool in his house, as many great men in those days had for their pleasure, to whom this lord gave a staff, and charged him to keep it till he should meet with one that was more fool than himself, and if he met with such a one, to deliver it over to him. Not many years after, this lord fell sick and indeed was sick unto death. His fool came to see him and was told by his sick lord that he must now shortly leave him. "And where will you go?" said the fool. "Into another world," said his lord. "And when will you return? Within a month?" "No." "Within a year?" "No." "When then?" "Never" "Never? And what provision have you made for your entertainment there?" "None at all." "No!" said the fool, "none at all? Here, take my staff. You are going away forever and have taken no care of how you shall fare in that other world from which you will never return! Take my staff, for I am not guilty of any such folly as this."

1850—Abbie Mills was an American religious writer of the nineteenth century who was profoundly influenced by the Holiness Movement. She was admired for her writings on "heart purity" (holiness) and for her verse, such as the hymn "Sing with Me." In her book Quiet Hallelujahs *(1886) she describes her three-day conversion and sanctification experience, which began on this day at an old-fashioned camp meeting near her home in New York City.*

———— ঙঁ ঃ৯ ————

I had never attended a meeting of this sort, . . . but when I arrived upon the ground, I heard some telling how the Lord had cleansed them from all sin and their happiness was complete. Others were exhorted to seek this full salvation. My heart was all turmoil again; but I thought I could not go to the altar where there was so much noise, so I went away out in the grove and sat down all alone and began to ask God most earnestly to show me if He did really mean that I might be free from sin in this life. Was Christian perfection really taught in the Bible?

How the Holy Spirit began to take the things of God and reveal them unto me! The Bible never seemed so full of holiness before. Passage after passage was presented to my mind until I cried, "It is enough; I believe God means I should be holy now." . . . I longed to possess the land of promised rest more and more; it attracted me. The command was "Go forward." But the giants! The crosses! That prayer meeting! The duty of speaking to the unconverted, social prayer, etc. How could I always be obedient? But the light shone only in the narrow way of self-renunciation and loyal following of my Divine Leader. I felt that I could not do as I had done on former occasions—put the subject away and be content to live as I had done. I had said in the presence of God that I believed He plainly taught in His word that I should be holy now and forevermore. To refuse to go forward was to be left in a desert land. . . .

Then I was assured I was dealing with the Faithful and True. His Word was truth. Would I give myself, my all, into His hands and test it? Oh, that never-to-be-forgotten moment when I said to my Redeemer, "I will; I do." Then there was a calm indeed. No voice; no sound; no emotion; but an inner consciousness that I was completely in the Lord's hands and I was being made clean. His promised words were mine.

1602—*The morality play* Cenodoxus, *written in Latin by German Jesuit writer Jacob Bidermann (1578–1639), was first performed on this day at the Jesuit college in Augsburg, Germany. The drama is based on a French legend of a famed doctor, Cenodoxus, who, though known for his piety and virtue, was condemned after death for having been a cunning hypocrite; as he approaches the judgment seat of Christ, he is forced to confront his own hypocrisy. In the following speech, Christ explains to Cenodoxus the magnitude of the gift he had rejected.*

--------------⊷⧼⧽⊶--------------

CHRIST: When you were nothing but dust and ash,
I gave you life and created you to do my will.
But you, still sinning, preferred the evil counsels
of the enemy and ignored my own counsels.
Though rejected, I remained your benefactor.
The more you hated me, the more my love for you grew;
in my fear of doing too little for you,
I did more and more. I came down from heaven
so that you might live there; I dwelt on the earth
so that you might be better able to leave it.
I scorned honors in the hope that you might follow
my example and scorn them too. I fasted for you,
I wept for you, I spent many nights watching over you,
keeping a constant vigil. With all my labors
I sought you like a lost sheep, and yet,
though I looked for you everywhere, I found you not.
For love of you I bore injuries and insults,
nor did I fear the hatred of the enemy
as long as I could depend on you to be my beloved.
I endured having my sinless body beaten
and whipped for your sins. I even suffered death
on the cross so that you might be free from death. . . .
Let all the works of earth proclaim
and all the heavenly host proclaim
that no greater work could I have performed,
nor needed to perform, to bind you
devotedly to me, and me to you.

1435—On this day an English Carmelite monk, Richard Misyn, completed his translation into English (from Latin) of The Fire of Love *by English hermit Richard Rolle of Hampole (c. 1290–1349). Rolle, considered the father of English mysticism, was the author of two sublimely beautiful books on the spiritual life, and he was the first to translate the Psalms into English. In the following selections from* The Fire of Love *(here adapted from Misyn's translation), Rolle describes love as a fire and as the "queen of virtues."*

From a clean conscience and an abundance of spiritual gladness and inward mirth rises the song of joy and the burning of endless love in the truly loving mind. . . . Truly, he who *does* great things is not great; but rather, whoever *loves* Christ greatly and *is beloved* by God is great. Philosophers have toiled much and then vanished without showing any fruit. And many people seem to do great things and to work many miracles, and yet they are still not worthy to be saved—for it is not the *doer*, but the *God-lover* to whom the heavenly crown is given. . . .

Love's power *spreads* and *binds* and *transforms*. It *spreads* because the beams of its goodness spread not only to friends and neighbors but to enemies and strangers as well. It *binds* because it unites the lover in action and will with Christ and other holy souls. . . . And it *transforms* because it turns the lover into the beloved and bears one to the other. Thus, the fire of the Holy Spirit, by possessing the heart, burns it and turns it into fire itself because in that form it is most like God. . . .

Love, queen of virtues, the fairest star, is the beauty of the soul; for in the soul it does these things: . . . it wounds it and fills it with longing; it moistens it and melts it and makes it beautiful; it gladdens the soul and enflames it so that its deeds and habits are beautiful.

All virtue, if it is to be truly called virtue, must doubtless be rooted in such love. No virtue can be held that is not grounded in God's love. Whoever tries to multiply virtues or good deeds without God's love is like a person who casts precious jewels into a bottomless mire pit. Clearly, all the deeds we do, in the end, will not heal our souls if those deeds are not done for the love of God and our neighbor. Therefore, since love alone can make us blessed, we should more desire to lose our lives than to defile love with mind or mouth or deed. In this, those who strive against sin may rejoice; in this, the victors are crowned.

1493—In London on this day, Norman printer Richard Pynson (who died in 1530) completed the printing of an anonymous treatise on the Ten Commandments called Dives and Pauper. *This delightful and earthy book is written in the form of a dialogue between a rich man, Dives, and a poor man, Pauper. Pauper is the wise hero of this book; with his homespun humor and wisdom, he catechizes Dives on the true meaning of the Commandments, often using folk tales to illustrate his points, as in the following excerpt. This modernized passage is from the chapter on the Ninth Commandment:* Thou shalt not covet.

———————— ◆§ ξ◆ ————————

PAUPER: The riches and wealth of this world are like the minstrel's horse. Once upon a time there came a proud thief into a stable and found a minstrel's horse standing next to his own. And since the minstrel's horse was the finer of the two, he took it and rode away on it, leaving his own feeble horse in the stable. The minstrel, who happened to see all this, ran by way of a short cut and met the thief as he was crossing a river. The minstrel cried, "Let us kneel!" The horse, who knew his master's voice well, kneeled down in the river, as he was accustomed to do when playing with his master. Then the minstrel said, "Arise!" and immediately the horse stood up, as he had been taught, and threw the proud thief into the water and ran again to his master.

This minstrel is the world, which plays with the folk of this world as does a minstrel or a juggler or a gambler. His horse is this world's wealth, which often, upon hearing the voice of its master, the world, plays "let us kneel" and brings people low and into great poverty and forsakes them in their greatest need and follows after the play of this world and not after the will of the covetous that would possess it. But often, those who toil most to be rich become the poorest. And, namely, evil-gotten goods play "let us kneel" with those who have misgotten their riches by cheating, withholding of debt, false accusation, mischief, or robbery. Therefore, it is a common proverb: Of evil-gotten gains— not even the third generation may enjoy them.

DIVES: Your speech is not pleasant to worldly, covetous men, and yet experience shows that you have spoken the truth.

1637—Samuel Rutherford (c. 1600–61) was a Scottish theologian and pastor, who, because of his strong religious convictions, was barred from preaching by the Scottish crown and sent into exile for two years (1636–38). During that time he wrote hundreds of letters to his friends, and together they make up one of the finest volumes on the subject of endurance in times of trial. (See also September 12.) On this day he wrote to a friend, William Glendinning, on the subject of seeing the living Christ at times when he seems most distant.

———— ✌ ✌ ————

I would seek no more happiness than a sight of him so near at hand—to see, hear, smell, and touch and embrace him. But oh, closed doors and veils and curtains and thick clouds hold me in pain, while I find the sweet burning of his love that many waters cannot quench! ... I should not refuse ten thousand years in Hell to have a wide soul enlarged and made wider, that I might be exceedingly, even to the running-over, filled with his love. Oh, what am I to love such a One or to be loved by that high and lofty One! I think the angels may blush to look upon him, and what am I to defile such infinite brightness with my sinful eyes! Oh, that Christ would come near and stand still and give me leave to look upon him! For to look seems the poor man's privilege, since he may, for nothing and without hire, behold the sun. I should have a king's life if I had no other thing to do than forevermore behold and eye my fair Lord Jesus. Nay, suppose I were kept out at Heaven's fair entry, I should be happy forevermore to look through a hole in the door and see my dearest and fairest Lord's face. O great King, why do you stand aloof? Why do you remain beyond the mountains? O Well-beloved, why do you pain a poor soul with delays? A long time out of your glorious presence is two deaths and two hells to me. We must meet. I must see him. ... Let me have no joy but the warmth and fire of Christ's love; I seek no other, God knows. If this love be taken from me, the bottom is fallen out of all my happiness and joy; and, therefore, I believe that Christ will never do me that much harm as to bereave a poor prisoner of his love. It were cruelty to take it from me; and He who is kindness itself cannot be cruel.

1936—*Eli Stanley Jones (1884–1973) was an American missionary to India and an author whose major work,* The Christ of the Indian Road *(1925), was a study of Indian missions. A decade later he wrote a daily devotional called* Victorious Living, *and the following reading from that book is his entry for this day. (For more information on Brother Lawrence, see August 3.)*

———————— ⋅⊰ ⊱⋅ ————————

We often quote with approval the man who said that he made shoes to pay expenses while he served God. But should he not have thought of serving God through the making of the shoes? Was not that material thing itself to become the manifestation of the spiritual? Is not the thing that attracts us to Brother Lawrence the fact that he practiced the presence of God in and through the washing of his pans and the scrubbing of his floors? The Old Testament says that every pot in Jerusalem shall have "holiness unto the Lord" written upon it. And was not this the thing that Brother Lawrence fulfilled? His pans had just that written on them.

Business people must be able to handle their ledgers with the same sense of sacredness and mission as the minister handles the sacred Book in the pulpit. Of course, that would mean the scrapping of many a business, for you cannot handle crookedness with sacredness. But it would be far better to scrap the business than to scrap one's soul. But legitimate business can be made a sacrament. "The extension of the incarnation" should mean just this: here today I stand in this business, in this workshop, in this schoolroom, to become the embodiment of the spirit of Christ in this situation. I shall work out His mind and spirit in my relationship with things and persons. As Peter offered his boat to Jesus to teach the multitudes from, so I offer to Him my boat, my business, my life from which He may teach in this situation the meaning of the Kingdom. I am an extension of the incarnation.

PRAYER: O Christ, we thank You that You can make life glow with meaning when we take You into the whole of it. Help me this day to do that very thing. I shall need power. But I know I can bank on You. Amen.

1741—At Enfield, Connecticut, on this day, Jonathan Edwards (1703–58) preached his now-famous sermon "Sinners in the Hands of an Angry God." Edwards, a brilliant thinker and inspired orator, is considered one of the greatest Calvinist philosophers that America produced. His preaching helped to initiate the so-called Great Awakening, the religious revival that swept through the colonies at that time. The following is an excerpt from his "Angry God" sermon.

The God that holds you over the pit of hell, much as one holds a spider or some loathsome insect over the fire, abhors you and is dreadfully provoked; his wrath towards you burns like fire; he looks upon you as worthy of nothing else but to be cast into the fire; he is of purer eyes than to bear to have you in his sight; you are ten thousand times more abominable in his eyes than the most hateful venomous serpent is in ours. You have offended him infinitely more than ever a stubborn rebel did his prince, and yet it is nothing but his hand that holds you from falling into the fire every moment. It is to be ascribed to nothing else that you did not go to hell last night, that you were suffered to awake again in this world after you closed your eyes to sleep. And there is no other reason to be given why you have not dropped into hell since you arose in the morning but that God's hand has held you up. There is no other reason to be given why you have not gone to hell, since you have sat here in the house of God, provoking his pure eyes by your sinful wicked manner of attending his solemn worship. Yea, there is nothing else that is to be given as a reason why you do not this very moment drop down into hell.

O sinner! Consider the fearful danger you are in; it is a great furnace of wrath, a wide and bottomless pit, full of the fire of wrath, that you are held over in the hand of that God, whose wrath is provoked and incensed as much against you as against many of the damned in hell. You hang by a slender thread with flames of divine wrath flashing about it. . . .

1721—Famed American Puritan Increase Mather (1639–1723) served as a chaplain for the British Army in the colonies, as a minister, and later as president of Harvard College. (See also December 11.) On this day, at the age of eighty-three, Mather preached in Boston on the subject "Advice to the Children of Godly Ancestors," from which these precepts are taken.

The children of godly ancestors should be careful that they themselves be godly. Now the children of New England are (or once were) for the most part the children of godly ancestors. What did our parents come into this wilderness for? Not to gain estates, as people do now, but for religion, and that they might leave their children in a hopeful way of being truly religious. . . . Oh turn to God, you that are children of godly parents. Remember that God calls you to it. . . . Children, you are concerned to turn to God, to make sure of Christ. Then you shall be happy; nothing else can make you happy. You cannot be sure of your lives. You may make sure of Christ. If you make sure of him, you will be happy whatever befalls you.

Seek God early. You read, "They that seek me early shall find me" (Proverbs 8:17). Oh, that there may be many early seekers of God, many that set themselves in good earnest to seek him. When you seek God, plead with him the relation with which you are advantaged, as Jacob once did: "O God of my father Abraham, O God of my father Isaac; my father and my grandfather did seek your face; they were your servants; Oh, let me be so too." . . .

Wait on God in the use of his own means that he would be merciful to you. Therefore, give diligent attention to the word of God when it is preached to you. . . . Cry to God that he would have mercy on you. Do as Paul did when, in the pangs of the new birth, it is said of him: "Behold, before that, he was a Pharisee; the Pharisees often prayed; but he did not pray in earnest. Now he prayed in good earnest"—as if his soul was concerned, as indeed it was. Pray for your life and soul, and God will hear and answer you. . . .

Now, may the God of our forebears mercifully preserve the children of New England, . . . may he be with them as he was with their parents, and in that faith and order of the Gospel which they walked in; and may he neither leave them nor forsake them.

1666—*The house of American colonial poet Anne Bradstreet (c. 1612–72) burned down today, inspiring her poem "Some Verses Upon the Burning of Our House July 10th, 1666," a portion of which follows. Known as Mistress Bradstreet, she was the first woman to publish poetry in the American colonies and was the author of the collection* The Tenth Muse *(1650).*

In silent night when rest I took
For sorrow near I did not look,
I wakened was with thundering noise
And piteous shrieks of dreadful voice. . . .

I, starting up, the light did spy,
And to my God my heart did cry
To strengthen me in my distress
And not to leave me succorless.
Then coming out beheld a space,
The flame consume my dwelling place.

And when I could no longer look,
I blessed His name that gave and took,
That laid my goods now in the dust:
Yea so it was, and so 'twas just.
It was His own: it was not mine;
Far be it that I should repine. . . .

Thou hast an house on high erect,
Framed by that mighty Architect,
With glory richly furnished,
Stands permanent though this be fled.
It's purchased and paid for too
By Him who hath enough to do.

A prize so vast as is unknown,
Yet by His gift, is made thine own.
There's wealth enough, I need no more;
Farewell my pelf, farewell my store.
The world no longer let me love,
My hope and treasure lies above.

1603—Dutchman Jacobus Arminius (1560–1609) was a Reformation theologian whose writings influenced the Wesleyans and Methodists and enraged the Calvinists, especially on the issue of predestination. On this day, the University of Leyden in Holland conferred upon Arminius the degree of Doctor of Divinity, and, by way of acceptance, he delivered an oration on the "Priesthood of Christ." Arminius vividly paints an imagined scene in heaven in which Justice and Mercy debate over the best way to deal with a sinful people. Justice demands a payment of a blood sacrifice for sin. Mercy cries out for forgiveness. That both might be satisfied, Wisdom steps in.

-------- ⊰ ⊱ --------

Wisdom was again desired in the Divine Council. She declared that [to resolve the conflict between Justice and Mercy] a man must be born from among men, who might have a nature in common with the rest of his brethren, that, being in all things tempted as they were, he might be able to sympathize with others in their suffering; and yet, that he should . . . not be under dominion of sin; that he should be one in whom Satan could find nothing worthy of condemnation, who should not be tormented by a consciousness of sin, and who should not even know sin, that is, one who should be "born in the likeness of sinful flesh, and yet without sin. For such a high priest became us, who is holy, harmless, undefiled, and separate from sinners" (Hebrews 7:26). But that he might have a community of nature with men, he ought to be born of a human being; and that he might have no participation in crime with them, but might be holy, he ought to be conceived by the Holy Ghost, because sanctification is his proper work. . . . Therefore, the Word of God, who from the beginning was with God and by whom the worlds and all things visible and invisible were created, ought himself to be made flesh, to undertake the office of the priesthood, and to offer his own flesh to God as a sacrifice for the life of the world.

We now have the person who was entrusted with the priesthood and to whom the province was assigned of atoning for the common offense: it is Jesus Christ, the Son of God and of man.

—from *The Writings of Arminius,*
translated by James Nichols

1893—Thérèse of Lisieux (1873–97), nicknamed "The Little Flower," was a French Carmelite nun (see January 10) and was made a saint of the Catholic Church after her death. Her touching autobiography, The Story of a Soul, *is still widely read and admired for its beauty and profound spirituality. She also wrote letters of wise spiritual counsel to her friends and family members. In the following letter, written on this day to her friend Sister Léonie, she shares an interesting thought: that we may take Christ captive with the small kindnesses we do in his name.*

————— ⋅⋦ ξ⋧⋅ —————

Even when the law of fear was in force, before our Lord's coming, the prophet Isaiah said, speaking in the name of the King of Heaven, "Can a woman forget her babe?... and if she should forget, yet will not I forget you" (Isaiah 49:15). What a touching promise! We who live under the law of love, shall we not profit by the loving advances made by our Spouse? How can anybody fear Him who allows Himself to be made captive "with one hair of our neck" (Canticles 4:9).

Let us learn to keep Him prisoner—this God, the Divine Beggar of Love. By telling us that a single hair can work this wonder, He shows us that the smallest actions done for His love are those that charm His heart. If it were necessary to do great things, we should be deserving of pity, but we are fortunate indeed, since Jesus lets Himself be led captive by the smallest action.... With you, dear Léonie, little sacrifices are never lacking. Is not your life made up of them? I rejoice to see you in possession of such wealth, especially when I remember that you know how to put it to good use, not only for yourself, but also for poor sinners. It is so sweet to help Jesus to save the souls which He has ransomed at the price of His precious blood, and which only await our help to hold them back from the abyss.

It seems to me that if our sacrifices take Jesus captive, our joys make Him prisoner too. All that is needful to attain this end is that, instead of giving ourselves over to selfish happiness, we offer to our Spouse the little joys He scatters in our path to charm our heart and draw them toward Him.

—translated by Thomas N. Taylor

1727—Johannes Amos Comenius (1592–1670) was a Moravian educator who lived and taught in Poland (his native country) and Holland. He believed that through education the world might be brought to a Utopian state of oneness with Christ. In an effort to achieve that goal, he wrote a children's "primer," or beginning reader, called the Orbis Pictus *(meaning the "illustrated world"), first translated into English in 1658. It contained illustrations of everyday objects and their names in English and Latin. The work was so valued that it was continually in print for more than two centuries. On this day, English publishers John and Benjamin Sprint announced a revised and updated eleventh edition of this best-selling book. The following readings are from that edition. (Note: the words in italics are the vocabulary words the children were expected to learn.)*

God. God is of himself from everlasting to everlasting. A most perfect and a most blessed *being*. In his *essence*, spiritual and one. In his *personality*, three. In his *will*, holy, just, merciful, and true. In his *power*, very great. In his *goodness*, very good. In his *wisdom*, immeasurable. A *light* inaccessible; and yet all in all. Everywhere and nowhere. The chiefest *good* and the only and inexhausted fountain of all good things. As the *Creator*, so the *Governor* and *Preserver* of all things, which we call the *world*....

Humanity. Men are made for one another's *good*; therefore let them be *kind*. Be sweet and lovely in your *countenance*, gentle and civil in your *behavior* and *manners*, affable and true-spoken with your *mouth*, affectionate and *candid* in your *heart*. So love, and so shall you be loved; and there will be a mutual *friendship*, as that of *turtle-doves*, hearty, gentle, and wishing well on both parts....

Thus you have seen in short, all things that can be shown, and have learned the *chief words* of the *English* and *Latin tongue*. Go on now and read other good *books* diligently, and you shall become *learned*, *wise*, and *godly*. Remember these things: fear God, and call upon him, that he may bestow upon you the *Spirit of Wisdom*. Farewell.

—Commenius's *Orbis Pictus*,
translated by Charles Hoole (1658)

1784—Rev. Henry Venn (1725–97) was an English divine and author of the popular book The Complete Duty of Man. *He was a founding member of the Clapham Sect, a group of prominent Christians who met informally to promote such causes as the abolition of the slave trade and the expansion of missionary work. On this day, while traveling apart from his family, he wrote a letter to his daughter in response to one he had received from her the day before. In her letter, she mentions a terrible thunderstorm that had recently caused much fear among their neighbors. Her father responds:*

———— ⋅⋗§⋖⋅ ————

The very same thunderstorm you were in, reached [here] in great violence. . . . It is good to be above fear that "hath torment" in such awful weather. Christians should labor much not to fear, as men without God have cause to do. And if fear of death makes us dismayed at the storm, we ought to examine from where that fear arises and not rest until we can say, "Death is ours." It is but a bad return for all His precious promises—and love stronger than death, which Christ has had for us—to tremble and quake, in case He should take us to Himself. I grant that our nerves are soon shaken, but our God has access to our spirits and can strengthen us and give us firmness; and [He] will when we pray to Him, that for the credit of our faith in His name, we may not fear for the body but sanctify the Lord God in our hearts and let Him be our fear and let Him be our dread. Wishing you much of His presence, much more knowledge and faith and love and every divine temper—and often, every day, thinking of you—with kind love from your dear mamma, I remain your affectionate father,

H. Venn

1923—In 1923 Canadian writer and evangelist Annie Richardson Kennedy published a daily devotional called A Year in John's Gospel, *from which the following reading for July 15 is taken. The Scripture on which the meditation is based is John 13:12–14: "So after he had washed their feet and had taken his garments and was set down again, he said to them, 'Do you know what I have done to you? You call me Master and Lord, and you say well, for so I am. If I, then, your Lord and Master, have washed your feet, you also ought to wash one another's feet.'"*

———————

Now Christ brings home the lesson of lowly service. James and John who wanted the highest place were taught by Christ wherein true ambition and real greatness consisted. No ordinance can give us a part with Christ and in none can we perform His service to others. We are to help each other keep clean by our mutual ministries of helpfulness and prayer. When the Greeks came the lesson was taught of self-sacrificing, lowly service. Paul speaks of restoring the brother in the spirit of meekness. Humility is the Christlike spirit. The Greek word for *humble* tells us what the pagans thought of this grace. They used it as a term expressing the groveling of a reptile. Christ takes humility and glorifies it. Augustine was once asked what was the first step to heaven. He replied, "Humility. The second step, humility. The third step, humility."

PRAYER: Our Christ, we are under obligation to imitate You here. Give us clean hands, we pray. May the water of the Word be applied. Lord, may we be willing that others perform this office for us! What a need we have of You along this line. Help us. Control us, Spirit of love. Use us for Jesus' sake. Amen.

1897—Rudyard Kipling (1865–1936), a major English literary figure, was famous for such books as Barrack-Room Ballads *(1892) and* The Jungle Book *(1894). In June of 1897 he was commissioned to write a hymn in honor of England's Queen Victoria on the occasion of her "Jubilee" (the sixtieth year of her reign). After much procrastination, he finally completed the assignment on this day. It is called "Recessional" (the first three verses of which are given below). This now-famous hymn, late as it was, was speedily sent to the* London Times *and published the next day.*

⋙⋘

God of our fathers, known of old,
   Lord of our far-flung battle-line,
Beneath whose awful Hand we hold
   Dominion over palm and pine—
Lord God of Hosts, be with us yet,
Lest we forget—lest we forget!

The tumult and the shouting dies;
   The Captains and the Kings depart:
Still stands Thine ancient sacrifice,
   An humble and a contrite heart.
Lord God of Hosts, be with us yet,
Lest we forget—lest we forget!

Far-called, our navies melt away;
   On dune and headland sinks the fire:
Lo, all our pomp of yesterday
   Is one with Nineveh and Tyre!
Judge of the Nations, spare us yet,
Lest we forget—lest we forget.

1854—Seventeen-year-old Frances Ridley Havergal (1836–79) was confirmed in Worcester Cathedral on this day. As an adult, she became one of the greatest English hymn writers of the nineteenth century and author of the influential book The Ministry of Song *(1870). She was a pioneer in exploring the uses of music as a special ministry of the church.*

———— ✥ ————

We were the first to go up, and I was the fourth or fifth on whom the bishop laid his hands. At first, the thought came as to who was kneeling next to me, but then the next moment I felt alone, unconscious of my fellow candidates, of the many eyes fixed upon us, and the many thoughts of and prayers for me, alone with God and His chief minister. My feelings when his hands were placed on my head (and there was solemnity and earnestness in the very touch and manner) I cannot describe, they were too confused; but when the words "Defend, O Lord, this Thy child with Thy heavenly grace, that she may continue Thine forever, and daily increase in Thy Holy spirit more and more, until she come unto Thy everlasting kingdom," were solemnly pronounced, if ever my heart followed a prayer it did then, if ever it thrilled with earnest longing not unmixed with joy, it did at the words "Thine forever."

[So impressed was Frances by the bishop's words, that later that day she wrote the following verse:]

> Oh! "Thine forever," what a blessed thing
> To be forever His who died for me!
> My Savior, all my life Thy praise I'll sing,
> Nor cease my song throughout eternity.

—from *Memorials of Frances Ridley Havergal*
by her sister, Maria V. G. Havergal (1880)

1738—Samuel Wesley (1662–1735) was an English minister, poet, hymn writer, and author, though he is now primarily remembered for being the father of John Wesley (1703–91) and his brother Charles (1707–88), the founders of Methodism. Among Samuel's hymns is one, "Behold the Savior of Mankind," that is unusual for having two remarkable stories attached to it. When the Wesleys' rectory home was destroyed by fire in 1709, Samuel's sole hand-written copy of this hymn was lifted into the air by the heat and recovered later on the ground near the house. And on this day in 1738, three years after Samuel's death and not long after Charles' own conversion, Charles visited the prisoners in Newgate Prison in London, and through the singing of this hymn, he was able to bring about the conversions of two condemned criminals on the eve of their executions. He wrote in his diary on this day, "It was one of the most triumphant hours I have ever known." Samuel's hymn is given here.

———— ⋅§ §⋅ ————

Behold the Savior of mankind
  Nailed to the shameful tree!
How vast the love that Him inclined
  To bleed and die for thee!

Hark how He groans while Nature shakes,
  And earth's strong pillars bend!
The Temple's veil in sunder breaks,
  The solid marbles rend.

'Tis done! The precious ransom's paid;
  "Receive my soul," He cries:
See where He bows His sacred head!
  He bows His head and dies.

But soon He'll break death's envious chain,
  And in full glory shine!
O Lamb of God, was ever pain,
  Was ever love like Thine!

1890—American writer E. M. Bounds (1835–1913) served as a Confederate chaplain, a pastor, an evangelist, and an editor, but he is chiefly remembered as the author of several outstanding books on prayer, such as Power Through Prayer *and* Preacher and Prayer. *The following excerpt is from an article, published on this day, that Bounds wrote for the* Christian Advocate *newspaper, in which he discusses the problem of money.*

—◦§ ﻉ◦—

Money has materialized the church. The money she does not give has earthened her. Money-loving, money-making, money-keeping, is the rock on which the spiritual movements of the church are stranded. ... The church is making earth her home instead of her battlefields; her members are demoralized by palaces instead of being hardened by tents. Her sighs and longings and struggles for the homeland are hushed in the embraces of a foreign love. Money has won on the church and holds it to earth in a more engaging and tasteful form than the memory of the onions and garlic held apostate Israel to Egypt. Public sentiment and church sentiment have fixed the worth of money so high that we hold it above the price of souls.

This covetousness which has materialized the church, and this material spirit which has rooted covetousness so thoroughly in the church, have arrested and almost destroyed the *grace* of giving, for our giving is too poor to dignify it by the name of a grace.... It arrests all the other graces; prayer, faith, self-denial, zeal, all are poisoned or perish by the same deadly influence.

This state of things can be remedied. The remedy is found, in the first place, in the genuine preaching of the genuine gospel. This age is too intent. Money and its allied forces are too strong to be impressed by a gospel of song, sentiment, or sham. Nothing but the unadulterated gospel—rock-founded, rock-ribbed, iron-cemented—will work this miraculous work. Nothing but God's real forceful gospel can reach this forceful earth-bent age; a gospel bathed in the blood of God, which finds all its mysteries solved and all its results summed up in heaven and hell.

No gospel of pseudo emasculating love can meet the case, but the whole of God's word must be declared, the full force of all its terrific revelations must be poured on the church like a tempest of shot and shell. The church must be deluged and impregnated with the truth that no man can have two heavens, that he who would gain eternal life must pay the price of this life.

1871—George MacDonald (1824–1905) was a Scottish minister, poet, novelist, and one of the most imaginative writers of all time. No less a writer than C. S. Lewis claimed MacDonald as a major influence. Among Mac-Donald's most famous books are At the Back of the North Wind, The Light Princess, Lilith, Phantastes, *and* The Princess and Curdie. *On this day, MacDonald wrote to a friend that his latest book of sermons,* The Miracles of Our Lord, *was about to come off the press. In this excerpt he ponders Jesus' reasons for allowing "no man to follow him" (Mark 5:37) when he raised Jairus' daughter from the dead.*

—————— ◦§ ◦§◦ ——————

Now it would appear that he stopped the crowd and would let them go no farther. They could not all see, and He did not wish them to see. It was not good for men to see too many miracles. They would feast their eyes and then cease to wonder or think. . . .

Jesus *must* have hated anything like display. God's greatest work has never been done in crowds, but in closets; and when it works out from thence, it is not upon crowds, but upon individuals. A crowd is not a divine thing. It is not a body. Its atoms are not members one of another. A crowd is a chaos over which the Spirit of God has yet to move, before each retires to his place to begin his harmonious works and unite with all the rest in the organized chorus of the human creation. The crowd must be dispersed that the church may be formed.

The relation of the crowd to the miracle is rightly reflected in what came to the friends of the house. To them, weeping and wailing greatly, after the Eastern fashion, He said when He entered, "Why do you make a tumult and weep? The child is not dead but sleeping" (Mark 5:39). They laughed Him to scorn. He put them all out. . . .

They knew she was dead, and their unfaithfulness blinded their hearts to what He meant. They were unfit to behold the proof of what He had said. Such as they, in such a mood, could gather from it no benefit. A faithful heart alone is capable of understanding the proof of the truest things. It is faith towards God which alone can lay hold of any of His facts. . . .

"Little girl, I say to you, arise." And her spirit returned "and immediately the girl got up and walked" (Mark 5:41–42).

1914—Today, American minister W. W. Staley, pastor of Suffolk Christian Church in Virginia, delivered an address at a conference for ministers. The conference, called "A Seaside Chautauqua and School of Methods," was held in Virginia Beach. This address and four others by Staley were later published in the book The Minister *and deal with ministerial lifestyle. Though meant for ministers, his talk on the subject of his love for books, "The Minister in His Study," is certainly true for many believers.*

A mighty host surrounds me in my library. Peter, James, and John did not see as much nor hear as much as the minister in his library. Jesus is here too, in the Bible and by the Spirit. There are more people in my library than in my church. They speak to me; they kindle the fires of my imagination; they quicken my faith, humble my pride, rebuke my wrong-doing and wrong-thinking, warn me against sin, and point my soul to the living Christ. I find tombs with angels, deserts with fountains, gardens with Saviors, prisons with praises, and crosses with crowns. Above the roar of the tempest, the flap of the split sails, the creak of the breaking timbers, and the cry of endangered men, I hear Jesus say, "Peace, be still." I hear Nebuchadnezzar say, "I see four men loose, walking in the midst of the fire, and they have no hurt; and the form of the fourth is like unto the Son of God." I hear Paul, in the midst of darkness and the raging sea, say, "There stood by me this night the angel of God, whose I am and whom I serve, saying, 'Fear not.'" The past is a mighty host, their thought, faith, love, and lives still speaking to our own. The library is a transfiguration scene, crowning lofty summits, silently and sweetly speaking to the minister so as to inspire him with renewed strength and satisfaction that arms him for the good fight of faith. Beyond this teeming past are the living millions moving to and fro, loving and hating, helping and hindering, neglecting age, crushing childhood, desecrating the Sabbath, greedily preying upon their fellows, preparing for war, and killing the flower of age. . . . The minister should seek to interpret the present age in the light of the Gospel and past civilizations. From his study as a tower, he should get his vision of mankind and God, and then go forth to preach salvation to a sinning world. His sermon should be a message from God, supported by His word, fired by His Spirit, and delivered in the spirit of love.

1609—Francis de Sales (1567–1622) was a French nobleman and priest. Because of his many beautiful writings he was, after his death, declared a "doctor of the church" and made a saint. He is now thought of as the patron saint of Christian writers. His most beloved work is his Introduction to the Devout Life, *the preface of which was written on this day. In the following selection he poetically describes the devout believer by using the symbol of Jacob's ladder.*

──────── ⋙⋘ ────────

Contemplate Jacob's ladder—it is a true metaphor for the devout life. Its two sides, between which we ascend and to which the rungs are attached, represent prayer, for it reaches up to the love of God, and to the sacraments, which confer it. The rungs are nothing less than the various degrees of charity by which we go from one virtue to another, descending by the practice of comforting and aiding our neighbor, and ascending by the contemplation of our loving union with God. Now look at those who are on the ladder: are they people with angelic souls or are they perhaps angels with human bodies? Though they are not young, they appear to be so because they are so full of vigor and spiritual agility. They have wings so that they might soar up to God in holy prayer; but they also have feet so they can walk among ordinary people and bless them with their friendly and edifying conversation. Their faces are beautiful and happy because they accept all circumstances with delight and contentment. Their legs and arms and heads are uncovered because all their thoughts, affections, and actions have no other intent, no other motive than to please God. The rest of their body is covered with a beautiful lightweight robe to show that they use only those earthly things that are most necessary to life, and that they use them with moderation and in accordance with their human state. Such are the devout souls.

Believe me, devotion is the delight of all delights, the queen of all virtues, and the perfection of all charity. If charity were milk, devotion would be the cream. If charity were a plant, devotion would be the flower. If charity were a precious stone, devotion would be its luster. If it were a precious balm, then devotion would be its sweet perfume, which comforts men and women, and causes angels to rejoice.

1899—In 1899 an English writer and scholar named Alexander Smellie (1857–1923) published a daily devotional book entitled In the Hour of Silence. *The following is his reading for July 23, which takes as its text Revelation 3:20: "Behold I stand at the door and knock."*

———— ఆక్ష్ ఏ —————

Let me marvel at the condescension and patience of the Lord. He stands at the door of my heart and knocks. He humbles Himself, and as a Suppliant begs to be permitted to enter in. And He is not easily driven away. Despite my repeated refusals, He waits and pleads. What sweetness of grace is His! What endurance of love—love unresentful of all wounds!

Let me be impressed and awed by my own responsibilities and dangers. I must open the door from the inside, and if it is still closed and barred, then it is I who am chargeable with that crime. Jesus will not force His way within against my will; if He is outside today, after so long a time, it is I who am keeping Him there on the wrong side of the threshold. What a contingency is this, and what a peril!

But let me receive the knocking Savior with all that He brings. When I say yes to Him, when I undo the bars of self-righteousness or of indifference or of cherished sin, when I throw wide the gates of my soul, it is the beginning of blessedness for me. It is a feast and a good day. At last I have begun to live. Blessed be God, as David Brainerd said, I "repair to a full fountain"; I have all and abound. "Well may this glowing heart rejoice and tell its raptures all abroad."

Come in, Thou Blessed of the Lord, why stand outside?

> The angel sought so far away
> I welcome at my door.

Nay, not the angel, but the Lord of the angels, before whom their glory pales and their love is cold and all their gifts are naught.

1885—Major Daniel Webster Whittle (1840–1901) served under General Sherman during the American Civil War. Later, through the influence of D. L. Moody, Whittle became an evangelist and wrote many books and familiar hymns. On this day, he wrote the following thoughts about prayer in his book The Wonders of Prayer. *(See also July 30 and October 19.)*

———— ✍ ————

Prayer is to bring us into communion with God, for the growth of the spiritual life that is ours by faith in Christ Jesus. To leave it upon any lower plane than this is to rob it of its highest functions and to paralyze it of lasting power for good in any direction. The promises of God are conditioned upon our being in this state of heart toward God. "If ye abide in me and my words abide in you, ye shall ask what ye will and it shall be done unto you" (John 15:7). Abiding in Christ, our will will be His will, as to desiring that which will most advance the divine life and promote confidence in God, and all our desires for material blessing will be subordinated to this motive. Right here must come in a line of truth that will lead us from the spirit of dictation in our prayers to God in all matters pertaining to our worldly concerns. We cannot tell what is for our highest spiritual good. The saving of our property or the taking it away. The recovery from sickness or the continuance of it; the restoration of the health of our loved one or his departing to be with Christ; the removing the thorn or the permitting it to remain. "In *everything*" it is indeed our blessed privilege to let *our requests* be made known unto God, but, praise His name, He has not passed over to us the awful responsibility of the assurance that *in everything* the requests we make known will be granted. He has reserved the decision, where we should rejoice to leave it, to His infinite wisdom and His infinite love. . . .

The highest use of prayer is to bring the soul nearer to God, and *not the making of it a mere matter of convenience to escape physical ills or supply physical necessities. . . .*

So in *all* things, that which God has given me intelligence and power to do, in avoiding evil or securing good, I am under direct command from Him to do, always depending upon His blessing to secure the needed result. A *true faith* in God will be made manifest by careful obedience to known commands. An *intelligent* faith can never allow dependence upon means used to take the place of dependence upon the living God, who alone makes them efficacious.

1935—Although Rev. Gary Davis (1896–1972) was an ordained minister, he found his most powerful ministry through music. This blind African-American singer, with his ragtime-influenced guitar and thundering vocal style, performed country gospel songs that have endured and been recorded by such artists as Bob Dylan and Peter, Paul, and Mary. Among his well-known songs are "Motherless Children," "Death Don't Have No Mercy," and "Samson and Delilah." On this day in New York City, Davis had his first gospel-music recording session. Among the songs he recorded is the following: "I Am the True Vine," which takes its inspiration from John 15:1.

———————— ⋘⋙ ————————

I went to the wilderness, didn't go to stay;
My soul got happy and I stayed all day.
Just let me tell you what a liar will do:
He won't serve God, and he won't let you.

    CHORUS: I am the True Vine,
    I am the True Vine,
    I am the True Vine,
    My Father is the Husbandman.

Stop sinning—let me tell you a natural fact:
If you ever go to hell you'll never come back....
You can talk about me just as much as you please,
I'll talk about you down on my knees.

If religion was a thing that money could buy,
The rich would live and the poor would die.
My soul thanks God it is not so;
If the rich don't pray, to hell they go.

One of these mornings, won't be long,
You're gonna call me and I'll be gone.
Bring it up, Christian, bring it up free,
Comfort the root of the tender tree.

1837—American religious leader Phoebe Palmer (1807–74) was not only one of the most influential women in revivalist and Holiness circles, she was also important for her advocacy of women's rights and for her support of social causes. (See also October 30.) In her spiritual autobiography, The Promise of the Father *(published in 1859), she describes her initial "sanctification," an experience that took place on this day.*

On the evening of July 26, 1837, between the hours of eight and nine o'clock, the Lord gave me such a view of my utter pollution and helplessness, apart from the cleansing, energizing influences of the purifying blood of Jesus and the quickening aids of the Holy Spirit, that I have ever since retained a vivid realization of the fact. I feel that I have received the sentence of death in myself; that I should not trust in myself, but in him who raises the dead. The tempter oftener makes attempts to paralyze the energies of my faith on this wise: "You know that you have received the sentence of death in yourself, and, without the living power of a living, indwelling Christ, momentarily purifying and quickening your being, you can do nothing. And dare you, with all your unworthiness, claim momentarily this cleansing, energizing power from on high?" Yes, I dare claim it. Alleluia! . . .

It was at this point in my career of discipleship that I received the promise of the Father. The sacrifice of all my entire being had now been made. The offering had not only been placed upon the altar, but it was also bound there in view of all coming time and in contemplation of every conceivable emergency.

Daily and hourly since that eventful period have I claimed it. But it is only by *a continuous act of surrender and a ceaseless act of faith* that I claim and retain the grace. Not an hour, I trust, has passed since that hallowed evening, twenty years since, in which I have not felt that I would rather die than knowingly offend God.

c. 250—The church has traditionally celebrated this day in honor of the Seven Sleepers of Ephesus. This early Christian legend has its roots in folk tale and was told in the early church as an encouragement to those suffering persecution. The legend is here recounted in a modern rendering of an anonymous medieval Anglo-Saxon sermon.

The Seven Sleepers were Maximianus, Malchus, Martinianus, Dionysius, Johannes, Seraphion, Constantinus. These seven believing soldiers of God were, in the days of Emperor Decius, dwelling in the city of Ephesus. They were of noble birth . . . and, in front of the heathen slayer [the Emperor Decius], were accused of being Christians. He would not slay them immediately but granted them time, on account of their noble birth, that they might bethink themselves and bow to his idol when he came again—or their bodies should be tortured with divers torments. Decius then went to other cities to torment the Christians, and the seven servants of God sold their possessions for money and secretly distributed it to the poor and went from the city into a great cave under a mountain and there continued in prayer day and night.

When Decius again came, he commanded them to be sent for. It was said to him that they were hidden in the cave, and he, then enraged, commanded the mouth of the cave to be closed with immense hewn stones. But the merciful God had, a little before, put them to sleep within the cave, and they so lay sleeping three hundred and seventy-two years, until Christianity spread over all the world. Subsequently, after this time, in the days of the Emperor Theodosius, who fervently believed in Christ, it happened that some workmen found the stone at the cave's mouth and rolled it away. Whereupon, the Almighty Creator gave to the seven saints that lay in the cave life and resurrection after so long a sleep, and they were then announced to the citizens. This miracle was then made known to the Christian Emperor Theodosius, and he, with joyful mind, journeyed thither with all the citizens and bishops and head men.

The holy martyrs then went out from the cave toward the emperor, and their countenances shone like the sun.

1942—Poet and novelist Charles Williams (1886–1945), on this day sent a copy of his book The Figure of Beatrice *to poet T. S. Eliot. Williams was highly influential among a small group of English writers of the time, including C. S. Lewis and W. H. Auden. In* The Figure of Beatrice, *a theological study of Dante's* Divine Comedy *(see September 14), Williams discusses two traditional ways that Christians have approached God: the "Way of Rejection," in which the believer shuns all the images of the world in order to focus only on the Image of God; and the "Way of Affirmation," in which the believer cherishes the things of the world as images and expressions of God's Creation. He considered Dante the greatest Christian poet of Affirmation.*

———— ⋘ ⋙ ————

Neither of these two Ways is, or can be, exclusive. The most vigorous ascetic, being forbidden formally to hasten his death, is bound to attend to the actualities of food, drink, and sleep . . . , however brief his attention may be. The most indulgent of Christians is yet bound to hold his most cherished images—of food, drink, sleep, or anything else— negligible beside the final Image of God. . . .

Our sacred Lord, in his earthly existence, deigned to use both methods. The miracle of Cana and all the miracles of healing are works of the affirmation of images; the counsel to pluck out the eye is a counsel of the rejection of images. It is said that he so rejected them for himself that he had nowhere to lay his head, and that he so affirmed them by his conduct that he was called a glutton and a wine-bibber. He commanded his disciples to abandon all images but himself and promised them, in terms of the same images, a hundred times what they had abandoned. The Crucifixion and the Death are rejection and affirmation at once, for they affirm death only to reject death; the intensity of that death is the opportunity of its own dissolution; and beyond that physical rejection of earth lies the re-affirmation of earth which is called the Resurrection.

As above, so below; as in him, so in us. The tangle of affirmation and rejection which is in each of us has to be drawn into some kind of pattern, and has so been drawn by all men who have ever lived.

1835—Danish writer and philosopher Søren Kierkegaard (1813–55) has been reviled by many Christians as "the Father of Existentialism," and yet his books show him to be a man of profound faith and spiritual insight. In the following excerpt from his Journals, written on this day, a twenty-two-year-old Kierkegaard describes a moving experience he had while standing by the sea. As he stood there, he reflected on the recent deaths of both his mother and his sister.

—————— ✦ ✦ ——————

It has always been one of my favorite places. As I stood there one quiet evening as the sea struck up its song with a deep and calm solemnity, whilst my eye met not a single sail on the vast expanse of water, and the sea set bounds to the heavens, and the heavens to the sea; whilst on the other side the busy noise of life subsided and the birds sang their evening prayer—the few that are dear to me came forth from their graves, or rather it seemed to me as though they had not died. I felt so content in their midst, I rested in their embrace, and it was as though I were out of the body, wafted with them into the ether above—and the hoarse screech of the gulls reminded me that I stood alone, and everything vanished before my eyes, and I turned back with a heavy heart to mix in the busy world, yet without forgetting such blessed moments. . . .

As I stood there alone and forsaken, and the power of the sea and the battle of the elements reminded me of my own nothingness, and on the other hand the sure flight of the birds recalled the words spoken by Christ: "Not a sparrow shall fall to the ground without your Father knowing": then all at once I felt how great and how small I was; then did those two mighty forces, pride and humility, happily unite in friendship. Lucky is the man to whom *that* is possible at every moment of his life; in whose breast those two factors have not only come to an agreement but have joined hands and been wedded. . . . His life will flow on peacefully and quietly and he will neither drain the intoxicating cup of pride nor the bitter chalice of despair. He has found what the great philosopher . . . desired, but did not find: that Archimedean point from which he could lift the whole world, the point which for that very reason must lie outside the world, outside the limitations of time and space.

—from *The Journals of Kierkegaard*,
translated by Alexander Dru

1864—The charming Victorian book The Wonders of Prayer *by Major Daniel Webster Whittle (1840–1901; see also July 24) records the following miraculous answer to prayer, which took place on this day. During the American Civil War, a certain Sunday school teacher who was a Northern sympathizer escaped the Southern troops who had ransacked his home. He found himself lost in the woods with his wife and several children. Having run out of provisions, he sat down by a tree to despair when his youngest daughter approached him.*

———— ∗§ §∗ ————

"Father, Father, I have found such a precious text in my little Testament which I brought to the mountain with me; for very joy I could not stop to read it to Mother but hastened to you with it. Please listen while I read."

To which he said, "Yes, my child, read it. There is comfort to be found in the Scriptures. We will not long be together on earth. . . ."

To which she replied: "Oh, Father, I believe that we will not die at this time; that we will not be permitted to starve; that God will surely send us relief; but do let me read." Then opening her dear little volume at the ninth verse of the sixth chapter of Matthew, she read as follows: "'Our Father, which art in heaven, hallowed be Thy name; Thy kingdom come; Thy will be done on earth as it is in heaven; give us this day our daily bread.' Oh, Father, to think that our dear Savior Himself taught His disciples to pray for their daily bread. These are His own words. It is not possible, therefore, that He will allow any person to starve, who, in His own appointed language, asks Him for food. Will He not, dear Father, hear our prayers for bread?"

At once and forever the scales fell from the eyes of that parent. With tears streaming down his cheeks, he clasped his child to his bosom and earnestly repeated the Lord's Prayer. He had scarcely finished it when a small dog ran to where he and his daughter were upon their knees and barked so fiercely as to attract to the spot its owner, a wealthy Pennsylvania farmer, who was upon the mountain in search of cattle that he had lost for several days. The kindhearted tiller of the soil immediately piloted the suffering family to his own comfortable home and properly provided for their wants.

1876—On this day a Cambridge scholar named Wynnard Hooper wrote, "It is somewhat remarkable that, in spite of the great interest attaching to the Gesta Romanorum as the most popular story book of the Middle Ages and as the source of much literature in that and later times, no English version of it should have appeared until 1824, when a translation was published by the Rev. Charles Swan." These words are part of Hooper's preface to a revised edition of Swan's monumental translation of the work. The Gesta Romanorum ("Roman Tales") was compiled by fourteenth-century monks for their entertainment. It contained anecdotes, folk tales, saints' lives, and droll stories of all kinds, each with a moralizing "application" attached. Chaucer, Shakespeare, and many other writers borrowed freely from the original Latin version. Here is a typical fable, with its "application," from Swan's translation.

———————◄§ §►———————

A king had two greyhounds, whom he kept alternately chained up. As long as they were thus fastened they mutually loved and fawned upon each other, but no sooner were they unloosed than they exhibited the most deadly signs of mutual hostility. The king was much concerned at this; because when he would have hunted with them, and for that purpose set them at liberty, they fought so fiercely that he was unable to follow his sport. This led him to consult some learned man, who recommended that the first of the dogs should be encountered by a strong and savage wolf; and then the second should be encouraged to the attack when his companion was in danger of being defeated. For when the first saw how the other aided him, they would in future be friends. This was accordingly done; and as the strength of the first dog failed, the second was let loose, who, after a severe struggle, killed the wolf. From this time, bound or unbound, they lived together in the most perfect friendship.

Application: My beloved, the king is Christ; the two dogs are the soul and body. If loosed by mortal sin, they are at war. The wolf is the devil, which being overcome, they live together in peace.

August

The martyrdom of St. Ignatius in the Colosseum at Rome
(see August 23). Illustration from *Menologium Graecorum*.

1851—At about half past ten at night on this day, an American pastor and missionary by the name of Reverend William Scott Downey had an unusual experience. (See also September 7.)

———————— •◦§ §◦• ————————

I dreamed I was in a sequestered spot. Tired and hungry with the travels of the day, I had seated myself upon a little hillock. Looking about, I beheld one flying from the clouds towards the place where I sat. As he approached me, he threw aside his veil and displayed a figure of unequaled beauty. Addressing me, "Child of sorrow," he said, "I am sent both to instruct and succor you." He then bade me take hold of his robe, which I did, when he bore me with him to the summit of a lofty mountain. Alighted there, I saw, at its base, a large field, and in its center an orchard, crowded with trees of every sort. It was surrounded by a high wall, at different points of which were four gates. . . .

We descended to the orchard and closely examined the trees, but could discover no fruit. "Will not the beauty of the orchard, the limbs of the trees, or their numerous leaves satisfy your hunger?" said he. "No," I replied. He then took from his bosom a wand, and pointing it to the trees, he pronounced, "Be fruitful!" Instantly every tree was loaded with the richest fruit. At his request I freely plucked and ate. My hunger was appeased.

He then addressed me as follows: "Open your ears, hear, and be wise. This field is the world. The orchard is the one true church, and Christ is its body. The different trees which you see are the different denominations of Christians. The branches and leaves, which could not satisfy your hunger, are the prayers of nominal Christians, which avail little in the sight of God. The fruits, which have since refreshed you, and made you glad, are the works of good men, which are ever well pleasing in the sight of God. Go upon your way," he said, "and be for the future more watchful over your own heart than you are to notice the conduct of others."

He then flew away and left me, and I awoke.

—from *Downey's Proverbs* (1853)

1903—On the fifteenth anniversary of her arrival in Okoyong, on the Calabar coast of West Africa, English missionary Mary Slessor (1848–1915) was honored at a special Communion service by the people of the town. In her time as a missionary, she had succeeded in allaying such practices as twin-murder, human sacrifice, and slavery. As the hymns were sung, she meditated.

———— ✺ ————

She seemed to be lost in a trance of thought, her face had a faraway look, and tears stood in her eyes. She was thinking of the greatness of God's love that could win the oppressed people of dark Okoyong.

She could not let the assembly break up without saying a few words. Now that they had the beginnings of a congregation they must, she said, build a church large enough for all who cared to come. And she pleaded with those who had been received to remain true to the faith. "Okoyong now looks to you more than to me for proof of the power of the gospel."

In the quiet of the evening in the Mission House, she seemed to dwell in the past. Long she spoke of what the conditions had been fifteen years before and of the changes that had come since. But her joy was in those who had been brought to confess Christ, and she was glad to think that, after all, the work had not been a failure. And all the glory she gave to her Father who had so marvelously helped her.

For a moment also her fancy turned to the future. She would be no longer there, but she knew the work would go on from strength to strength, and her eyes shone as she saw in vision the gradual ingathering of the people and her beloved Okoyong at last fair and redeemed.

—from W. P. Livingstone's *Mary Slessor of Calabar* (1916)

1666—On this day a French ecclesiastic, the Abbé de Beaufort, first met Nicolas Herman, who is better known as Brother Lawrence (c. 1605–91). Lawrence was a French Carmelite lay brother who, as a humble kitchen worker in the monastery, believed that one could "practice the presence of God" in all circumstances. Beaufort was so impressed with Lawrence's devotion that he published a volume of his sayings in 1792 and a volume of recollections in 1794. Together these books are known in English as The Practice of the Presence of God, *from which the following is taken.*

———— ✥ ————

He told me . . . that the most excellent method he had found of going to God was that of doing our common business without any view to pleasing men and, as far as we are capable, purely for the love of God. That it was a great delusion to think that the times of prayer ought to differ from other times; that we are as strictly obliged to adhere to God by action in the time of action as by prayer in the season of prayer. That his prayer was nothing else but a sense of the presence of God, his soul being at that time insensible to everything but divine love; and that when the appointed times of prayer were past, he found no difference because he still continued with God, praising and blessing Him with all his might, so that he passed his life in continual joy; yet hoped that God would give him somewhat to suffer when he should grow stronger. That we ought, once and for all, heartily to put our whole trust in God and make a total surrender of ourselves to Him, secure that He would not deceive us. That we ought not to be weary of doing little things for the love of God, who regards not the greatness of the work, but the love with which it is performed. That we should not wonder if, in the beginning, we often failed in our endeavors, but that at last we should gain a habit, which will naturally produce its acts in us, without our care and to our exceeding great delight. That the whole substance of religion was faith, hope, and charity, by the practice of which we become united to the will of God; that all besides is indifferent and to be used as a means that we may arrive at our end and be swallowed up therein, by faith and charity. That all things are possible to him who believes; that they are less difficult to him who hopes; that they are more easy to him who loves; and still more easy to him who perseveres in the practice of these three virtues.

—translator unknown

1856—John Keble (1792–1866) was a poet and professor of poetry at Oxford, and also one of the most influential religious leaders in Victorian England. He is best remembered for his leadership in the Oxford Movement, which attempted to reassert "high church" values in the Church of England. On this day, Keble, now in his mid-sixties and in the mood to look back on his eventful life, wrote this touching poem/prayer called "Harvest."

Lord, in thy name thy servants plead,
And thou hast sworn to hear;
Thine is the harvest, thine the seed,
The fresh and fading year:

Our hope, when autumn winds blew wild,
We trusted, Lord, with thee;
And still, now spring has on us smiled,
We wait on thy decree.

The former and the latter rain,
The summer sun and air,
The green ear and the golden grain—
All thine—are ours by prayer.

Thine too by right, and ours by grace,
The wondrous growth unseen,
The hopes that soothe, the fears that brace,
The love that shines serene.

So grant the precious things brought forth
By sun and moon below,
That thee in thy new heaven and earth
We never may forego.

1888—On this day Bishop Herbert of Salford, England, wrote to Irish author and priest Father Dean Kinane: "Like your other exquisite works, St. Patrick's Life will find a wide circulation in England." The following charming excerpt from Kinane's book, published in 1888, describes the legendary conversion of the daughters of pagan Irish King Laeghaire. St. Patrick (c. 389–c. 461), Ireland's greatest saint, is credited with converting the island to Christianity in the fifth century.

———— ❧ ❧ ————

Laeghaire McNeill's two daughters, Ethne the Fair and Fieldelm the Red, ... questioned Patrick, ... "Who is your God and in what place is He—in Heaven or in earth? Is it under the earth or on the earth or in the seas or in the streams or in hills or in valleys? Has He sons or daughters? Has He gold and silver? Is there a profusion of every good in His kingdom? Tell us plainly how we shall see Him and how He is to be loved and how He is to be found. Is He young or old, or is He ever living? Is He beautiful ... ?"

St. Patrick, full of the Holy Spirit, responded: "Our God is the God of all, the God of heaven and earth, the God of the seas and the rivers, the God of the sun and the moon and of all the other planets; the God of the high hills and the low valleys; God over heaven, in heaven, and under heaven; ... He inspires all things; He quickens all things; He enkindles all things; He gives light to the sun and to the moon. He created fountains in the dry land and placed dry islands in the sea and stars to minister to the greater lights. He has a Son co-eternal and co-equal with Himself; and the Son is not younger than the Father, nor is the Father older than the Son. And [the Father and the Son] and the Holy Ghost are not divided. I desire, moreover, to unite you to the Son of the heavenly King, for you are daughters of an earthly king."

And the daughters said, as if with one mouth and heart, "How shall we come to believe in that King? Teach us duly that we may see the Lord face to face...."

And St. Patrick said, "Do you believe that through baptism the sin of your mother and your father shall be put away from you?... [And] do you believe in repentance after sin?"

"Yes."

And they were baptized.

1912—James Russell Miller (1840–1912) was an American clergyman and author of numerous best-selling devotional books. At the time of his death, his final manuscript was almost complete. A friend of Miller's, John T. Faris, completed the book and wrote the preface on this day. An excerpt from Miller's completed book, called The Book of Comfort, *follows. (See also May 13.)*

————— ✺ —————

There is a great waste of power in our failure to appreciate our opportunities. "If I only had the gifts that this man has I would do the large and beautiful things that he does. But I never have the chance of doing such things. Nothing ever comes to my hand but opportunities for little commonplace things." Now, the truth is that nothing is commonplace. The giving of a cup of cold water is one of the smallest kindnesses anyone can show to another, yet Jesus said that God takes notice of this act amid all the events of the whole world, any busy day, and rewards it. It may not be cabled half round the world and announced with great headlines in the newspapers, but it is noticed in heaven. We do not begin to understand what great waste we are allowing when we fail to put the true value on little opportunities of serving others. Somehow we get the feeling that any cross-bearing worthwhile must be a costly sacrifice, something that puts nails through our hands, something that hurts till we bleed. . . .

When the great miracle of the loaves had been wrought, Jesus sent his disciples to gather up the broken pieces, "that nothing be lost." The Master is continually giving us the same command. Every hour's talk we have with a friend leaves fragments that we ought to gather up and keep to feed our heart's hunger or the hunger of others' hearts, as we go on. When we hear good words spoken or read a good book, we should gather up the fragments of knowledge, the suggestions of helpful thoughts, the broken pieces, and fix them in our hearts for use in our lives. We allow large values of the good things we hear or read to turn to waste continually because we are poor listeners or do not try to keep what we hear. We let the broken pieces be lost and thereby are great losers. If only we would gather up and keep all the good things that come to us through conversations and through reading, we would soon have great treasures of knowledge and wisdom.

1692—*The colonists of the Plymouth Church in Massachusetts voted unanimously on this day to supplement their old English Psalter, the tunes of which were often difficult to sing, with the* Bay Psalm Book. *This hymnal, also known as the* New England Version, *was first printed in 1640 by printer Stephen Daye and was the first book to be printed in British North America. Here is Psalm 23 as versified in the* Bay Psalm Book. *The versifications were done by a panel of Congregationalist clergymen, including Richard Mather (1596–1669), father of noted preacher Increase Mather (see July 9 and December 11).*

The Lord to me a shepherd is;
   Want therefore shall not I.
He in the folds of tender grass
   Doth cause me down to lie.

To waters calm me gently leads;
   Restore my soul doth he;
He doth in paths of righteousness
   For his name's sake lead me.

Yea though in valley of death's shade
   I walk, none ill I'll fear;
Because thou art with me, thy rod
   And staff my comfort are.

For me a table thou hast spread
   In presence of my foes;
Thou dost anoint my head with oil;
   My cup it overflows.

Goodness and mercy surely shall
   All my days follow me,
And in the Lord's house I shall dwell
   So long as days shall be.

1555—Robert Smith, an English clergyman, was martyred on this day for his faith. Instead of directing recrimination toward his persecutors, he left the following gentle advice in poetic form to his children, written shortly before his execution. It is called "The Exhortation of a Father to His Children."

Ye are the temples of the Lord,
    For ye are dearly bought;
And they that do defile the same
    Shall surely come to naught.

Possess not pride in any wise,
    Build not your house too high;
But have always before your eyes
    That ye be born to die.

Defraud not him that hired is,
    Your labor to sustain
But give him always out of hand,
    His penny for his pain.

And as you would that other men
    Against you should proceed,
Do you the same to them again
    When they do stand in need.

And part your portion with the poor
    In money and in meat;
And feed the fainted feeble soul
    With that which ye should eat.

Ask counsel always of the wise,
    Give ear unto the end;
Refuse not you the sweet rebuke
    of him that is your friend.

Be thankful always to the Lord,
    With prayer and with praise,
Desiring Him in all your works
    For to direct your ways.

1884—On this day, a woman named Irene H. Ovington dedicated her anthology of thoughts from the sermons of Henry Ward Beecher (1813–87) to "the many sorrowing ones of the earth"; her compilation is called Comforting Thoughts. Beecher, a popular American preacher of the time, was particularly known for his simple but vivid metaphors for describing the Christian experience, as the following thoughts about death show.

———— ❦ ————

• All burden-bearers may feel the touch of God and his strength. May those who have but little faith have at least the faith of the hem, and, touching the garment of Christ, may they know that there is healing in him. . . .

• To some, suffering comes only to make them howl and cry and whine, and ask to know how to get rid of it. Put the saddle of patience on your back, and say to suffering, "Mount and ride me"; and take the bit in your mouth and be "exercised." Be broken. Be trained. Be disciplined. Go through the drill. Bear your suffering till you know that you are master of it, as at first it was the master of you. . . .

• The grave is but the shutting of the angel hand that keeps the treasure and conveys it safely to the other side. As they who sail over the seas go down into the vessel and are hid, so the grave is but the resting place of the dead for a little time—not decay, not loss, not final separation in darkness. . . .

• Dying is like the folding of the flower. It is a gentle wind dying away. It is a tide flowing out to the depths beyond. It is a taper going out. It is a spark extinguished. It is a silent bird at twilight shooting through the sky, half rosy-lit, to its nest. . . .

• The world is but an out-building of creation. We have not seen the whole. What barns are to mansions, this world is to heaven. . . .

• God forbid that we should bury anything. There is no earth that can touch my companion. There is no earth that can touch my child. The jewel is not in the ground. The jewel is gone from the casket, and I have buried the casket, not the jewel.

1804—On this day, an English minister, Rev. Isaac Nicholson, wrote the preface for the first edition of A Treatise Upon Growth in Grace *by popular English preacher and writer Samuel Eyles Pierce (1746–1829). The following is one of Pierce's prayers from that work.*

————— ✦ —————

O Holy Father! It has pleased you to record in your Word the everlasting perfection of your Son Jesus Christ and his great salvation; and the revelation which you have made of it therein with your testimony is very clear and plain. I believe your record worthy of full credit, and the work of Jesus to be a finished salvation. Help me to walk with you in the true belief of your own authority and word. Grant me grace to live by faith, to walk by faith, to fight the good fight of faith, and to persevere in my spiritual warfare; believing that you "have given me eternal life, that this life is in your Son," and "that he who has the Son has life." Let me receive your word and oath as my full security for everlasting life.

O most blessed and precious Jesus! Keep me looking to you and leaning on you for everything. Be with me in my walk and warfare, in sickness and in death. When you bring me to it, let me glorify you by dying in the full belief of your everlasting and complete salvation, and of your complete victory over death and all the powers of darkness. Let me glorify you with my last breath by putting honor on you, as God-man Mediator, as "my all on earth" and "all in heaven."

O Holy Ghost! I bless you for all your divine teachings, gracious quickenings, comforts, and strengthenings. Keep, oh, keep my eye on Jesus, till I see him in eternal glory. In my last moments, when all the springs of natural life shall cease in me, fill me with hopes full of immortality. I ask it for the honor of Christ, the conqueror of death, who by his resurrection and ascension has opened the way into the holiest of all. To whom, with you, Holy Father, and you, blessed Spirit, be equal and unceasing praise. Amen.

1246—On this day Brothers Leo, Rufino, and Angelo, known as the "Three Companions," completed the writing of The Legend of St. *Francis, one of the earliest biographies of Francis of Assisi (1182–1226). All three men had been disciples of the saint. In the following excerpt, they recall how Francis encouraged his earliest disciples to go out into the world to tell people about the love of God.*

———————— ✌ ❧ ————————

Francis called the six brethren to him and foretold to them those things that were to come: "Dearest brethren, let us consider our vocation to which God in His mercy has called us, not so much for our own salvation as for that of the many; therefore, let us go through the world admonishing all people both by example and word to do penance and to be mindful of the commands of God. Fear not if you seem weak and despised and foolish, but with easy minds preach repentance in simplicity, trusting in the Lord who has overcome the world, for by His Spirit He speaks through you and in you to admonish all men to turn to Him and keep His commandments. You will find some people that are faithful, gentle, and gracious, who will receive you and your words with joy; and others, the larger part, will be faithless, proud, and blasphemous, who, with reviling, will oppose you, and against these you shall speak. Be it set, therefore, in your hearts to bear all things patiently and humbly."

And he gave them his blessing. And thus blessed the men of God departed, devoutly observing his behests. When they came on any church or wayside crucifix, they would bow in prayer and say devoutly, "We adore You, O Christ, and bless You in all Your churches in the whole world, for by Your Holy Cross You have redeemed the world." For Francis was persuaded that it was always a place of the Lord wherever they found even so much as one crucifix. And all the people who saw them marveled exceedingly, for in their habits and way of life they were unlike all others and seemed outlandish. Wherever they entered, be it city or castle or farm or house, they brought a message of peace, consoling all, and bidding them to fear and love the Maker of heaven and earth and to keep His commandments.

1837—Angelina Grimké (1805–79) and her sister, Sarah (1792–1873), were Quaker women known for their vocal opposition to slavery in the 1820s and 1830s, an opposition deeply rooted in their Christian faith. Angelina, in particular, was a powerful and gifted speaker, but she drew criticism from those who felt it unbiblical for women to speak in public, let alone from the pulpit. She was, therefore, almost inadvertently forced to defend the rights of women, and became one of the movement's earliest exponents, as the following letter, written on this day to one of her critics, shows.

———— ✺ ————

My Dear Brother,

No doubt thou hast heard by this time of all the fuss that is now making in this region about our stepping so far out of the bounds of female propriety as to lecture to promiscuous assemblies. My auditors literally sit sometimes with "mouths agape and eyes astare" so that I cannot help smiling in the midst of "rhetorical flourishes" to witness their perfect amazement at hearing a woman speak in the churches. . . . But seriously speaking, we are placed very unexpectedly in a very trying situation, in the forefront of an entirely new contest—a contest for the *rights of women* as a moral, intelligent, and responsible being. . . .

Who will stand by woman in the great struggle? As to our being Quakers being an *excuse* for our speaking in public, we do *not* stand on this ground at all, we ask *no* favors for ourselves, but *claim* rights for our *sex*. If it is wrong for woman to lecture or preach then let the Quakers give up their false views, and let other sects refuse to hear their women, but if it is *right* then let *all* women who have gifts "mind their calling" and enjoy "the liberty wherewith Christ has made them free," in that declaration of Paul, "in Christ Jesus there is neither male nor female." O! if in our intercourse with each other we realized this great truth, how delightful, ennobling, and dignified it would be, but as I told the Moral Reform Society of Boston in my address, *this* reformation *must begin with ourselves.*

—Angelina Grimké

1727—After years of divisiveness, a group of Christians in Herrnhut, Bohemia, began a revival at a Communion service under the direction of the young Count N. L. von Zinzendorf (1700–60; see also September 6). The renewed community became known as the Moravian Brethren. Moravian poet and hymn writer James Montgomery (1771–1854; see also October 14) described this day—"the birthday of the renewed church"—as follows:

They walked with God in peace and love,
    But failed with one another;
While sternly for the faith they strove,
    Brother fell out with brother;
But He in Whom they put their trust,
Who knew their frames that they were dust,
    Pitied and healed their weakness.

He found them in His house of prayer
    With one accord assembled,
And so revealed His presence there
    They wept for joy and trembled;
One cup they drank, one bread they break,
One baptism shared, one language spake,
    Forgiving and forgiven.

Then forth they went, with tongues of flame
    In one blest theme delighting,
The love of Jesus, and His name,
    God's children all uniting!
That love our theme and watchword still;
That law of love may we fulfill,
    And love as we are loved.

1955—Swiss theologian Karl Barth (1886–1968) was a brilliant and monumentally influential figure in modern theology and was called by one writer "the most notable Christian prophet of our times." In his writing and preaching, Barth worked to extricate the Christian faith from the trappings of culture, art, politics, technology, philosophy, and other trendy distractions of the modern church. He insisted, instead, on a wholehearted return to the essentials of Christian belief. A good example can be found in the following passage from a sermon he preached on this day to the prisoners at the Basle Prison in Switzerland. In it he takes Ephesians 2:5 as his text: "By grace you have been saved." It was later published in the collection Deliverance to the Captives.

———— ᴂᵹ ᶘᴥ ————

You probably all know the legend of the rider who crossed the frozen Lake of Constance by night without knowing it. When he reached the opposite shore and was told whence he came, he broke down, horrified. This is the human situation when the sky opens and the earth is bright, when we may hear: *By grace you have been saved!* In such a moment we are like that terrified rider. When we hear this word we involuntarily look back, do we not, asking ourselves: Where have I been? Over an abyss, in mortal danger! What did I do? The most foolish thing I ever attempted! What happened? I was doomed and miraculously escaped and now I am safe! You ask: "Do we really live in such danger?" Yes, we live on the brink of death. But we have been saved. Look at our Savior and at our Salvation! Look at Jesus Christ on the cross, accused, sentenced, and punished instead of us! Do you know for whose sake he is hanging there? For *our* sake—because of *our* sin—sharing *our* captivity—burdened with *our* suffering! He nails *our* life to the cross. This is how God had to deal with *us*. From this darkness he has saved *us*. He who is not shattered after hearing this news may not yet have grasped the word of God: *By grace you have been saved.*

—translated by Marguerite Wieser

c. 1280—Angela of Foligno (c. 1248–1309) was an Italian mystic and follower of Francis of Assisi. After the death of her husband, she converted and soon became famous for her piety and her many spiritual visions. On this day, shortly after her conversion, she prayed that God would inform her of the authenticity of her visions, or "conversations," as she called them, for she feared that perhaps they were merely imaginary. She was rewarded with the following assurance. (See also January 3.)

———————— ·◦§ §◦· ————————

Then came to me a heavenly voice promising me that my request should be granted and saying further: "God has shown Himself to you, has spoken with you, and has endowed you with understanding of Himself; take heed, therefore, that you neither speak, behold, nor hearken to anything whatsoever save according to His will." I perceived that these things were said to me with much discretion and ripe wisdom. The aforesaid conversations had left me with great joy and the hope of obtaining that for which I had asked, and the foregoing words did, moreover, tell me that God would grant the grace that everything I did should be done with His permission.

I began therefore, to do the three things which had been told to me. Accordingly my heart was uplifted from all things earthly and fixed on God. And nothing that I did or ate or spoke prevented my heart from being always fixed on God; neither could I see or think or feel save according unto God's will. . . .

This lasted three days and three nights. Finally I beheld God in spirit during Mass at about the time of the elevation of the Body of Christ. After this vision there remained with me an indescribable sweetness and great joy, which I do think will never fail me all the days of my life. And in this vision was I assured of all that I had asked; there remained in me no doubt whatsoever, but I was fully satisfied and persuaded that I had not been deceived in the foregoing conversations.

—from Angela of Foligno's *Book of Divine Consolation,*
translated by Mary G. Steegmann

1578—Spanish monk, poet, and mystic St. John of the Cross (1542–91) escaped imprisonment on this day after eight months of captivity. During that time he is believed to have written his most famous poem, "The Dark Night of the Soul," an abridged version of which follows. In the amatory style of the Song of Solomon, John describes the soul's longing for union with Christ. (For part of John's own interpretation of this poem, see December 2.)

On a dark night,
Burning with the longings of love—
Oh happy circumstance!—
I slipped out of my house unnoticed,
While all within lay sleeping. . . .

Secretly, in the night,
Where no one saw me,
And where I saw no one,
I went out with no light to guide me
Except that which burned in my heart.

It led me farther on,
As clearly as the midday sun,
To where He waited—
He whom I know so well—
To a place where no one else appeared.

O night that guided me!
O night more lovely than the dawn!
O night that joined
The lover to the Beloved One,
Transforming the lover into the Beloved One. . . .

And there I stayed
And leaned my head on the Beloved,
And everything seemed to vanish
As I lost myself in Him and left
All my cares forgotten among the lilies.

1919—William Temple (1881–1944) was an outstanding English preacher and theologian between the wars. (See May 19.) One might call him an Anglican by heredity, since he was the son of an Archbishop of Canterbury. Temple himself became the Archbishop of Canterbury during World War II. Known for his concern for the poor, he preached, on this day, a sermon entitled "Inasmuch" in Westminster Abbey, the concluding portion of which is given here.

———————— ⋙⋘ ————————

It is Christ who pines when the poor are hungry; it is Christ who is repulsed when strangers are not welcome; it is Christ who suffers when rags fail to keep out the cold; it is Christ who is in anguish in the long-drawn illness; it is Christ who waits behind the prison doors. You come upon one of those who have been broken by the tempests of life, and if you look with eyes of Christian faith and love, he will lift a brow "luminous and imperial from the rags," and you will know that you are standing before the King of Kings, Lord of Lords.

Christ brought to the world a new conception of royalty. He rules by love and not by force. That, as he expressly said, is the difference between his Kingdom and the kingdoms of this world. His most regal act was the supreme self-sacrifice whereby he would draw all men to himself and make them willingly obedient to him forever. In full harmony with this, he never speaks of himself as King except on one occasion only, . . . when, in the parable of the sheep and the goats, he identifies himself with the failures of the world and the outcasts of society. "Then shall the King say unto them on his right hand. . . . I was an hungered and ye gave me meat; I was a stranger and ye took me in; naked and ye clothed me; I was sick and ye visited me; I was in prison, and ye came unto me."

Civilization, as we know it, produces much human refuse. Slum dwellings, long hours of work, underpayment, child labor, lack of education, prostitution—all these evils are responsible for stunting and warping the development of souls. Things are improving, we hope. But unless we are exerting all the strength that Christ gives us in ending these bad conditions, then the responsibility for wasted lives lies at our door, and from the streets of cities or the lanes of countrysides the cry goes up through the lips of their Savior and our Judge: "Inasmuch as ye did it not unto one of these least, ye did it not unto me."

1688—John Bunyan (1628–88) is perhaps the most beloved of all English religious writers, and his classic Pilgrim's Progress *is still read by millions in dozens of languages (see also February 18). He was a Nonconformist preacher who spent much time in prison for his faith. On this day, he preached his final sermon, a portion of which is quoted below. In it, he compares the birth of a child to the believer's new life in Christ. Bunyan died two weeks later.*

———— ✺ ————

A child, you know is [inclined] to cry as soon as it comes into the world; for if there be no noise, they say it is dead. You that are born of God and Christians, if you be not criers, there is no spiritual life in you; if you be born of God, you are crying ones; as soon as he has raised you out of the dark dungeon of sin, you cannot but cry to God, "What must I do to be saved?" As soon as ever God had touched the jailer, he cries out, "Men and brethren, what must I do to be saved?" ...

A child that is newly born, if it have not other comforts to keep it warm than it had in its mother's womb, it dies. It must have something for its succor; so Christ had swaddling clothes prepared for him; so those that are born again, they must have some promise of Christ to keep them alive. Those that are in a carnal state, they warm themselves with other things, but those that are born again, they cannot live without some promise of Christ to keep them alive, as he did the poor infant in Ezekiel 17: "I covered you with embroidered gold." And when women are with child, what fine things they will prepare for their child! Oh, but what fine things has Christ prepared to wrap all in that are born again! Oh, what wrappings of gold has Christ prepared for all that are born again! Women will dress their children, that everyone may see them [and] how fine they are; so he in Ezekiel 16:11: "I decked you also with ornaments, and I also put bracelets upon your hands and a chain on your neck. And I put a jewel on your forehead," and he says in the thirteenth verse: "You did gain a kingdom." This is to set out nothing in the world but the righteousness of Christ and the graces of the spirit, without which a newborn babe cannot live, unless he have the golden righteousness of Christ.

1565—The name John Knox (1505–72) is synonymous with the Scottish Reformation. Not only was Knox a writer, preacher, and statesman, but he was also one of the founders of the Presbyterian Church. In our own time many churches still bear his name. On this day in Edinburgh, Scotland, Knox delivered one of his most famous sermons, "A Sermon on Isaiah 26." The following passage from that sermon beautifully explains Isaiah 26:19: "Your dead shall live, together with my dead body shall they arise. Awake and sing, you that dwell in dust; for your dew is as the dew of the herbs, and the earth shall cast out the dead."

———————— ⋅⊰ ⊱⋅ ————————

Do you think this impossible—that God should give life to you and bring you to a state of commonwealth again after you are dead? But why do you not consider what God works from year to year in the order of nature? Sometimes you see the face of the earth decked and beautified with herbs, flowers, grass, and fruits; again you see the same utterly taken away by storms and the vehemence of the winter. What does God do to replenish the earth again and to restore the beauty thereof? He sends down his small and soft dew, the drops of which, in their descending, are neither great nor visible, and yet thereby are the pores and secret veins of the earth, which before by vehemence of frost and cold, were shut up, opened again, and so does the earth produce again the herbs, flowers, and fruits. Shall you then think that the dew of God's heavenly grace will not be as effectual in you to whom he has made his promise, as it is in the herbs and fruits, which from year to year bud forth and decay? If you do not think so, the prophet would say your incredulity is inexcusable because you neither rightly weigh the power nor the promise of your God. . . .

Now, if the power of God is so manifest in raising up the fruits of the earth, to which no particular promise is made by God, what shall be his power and virtue in raising up our bodies, seeing that he is bound to do so by the solemn promise of Jesus Christ, by his eternal wisdom, and by the Verity itself that cannot lie? Yea, seeing that the members must once communicate with the glory of the Head, how shall our bodies, which are flesh of his flesh and bone of his bones, lie still forever in corruption, seeing that our Head, Jesus Christ, is now exalted in his glory?

1153—Bernard of Clairvaux (1091–1153) died on this day, and the church has since honored August 20 in his memory. Bernard was a French Cistercian monk, a writer and mystic, and a staunch opponent of rationalistic theology. He was beloved for his sublime writings and warm spirituality. Perhaps his most beautiful work is his On Loving God. *The following passage from that work seems particularly appropriate on this day when Bernard went to be with the Lord.*

──────── ◦§ §◦ ────────

Since Scripture says that God made everything for Himself, a day will come when the creation conforms itself to the Creator and is in complete accord with Him. Consequently, it is necessary for us to enter into a state in which, just as God willed that everything exist for Himself, we too must desire to exist not for ourselves or anything else, nor seeking our own pleasure, but for His will alone. What will make us rejoice in that day will not be so much the satisfying of our own needs or attaining happiness as the final accomplishment of His will in us. That is what we ask of Him each day when we pray, "Your will be done on earth as it is in heaven." O holy and pure love! O sweet and pleasant affection! O pure and uncorrupted intention of the will, all the more pure and uncorrupted because it is unmixed with our own selfish will, all the more sweet and pleasant because all that is within it is divine! It is deifying to arrive at such a state. Just as a drop of water seems to lose itself entirely in a large quantity of wine, assuming the wine's own savor and color; just as red hot iron seems to become so much like fire that it loses its original character; just as the air, full of sunlight, is not just illumined but transformed by the brilliance of that light—so too it is necessary among the saints for all human affections to be melted down so that they can entirely flow, if one may express it that way, into the will of God. Otherwise, how will God be all in all if something human remains? Certainly, our human substance will remain but in another form, with another glory, with another power. When will this happen? Who will see and possess such things? . . . Do you think, Lord, I will ever see Your holy temple?

As for myself, I believe I shall, but not before having perfectly fulfilled the commandment: "You shall love the Lord your God with all your heart, soul, and strength, and your neighbor as yourself."

1864—Chambers' Book of Days *was a popular book of family reference and entertainment in the last half of the nineteenth century. Edited by Scottish author and publisher Robert Chambers (1802–71), it gathered together readings, as the title page states, "connected with the calendar including anecdote, biography, and history, curiosities of literature and oddities of human life and character." For this day, Chambers records what he calls a "Curious Prayer" (which he says he found in an old book called* Fog's Journal) *as a satiric example of the kind of selfish prayer wealthy people are too apt to pray.*

⎯⎯⎯⎯ ⋖ৡ ৡ⋗ ⎯⎯⎯⎯

O Lord, Thou knowest that I have nine houses in the city of London, and likewise that I have lately purchased an estate in . . . the county of Essex. Lord, I beseech Thee to preserve the two counties of Essex and Middlesex from fires and earthquakes; and as I have a mortgage in Hertfordshire, I beseech Thee likewise to have an eye of compassion on that county. And, Lord, for the rest of the counties, Thou mayest deal with them as Thou art pleased. O Lord, enable the Bank to answer all their bills and make all my debtors good men. Give a prosperous voyage and return to the *Mermaid* sloop, which I have insured; and Lord, Thou hast said, "that the days of the wicked are short," and I trust Thou wilt not forget Thy promises, having purchased an estate in reversion of Sir J. P., a profligate young man. Lord, keep our funds from sinking; and if it be Thy will, let there be no sinking funds. Keep my son Caleb out of evil company and gaming houses. And sanctify, O Lord, this night to me by preserving me from thieves and fire, and make my servant honest and careful, whilst I, Thy servant, lie down in Thee, O Lord. Amen.

1535—Along with Martin Luther, French theologian John Calvin (1509–64) was the preeminent personality behind the Protestant Reformation of the sixteenth century. Calvin's greatest work, The Institutes of Christian Religion, *was written in Latin and is believed to have been completed on or shortly before this day. It was published in the spring of the next year. The lengthy* Institutes *are a comprehensive text of Reformation doctrine, stressing God's sovereignty, man's fallen nature, and the primacy of Scripture. This last point is elegantly made in the following extract from* The Institutes.

———————— ·ঙ্গ ঙ্গ· ————————

As persons who are old or whose eyes are by any means become dim, if you show them the most beautiful book, though they perceive something written, can but scarcely read two words together, yet, by the assistance of spectacles, will begin to read distinctly—so the Scripture, collecting in our minds the otherwise confused notions of Deity, dispels the darkness and gives us a clear view of the true God. This, then, is a singular favor that, in the instruction of the Church, God not only uses mute teachers, but even opens his own sacred mouth; not only proclaims that some god ought to be worshiped, but at the same time pronounces himself to be the Being to whom this worship is due; and not only teaches the elect to raise their view to a Deity, but also exhibits himself as the object of their contemplation. This method he has observed toward his church from the beginning; besides those common lessons of instruction, to afford them also his word, which furnishes a more correct and certain criterion to distinguish him from all fictitious deities.... Therefore, though every man should seriously apply himself to a consideration of the works of God, being placed in this very splendid theater to be a spectator of them, yet he ought principally to attend to the word that he may attain superior advantages.... No man can have the least knowledge of true and sound doctrine without having been a disciple of the Scripture. Hence originates all true wisdom, when we embrace with reverence the testimony that God has been pleased to deliver concerning himself.... "The law of the Lord is perfect, converting the soul: the testimony of the Lord is sure, making wise the simple: the statutes of the Lord are right, rejoicing the heart: the commandment of the Lord is pure, enlightening the eyes" (Psalm 19:7–8).

—translated by John Allen (1813)

c. 107—Ignatius (c. 35–c. 107), Bishop of Antioch, wrote a letter to the Christians in Rome on this day. He wrote it from Smyrna while under the guard of Roman soldiers who were taking him to Rome to be executed for his faith. Tradition says that he was martyred in the infamous Colosseum. In this letter (which is considered authentic by most scholars), he pleads with his fellow Christians in Rome not to attempt to intercede in his behalf when he arrives.

———————— ≈§ §≈ ————————

I am willing to die for God, unless you hinder me. I beseech you not to show an unseasonable good will toward me. Allow me to be food of the wild beasts by whom I shall attain to God. For I am the wheat of God, and I shall be ground by the teeth of the wild beasts so that I may be found the pure bread of Christ. . . . From Syria even to Rome, I fight with beasts both by sea and land, both night and day, being bound to ten leopards—that is to say, to such a band of soldiers who, though they treat me with all manner of kindness, are the worse for it. . . .

Pardon me in this matter; I know what is profitable for me. Now I begin to be a disciple. Nor shall anything dissuade me, whether visible or invisible, that I may attain to Jesus Christ. Let fire and the cross, let the companies of wild beasts, let the breakings of bones and tearing of members, let the shattering in pieces of the whole body, and all the wicked torments of the devil come upon me—only let me enjoy Jesus Christ. All the ends of the world and all its kingdoms will profit me nothing. I would rather die for Jesus Christ than rule to the utmost ends of the earth. Him I seek who died for us; him I desire that rose again for us. This is the gain that is laid up for me. Pardon me, my brethren, you shall not hinder me from living, nor, seeing I desire to go to God, can you separate me from him for the sake of this world, nor reduce me by any of the desires of it. Suffer me to enter into pure light, where I shall be indeed the servant of God.

—translator unknown

410—St. Augustine (354–430) was the Bishop of Hippo, a city in northern Africa, and one of the most influential and prolific theological writers of all time. He was responsible for defeating many heretical doctrines that threatened the early church, and his autobiography, The Confessions, *is still widely read and justifiably admired. Augustine lived during the final collapse of the Roman empire, and after a barbarian army began an invasion of Rome on this day, many Christians wondered why God would allow their holy city to be sacked. Augustine was moved to respond by writing his greatest work,* The City of God. *In the following excerpt Augustine asks some hard questions of those who feel that God had abandoned Rome.*

They [the Christians in Rome] lost all that they had. What? Their faith? Their zeal? Their goods of the inward man, which enrich the soul before God? These are a Christian's riches. . . .

The extremity of famine, they say, destroyed many Christians in these invasions. Well, even of this also the faithful, by enduring it faithfully, have made good use. For such as the famine made an end of, it delivered from the evils of this life as well as any other bodily disease could do; such as it ended not, it taught them a sparing diet and the ability to fast. Yes, but many Christians were destroyed by the foulest variety of means that might be, falling by so many sorts of death; but this ought not to be a burden grievous to be endured, since it is common to all that ever have been born. . . . A bad death never follows a good life, for there is nothing that makes death bad but that estate that follows death. Therefore let not our concern for those who needs must die be employed upon the manner of their death, but upon the estate that they are eternally to inherit after death. Wherefore seeing that all Christians know that the death of the religious beggar amongst the dogs, licking his sores, was better than the death of the wicked rich man in all his silks and purples, what power does the horror of any kind of death have to affright their souls who have led a virtuous life?

—translated by John Healey (1620)

1832—Albert Barnes (1798–1870) was an American Presbyterian clergy-man whose Bible commentary, Notes, Explanatory and Practical, on the Gospels, *was once widely used in Sunday schools and Bible classes. On this day he wrote the preface to the first edition of that work, and the following is his gloss of Matthew 6:6: "When you pray enter into your closet, and, when you have shut your door, pray to your father who is in secret; and your Father, who sees in secret, shall reward you openly."*

———————— ⋅≈§ ξ≈⋅ ————————

The Savior does not specify the times when we should pray in secret. He does not say how often it should be done.... Yet without giving rules—where the Savior has given none—we may suggest the following as times when secret prayer is proper. (1) In the morning.... (2) In the evening.... (3) We should pray in times of embarrassment and perplexity.... (4) We should pray when we are beset with strong temptations.... (5) We should pray when the Spirit prompts us to pray; when we feel just like praying; when nothing can satisfy the soul but prayer. Such times occur in the life of every Christian—and they are "springtimes" of piety—favorable gales to waft us on to heaven. Prayer to the Christian at such times is just as congenial as conversation with a friend when the bosom is filled with love; as the society of father, mother, sister, child is when the heart glows with attachment; as the strains of sweet music are to the ear best attuned to the love of harmony; as the most exquisite poetry is to the heart enamored with the muses; and as the most delicious banquet is to the hungry. Prayer, then, is the element of being; the breath; the vital air; and then the Christian must and should pray. He is the most eminent Christian who is most favored with such strong emotions urging him to prayer. The heart is full. The soul is tender. The sun of glory shines with unusual splendor. No cloud intervenes. The Christian rises from the earth and pants for glory.

1772—American Quaker John Woolman (1720–72) was an itinerant preacher and passionate abolitionist. His Journals, published posthumously in 1774, continue to be read and loved, and they are considered one of the great documents of Christian social conscience. On this day, near the end of his life, he wrote in his journal, "I feel a concern to commit to writing that which to me hath been a case uncommon." He then related a dream that he had had during a severe illness more than two and a half years before.

———— ❧ ❦ ————

I heard a soft melodious voice, more pure and harmonious than any I had heard with my ears before; I believed it was the voice of an angel who spoke to the other angels; the words were, "John Woolman is dead." I soon remembered that I once was John Woolman, and being assured that I was alive in the body, I greatly wondered what the heavenly voice could mean. I believed beyond doubting that it was the voice of a holy angel. . . .

All this time the song of the angel remained a mystery; and in the morning, my dear wife and some others coming to my bedside, I asked them if they knew who I was, and they, telling me I was John Woolman, thought I was light-headed, for I told them not what the angel said, nor was I disposed to talk much to anyone but was very desirous to get so deep that I might understand this mystery.

My tongue was often so dry that I could not speak till I had moved it about and gathered some moisture, and as I lay still for a time, at length I felt Divine power prepare my mouth that I could speak, and I then said, "I am crucified with Christ, nevertheless I live; yet not I, but Christ lives in me. And the life which I now live in the flesh I live by the faith of the Son of God, who loved me and gave himself for me." Then the mystery was opened, and I perceived there was joy in heaven over a sinner who had repented and that the language "John Woolman is dead" meant no more than the death of my own will.

1819—On this day English visionary poet and artist William Blake (1757– 1827) sold a copy of his most famous collection of "illuminated" poetry, Songs of Innocence and Experience, *to his friend and patron John Linnell (1792–1882). Only a handful of original copies are now known to exist. Blake meticulously engraved, hand printed, and hand colored numerous illustrated books in small editions, many of them containing his prophetic visions in verse form. Today they are some of the most cherished and priceless books of all time. (See also December 30.) The following tender children's poem from* Songs of Innocence and Experience *is called "On Another's Sorrow."*

Can I see another's woe,
And not be in sorrow too?
Can I see another's grief,
And not seek for kind relief?

Can I see a falling tear,
And not feel my sorrow's share?
Can a father see his child
Weep, nor be with sorrow filled?

Can a mother sit and hear
An infant groan, an infant fear?
No, no! never can it be!
Never, never can it be!

And can he who smiles on all
Hear the wren with sorrows small,
Hear the small bird's grief & care,
Hear the woes that infants bear,

And not sit beside the nest,
Pouring pity in their breast;
And not sit the cradle near,
Weeping tear on infant's tear;

Wiping all our tears away?
And not sit both night & day,
O! no, never can it be!
Never, never can it be!

He doth give his joy to all;
He becomes an infant small;
He becomes a man of woe;
He doth feel the sorrow too.

Think not thou canst sigh a sigh,
And thy maker is not by;
Think not thou canst weep a tear,
And thy maker is not near.

O! he gives to us his joy
That our grief he may destroy;
Till our grief is fled & gone
He doth sit by us and moan.

1812—While traveling through Persia on this day, a month and a half before his death from fever, English missionary Henry Martyn (1781–1812) wrote his last letter to his fiancée, Lydia Grenfell. Martyn's goal was to spread the Gospel throughout Persia and convert the Sufis (Muslim mystics). Shunning the conventional techniques of missionary endeavor, Martyn was known for boldly adopting Persian dress and customs so that he might more effectively reach the people.

I wrote to you last, my dear Lydia, in great disorder. My fever had approached nearly to delirium, and my debility was so great that it seemed impossible I could withstand the power of disease many days. Yet it has pleased God to restore me to life and health again; not that I have recovered my former strength yet but consider myself sufficiently restored to prosecute my journey. My daily prayer is that my late chastisement may have its intended effect and make me all the rest of my days more humble and less self-confident. Self-confidence has often let me down fearful lengths and would, without God's gracious interference, prove my endless perdition. I seem to be made to feel this evil of my heart more than any other at this time. In prayer, or when I write or converse on the subject, Christ appears to me my life and strength; but at other times I am as thoughtless and bold as if I had all life and strength in myself. Such neglect on our part works a diminution of our joys; but the covenant, the covenant! stands fast with Him, for His people evermore. I mentioned my conversing sometimes on Divine subjects, for though it is long enough since I have seen a child of God, I am sometimes led on by the Persians to tell them all I know of the very recesses of the sanctuary, and these are the things that interest them. But to give an account of all my discussion with these mystic philosophers must be reserved to the time of our meeting. Do I dream? That I venture to think and write of such an event as that? Is it possible that we shall ever meet again below? Though it is possible, I dare not indulge such a pleasing hope yet. I am still at a tremendous distance, and the countries I have to pass through are many of them dangerous to the traveler. . . . But I trust I shall shortly see thee face to face.

Believe me to be yours ever, most faithful and affectionately, H. Martyn

—from *The Life and Letters of Henry Martyn* (1819)

1923—On this day American hymnologist Carl F. Price (1881–1948) wrote the preface to his popular volume One Hundred and One Hymn Stories, *in which he states: "Every hymn has a real story, if only we could discover it." The following is typical of the stories that Price was able to uncover. It concerns the author of the hymn "I Love to Steal Away Awhile," Phebe Hinsdale Brown (1783–1861), who was married to a poor Connecticut house-painter and took care of four children and a bed-ridden sister.*

Therefore at twilight she would frequently slip away from home and walk alone along the road as far as the garden of the next house, where the fragrance of the flowers and the beauty of the sunset hour gave her opportunity for meditation and communion with God. But her neighbors wondered, and gossips talked, and the woman who owned the garden once asked her somewhat haughtily: "Mrs. Brown, why do you come up at evening so near our house and then go back without coming in? If you want anything, why don't you come in and ask for it?"

That night, with all the children abed, save the baby in her arms, she burst into tears. Taking a pen, she wrote in verse, "An Apology for My Twilight Rambles, Addressed to a Lady," from which the verses of this hymn are taken.

I love to steal away awhile
From every cumbering care,
And spend the hours of setting day
In humble, grateful prayer.

I love in solitude to shed
The penitential tear,
And all his promises to plead
Where none but God can hear.

I love to think on mercies past,
And future good implore,
And all my cares and sorrows cast
On him whom I adore.

1866—Robert Stephen Hawker (1803–75) was an English poet and clergyman who served as vicar of Morwenstow in Cornwall. His lovely poetry is sadly neglected in our time. On this day, he wrote the poem "A Thought," which was inspired by his reading of Genesis 18:1–3: "And the Lord appeared to [Abraham] in the plains of Mamre: and he sat in the tent door in the heat of the day; and he lifted up his eyes and looked, and, lo, three men stood by him: and when he saw them, he ran to meet them from the tent door, and bowed himself toward the ground, and said, 'My Lord, if now I have found favor in your sight, pass not away, I pray you, from your servant.'"

A fair and stately scene of roof and walls
Touched by the ruddy sunsets of the west,
Where, meek and molten, eve's soft radiance falls
Like golden feathers in the ringdove's nest.

Yonder the bounding sea, that couch of God!
A wavy wilderness of sand between;
Such pavement, in the Syrian deserts, trod
Bright forms, in girded albs, of heavenly mien.

Such saw the patriarch in his noonday tent:
Three severed shapes that glided in the sun,
Till lo, they cling, and, interfused and blent,
A lovely semblance gleams, the three in one!

Be such the scenery of this peaceful ground,
This leafy tent amid the wilderness;
Fair skies above, the breath of angels round,
And God the Trinity to beam and bless.

1656—Thomas Watson (who died in 1686) was a Puritan preacher and pastor of St. Stephen's Church, Walbrook, in London, England. On this day, at St. Paul's Cathedral, before the lord mayor and aldermen of London, he preached his most famous sermon, called "The One Thing Necessary"—that is, salvation. In this excerpt, he defines three things conducive to salvation.

The first is . . . "fear and trembling." This is not a fear of doubting, but a fear of diligence. This fear is requisite in the working out of salvation. "Let us fear lest we come short" (Hebrews 4:1). Fear is a remedy against presumption. Fear is that flaming sword that turns every way to keep sin from entering. Fear quickens; it is an antidote against sloth. "Noah, being moved with fear, prepared an ark" (Hebrews 11:8). The traveler, fearing lest night should overtake him before he gets to his journey's end, spurs on the faster. . . .

Secondly, another great help in working out salvation is love. Love makes the work come off with delight. Seven years' labor seemed as nothing to Jacob because of the love that he bore for Rachel. Love facilitates everything. It is like wings to the bird, like wheels to the chariot, like sails to the ship. It carries on swiftly and cheerfully in duty. Love is never weary. It is an excellent saying of Gregory, "Let but a man get the love of the world in his heart, and he will quickly be rich." So if you will but get the love of religion in your heart, you will quickly be rich in grace. Love is a vigorous, active grace. It despises dangers; it tramples upon difficulties. Like a mighty torrent, it carries all before it. This is the grace which takes heaven by violence. Get but your hearts well heated with this grace and you will be fitted for work. . . .

Lastly, work in hope. The Apostle said, "He that plows shall plow in hope" (1 Corinthians 9:10). Hope is the soul's anchor (Hebrews 6:19). Cast this anchor upon the promise, and you shall never sink. Nothing more hinders us in our working than unbelief. "Sure," said a Christian, "I may toil all the day and catch nothing." What? Is there no balm in Gilead? Is there no mercy seat? Oh, sprinkle faith in every duty, look up to free grace, fix your eye upon the blood of Christ. Would you be saved? To your working, join believing.

September

❧ ❧

Francis of Assisi preaching to the birds (see September 16).
Illustration based on a painting by Giotto.

1909—American clergyman and journalist William Allen Knight (1863–1957) was known for his warmhearted parables about working people and what the simple details of Jesus' life mean to them. His most famous book is The Song of the Syrian Guest. *On this day was published his fictional story* The Shepherd of Jebel Nur, *which portrays a thoughtful aged shepherd in the modern Middle East as he ponders the meaning of Christ's role as a shepherd. The shepherd speaks:*

————— ⋙ ⋘ —————

When [Jesus] saw the multitudes, you know how he was moved with compassion because they seemed distressed and scattered like sheep having no shepherd. When he sought to show his love for a little child in the rough world or a wayward one lost and helpless, he talked of the shepherd leaving the many safe in the fold and going into the mountains seeking the one stray and bringing it in—"laying it on his shoulder," says he—and rejoicing over it most of all. When his heart rose within him at the last to forgive a sinning old fisherman and let the man know that he would trust him still—do you not remember?—he said naught of making him a fisher of men as he did at first; but right there, with boats and nets all about, the best words he could find were: "Feed my lambs—tend my sheep."

And strangest of all—I never cease wondering at this, sirs—in all he ever said about giving his life for men, he found no words so fine for his fullest utterance about that as when he talked of the flock and the fold and the door and the pasture, of thief and wolf, and the shepherd laying down his life for the sheep. Aye! A bonny thing that—a bonny thing to think on!

1897—Canadian-American minister Albert Benjamin Simpson (1844– 1919) was a tireless evangelist, the founder of Christian and Missionary Alliance, and the author of more than seventy books. In his preaching he stressed what he called "the four-fold gospel": that is, Christ as "Savior, Sanctifier, Healer, and Coming King." In 1897 he published a daily devotional book entitled Days of Heaven upon Earth: A Year Book of Scripture Texts and Living Truths. *The following is Simpson's reflection for this day, September 2, and he takes as his Scripture text Zechariah 4:10: "Who has despised the day of small things?"*

———— ⋖§ §⋗ ————

The oak comes out of the acorn, the eagle out of that little egg in the nest, the harvest comes out of the seed; and so the glory of the coming age is all coming out of the Christ life now, even as the majesty of His kingdom was all wrapped up that night in the babe of Bethlehem.

Oh, let us take Him for all our life. Let us be united to His person and His risen body. Let us know what it is to say, "The Lord is for the body and the body is for the Lord!" We are members of His body and His flesh and His bones.

He that gave that little infant, His own blessed babe and His only begotten Son, on that dark winter night to the arms of a cruel and ungrateful world, will not refuse to give Him in all His fullness to your heart if you will but open your heart and give Him right of way and full ownership and possession. Then shall you know in your measure His quickening life, even in this earthly life, and by-and-by your hope shall reach its full fruition when you shall sit with Him on His throne with every fiber of your immortal being even as He.

1516—Sir Thomas More (1478–1535) was an author, a statesman, and the Lord Chancellor of England during the reign of Henry VIII. He was also a close friend of Dutch scholar Desiderius Erasmus (c. 1466–1536), a leading figure of the Renaissance. On this day More sent Erasmus the Latin manuscript of a book More had just completed, a satirical fantasy called Utopia, *which is now regarded as a masterpiece of world literature.* Utopia *(meaning "Nowhere") is a mythical place where peace and balance rule. More creates a world of harmony and toleration that contrasts sharply with the present world. Here he describes the Utopian form of worship.*

———— ◦§ §◦ ————

In one thing they very much exceed us: all their music, both vocal and instrumental, is adapted to imitate and express the passions, and is so happily suited to every occasion that . . . [it] affects and kindles the passions, and works the sentiments deep into the hearts of the hearers. When this is done, both priests and people offer up very solemn prayers to God in a set form of words; and these are so composed that whatsoever is pronounced by the whole assembly may be likewise applied by every man in particular to his own condition. In these they acknowledge God to be the author and governor of the world, and the fountain of all the good they receive, and therefore offer up to Him their thanksgiving; and in particular bless Him for His goodness in ordering it so that they are born under the happiest government in the world and are of a religion that they hope is the truest of all others: but if they are mistaken, and if there is either a better government or a religion more acceptable to God, they implore Him to let them know it, vowing that they resolve to follow Him whithersoever He leads them. . . . Then they pray that God may give them an easy passage at last to Himself; not presuming to set limits to Him, how early or late it should be; but if it may be wished for, without derogating from His supreme authority, they desire to be quickly delivered and to be taken to Himself, though by the most terrible kind of death, rather than to be detained long from seeing Him by the most prosperous course of life. When this prayer is ended, they all fall down again upon the ground, and after a little while they rise up, go home to dinner, and spend the rest of the day in diversion or military exercises.

—translator unknown

1847—Scotsman Henry Francis Lyte (1793–1847) ministered to the poor fishermen of Lower Brixham, Devonshire, England, for twenty-three years. According to his daughter Anna, Lyte wrote his most famous hymn, "Abide with Me," on this day, though there is considerable evidence that the hymn was actually written before this time. Lyte, in rapidly failing health and having delivered his final sermon in Brixham, walked a solitary garden path toward the sea, where he is said to have composed the words to this hymn. When he died only a few weeks later, his final words were, "Peace! Joy!"

Abide with me; fast falls the eventide;
The darkness deepens; Lord, with me abide.
When other helpers fail, and comforts flee,
Help of the helpless, O abide with me.

Swift to its close ebbs our life's little day;
Earth's joys grow dim, its glories pass away;
Change and decay in all around I see;
O Thou who changest not, abide with me.

I need Thy presence every passing hour;
What but Thy grace can foil the tempter's power?
Who like Thyself my guide and stay can be?
Through cloud and sunshine, O abide with me.

I fear no foe with Thee at hand to bless;
Ills have no weight, and tears no bitterness.
Where is death's sting? where, grave, thy victory?
I triumph still, if Thou abide with me.

Hold Thou Thy cross before my closing eyes;
Shine through the gloom, and point me to the skies.
Heaven's morning breaks, and earth's vain shadows flee.
In life, in death, O Lord, abide with me.

1872—American poet Marian Longfellow was the niece of poet Henry Wadsworth Longfellow (1807–82) and the author of many beautiful devotional poems. On this day she wrote a poem entitled "Litany." The Latin phrase that ends each stanza, "Jesu, audi nos," is taken from the Latin Mass and means "Jesus, hear us."

By thy sorrow and thy pain,
By thy form once bruised and slain,
By thy blood poured out like rain—
    Jesu, audi nos!

By thy toil and bitter grief,
By thy tears without relief,
By thy life so grand, so brief—
    Jesu, audi nos!

By thy death and agony,
By thy sweet humility,
By thy boundless charity—
    Jesu, audi nos!

By thy Resurrection morn,
By thy glorious face that shone,
O thou Holy, Sinless One!
    Jesu, audi nos!

1746—Nikolaus Ludwig Count von Zinzendorf (1700–60), a German nobleman, helped to organize the Moravian Brethren in 1737. (See also August 13.) Because of persecution, Zinzendorf and the Moravians first moved to London, then to the Americas in 1741. On this day, in the Brethren's Chapel in London, England, Zinzendorf, now Bishop of the Moravian church, delivered one of his most famous sermons, "Concerning Saving Faith," an excerpt of which follows.

In the Savior's affairs [Peter] was not just a natural, unconverted, unfamiliar man (which indeed is in itself sin enough), but rather he was a deliberate denier, what today is called a renegade. He would rather not know his Lord; he was ashamed of his Lord; he abjured his Lord three times. And a few days later his Lord came up and rose from the dead and was loved by those people who had followed Him to death itself, by the women who had helped to place Him into the grave and who came back at early dawn and looked for Him out of love. "Ah," says the Savior to them, "you dear children, I absolutely beg of you not to delay here with me, but go and tell my Peter that I am here again" (Mark 16:7 paraphrased).

This must have been an astonishing message to Peter. Was this all his punishment, to be notified that his Lord is risen again? And if so, should he have been the very first who was comforted, whose heart was revived? Thus, when the Savior said to him afterward, "Do you love me more than these do?" he said, "You know all things; you know how much I love you" (John 21:15ff.). And at that time he really did love Him more than all the others. Before he had loved Him in his imagination; he had honored Him and out of esteem for Him had rashly claimed to be ready to suffer death for Him rather than forsake Him. He did make a bold beginning, but he got stuck, because his love was dry and intellectual. But when the Savior forgave him everything, when He acquitted him of his sins, when He declared a renegade to be His apostle, then Peter could hold back no longer. If anyone said anything about his Lord to him, tears filled his eyes, and his body and soul were humbled. Already in the high priest's palace the bare presentiment of the character of his Lord had made his eyes fountains of tears.

—from Zinzendorf's *Nine Public Lectures*,
translated by George W. Forell

1853—American pastor and missionary Rev. William Scott Downey (see also August 1), on this day, received a letter from the secretary of England's Queen Victoria, acknowledging receipt of Downey's gift of his recently published book, Downey's Proverbs, and thanking him on behalf of the queen. Downey composed more than 250 original proverbs for this collection. Among them are the following:

———— ◈ ————

• An eastern bashaw once complained that he had no shoes, but when he saw a man without legs he was content.

• Those who are not full grown ought not to laugh at giants.

• When the lion becomes infirm, asses kick him with impunity.

• While traveling I have often noticed bull dogs lying still while puppies were barking.

• It is far better to die a porter in the fear of the Lord than a courtier in the fear of the devil.

• No man's sight is so strong that he can read in the dark; neither can reason without revelation guide us to heaven.

• The mind is nothing less than a garden of inestimable value, which man should strive to cultivate.

• It is better to drink the water of industry from an earthen cup than the wine of indolence from a silver tankard.

• Never be angry with your neighbor because his religious views differ from your own; for all the branches of a tree do not lean the same way.

• The difference between the humble minister of Jesus and the fashionable popular preacher is this: the former studies the pasturage for his flock; the latter the transferability of their wool.

• A good sermon, like a safe channel, ought to be more appreciated for its depth than for its length.

• As large trees are not the most productive, neither are wealthy men the most liberal.

• Riches have benefited tens and ruined thousands.

• As the furnace purifies the silver, so does charity rid wealth of its dross.

1861—On this Sunday, Charles Haddon Spurgeon (1834–92), one of the greatest preachers England ever produced, delivered a sermon at the Metropolitan Tabernacle in London that proved to be one of his most enduring. Called "Accidents, Not Punishments," the sermon was his response to a series of tragic disasters during the preceding week in London. In the following passage, he answers those who claim that such disasters are God's punishment for human sin. (See also January 6.)

———— ⋙ ⋘ ————

If a calamity were always the result of some sin, providence would be as simple as that twice two made four. It would be one of the first lessons that a child might learn. But Scripture teaches us that providence is a great depth in which the human intellect may swim and dive, but it can neither find a bottom nor a shore. If you and I pretend that we can find out the reasons of providence and twist the dispensations of God over our fingers, we only prove our folly, but we do not prove that we have begun to understand the ways of God. Why suppose for a moment there were some great performance going on, and you should say, "Yes, I understand it." What a simpleton you would be!

Do you not know that the great transactions of providence began six thousand years ago? You have only stepped into this world for thirty or forty years and have seen one actor on the stage, and you say you understand it. You have only begun to know. Only God knows the end from the beginning; only He understands what are the great results, what is the great reason for which the world was made and for which He permits both good and evil to occur. Think not that you know the ways of God. It is to degrade providence and to bring God down to the level of men when you pretend that you can understand those calamities and find out the secret designs of wisdom.

But next, do you not perceive that such an idea as this would encourage Pharisaism? The people who were crushed to death or scalded or destroyed under the wheels of railway trains were worse sinners than we are? ... I have never read in the Scriptures, "We know that we have passed from death unto life because we have traveled from London to Brighton safely twice a day."

1643—On this day a nineteen-year-old English shoemaker named George Fox (1624–91) experienced a spiritual crisis. It began when two friends, calling themselves Christians, invited him to drink with them at an inn, but they tricked Fox into paying the bill. Having been raised a Christian, Fox saw this incident as symbolic of the hypocrisy in much of the church, and on this day he embarked on a pilgrimage that led him to become an itinerant preacher and writer, eventually forming the Society of Friends, better known as the Quakers. Concerning Fox's crisis, Quaker missionary and writer Thomas Kelly (1893–1941, see also January 17) wrote in his exquisite devotional classic, A Testament of Devotion, *the following reflection.*

Only now and then comes a man or a woman who, like John Woolman or Francis of Assisi, is willing to be utterly obedient, to go the other half, to follow God's faintest whisper. But when such a commitment comes in a human life, God breaks through, miracles are wrought, world-renewing divine forces are released, history changes. . . .

Many of us have become as mildly and as conventionally religious as were the church folk of three centuries ago, against whose mildness and mediocrity and passionlessness George Fox and his followers flung themselves with all the passion of a glorious and a new discovery and with all the energy of dedicated lives. In some, says William James, religion exists as a dull habit, in others as an acute fever. Religion as a dull habit is not that for which Christ lived and died. . . .

George Fox as a youth was religious enough to meet all earthly standards and was even proposed as a student for the ministry. But the insatiable God-hunger in him drove him from such mediocrity into a passionate quest for the real whole-wheat Bread of Life. Sensible relatives told him to settle down and get married. Thinking him crazy, they took him to a doctor to have his blood let—the equivalent of being taken to a psychiatrist in these days. . . . Parents, if some of your children are seized with this imperative God-hunger, don't tell them to snap out of it and get a job, but carry them patiently in your love, or at least keep your hands off and let the holy work of God proceed in their souls.

1826—On this day English preacher William Jay (1769–1853) wrote the preface to his collection of lectures delivered at Argyle Chapel in Bath, England. The collection was entitled The Christian Contemplated. *A passage from the first lecture of that book is given below. Jay is considered one of the greatest English preachers of the nineteenth century and was also the author of the best-selling devotional* Evening and Morning Exercises. *(See also February 26.)*

How ought they that are in Christ to conduct themselves? How cheerfully, how gratefully ought you to feel! Once far off, and now nigh! Once strangers and enemies, and now fellow citizens with the saints and of the household of God! Once having nothing, and now possessing all things! You have had much forgiven—you should love much. He has done great things for you—you should largely inquire what you can do for him; and "by the mercies of God present your body a living sacrifice, holy and acceptable, which is your reasonable service." O you who live by this Savior, make him known. Recommend him. Begin with your own family. You are concerned to provide for your children, but how is your love operating? Is it not in laying up for them treasure on earth? Or seeking great things for them in the world? It will be infinitely better to leave them in Christ than to leave them with thousands of gold and silver or to leave them with kings upon the throne. Forget not your friends and your neighbors. Hold forth the Word of Life impressively and invitingly to all around you. Teach transgressors his ways and let sinners be converted unto him. What says the Poet?

> O 'tis a Godlike privilege to save;
> And he that scorns it is himself a slave.
> Inform the mind; one beam of heavenly day
> Will heal the heart and melt his chains away.

1903—*This is the day on which H. Clay Trumbull (1830–1903) wrote the introduction to his book* How to Deal with Doubts and Doubters. *Trumbull was an American Congregational minister who had served as a military chaplain during the American Civil War. In his book, he outlines ways of dealing with various kinds of religious doubt, as in the following excerpt.*

———— ⋅§ §⋅ ————

A church-goer, who desired to be right and to do right, when urged to connect himself with the church, expressed the fear that he was not good enough. This seemingly was his sincere feeling. For years he waited outside in the hope that he would grow better. Appeals from his friends for another course were of no avail. Then he was taken seriously ill, and he was brought to face death. As he prayed for recovery, and as he was prayed for, he seemed to have a different view of Christ; and when he was restored to health, he was glad to think of his Savior as one to whom he ought to show gratitude. When his pastor urged him to come into the church, as one who desired to evidence his thankfulness and trust, he came forward as a loving, trusting follower of Christ. It were better to come just as he was, he thought, than to wait outside indefinitely to grow better. . . .

It is important for every person who is in the church to bear in mind this truth as to the nature and mission of the church. It is not as an exhibition hall but as a hospital that it calls for members and that members continue in it. No man has made such progress in the Christian life that he no longer needs the helps that the church supplies him. The more progress one makes, the more he desires progress. If he feels that he is good enough to be a church member, he gives evidence that he has no right view of the church of Christ or of right life in Christ.

1637—Scottish pastor, theologian, and author Samuel Rutherford (c. 1600–61) wrote several works of theology, but it is for his letters that he is chiefly remembered today. Having been forbidden to preach by the Scottish crown in 1636, he spent two years' exile in Aberdeen, Scotland. His letters from this period, which were published posthumously, are among the treasures of Christian literature. (See also July 6.) In the following letter, written on this day, he encourages a friend, Alexander Gordon, in his suffering.

————— ❧ ❧ —————

Our crosses for Christ are not made of iron; they are softer and of more gentle metal. . . .

I see that Christ can borrow a cross for some hours and set his servants beside it, rather than under it, and win the plea, too, and make glory to himself and shame to his enemies and comfort his children out of it. But whether Christ buy or borrow crosses, he is King of crosses and King of devils and King over Hell and King over malice. When he was in the grave, he came out and brought the keys with him. He is Lord Jailer: nay, what am I saying? He is Captain of the castle, and he has the keys of death and Hell; and what are our troubles but little deaths, and He who commands the great castle commands the little also.

I see that a hardened face and two skins upon our brows, against the winter hail and stormy wind, is most appropriate for a poor traveler in a winter journey to Heaven. Oh, what art it is to learn to endure hardness and to learn to go barefooted either through the Devil's fiery coals or his frozen waters.

I am persuaded that a sea venture with Christ makes great riches. Is not the ship of our King Jesus coming home, and shall not we get part of the gold? Alas! We fools miscount our gain when we seem losers. Believe me, I have no challenges against this well-born cross; for it is come to Christ's house and is honorable and is a gift: "To you it is given to suffer." Oh, what fools are we to undervalue his gifts and to make light of that which is true honor! For if we could be faithful, our tackle shall not loosen or our mast break or our sails blow into the sea. The bastard crosses, the kinless and base-born crosses of worldlings for evil-doing, must be heavy and grievous; but our afflictions are light and momentary.

1845—The beloved hymn "Sweet Hour of Prayer" was first published on this day in the New York Observer. *The words are usually attributed to an English Congregational preacher named William Walford (1772–1850). The third stanza takes Deuteronomy 3:27 as its text: "Go to the top of Pisgah, and lift up your eyes westward and northward and southward and eastward and behold it with your eyes."*

Sweet hour of prayer, sweet hour of prayer,
That calls me from a world of care
And bids me at my Father's throne
Make all my wants and wishes known!
In seasons of distress and grief,
My soul has often found relief,
And oft escaped the tempter's snare
By thy return, sweet hour of prayer.

Sweet hour of prayer, sweet hour of prayer,
Thy wings shall my petition bear
To him whose truth and faithfulness
Engage the waiting soul to bless:
And since he bids me seek his face,
Believe his word and trust his grace,
I'll cast on him my every care,
And wait for thee, sweet hour of prayer.

Sweet hour of prayer, sweet hour of prayer,
May I thy consolation share,
Till from Mount Pisgah's lofty height,
I view my home and take my flight:
This robe of flesh I'll drop and rise
To seize the everlasting prize;
And shout, while passing through the air,
"Farewell, farewell, sweet hour of prayer."

1321—Italian poet Dante Alighieri (1265–1321) was one of the greatest poets of all time. In his famous epic, The Divine Comedy, which is divided into three parts, "Inferno," "Purgatory," and "Paradise," he recounts a dreamlike journey through hell, purgatory, and heaven. On this day, only hours before his own death, Dante completed the concluding "Paradise" portion of The Divine Comedy, from which the following lines are taken. In them, he describes a heavenly vision of the church (the white rose) surrounded by all the angels and saints (the bees).

In fashion then as of a snow-white rose
    Displayed itself to me the saintly host,
    Whom Christ in his own blood had made his bride,
But the other host, that flying sees and sings
    The glory of Him who doth enamor it,
    And the goodness that created it so noble,
Even as a swarm of bees, that sinks in flowers
    One moment, and the next returns again
    To where its labor is to sweetness turned,
Sank into the great flower, that is adorned
    With leaves so many, and thence reascended
    To where its love abideth evermore.
Their faces had they all of living flame,
    And wings of gold, and all the rest so white
    No snow unto that limit doth attain.
From bench to bench, into the flower descending,
    They carried something of the peace and ardor
    Which by the fanning of their flanks they won.
Nor did the interposing 'twixt the flower
    And what was o'er it of such plenitude
    Of flying shapes impede the sight and splendor;
Because the light divine so penetrates
    The universe, according to its merit,
    That naught can be an obstacle against it.

—from Canto 31 of the "Paradiso,"
translated by Henry Wadsworth Longfellow (1867)

1648—The publication of The Westminster Shorter Catechism, *largely the work of English Puritan thinker and Cambridge professor Anthony Tuckney (1599–1670), was approved by England's Parliament on this day. It is probably the most well-known catechism in English, and it has been used by Presbyterians, Congregationalists, and Baptists for more than three centuries for training new believers in the fundamentals of the faith. The famous opening section of that document follows.*

————————— ❧ ❦ —————————

QUESTION 1: What is the chief end of man?

ANSWER: Man's chief end is to glorify God and to enjoy Him forever.

QUESTION 2: What rule has God given to direct us how we may glorify and enjoy Him?

ANSWER: The Word of God, which is contained in the Scriptures of the Old and New Testaments, is the only rule to direct us how we may glorify and enjoy Him.

QUESTION 3: What do the Scriptures principally teach?

ANSWER: The Scriptures principally teach what man is to believe concerning God, and what duty God requires of man.

QUESTION 4: What is God?

ANSWER: God is a Spirit, infinite, eternal, and unchangeable, in His being, wisdom, power, holiness, justice, goodness, and truth.

QUESTION 5: Are there more Gods than one?

ANSWER: There is but one only, the living and true God.

QUESTION 6: How many persons are there in the Godhead?

ANSWER: There are three persons in the Godhead: the Father, the Son, and the Holy Ghost; and these three are one God, the same in substance, equal in power and glory.

1224—Francis of Assisi (1181–1226) is said to have received the stigmata (the wounds of Christ) on this day or the next. To those who find this event unbelievable, modern South African poet Arthur Shearly Cripps offers this stunning response. He sees it as Francis's deeper understanding of Christ's suffering, something all of us would do well to reflect upon. Francis is the imagined narrator in the following passage from Cripps' poem "The Death of Saint Francis."

———— ❧ ————

I knew in blissful anguish what it means
To be a part of Christ and feel as mine
The dark distresses of my brother limbs,
To feel it bodily and simply true,
To feel as mine the shadow of curse on all,
Hard words, hard looks, and savage misery,
And struggling deaths, unpitied and unwept.
To feel rich brothers' sad satieties,
The weary manner of their lives and deaths,
That want in love, and lacking love lack all.
To feel the heavy sorrow of the world
Thicken and thicken on to future hell,
To mighty cities with their miles of streets,
Where men seek work for days, and walk and starve. . . .
The horror of the things our brothers bear!
It was but naught to that which after came,
The woe of things we make our brothers bear,
Our brothers and our sisters! In my heart
Christ's Heart seemed beating, and the world's whole sin,
Its crimson malice and grey negligence—
Rose up and blackening hid the Face of God.
But oh! that Sacred heart rushed out to them
In veriest anguish and in veriest bliss,
Demanding, craving, in sure hope of them,
"Father, forgive, they know not what they do."
. . . When I woke His prints were in my hands,
And in my feet, while in my side there showed,
As it were, the Heart-Wound from the soldier's lance.

1179—On this day the church has traditionally honored German abbess Hildegard of Bingen (born in 1098), who died on this date in 1179. She possessed one of the most remarkable creative minds of all time. She composed music (which is still performed), she painted visionary paintings and interpreted them, she was an inventor of great ingenuity, and she wrote some of the most sublimely mystical books of the Middle Ages. The following passage, about the power of music, is from her most famous work, Scivias *("Knowing God's Ways").*

———————— ⋅≼ ≽⋅ ————————

Just as the power of God, extending everywhere, surrounds all things without encountering any resistance, so too, the rationality of man has the great ability to sound through living voices and to rouse listless souls to wakefulness in music.

Even David demonstrates this in the music of his prophecy, and Jeremiah shows it in the sorrowful voice of his lamentation. So it is that even [I]—a poor, weak-natured little woman—hear, in music, the sound of fiery ardor in the virgin's blush, in the embracing words of the budding twig; the sound of keenness from the living lights that shine in the celestial city; the sound of prophecy in deep sermons; the sound of marvelous words from the enlarging of the apostleship; the sound of blood being poured out by those who offer themselves up in faith; the sound of the priestly mysteries being observed; and the sound of the virgin's step on the heavenly greenness of flowering things. For faithful creation echoes back to the heavenly Creator with its voice of exultation and joy, returning frequent thanks. . . . Music not only rejoices in the unanimity of exultation of those who bravely persevere along the path of righteousness, it also exults in the concord of reviving those who have fallen away from the path of justice and are lifted up at last to blessedness. For even the good shepherd joyfully led back to the flock the sheep that had been lost.

Musical harmony softens hard hearts, inducing in them the moisture of contrition and summoning the Holy Spirit. So it is that those voices that you hear are like the voice of the multitude when they lift up their voices on high. For the faithful carry their jubilant praises in the singleness of unanimity and revealed love, towards that unity of mind where there is no discord, when they make those on earth sigh with heart and mouths for their heavenly reward.

—translated by Robert Carver

1738—Samuel Johnson (1709–84), known to history as "Dr. Johnson," is one of the towering figures of English literature. (See also March 28.) He was a renowned critic and author and one of the most sparkling wits of any age. In 1755 he published his most famous work, his monumental Dictionary of the English Language, *the first of its kind. Before he achieved fame, however, he lived as a poor struggling writer and teacher in London. On this day, he wrote the following prayer to commemorate the occasion of his twenty-ninth birthday. His piety was sincere and deeply felt, and he continued to write such moving birthday prayers until the last year of his life.*

O God, the Creator and Preserver of all mankind, Father of all mercies, I, Your unworthy servant, do give You most humble thanks for all Your goodness and loving-kindness to me. I bless You for my creation, preservation, and redemption, for the knowledge of Your Son Jesus Christ, for the means of Grace and the hope of glory. In the day of childhood and youth, in the midst of weakness, blindness, and danger, You have protected me; amid afflictions of mind, body, and estate, You have supported me; and amid vanity and wickedness You have spared me. Grant, O merciful Father, that I may have a lively sense of Your mercies. Create in me a contrite heart, that I may worthily lament my sins and acknowledge my wickedness and obtain remission and forgiveness, through the satisfaction of Jesus Christ. And, O Lord, enable me, by Your grace, to redeem the time that I have spent in sloth, vanity, and wickedness; to make use of Your gifts to the honor of Your name; to lead a new life in Your faith, fear, and love; and finally to obtain everlasting life. Grant this, Almighty Lord, for the merits and through the mediation of our most holy and blessed Savior Jesus Christ; to whom, with You and the Holy Ghost, Three Persons and One God, be all honor and glory, world without end. Amen.

1853—English physician J. Hudson Taylor (1832–1905) was one of England's great missionaries and the founder of the China Inland Mission in 1865. He believed that missionaries should adopt, as far as possible, the dress and customs of the country to which they were called. He spent his final years in China, therefore, dressed in Chinese garb and wearing his hair in the Chinese fashion. His influence on contemporary missions is enormous. On this day, he first left England for China, and he later recalled his emotion at that time in his autobiographical book, A Retrospective.

On September 19, 1853, a little service was held in the stern cabin of the *Dumfries*, which had been secured for me by the Committee of the Chinese Evangelization Society, under whose auspices I was going to China.

My beloved, now sainted mother had come to see me off from Liverpool. Never shall I forget that day, nor how she went with me into the little cabin that was to be my home for nearly six long months. With a mother's loving hand she smoothed the little bed. She sat by my side and joined me in the last hymn that we should sing together before the long parting. We knelt down, and she prayed—the last prayer I was to hear before starting for China. Then notice was given that we must separate, and we had to say good-bye, never expecting to meet on earth again.

For my sake she restrained her feelings as much as possible. We parted; and she went on shore, giving me her blessing; I stood alone on deck, and she followed the ship as we moved toward the dock gates. As we passed through the gates, and the separation really began, I shall never forget the cry of anguish wrung from that mother's heart. It went through me like a knife. I never knew so fully, until then, what "God so loved the world" meant. And I am quite sure that my precious mother learned more of the love of God to the perishing in that hour than in all her life before.

1931—In the early morning hours of this day, Oxford dons C. S. Lewis (1898–1963) and J. R. R. Tolkien (1892–1973), along with another professor, Hugo Dyson, finished a lengthy discussion of myth and Christianity. The conversation had begun the evening before as the friends strolled along Addison's Walk in Oxford, England. The talk, said Lewis, brought him, "from believing in God to definitely believing in Christ." Of course, Lewis went on to become probably the most popular Christian writer of the twentieth century, and Tolkien's Fellowship of the Ring *series of fantasy novels have been perennial best-sellers for several decades. Lewis describes their conversation as follows.*

———————⋅෴ ෴⋅———————

Now what Dyson and Tolkien showed me was this: that if I met the idea of sacrifice in a Pagan story I didn't mind it at all: again, that if I met the idea of a god sacrificing himself to himself . . . I liked it very much and was mysteriously moved by it: again, that the idea of the dying and reviving god (Balder, Adonis, Bacchus) similarly moved me provided I met it anywhere except in the Gospels. . . .

Now the story of Christ is simply a true myth: a myth working on us in the same way as the others, but with this tremendous difference that *it really happened*: and one must be content to accept it in the same way, remembering that it is God's myth where the others are men's myths: i.e. the Pagan stories are God expressing Himself through the minds of poets, using such images as He found there, while Christianity is God expressing Himself through what we call "real things." . . .

Does this amount to a belief in Christianity? At any rate I am now certain (a) That this Christian story is to be approached, in a sense, as I approach the other myths. (b) That it is the most important and full of meaning. I am also nearly certain that it really happened.

—from *They Stand Together: The Letters of C. S. Lewis to Arthur Greeves*

1833—Mrs. Maria W. Stewart was a popular African-American preacher of the nineteenth century. She left only a handful of writings, but among them is a beautiful "Farewell Address," delivered on this date in Boston on the occasion of her stepping down from the pulpit. She had encountered much resistance to her ministry on account of both her race and her gender. In the following excerpt from her "Farewell Address" she addresses her critics.

———————— ⋙ ⋘ ————————

What if I am a woman? Is not the God of ancient times the God of these modern days? Did he not raise up Deborah to be a mother and a judge in Israel? Did not queen Esther save the lives of the Jews? And Mary Magdalene first declare the resurrection of Christ from the dead? Come, said the woman of Samaria, and see a man that has told me all things that ever I did—is not this the Christ? St. Paul declared that it was a shame for a woman to speak in pubic, yet our great High Priest and Advocate did not condemn the woman for a more notorious offense than this; neither will he condemn this worthless worm. The bruised reed he will not break, and the smoking flax he will not quench till he sends forth judgment unto victory. Did St. Paul but know of our wrongs and deprivations, I presume he would make no objections to our pleading in public for our rights. Again, holy women ministered to Christ and the apostles; and women of refinement in all ages, more or less have had a voice in moral, religious, and political subjects. Again, why the Almighty has imparted to me the power of speaking thus, I cannot tell. "And Jesus lifted up his voice and said, I thank you, O Father, Lord of heaven and earth, that though you have hidden these things from the wise and prudent, you have revealed them to babes: even so, Father, for so it seemed good in your sight."

. . . Be no longer astonished then, my brethren and friends, that God at this eventful period should raise up your own females to strive, by their example both in public and private, to assist those who are endeavoring to stop the strong current of prejudice that flows so profusely against us at present. No longer ridicule their efforts, it will be counted for sin. For God makes use of feeble means sometimes, to bring about his most exalted purposes.

286—Englishman John Foxe (1516–87) is one of Protestantism's most popular authors for his famous martyrology Foxe's Book of Martyrs, *which was originally called* Acts and Monuments *(published in 1554; revised and expanded in 1563). Many readers believe the work is seriously flawed, however, by its lack of careful scholarship and its bitter anti-Catholic tone. Although Foxe himself publicly denounced Protestant persecution of Catholics, his book focuses largely on Catholic abuses. Early in the book, Foxe relates stories of martyrdoms that are not of the Catholic-versus-Protestant variety, and among them is the following. Although most certainly a legend, the massacre of the "Theban legion" took place, according to Foxe, on this day.*

———————— ·◦§ ◦§◦ ·————————

[The Theban legion] contained none but Christians.... They were quartered in the East till the emperor Maximian ordered them to march to Gaul to assist him against the rebels of Burgundy.... About this time, Maximian ordered a general sacrifice at which the whole army was to assist, and he commanded that they should take oaths of allegiance and swear at the same time to assist him in the extirpation of Christianity in Gaul.

Terrified at these orders, each individual of the Theban legion absolutely refused either to sacrifice or take the oaths prescribed. This so greatly enraged Maximian that he ordered the legion to be decimated, that is, every tenth man to be selected from the rest and put to the sword. This cruel order having been put into execution, those who remained alive were still inflexible, when a second decimation took place, and again every tenth man of those living was put to the sword.

But this second severity made no more impression than the first; the soldiers preserved their fortitude and their principles but, by the advice of their officers, drew up a remonstrance to the emperor in which they told him "that they were his subjects and his soldiers but could not at the same time forget the Almighty...."

Such a declaration, it might be presumed, would have softened the emperor, but it had a contrary effect; for, enraged at their perseverance and unanimity, he commanded that the whole legion should be put to death.

1666—Mary Boyle, Countess of Warwick (1624–78), was a noblewoman who was well acquainted with English courtly life of the seventeenth century. Her Diary, published long after her death, is both beautiful and full of profound devotional wisdom. In her diary entry for this day, she records a wonderful faith-affirming experience. (See also April 23.)

———— ⋙ ⋘ ————

I rose very early and went into my closet; and upon reading that passage in Scripture of Christ's asking Peter whether he loved Him, and Peter's answering that he knew He loved him, God was pleased to melt my heart exceedingly and to make me, with abundance of tears, to say, as he did, that He knew I loved Him above all things in heaven and earth. I felt the love of God made great work in my breast; then I went and meditated upon the passion of Christ, in order thoroughly to melt my heart; and God was pleased to encourage me to come to His [communion] table by bringing most sweet promises to my mind. I had great encouragement to come, by finding some inward persuasion that God, through Christ, would accept me; He was pleased then to give me sweet communion with Him. When I had prayed earnestly to God and blessed Him heartily for giving me leave to come, I went to the chapel. In the prayer, the desires of my heart went out exceedingly after God. When the sacrament was brought to me, my heart did pant and breathe after it, and God was pleased to give a great deal of comfort in that ordinance and much assurance of His love; I had then a lively sense of His love in my heart and could steadfastly believe that I was my Beloved's, and He was mine. After the sacrament was over, I instantly went up from there, while my heart was warm, to bless God and to beg strength to keep the promises I had made of new obedience. God was pleased there to give me sweet communion with Him and much soul-satisfaction. After the public duties of the day were over, in which my heart continued still to breathe after God, I did alone, in the evening, meditate upon the privileges of God's children and upon His unchangeable love to them, which made the meditation of Him to be very sweet to me; then, after supper, I committed myself to God in a short prayer before bedtime. Lord, I bless You for this day; oh, that I might have many more such!

1915—American writer and minister David de Forest Burrell was one of the most popular authors to publish with the American Tract Society, one of the most influential religious publishers of that time. One of Burrell's books, Letters from the Dominie (1916), collected a series of letters on "his view from the pew" addressed to "no one in particular, but with many in mind whom I have known and loved." Here is a sample, written on this day.

———— ❧ ❧ ————

I wish I could work a wonder in this day. Do you know what it would be? It would be to transform a certain prayer-meeting pessimist into an all-around optimist. Why is it that some folks cannot even talk with God in a cheerful, hopeful tone of voice?

Of course, the pessimist, like the poor, is always with us; but he is not nearly so good company as the other ubiquitous person, especially in prayer meeting! I meet him in many places. So do you.

He talks politics, and we feel as if the country were going to ruin; business, and we are sure the bottom has dropped out of the industrial world; household matters, and we are convinced that every grocer and butcher is a thief; or religion, and we feel that the Church is going fast to decay and that God is in desperate straits! . . .

But surely if the pessimistic spirit is out of place anywhere, it is in the Church of the living God. For no one need expect flawless perfection in the Church on earth until Christ comes again. There is here no perfect music, nor perfect sermon, nor perfect ventilation, nor perfect society, nor even a single perfect Christian! It is the glory of the Church that, with all its faults, it is chosen and used by its Lord as the divinely appointed tool for His hand. . . .

And we ought not to forget that optimism, as well as pessimism, is contagious. Spread it! Be a "promoter" of the right sort, an enthusiast for your church. It is Christ's church; and the optimist can serve Him in it far better than the pessimist can.

I have been reading Isaiah the Optimist. What an inspiriting challenge he issues to Israel on Jehovah's behalf: "Enlarge the place of thy tent, and let them stretch forth the curtains of thy habitations; spare not; lengthen thy cords and strengthen thy stakes. For thou shalt spread abroad on the right hand and on the left." . . . Let us, like Carey, "Expect great things from God."

1908—Gilbert Keith Chesterton (1874–1936) was an enormously popular English journalist, author, and controversialist. To this day, a large number of his books remain in print, beloved for their riotous humor, wit, occasional mystery, and deep personal faith. Among his greatest works of lay theology is his book Orthodoxy, an extended essay on the basic tenets of Christian faith, which was first published on this day. The following is an excerpt.

We are perhaps permitted tragedy as a sort of merciful comedy: because the frantic energy of divine things would knock us down like a drunken farce. We can take our own tears more lightly than we could take the tremendous levities of the angels. So we sit perhaps in a starry chamber of silence, while the laughter of the heavens is too loud for us to hear.

Joy . . . is the gigantic secret of the Christian. And as I close this chaotic volume I open again the strange small book from which all Christianity came; and I am again haunted by a kind of confirmation. The tremendous figure which fills the Gospels towers in this respect, as in every other, above all the thinkers who ever thought themselves tall. His pathos was natural, almost casual. The Stoics, ancient and modern, were proud of concealing their tears. He never concealed His tears; He showed them plainly on His open face at any daily sight, such as the far sight of His native city. Yet He concealed something. Solemn supermen and imperial diplomatists are proud of restraining their anger. He never restrained His anger. He flung furniture down the front steps of the Temple, and asked men how they expected to escape the damnation of Hell. Yet He restrained something. I say it with reverence; there was in that shattering personality a thread that must be called shyness. There was something that He hid from all men when He went up a mountain to pray. There was something that He covered constantly by abrupt silence or impetuous isolation. There was some one thing that was too great for God to show us when He walked upon our earth; and I have sometimes fancied that it was His mirth.

1635—Pietro Aretino (1492–1556) was an Italian satirist, called "the Scourge of Princes" for his attacks on the rich and powerful of his time. He wrote a religious work, A Paraphrase Upon the Seven Penitential Psalms, *the anonymous English translation of which received its imprimatur on this day (the official seal that it contained no doctrinal error). In the following adapted extract, Aretino describes God by using the metaphor of three birds: the pelican (thought to revive its young with blood drawn from its own breast and therefore a symbol of the Crucifixion), the owl (a symbol of Christ's death), and the sparrow (a symbol of the Resurrection).*

⋅◈ ◈⋅

"I will become like the pelican," says God. "I will open my breast with the beak of my merciful will; and in the solitude of the world, with my blood I will resuscitate and raise the nations, just as the pelican raises his young, who, being dead, will reassume life by the blood of the bird that brought them forth.

"But as the owl on his perch sees nothing but darkness, so too in the world I shall see nothing but obscurities, heavy, gloomy darkness of sin, fogs, mists of pride, and smokes of vanity." . . .

On the day before your resurrection, my Lord, before rising again, you will seem to have slept. But while you slept, you completed your miraculous work, which your will decreed to expedite. To completely finish your work, you will sweat and take heavy pains for the common good, for the common safety of all the Universe and of all the world. By rending asunder the gates of Hell with the force of your pity and tender mercy, by binding, banishing, and condemning our old adversary to everlasting fire, you will demonstrate that in this seeming slumber you were attentive, always watchful, that you were fully alert to the need of your creatures.

And in so doing you will resemble a lovely, retired, solitary sparrow, who after his flight from elsewhere, strangerlike and alone, perches upon a house, wherein many people are lodged. And then, having completed that which you had to do upon the earth, you will mount to Heaven and remain ever after in paradise with the angels: one only God and one only Savior of the world.

1704—Englishman John Locke (1632–1704), considered one of the greatest philosophical thinkers England ever produced, was a staunch defender of religious freedom and author of the famous Essay Concerning Human Understanding. *He spent seventeen years pondering the issues included in that book, which was published in 1690. He also wrote an influential volume entitled* The Reasonableness of Christianity *(1695). Though Locke was described as "cold and unimaginative" by some, his personal faith was warm and earnest, as can be seen in the following letter, written near the end of his life, on this day, to a man who had asked him the best method of studying religion.*

————— ❧ ❧ —————

What is the best method to study religion? . . . I can make you no other answer than . . . that the only way to attain a certain knowledge of that is the study of the Holy Scripture. And my reason is, because the Christian religion is a revelation from God Almighty, which is contained in the Bible; and so all the knowledge we can have of it must be derived from thence. But if you ask, "Which is the best way to get knowledge of the Roman, Lutheran, or reformed religion, of this or that particular church?" Each whereof entitles itself to be the true Christian religion, with some kind of exclusion or diminution of the rest, that will not be hard to tell you. But then, it is plain that the books that best teach you any one of these, do most remove you from all the rest, and, in this way of studying, you pitch upon one as the right, before you know it to be so; whereas that choice should be the result of your study of the Christian religion in the Sacred Scriptures. And the method I have proposed would, I presume, bring you the surest way to that Church which, I imagine, you already think most conformable to the Word of God.

. . . What is the best way of interpreting the Sacred Scripture (taking *interpreting* to mean *understanding*)? I think the best way for understanding the Scripture . . . is to read it assiduously and diligently, and, if it can be, in the original. I do not mean to read every day some certain number of chapters, as is usual, but to read it so as to study and consider and not leave till you are satisfied that you have got the true meaning.

Eighteenth century—Although forgotten in our time, Karl Heinrich von Bogatzky (1690–1774) was a renowned German hymn writer and author of one of the world's most popular daily devotionals, The Golden Treasury for the Children of God. *In over sixty editions in English and translated into dozens of languages, it was until recently second only to Bunyan's* Pilgrim's Progress *in worldwide popularity. The Golden Treasury, in an anonymous English translation, gives the following reading for this day.*

───────── ❧ ❧ ─────────

Scripture verse: *The penitent's prayer: "What must I do to be saved?" The Divine answer: "Believe on the Lord Jesus, and you will be saved, and your house" (Acts 16:31).*

Faith is not a confidence of our own making; it is God who molds it in a broken and repenting heart. This faith purifies the heart, crucifies the old Adam, overcomes the world, changes us in heart, mind, and all the power and faculties of the soul—which is true faith. It is not merely that we think and say, "I believe." We must test our faith. All true believers have received it with a sense of godly sorrow and with brokenness of heart. If we feel something of this and ask Christ in prayer for faith and grace, then we have a sure mark of faith already—for if we did not believe, we would not pray. And the person who daily asks to be cleansed by the blood of Christ has true faith and hope already, even if that person still feels weak and does not taste any joy. May the Lord grant to all our souls such repentance unto life and such faith in Jesus Christ, which are the saving graces of the Spirit, so that, in due time, when the end comes, we may receive a crown of glory to wear forever in the presence of the Prince of Life and of God Himself.

> Ye dying souls who sit
>   In darkness and distress,
> Look from the borders of the pit
>   To Christ's recovering grace.
>
> Sinners shall hear His sound;
>   Their thankful tongues shall own
> That their righteousness and strength is found
>   In Christ the Lord alone.

1899—*Alexander Carmichael (1832–1912) was a Scottish civil servant whose passion and scholarly pastime was the collecting of Gaelic prayers, invocations, and songs, many with ancient Celtic roots, from the islands and highlands of Scotland. On this day, he completed the writing of the preface of his monumental anthology of these pieces,* Carmina Gadelica *("Songs of the Gaels"). The following primitive chant in praise of Christ is from that wonderful collection.*

Hey the Gift, ho the Gift,
Hey the Gift, on the living.

Son of the dawn, Son of the clouds,
Son of the planet, Son of the star,
Hey the Gift, ho the Gift,
Hey the Gift, on the living.

Son of the rain, Son of the dew,
Son of the welkin, Son of the sky,
Hey the Gift, ho the Gift,
Hey the Gift, on the living.

Son of the flame, Son of the light,
Son of the sphere, Son of the globe,
Hey the Gift, ho the Gift,
Hey the Gift, on the living.

Son of the elements, Son of the heavens,
Son of the moon, Son of the sun,
Hey the Gift, ho the Gift,
Hey the Gift, on the living.

Son of Mary of the God-mind,
And the Son of God first of all news,
Hey the Gift, ho the Gift,
Hey the Gift, on the living.

1654—On this day Henry Vaughan (1622–95), English doctor and poet, wrote the preface to the second volume of his collected devotional verse, Silex Scintillans ("A Sparkling Stone"). In it, he apologizes for the "remote" quality of some of his poems, but as he explains, he "was nigh unto death" when he wrote many of them. It was during that illness that Christ first became real to him. The following poem from that collection takes for its text John 1:38–39: "Then Jesus turned, and saw them following, and said to them, 'What do you seek?' They said to him, 'Rabbi,' (which is to say, being interpreted, Master,) 'where are you staying?' He said, 'Come and see.' They came and saw where he was living, and stayed with him that day: for it was about the tenth hour."

———— ◆◇ ————

What happy, secret fountain,
Fair shade, or mountain,
Whose undiscovered virgin glory
Boasts it this day, though not in story,
Was then thy dwelling? Did some cloud
Fixed to a Tent, descend and shroud
My distressed Lord? Or did a star
Beckoned by thee, though high and far,
In sparkling smiles haste gladly down
To lodge light, and increase her own?
My dear, dear God! I do not know
What lodged thee then, nor where, nor how;
But I am sure, thou dost now come
Oft to a narrow homely room,
Where thou too hast but the least part,
My God, I mean *my sinful heart.*

Ocrober

English poet and hymn writer Frances Ridley Havergal
(see October 13). Frontispiece to her collection of
meditations *Royal Grace and Loyal Gifts*.

1813—An American woman named Sally Thomas (1769–1813) died on this day. Her story is movingly told in Edith Deen's classic Great Women of the Christian Faith, *first published in 1959.*

———————— ☙ ❧ ————————

Sally Thomas was a servant girl in Cornish, New Hampshire, who, like the New Testament widow with the two mites, gave all she had to the Christian cause. Her wages never exceeded fifty cents a week, yet because she was industrious and thrifty, she managed to save the remarkable sum of $345.83, which she gave to missions. This was the first gift actually paid to the treasurer of the American Board of Commissioners for Foreign Missions.

Little is known of Sally Thomas's life except the facts on her gravestone in Cornish, where she lived and worked for twenty-three years with the family of Daniel Chase, one of the first settlers in the town. Her gravestone reads: "In memory of Miss Sally Thomas, who died October 1, 1813, aged 44. By the labor of her hands she had acquired property amounting to about $500; which by her last will, excepting a few small legacies, she gave for the spread and support of the Gospel among the heathen."

Thirty-six years after her death, her pastor's son, Reverend Joseph Rowell, prepared a statement about her gift and her life for the *Missionary Herald* of October 1878. In this article, the author tells of her membership in the Congregational Church in Cornish during the ministry of his father. He speaks of the family for whom she worked and how from them and their friends Sally caught the religious spirit of the time and willingly gave all she had to further the work of the Church overseas.

The fact that she gave so much when she had so little has placed her among the immortals in the records of foreign missions. Though she lived a century and a half ago, her gift still inspires church people everywhere.

1528—English reformer William Tyndale (c. 1492–1536) was an influential preacher, tract writer, and Bible translator. He translated the Pentateuch, the Book of Jonah, and the entire New Testament, all of which had a profound influence on the translation of the King James Bible less than a century later. On this day Tyndale wrote the preface to one of his most renowned tracts, "The Obedience of Christian Men," from which the following reflection comes: on tribulation in the Christian life. Tyndale himself suffered persecution and was martyred in 1536.

✧

Joseph saw the sun and the moon and the eleven stars worshiping God. Nevertheless, before that came to pass, God laid him where he could neither see sun nor moon nor any star of the sky, and for many years and also undeservedly—to nurture him, to humble him, to make him meek, to teach him God's ways, and to make him apt and ready for his later place of honor, so that he might perceive and feel that it came from God and that he might be strong in the Spirit to minister it in a godly manner.

God promised the children of Israel a land with rivers of milk and honey, but He brought them for the space of forty years into a land where not only rivers of milk and honey did not flow, but where not so much as a drop of water flowed—to nurture them and to teach them, as a father does his child, and to do them good at the latter end, so that they might be strong in their spirit and souls, and to use his gifts and benefits in a godly manner and after his will.

He promised David a kingdom and immediately stirred up king Saul against him to persecute him, to hunt him as men do hares with greyhounds, and to ferret him out of every hole, and that for the space of many years. This was to tame him, to make him meek, to kill his lusts, to make him feel other men's diseases, to make him merciful, to make him understand that he was made a king to minister to and serve his brethren. . . .

The Spirit, through tribulation, purges us and kills our fleshly wit, our worldly understanding, our belly wisdom, and fills us full of the wisdom of God. Tribulation is a blessing that comes of God; as Christ says (in Matthew 5), "Blessed are they that suffer persecution for righteousness' sake, for theirs is the kingdom of heaven." Is not this a comfortable word?

1259—Bonaventure (1221–74), one of the great "doctors of the church," was a highly regarded Franciscan philosopher and theologian. On or shortly before this day, the thirty-fifth anniversary of the death of St. Francis, he went on a retreat to write his book The Soul's Journey into God, *from which the following is taken. In this passage he reflects on the fact that, like St. Francis, we all have access to God through pure minds and sensitive, longing hearts. (See also May 23.)*

———— ⋅⋚ ⋛⋅ ————

Let us say with Dionysius: "Concerning mystical visions, my friend, redouble your efforts and abandon the senses and the workings of the intellect, both visible and invisible things, and all things that exist and don't exist; and so far as possible, allow yourself to be brought back to a unity with Him who is beyond all essence and knowledge. And then, transcending yourself and all things, with the immeasurable and absolute transport of a pure soul, ascend to the superessential radiance of the divine darkness."

If you wish to know how these things are done, ask grace not doctrine, ask desire not intellect, ask the groanings of prayer not studious reading, ask the Bridegroom not the professor, ask God not man, ask darkness not clarity, not light but the fire that totally inflames you and carries you into God by means of ecstatic fervor and consuming affections. God Himself is this fire, and "his furnace is in Jerusalem" (Isaiah 31:9); and it is Christ who, in the flame of His most ardent passion, kindles it; this fire is only perceived by that person who says, "My soul chooses hanging and my bones death" (Job 7:15). Whoever loves this death is able to see God, for it is undoubtedly true that "no one shall see me and live" (Exodus 33:20).

Let us die, then, and enter into this darkness; let us impose a silence upon our cares and our desires and our imaginings. With the crucified Christ let us pass "out of this world to the Father" (John 13:1) so that when the Father is shown to us we can say with Philip, "It is enough for us" (John 14:8); so that we can hear with Paul, "My grace is sufficient for you" (2 Corinthians 12:9); and so that we can rejoice with David, saying, "My flesh and my heart have fainted away; You are the God of my heart, and the God who is my portion forever. Blessed be the Lord forever and let all the people say: Let it be; let it be. Amen" (Psalms 72:26, 105:48).

1912—Considered a modern prophet by some and reviled by many, American Baptist minister Walter Raushenbusch (1861–1918) was an outspoken advocate of a radical social interpretation of the Bible, an approach that earned him the epithet "The Father of the Social Gospel." On this day he completed the preface of his classic Christianizing the Social Order. *The prophetic spirit of his writing can be seen in the following excerpt from that book.*

———— ⋘ ⋙ ————

The Christian indictment of Capitalism [is] summed up in this single challenge, that Capitalism has generated a spirit of its own which is antagonistic to the spirit of Christianity; a spirit of hardness and cruelty that neutralizes the Christian spirit of love; a spirit that sets material goods above spiritual possessions. To set Things above Men is the really dangerous practical materialism. To set Mammon before God is the only idolatry against which Jesus warned us.

As Capitalism has spread over the industrial nations, a smoke bank of materialism has ascended from it and shut the blue dome of heaven from the sight of men. All the spiritual forces of society have felt themselves in the grip of a new, invisible adversary with whom they had to wrestle, and whose touch made their hearts like lead.

[For instance,] the taste for pure literature, especially for poetry, has declined in the classes that once had it. A person who cultivates poetry as our fathers used to do must do it with a smile, or he will pass for a freak. In spite of the vast public created by the spread of education and reached by modern methods of publicity, the amount of enduring literature produced is slight. Authors who cannot produce what will make a commercial profit can get no hearing. Authors who do produce what is commercially profitable are overstimulated, rushed, and drained. Department store novels and Sunday editions are drowning the intellect of the people in a sea of slush. They furnish the sensations of thinking without its efforts. . . .

When literature, art, education, the learned professions, and all other organized expressions of the spiritual life are being blanketed by the materialistic spirit generated in our business world, how can religion and the Church escape?

1683—Perhaps the most influential of all children's religious books, The New England Primer, or Milk for Babes, was first licensed for publication on this day. This classic is the source for many well-known children's verses.

In Adam's fall
We sinned all.

Young Obadias,
David, Josias—
All were pious.

Young Timothy
Learnt sin to flee.

Now I lay me down to sleep,
I pray the Lord my soul to keep;
If I should die before I wake,
I pray the Lord my soul to take.

Have communion with few,
Be intimate with One.
Deal justly with all,
Speak evil of none.

Good Children must
Fear God all day,
Parents obey,
No false thing say,
By no sin stray,
Love Christ alway,
In secret pray,
Mind little play,
Make no delay
In doing good.

First in the morning
when thou dost awake,
To God for his grace
thy petition make,
Some heavenly petition
use daily to say,
That the God of heaven
may bless thee alway.

1871—On this day a group of eleven African-American singers—six women and five men, all students at Fisk University—set off from Nashville, Tennessee, on a boat trip up the Mississippi and Ohio Rivers. By singing gospel songs and traditional spirituals in local churches, they hoped to raise enough money to rescue their financially strapped school from bankruptcy. The effort succeeded, and they eventually became the most renowned gospel choir of all time, touring the world as the Fisk Jubilee Singers. They first popularized many songs that are still familiar today, such as "Swing Low, Sweet Chariot," "Old Time Religion," "Go Down, Moses," "Nobody Knows the Trouble I See," and the following, called "Didn't My Lord Deliver Daniel."

He delivered Daniel from the lion's den,
Jonah from the belly of the whale,
And the Hebrew children from the fiery furnace,
And why not everyone?

> CHORUS: Didn't my Lord deliver Daniel,
> Deliver Daniel, deliver Daniel,
> Didn't my Lord deliver Daniel,
> And why not everyone?

Though the moon run down in a purple stream
And the sun forbear to shine,
Though every star shall disappear,
King Jesus shall be mine.

The wind blows East and the wind blows West,
It blows like judgment day,
And every poor soul that never did pray
Will be glad to pray that day.

> CHORUS: Didn't my Lord deliver Daniel,
> Deliver Daniel, deliver Daniel,
> Didn't my Lord deliver Daniel,
> And why not everyone?

1347—St. Sergius (1314–92) is one of the most beloved and popular saints of Russia. He founded a famous monastery and contributed to the general spiritual renewal of his country. On this day, as a young man, he "received his tonsure," that is, he became a monk. This day also marks the beginning of his famed asceticism, for he soon left to live alone in the wilderness for several years. A monk named Epiphanius, an early biographer and disciple of Sergius, wrote the following account in his Life, Acts, and Miracles of Our Reverence and Holy Father Abbot Sergius.

Who can recount his labors? Who can number the trials he endured living alone in the wilderness? Under different forms and from time to time the devil wrestled with the saint, but the demons beset St. Sergius in vain; no matter what visions they evoked, they failed to overcome the firm and fearless spirit of the ascetic. At one moment it was Satan who laid his snares, at another incursions of wild beasts took place, for many were the wild animals inhabiting this wilderness. Some of these remained at a distance; others came near the saint, surrounded him, and even sniffed him. In particular a bear used to come to the holy man. Seeing the animal did not come to harm him but in order to get some food, the saint brought a small slice of bread from his hut and placed it on a log or stump, so the bear learned to come for the meal thus prepared for him and, having eaten it, went away again. If there was no bread and the bear did not find his usual slice, he would wait about for a long while and look around on all sides, rather like some money-lender waiting to receive payment of his debt. At this time Sergius had no variety of food in the wilderness, only bread and water from the spring—and a great scarcity of these. Often bread was not to be found, then both he and the bear went hungry. Sometimes, although there was but one single slice of bread, the saint gave it to the bear, being unwilling to disappoint him of his food.

He diligently read the Holy Scriptures to obtain a knowledge of all virtue; in his secret meditations training his mind in a longing for eternal bliss. Most wonderful of all, none knew the measure of his ascetic and godly life spent in solitude. God, the beholder of all hidden things, alone saw it.

—from *A Treasury of Russian Spirituality*,
translated by Nicholas Zernov (1948)

1871—While world-renowned American evangelist Dwight L. Moody (1837–99; see also January 30) was preaching in Chicago on this day, a fire bell rang nearby. He quickly brought his sermon to a close and sent the people home. The bell was announcing the beginning of one of the greatest disasters of the nineteenth century: the Great Chicago Fire. Twenty-two years later Moody reflected on his experience:

———— ◈ ————

I intended to devote six nights to Christ's life. I had spent four Sunday nights on the subject and had followed Him from the manger along through His life to His arrest and trial, and on the fifth Sunday night, October 8, I was preaching to the largest congregation I had ever had in Chicago, quite elated with my success. My text was, "What shall I do then with Jesus which is called the Christ?" That night I made one of the greatest mistakes of my life. After preaching . . . with all the power that God had given me, urging Christ upon the people, I closed the sermon and said, "I wish you would take this text home with you and turn it over in your minds during the week, and next Sunday we will come to Calvary and the cross, and we will decide what we will do with Jesus of Nazareth."

I have never seen that congregation since. I have hard work to keep back the tears today. . . . I have a great many old friends and am pretty well acquainted in Chicago, but twenty-two years have passed away . . . and I will never meet those people again until I meet them in another world. But I want to tell you one lesson I learned that night, which I have never forgotten, and that is, when I preach to press Christ upon the people then and there, I try to bring them to a decision on the spot. I would rather have that right hand cut off than give an audience a week to decide what to do with Jesus.

—from Dwight L. Moody's "Fire Sermon"

*1851—Richard Chenevix Trench (1807–86) was an Irish-born poet, pro-
fessor, and prelate in the Church of England. He was a gifted linguist and
hymn writer as well. Among his many notable books is On the Study of
Words, the preface of which he wrote on this day. The book was one of the
first to attempt a systematic study of word origins and meanings, and it influenced many later writers and thinkers such as Owen Barfield and C. S.
Lewis. Trench believed words and their origins contained profound moral
lessons, if only we paid attention to them. In the following excerpt, for
example, Trench looks at the origin of the word tribulation.*

———————— ⋅⋟ ⋞⋅ ————————

On every side we are beset with poetry. Popular language is full of
it, of words used in an imaginative sense, of things called . . . by names
having immediate reference not to what they are, but to what they are
like. All language is in some sort, as one has said, a collection of faded
metaphors. . . .

Let me illustrate my meaning more at length by the word *tribulation*. We all know in a general way that this word, which occurs not seldom in Scripture and in the Prayer Book, means affliction, sorrow,
anguish; but it is quite worth our while to know *how* it means this, and
to question *tribulation* a little closer. It is derived from the Latin *tribu-
lum*, which was the threshing instrument, or harrow, whereby the
Roman husbandman separated the corn from the husks; and *tribulatio*
in its primary signification was the act of this separation. But some Latin
writer of the Christian Church appropriated the word and image for the
setting forth of a higher truth; and sorrow, distress, and adversity being
the appointed means for the separating in men of whatever in them was
light, trivial, and poor from the solid and the true, their chaff from their
wheat. He therefore called these sorrows and trials "tribulations,"
threshings, that is, of the inner spiritual man, without which there
could be no fitting him for the heavenly garner. . . .

This deeper religious use of the word *tribulation* was unknown to
classical antiquity, belonging exclusively to the Christian writers.

1821—American lawyer Charles G. Finney (1792–1875) first began reading the Bible because he noticed how often his law books referred to it. Then, on this day, he had a powerful conversion experience that redirected the entire course of his life. He eventually became one of the most renowned revivalists of the nineteenth century as well as a lecturer, minister, and educator. Later in his life, he wrote about his extremely mystical conversion experience.

———— ✥ ————

There was no fire and no light in the room; nevertheless, it appeared to me as if it were perfectly light. As I went in and shut the door after me, it seemed as if I met the Lord Jesus Christ face to face. . . . He said nothing, but looked at me in such a manner as to break me right down at his feet. I have always since regarded this as a most remarkable state of mind; for it seemed to me a reality that he stood before me, and I fell down at his feet and poured out my soul to him. I wept aloud like a child and made such confessions as I could with my choked utterance. It seemed to me that I bathed his feet with my tears. . . .

As soon as my mind became calm enough to break off from that interview, I returned to the front office and found that the fire that I had made of large wood was nearly burned out. But as I turned and was about to take a seat by the fire, I received a mighty baptism of the Holy Ghost. Without any expectation of it, without ever having the thought in my mind that there was any such thing for me, without any recollection that I had ever heard the thing mentioned by any person in the world, the Holy Spirit descended upon me in a manner that seemed to go through me, body and soul. I could feel the impression, like a wave of electricity, going through and through me. Indeed it seemed to come in waves and waves of liquid love; for I could not express it in any other way. It seemed like the very breath of God. I can recollect distinctly that it seemed to fan me, like immense wings.

—from *The Memoirs of Rev. Charles G. Finney* (1876)

1810—*On this day the copyright was granted to the first edition of* Wyeth's Repository of Sacred Music *by John Wyeth (1770–1858). What sets this hymnal apart is that it was among the first to use the "shape note" system of musical notation, in which notes are printed in different shapes to aid those who cannot read standard notation. Surprisingly, Wyeth himself was not a musician, but an American bookseller who was able to capitalize on the vogue for new hymnals. The following hymn, "Guide Me, O Thou Great Jehovah," though already popular and widely known, was included in that collection. Its authorship is credited to Welsh hymn writer and Methodist minister William Williams (1717–91).*

———— ⋙ ⋘ ————

Guide me, O thou great Jehovah,
 Pilgrim through this barren land;
I am weak, but thou art mighty,
 Hold me in thy powerful hand;
 Bread of Heaven, Bread of Heaven,
Feed me till I want no more.

Open, Lord, the crystal fountain,
 Whence the healing streams do flow;
Let the fiery cloudy pillar
 Lead me all my journey through;
 Strong Deliverer, Strong Deliverer,
Be thou still my strength and shield.

When I tread the verge of Jordan,
 Bid my anxious fears subside;
Death of death, and hell's destruction,
 Land me safe on Canaan's side;
 Songs of praises, songs of praises
I will ever give to thee.

1915—In Jolo, Philippine Islands, on this day, Canadian missionary C. H. Brent (1862–1929), Bishop of the Philippines, completed the writing of the preface of his book The Conquest of Trouble and the Peace of God. *In the first half of the book, he writes short expository "musings," as he calls them, on every instance of the word* trouble *in the book of Psalms. In the second half of the book, he does the same for every use of the word* peace *in the four gospels. The book is both tender and profound, as can be seen by the following entry.*

───────── ·◄§ §►· ─────────

"My soul also is sore troubled" (Psalm 6:3).

This whole psalm is by one deeply troubled in body and soul: "My beauty is gone for very trouble" (verse 7).

God is called upon to spare, and in the end faith anticipates His sure response. Relief comes with the conviction that God heeds. We can hail the dawn even before day breaks if we have the foresight of faith. Comeliness is corroded by unbeaten trouble; it is transfigured by conquered trouble. There is in this Psalm something of self-pity, that enemy of God's pity. Without God's pity, the certainty that He is effectively operating upon our trouble, the mind must turn in upon itself and self-pity ensues.

It is very easy to aggravate trouble by dwelling too intently upon it and watching its clouds as they drift in, very much as the fascinated bird watches the serpent about to devour it. Nothing intensifies trouble like timidity and passivity. There is an oriental proverb which says that "you cannot prevent the birds of despair from flying over your head, but you need not ask them to nest in your hair."

1877—On this day, poet Frances Ridley Havergal (1836–79), one of Victorian England's most popular and beloved hymn writers, wrote the hymn "Who Is on the Lord's Side?" She included it her collection of verse Royal Grace and Loyal Gifts, *and it is based on 1 Chronicles 12:18: "Thine are we, David, and on thy side." The opening verses of that lovely hymn follow.*

────────── ✦ ──────────

Who is on the Lord's side?
   Who will serve the King?
Who will be his helpers,
   Other lives to bring?
Who will leave the world's side?
   Who will face the foe?
Who is on the Lord's side?
   Who for him will go?

RESPONSE: By thy call of mercy,
   By thy grace divine,
We are on the Lord's side;
   Savior, we are thine.

Not for weight of glory,
   Not for crown and palm,
Enter we the army,
   Raise the warrior psalm;
But for Love that claimeth
   Lives for whom he dies;
He whom Jesus nameth
   Must be on his side.

RESPONSE: By thy love constraining,
   By thy grace divine
We are on the Lord's side;
   Savior, we are thine.

1816—In the evening of this day a British minister named Thomas Taylor (1738–1816) delivered a stirring sermon in which he stated that he "hoped to die as an old soldier of Jesus Christ, with his sword in his hand." The next morning he died in his sleep. The sermon, followed so soon by the minister's death, so moved British poet and hymn writer James Montgomery (1771–1854; see also August 13) that he wrote the hymn "The Christian Soldier" in memory of Reverend Taylor.

———— ❧ ❧ ————

Servant of God, well done!
   Rest from thy loved employ:
The battle fought, the victory won,
   Enter thy Master's joy!

The voice at midnight came;
   He started up to hear;
A mortal arrow pierced his frame;
   He fell, but felt no fear.

His spirit with a bound
   Left its encumbering clay:
His tent, at sunrise, on the ground
   A darkened ruin lay.

The pains of death are past,
   Labor and sorrow cease,
And life's long warfare closed at last,
   His soul is found in peace.

Soldier of Christ, well done!
   Praise by thy new employ;
And, while eternal ages run,
   Rest in thy Savior's joy.

—from James Montgomery's *Greenland and Other Poems* (1819)

1926—Englishwoman Lilias Trotter (1853–1928) gave up a promising career as an artist to become a missionary to North Africa. Her special calling was to witness to the Sufis (Muslim mystics), an act that was punishable by death in many parts of the Muslim world at the time. In her greatest book, The Way of the Sevenfold Secret, *she attempts to explain the Gospel of Christ in a way that might be understood by the Sufis. On this day, the Bishop of Jerusalem, Rennie MacInnes, wrote the preface to the first edition of Miss Trotter's book. The following excerpt from chapter 3 of* The Way of the Sevenfold Secret *takes John 10:7 as its text: "Then said Jesus unto them again, 'Verily, verily, I say unto you, I am the Door of the sheep.'"*

———— ❧ ❧ ————

Just as in human friendship those sharing it must be brought near together before there can be the linking of their hearts, so it must be in the Divine Friendship.

In the words of Christ, we have the step of drawing near to God set forth to us by the symbol of a door—the door into a sheepfold.

Now a sheepfold is a place of safety in the midst of danger: the wilderness may be all around, and wild beasts may be heard growling only a stone's throw off, but the sheep in the fold are as safe as if no enemies were there. They have entered in and they are saved.

So, in this new secret, God makes known to us that there is a place where even now in the wilderness of this world, with evil prowling all around, we may rest in safety as sheep within the fold. There is a place of nearness to God where the devil dares not venture that he may snatch the soul away; there is a salvation that is here and now.

We know, our brothers, that this is to you a new thought. Your belief is that no one can tell with certainty that he is saved until the day of account. You feel yourselves like sheep that may at any moment become a prey. Listen, for Christ speaks of a sheepfold right here in the wilderness, and of a door whereby we may enter in. . . .

There is no other way: the sheepfold has only one door. . . . Make haste to enter, my brother. . . . Dare to enter in.

1893—In this year an American woman named Adelaide S. Seaverns published a daily devotional called Thoughts for the Thoughtful *in which she collected her favorite thoughts from the great Christian writers. Her reading for this day is taken from the devotional writings of Christopher Newman Hall (1816–1902), an English Congregational clergyman, hymn writer, and devotional book writer.*

———————— ⋙⋘ ————————

The sight of falling leaves is saddening. Yet if we really fade as they, there is cause for grateful rejoicing. The leaf fades when its work is done. It has an important function as the lungs of the tree. The sap circulating through its surface receives the oxygen breathed in from the atmosphere. This combines with the carbon and, by the influence of light, is so changed as to be capable of depositing new material as the vitalizing current descends behind the bark, forming each year an additional ring around the stem. Thus every leaf, however weak and small, helps to build up the solid tree. The strongest portion of the oak is formed by the weakest. So the soul of a person, breathing the air of heaven and basking in the Sun of righteousness, by a divine chemistry transforms the natural into the spiritual, and not only becomes strong but insensibly builds up the great tree of humanity, the nation, and the church. Each single leaf, the young, the small, the obscure, renders help and adds to the beauty of the forest though it is itself unobserved. And each one of us by righteousness and love may help to beautify the moral world and make the wilderness rejoice. . . . We do not live in vain if we have helped to make life less burdensome and have comforted any of God's children—the least of Christ's brethren in the dusty highway. We need not regret if we do fade as a leaf, fulfilling its purpose before it falls.

1881—Theodore Parker (1810–60) was a highly respected though contro-versial American minister (see March 4 for more details). On this day, beloved American novelist Louisa May Alcott (1832–88) wrote in her pref-ace to the posthumously published Prayers of Theodore Parker: *"Some of his prayers were like poems, rich in lovely, quaint, and striking figures." Here is a sample.*

———————— ❧ ☙ ————————

Our Father, who is always with us, we thank you for the material world you have given us, this great foodful ground underneath our feet, this wide overarching heaven above our heads, and for the greater and lesser lights you have placed therein. We bless you for the moon that measures out the night, walking in brightness her continuous round, and for the sun that pours out the happy and the blessed day all round your many-peopled world. We thank you for the green grass, springing in its fair prophecy, for the oracular buds that are promising glorious things in weeks to come. We thank you for the power of vegetative and animative life that you have planted in this world of matter, which comes up this handsome growth of plant and tree, this noble life of fish, insect, reptile, bird, beast, and every living thing.

We thank you for the human world whereof you have created us. We bless you for the great spiritual talents wherewith you have endowed humanity, the crown of your visible creation on the earth. We thank you for our mind and our conscience and our heart, and all the mani-fold faculties that you have given us. . . .

We thank you for the work you give us to do on earth, in our vari-ous callings, widespread in the many-peopled town, or in some lonely spot hid in the green world that encompasses the town. We thank you for all these things that our hands find to do, by fireside and fieldside, in school or shop or house or ship or mart or wherever you summon us in the manifold vocations of our mortal life. . . .

Day by day, may we proclaim our religion by our faithful industry, doing what should be done, bearing what must be borne. . . . So may your kingdom come and your will be done on earth as it is in heaven. Amen.

1868—*A few days before he was to preach at a church in Philadelphia, Congregational minister Daniel March (1816–1909) could not find an appropriate closing hymn to accompany his text, "Here am I; send me" (Isaiah 6:8). So he wrote his own hymn. He set his words to a traditional folk-hymn tune that he found in an earlier hymnal, The Christian Lyre (1831). The resulting hymn, "Hark, the Voice of Jesus Calling," was first performed on this day.*

———— ✒ ✑ ————

Hark, the voice of Jesus calling,
"Who will go and work today?
Fields are white, and harvest's waiting,
Who will bear the sheaves away?"
Loud and long the Master calleth,
Rich reward He offers free;
Who will answer, gladly saying,
"Here am I; send me, send me"?

If you cannot be the watchman
Standing high on Zion's wall,
Pointing out the path to heaven,
Offering life and peace to all,
If you cannot speak like angels,
If you cannot preach like Paul,
You can tell the love of Jesus,
You can say, "He died for all."

Let none hear you idly saying,
"There is nothing I can do,"
While the souls of men are dying,
And the Master calls for you;
Take the task He gives you gladly;
Let His work your pleasure be;
Answer quickly when He calleth,
"Here am I; send me, send me."

1876—In a letter to the editor of an English magazine called The Christian, *an anonymous sea captain relates the story of a miraculous occurrence that began on this day. This anecdote is recorded in Major Daniel Webster Whittle's book* The Wonders of Prayer *(1885). (See July 24 for more information about this author.)*

"About one hundred and fifty miles west of the Bahamas, we encountered very disagreeable weather. For five or six days we seemed held by shifting currents or some unknown power in about the same place. We would think we had sailed thirty or forty miles, when on taking our observations we would find we were within three of four miles of our position the day before. This circumstance occurring repeatedly proved a trial to my faith, and I said within my heart, 'Lord, why are we so hindered and kept in this position?' Day after day we were held as if by an unseen force, until at length a change took place and we went on our way.

"Reaching our port they inquired, 'Where have you been through the gale?'

'What gale?' we asked. 'We have seen no gale.'

"We then learned that a terrible hurricane had swept through that region and that all was desolation. We afterward learned that this hurricane had swept around us and had almost formed a circle around the place occupied by us during the storm. A hundred miles in one direction all was wreck and ruin, fifty miles in the opposite direction all was desolation; and while that storm was raging in all its fury, we were held in perfect safety, in quiet waters, and in continual anxiety to change our position and pursue our voyage. One day of ordinary sailing would have brought us into the track of the storm and sent us to the bottom of the sea. We were anxious to sail on, but some unseen power held us where we were and we escaped."

The captain was a prayerful man, trusting in his Lord, though his faith was tried and he thought the Lord was not helping him. Yet the Lord was keeping his promise to him: "The beloved of the Lord shall dwell in safety by him, and the Lord shall cover him all the day long" (Deuteronomy 33:12).

1653—On this day a group of Dutch artists, known as the Guild of St. Luke, held a feast in honor of Dutch dramatist and poet Joost van den Vondel (1587–1679), one of the most renowned writers of the Dutch Renaissance. At that very moment, Vondel's crowning achievement, a poetic drama called Lucifer, was in the process of being printed. It appeared the next year and would soon become an influence on another landmark of Christian literature: Milton's Paradise Lost (1667). The following speech from Lucifer is spoken by the angel Michael after the armies of heaven have defeated Satan and the rebel angels, and cast them into hell.

———————— ◄§ §► ————————

MICHAEL: Praise be to God! The state of things above
Has changed. Our Grand Foe has met his defeat;
And in our hands he leaves his standard, helm,
And morning-star, and shield and banners bold.
Which spoil, gained in pursuit, even now does hang,
'Mid joys triumphant, honors, songs of praise,
And sounds of trump, on Heaven's axis bright,
The mirror clear of all rebelliousness,
Of all ambition that would rear its crest
'Gainst God, the stem immovable—grand fount,
Prime source, and Father of all things that are,
Which from His hand their nature did receive,
And various attributes. No more shall we
Behold the glow of Majesty Supreme
Dimmed by the damp of base ingratitude.
There, deep beneath our sight and these high thrones,
They wander through the air and restlessly
Move to and fro, all blind and overcast
With shrouding clouds, and horribly deformed.
Thus is his fate, who would assail God's Throne.
CHORUS: Thus is his fate, who would assail God's Throne.
Thus his fate, who would, through envy, man,
In God's own image made, deprive of light.

—from Act V of Vondel's *Lucifer*,
translated by Leonard Charles Van Noppen (1898)

1726—*Today the* Boston Gazette *newspaper carried this advertisement:* "*Just published:* An Introduction to the Singing of Psalm Tunes in a Plain and Easy Method . . . *by the Rev. Mr. Tufts.*" *This manual, intended for* "*children and people of the meanest capacities,*" *sets forth the rudiments of musical notation for the untrained. An anonymous poem,* "*On the Divine Uses of Music,*" *stands as the epigraph of the book and imaginatively describes the importance of song in the life of believers.*

We sing to You whose wisdom formed
The curious organ of the ear;
And You who gave us voices, Lord,
Our grateful songs in kindness hear.

We'll joy in God who is the spring
Of lawful joy and harmless mirth,
Whose boundless Love is fitly called
The harmony of heaven and earth.

These praises, dearest Lord, aloud
Our humblest sonnets shall rehearse,
Which rightly tuned are rightly styled
The music of the universe. . . .

Thus we poor mortals still on earth
Will imitate the heavenly choirs,
And with high notes above the clouds
We'll send with words more raised desires.

And that above, we may be sure,
When we come there our part to know;
While we live here at home and church,
We'll practice singing oft below.

1868—On this day American religious novelist Elizabeth Stuart Phelps (1844–1911) dedicated her novel Gates Ajar to her father, "whose life, like a perfume from beyond the Gates, penetrates every life which approaches it." The book proved immensely popular. It is the story of Mary Cabot, a young woman living in New England, who loses her faith after her brother is killed in the American Civil War. When her Aunt Winifred visits from Kansas, Mary's attitudes begin to change. Aunt Winifred's homespun wisdom and deep faith cause Mary to take a new view of God and life after death. In the following passage, Aunt Winifred discusses her ideas about heaven.

――――――――⋖⋗――――――――

One thing I have thought much about; it is that, whatever may be our first experience after leaving the body, it is not likely to be a *revolutionary* one. It is more in analogy with God's dealings that a quiet process, a gentle accustoming, should open our eyes on the light that would blind if it came in a flash. Perhaps we shall not see Him— perhaps we could not bear it to see Him at once. It may be that the faces of familiar human friends will be the first to greet us; it may be that the touch of the human hand dearer than any but His own shall lead us, as we are able, behind the veil, till we are a little used to the glory and the wonder and lead us so to Him.

Be that as it may, and be heaven where it may, I am not afraid. With all my guessing and my studying and my dreaming over these things, I am only a child in the dark. Nevertheless, I am not afraid of the dark. . . .

[Will heaven] disappoint me? No, I have settled that in my heart with God. I do not *think* I shall be disappointed. The truth is, he has obviously not *opened* the gates which bar heaven from our sight, but he has as obviously not *shut* them; they stand ajar, with the Bible and reason in the way, to keep them from closing; surely we should look in as far as we can, and surely, if we look with reverence, our eyes will [behold just enough so] that we may not cheat ourselves with mirages. And as the little Swedish girl said the first time she saw the stars: "O father, if the *wrong side* of heaven is so beautiful, what must the *right side* be?"

4004 B.C.—*Irish archbishop James Ussher (1581–1656) was a man of wide learning, famous for his "Bible chronology," which still appears in the margins of some Bibles. According to his calculations, which are now largely discredited, the actual moment of Creation took place at 9:00 in the morning on this day. Whether accurate or not, his calculations provide an opportunity to read the opening stanzas of "The Creation" from God's Trombones by African-American writer James Weldon Johnson (1871–1938). Aside from being a leading writer of the Harlem Renaissance, Johnson was also a lawyer, diplomat, professor, and secretary of the NAACP.*

————— ❧ ❧ —————

And God stepped out on space,
And he looked around and said:
I'm lonely—
I'll make me a world.
And far as the eye of God could see
Darkness covered everything,
Blacker than a hundred midnights
Down in a cypress swamp.

Then God smiled,
And the light broke,
And the darkness rolled up on one side,
And the light stood shining on the other,
And God said: That's good!

Then God reached out and took the light in his hands,
And God rolled the light around in his hands
Until he made the sun;
And he set that sun a-blazing in the heavens.
And the light that was left from making the sun
God gathered it up in a shining ball
And flung it against the darkness,
Spangling the night with the moon and stars.
Then down between
The darkness and the light
He hurled the world;
And God said: That's good!

1890—On this day the imprimatur was granted to a new translation, by Kegan Paul and Rev. Thomas Pope, of The Imitation of Christ *by German monk Thomas à Kempis (1380–1471). English publisher and author Kegan Paul (1828–1902) published many of the landmarks of English literature of his time.* The Imitation of Christ, *traditionally ascribed to Thomas, is one of the most popular Christian classics of all time. Countless readers consider it their favorite devotional book. Here, in Paul's and Pope's translation, is how Thomas à Kempis describes love.*

———— ⋞ ⋟ ————

Love is a great thing, a great good indeed, which alone makes light all that is burdensome and bears with even mind all that is uneven. For it carries a burden without being burdened, and it makes all that which is bitter, sweet and savory. The love of Jesus is noble and spurs us on to do great things and excites us to desire always things more perfect. Love desires to have its abode above and not to be kept back by things below. Love desires to be at liberty and estranged from all worldly affection, lest its inner view be hindered, lest it suffer itself to be entangled through some temporal interest or give way through mishap.

Nothing is sweeter than love; nothing stronger, nothing higher, nothing broader, nothing more pleasant, nothing fuller or better in heaven and in earth; for love is born of God and can rest only in God above all things created. The lover flies, runs, and rejoices; he is free and not held. He gives all for all and has all in all because he rests in one supreme above all, from whom all good flows and proceeds. He looks not at the gifts but turns himself above all goods to the giver. . . .

Whosoever loves knows the cry of this voice. A loud cry in the ears of God is that ardent affection of the soul which says, "My God, my love, you are all mine and I am all yours. Enlarge me in your love that I may learn to taste with the inner mouth of the heart how sweet it is to love and to be dissolved and swim in a sea of love. Let me be possessed by love, going above myself through excess of fervor and awe. Let me sing the song of love; let me follow you, my beloved, on high; let my soul lose herself in your praises, exulting in love. Let me love you more than myself, and myself only for you.

1882—Hannah Whitall Smith (1832–1911) was a popular American religious writer and an early advocate of women's rights. She is best remembered for her classic book The Christian's Secret of a Happy Life, *which for many years was the best-selling devotional book of all time. On this day, Hannah wrote to her daughter Mary concerning her book: "Wherever I go I am met with stories of its value and blessing. So many people even here have told me that it is 'next to their Bibles.' I would rather have written that book that has brought comfort and joy to so many sad and weary hearts than be the Queen of England." A passage follows. (See also November 28.)*

───────── ❧ ─────────

The Bible tells us that when God went forth for the salvation of His people, then He "did ride upon His horses and chariots of salvation." And it is the same now. Everything becomes a "chariot of salvation," when God rides upon it. . . . The great point, then, is to have our eyes opened to see in everything that comes to us a "chariot of God" and to learn how to mount into these chariots. We must recognize each thing that comes to us as being really God's chariot for us and must accept it as from Him. He does not command or originate the thing perhaps; but the moment we put it into His hands it becomes His, and He at once turns it into a chariot for us. He makes all things, even bad things, work together for good to all those who trust Him. All He needs is to have them entirely committed to Him.

When your trial comes, then, put it right into the will of God, and climb into the will as a little child climbs into its mother's arms. The baby carried in the chariot of its mother's arms rides triumphantly through the hardest places and does not even know they are hard. And how much more we who are carried in the chariot of the "arms of God!"

Get into your chariot, then. Take each thing that is wrong in your lives as God's chariot for you. No matter who the builder of the wrong may be, whether men or devils, by the time it reaches your side it is God's chariot for you and is meant to carry you to a heavenly place of triumph. Shut out all the second causes and find the Lord in it. Say, "Lord, open my eyes that I may see, not the visible enemy, but your unseen chariots of deliverance."

1892—Joseph Jacobs (1884–1916), a well-known English writer and scholar, is now remembered chiefly for his outstanding compilations of English and Celtic fairy tales. On this day, from his home in Kilburn, England, he dedicated his translation of Gracian's Art of Worldly Wisdom *to a Mrs. G. H. Lewis, saying, "Gracian . . . sees clear, but he looks upward." Baltasar Gracian (1601–58) was a Spanish Jesuit writer whose* Art of Worldly Wisdom *has become a widely beloved "self-help" classic. In it he catalogs earthy advice for advancing in the world and stresses moderation, morality, intensity, and wisdom. If his advice is not always particularly spiritual, it is at least practical. Here is a sampling from Jacobs' translation.*

———————— ∙◦§ ◦∙ ————————

• *Find the Good in a Thing at Once.* 'Tis the advantage of good taste. The bee goes to the honey for her comb, the serpent to the gall for its venom. So with taste: some seek the good, others the ill. There is nothing that has no good in it, especially in books, as giving food for thought....

• *Look into the Interior of Things.* Things are generally other than they seem, and ignorance that never looks beneath the rind becomes disabused when you show the kernel. Lies always come first, dragging fools along by their irreparable vulgarity. Truth always lags last, limping along on the arm of time....

• *Trust Your Heart,* especially when it has been proved. Never deny it a hearing. It is a kind of house oracle that often foretells the most important. Many have perished because they feared their own heart, but of what use is it to fear it without finding a better remedy? Many are endowed by nature with a heart so true that it always warns them of misfortune and wards off its effects. It is unwise to seek evils, unless you seek to conquer them....

• *Noble Qualities.* Noble qualities make noble humans; a single one of them is worth more than a multitude of mediocre ones. There was once a man who made all his belongings, even his household utensils, as great as possible. How much more ought a great man see that the qualities of his soul are as great as possible. In God all is eternal and infinite, so in a hero everything should be great and majestic, so that all his deeds, nay, all his words, should be pervaded by a transcendent majesty.

1769—English minister William Romaine (1714–95) was such a popular preacher that his parishioners grew resentful of the growing crowd of new faces in their midst. His posthumously published letters have long proven a source of great inspiration to Christian readers. For example, on this day he wrote to a friend concerning the value of getting beyond self in the spiritual life.

———— ❧ ❧ ————

The more we get outside of self, the more we grow in Jesus. Tired of our works and duties, we learn to value His righteousness. Feeling we cannot keep ourselves, we know how to trust His faithfulness, who has undertaken to keep His people to the end. O what a friend is this, whose love is like Himself—the same yesterday, today, and forever! This sense of His love makes His people loving, and His love to them is the bond of all their holy love to one another. Having put on Christ, they put on with Him kindness, brotherly love, bowels of mercy, etc. . . . The love of Christ will constrain to this; it spreads like leaven. Every act not only brings forth but also diffuses its sweet influence. . . . The holy flame spreads as it burns; so that every affection, as it increases its attachment to our glorious Head, makes us more truly loving to all His members.

My dear friend, I wish you were more intimate with this loving Jesus. And why not? What has He done to make you shy of Him? All your complaints about yourself are no bar; they are so many ties and bonds, constraining you to love Him. Yea, He will love to bear them for you, as matters of faith. Whatever you are, or whatever you feel of sin, misery, helplessness, etc., if rightly managed should increase your knowledge of and dependence on the Lord Jesus Christ. Indeed, all that you meet with, till you meet Him face to face, should bring you into more experience of His perfect salvation and of His free love to bestow it on such as you—by which means you would be growing daily in the excellency of the knowledge of your Lord and would be more conformed to His image and example. May you and I increase daily in this heavenly friendship, and may we love Him in our measure as He loved us.

1885—Andrew Murray (1828–1917) was a South African missionary, writer, and divine, whose most famous and enduring work is With Christ in the School of Prayer. *In that book's preface, which Murray wrote on this day, he states, "Many complain that they have not the power to pray in faith, to pray the effectual prayer that availeth much. The message I would fain bring them is that the blessed Jesus is waiting, is longing, to teach them this." Throughout the book he uses the metaphor of Jesus as a schoolmaster in whose school the beginner in prayer is enrolled.*

Blessed Lord! who ever lives to pray, You can teach me too to pray, me to live ever to pray. In this You love to make me share Your glory in heaven, that I should pray without ceasing and ever stand as a priest in the presence of my God.

Lord Jesus! I ask You this day to enroll my name among those who confess that they know not how to pray as they ought, and especially ask You for a course of teaching in prayer. Lord! Teach me to tarry with You in the school and give You time to train me. May a deep sense of my ignorance, of the wonderful privilege and power of prayer, of the need of the Holy Spirit as the Spirit of prayer, lead me to cast away my thoughts of what I think I know, and make me kneel before You in true teachableness and poverty of spirit.

And fill me, Lord, with the confidence that with such a teacher as You are, I shall learn to pray. In the assurance that I have as my teacher, Jesus, who is ever praying to the Father, and by His prayer rules the destinies of His Church and the world, I will not be afraid. As much as I need to know of the mysteries of the prayer world, You will unfold for me. And when I may not know, You will teach me to be strong in faith, giving glory to God.

Blessed Lord! You will not put to shame Your scholar who trusts You, nor, by Your grace, would he You either. Amen.

1902—Abraham Kuyper (1837–1920) was a famed Dutch theologian and statesman, who, while spending an active life in politics, was able to write warm and compelling works of theology that proved popular among scholars and lay readers alike. The following passage, for example, is from his book-length meditation on death, called Asleep in Jesus, *the foreword of which was written on this day.*

———— ⋅᠍᠍⊰ ⊱⋅ ————

No one on earth has ever fathomed his own being.

Until we die we remain to ourselves the *deepest* mystery.

But this then is the glory that awaits us after dying—that the veil will be taken away from our face, and as in a clear mirror God will show us our own being.

Then only. Not before.

And herein is grace. If here on earth we were ever to have a sight of our own being as we actually are, we would be terrified at ourselves. Even as the loving wife, hastening to the hospital to see her husband who had been wounded on the field of battle—when she saw his misshapen, bandaged face, involuntarily recoiled; so would our soul shrink back from ourselves if we were to see in clearness our own being soiled by sin and enwound by grace.

And therefore Jesus tarries. And He will only let you see yourself when the latest trace of sin is gone and the last bandage has been removed and you can see yourself as a model of Christ's redeeming love, altogether sound and altogether healed.

Then the mystery of your person falls away from before you.

And God Who *alone* knows your being, because He Himself has foreordained and created you and has kept you and has restored you, will then discover you to yourself, reveal your own being to you and in your own being, *for God's sake*, make you rich.

—adapted from the translation of John Hendrik de Vries (1929)

1857—American religious leader Phoebe Palmer (1807–74) was one of the most prominent female evangelists of the nineteenth century. (See also July 26.) She worked tirelessly for women's rights and radical social reform. On this day in London, after a successful revival tour of England, as she waited at a train station, she and a company of coworkers and friends determined to form themselves into a "soul-saving band." To that end, they made the following resolutions.

———— ⁓ঔ৯ ————

1. Resolved: That while we would not be unmindful of the divine injunction to be "diligent in business," we will, through the assistance of almighty grace, manifest our fervor of spirit by endeavoring to make every earthly consideration, whether it be secular business or domestic avocations, specifically subservient to the service of Christ.

2. Resolved: That we will endeavor to save at least one half hour daily, and more, if possible, in specific, direct efforts to win souls to Christ. . . .

3. Resolved: That we will make earnest and prayerful efforts to engage all who love our Lord Jesus Christ to unite in this, the most momentous and ennobling Christian enterprise that can command the attentions of a redeemed world: enlisting, as far as in us lies, the interest of all professed Christians, whether young or old, and irrespective of denomination, inasmuch as all professed Christians are called to be *workers together* with God in bringing a revolted world back to the world's Redeemer.

4. Resolved: That we will, as far as circumstances permit, meet together weekly at such time and place as, by mutual agreement, shall be deemed most expedient; in order—first: To seek counsel of God, "Who teaches our hands to war and our fingers to fight," and through whom alone we can wage a successful warfare against the hosts of sin. Second: To present cases demanding special prayer, to report conversions or cases of hopeful interest, for mutual counsel, and especially for the encouragement of the weak and timid in order that the graces of the Spirit, in the weakest believer may be brought into continuous requisition and thereby be continually multiplied, and thus the timid and weak in Zion become courageous and strong as David.

—from Phoebe Palmer's *The Promise of the Father* (1859)

1742—Presbyterian minister Philip Doddridge (1702–51) was a Nonconformist divine and hymn writer of note in eighteenth-century England. Among his hymns are "O Happy Day" and "O God of Bethel, by Whose Hand." On this day, while his wife was traveling apart from him for a month, he wrote her a charming letter describing his life in her absence.

———— ⚜ ————

My days begin, pass, and end in pleasure and seem short because they are so delightful. It may seem strange to say it, but really so it is, I hardly feel that I want anything. I often think of you and pray for you and bless God on your account and please myself with the hope of many comfortable days and weeks and years with you; yet I am not at all anxious about your return or indeed about anything else. And the reason— the great and sufficient reason—is that I have more of the presence of God with me than I remember ever to have enjoyed in any one month of my life. He enables me to live for Him and to live with Him. When I awake in the morning, which is always before it is light, I address myself to Him and converse with Him, speak to Him while I am lighting my candle and putting on my clothes, and have often more delight before I come out of my chamber, though it be hardly a quarter of an hour after my awaking, than I have enjoyed for whole days or perhaps weeks of my life. He meets me in study, in secret, in family devotions. It is pleasant to read, pleasant to compose, pleasant to converse with my friends at home; pleasant to visit those abroad—the poor, the sick; pleasant to write letters of necessary business by which any good can be done; pleasant to go out and preach the gospel to poor souls, of which some are thirsting for it, and others dying without it; pleasant in the weekday to think how near another Sabbath is; but, oh! much, much more pleasant to think how near eternity is and how short the journey through this wilderness and that it is but a step from earth to heaven.

... But the postman calls, and I must therefore conclude, wishing you all the happiness I feel—and more if your heart could contain it. My dearest, your ever affectionate friend, who hopes to love you forever,

P. Doddridge

November

Spanish mystic Teresa of Ávila writing
in her cell (see November 29). Illustration from
Sabine Baring-Gold's *Lives of the Saints*.

c. 710—Bede (673–735), a medieval English scholar, was called "The father of English church history" for his extensive historical writings. Shortly after his death (see May 26) he was not only canonized, but dubbed "The Venerable Bede." The following excerpt is from a sermon Bede delivered on All Saints' Day, which, in Bede's time, was a movable feast. A few years after Bede's death, Pope Gregory III fixed the date of All Saints as November 1, where it has remained ever since. What follows is Bede's picture of our arrival in heaven to meet "all the saints."

--------- ❧ ❦ ---------

The multitude of the faithful shall ... enter the palace of that eternal court, who in peaceful union have observed the heavenly commandments and have maintained the purity of the faith.

But above all these things [we will associate] with the companies of angels and archangels, thrones and dominions, principalities and powers, and the enjoyment of the watches of all the celestial virtues— to behold the squadron of the saints, adorned with stars; the patriarchs, glittering with faith; the prophets, rejoicing in hope; the apostles, who in the twelve tribes of Israel, shall judge the whole world; the martyrs, decked with the purple diadems of victory; the virgins, also, with the wreaths of beauty. But of the King, who is in the midst, no words are able to speak. That beauty, that virtue, that glory, that magnificence, that majesty, surpasses every expression, every sense of the human mind. For it is greater than the glory of all saints. But to attain to that ineffable sight and to be made radiant with the splendor of His countenance, it were worthwhile to suffer torment every day—it were worthwhile to endure hell itself for a season, so that we might behold Christ coming in glory and be joined to the number of the saints. So is it not then well worthwhile to endure earthly sorrows, that we may be partakers of such good and such glory?

Let us consider that Paradise is our country, as well as theirs, and so we shall begin to reckon the patriarchs as our fathers. Why do we not, then, hasten and run, that we may behold our country and salute our parents?

—translated by John Mason Neale

1855—The excerpt below is from a sermon delivered by Father F.-J.-F. Fortin, French priest and curé of St. Étienne Church in Auxerre, France, on All Souls' Day. It was published in his book Parish Sermons *in 1855. (See also April 19.) Catholic and Protestant churches alike celebrate All Souls' Day in memory of all those who have died in the faith, as Father Fortin describes here.*

————— ◦§ §◦ —————

My friends, nothing is more consoling that the death of the just.... They bless the Lord who has uprooted them from the earth and transplanted them in that delicious country where streams flow with milk and honey. They have left Egypt, marked with the blood of the lamb, nourished by his mysterious flesh, and laden with the spoils of his enemies. In vain, impious Pharaoh deploys his trickery and violence against them; but the tyrant is vanquished, the Red Sea crossed. Their long and perilous journey through the desert has reached its end. All battles are ended. All victories are sealed. They reach the borders of their homeland. With saintly transports they greet these new regions where they will forever be reunited with their own people.

If you were to ask me, my friends, how the just are able to be enlivened by such confidence at death, I would tell you that the memory of their justice consoles them, that the succors of religion fortify them, that their hope of immortality reassures them. They will appear before their Judge, but for a long time they have known that He will rule in their favor because of the virtues that He Himself practiced. They will enter into the vast expanses of eternity, but they will only do so because they have been preceded by His works of salvation. If the gates of the celestial realm are difficult to pass through, then they will know that the guardians of those eternal doors are the same poor whose hunger they satisfied, whose nakedness they covered, whose tears they dried. They know that even while the world itself disappears, it cannot take with it the works of mercy they have done. Without regret they will see all their honor and dignity and wealth fall away and vanish. But the kindnesses they have done will remain.... The humiliations that helped you overcome your pride, the ability to forgive that helped you deny your anger, and the many saintly instances of love that helped you tame your avarice—all these will abundantly console your heart when you lie upon your deathbed.

1829—Robert Hawker (1753–1827) was a beloved English religious writer and vicar in Charles Church in Plymouth, England. His outstanding daily devotional, The Poor Man's Morning and Evening Portions (1829), was published after his death. His evening reflection for this day takes Isaiah 55:8 as its theme: "For my thoughts are not your thoughts, neither are your ways my ways, says the Lord."

———— ⋅⋙ ⋘⋅ ————

My soul, have you ever considered the blessedness in this verse as it concerns the great work of salvation? Ponder over it this evening. There is nothing, perhaps, in which there is a greater and more striking difference than there is between our crude and contracted notions of redemption, and the perfect and unerring thoughts of Jehovah on this point. Our conduct toward each other is so limited on the score of pardon that though we may forgive a first or second offense, yet if it be repeated too many times, nature revolts at the offender and seems to take a kind of justification in withholding any farther acts of clemency. . . . But with God, abounding sin calls forth abounding grace and, like the tide, rises above high watermark—yea, overflows all the banks and surrounding ground; so much so, indeed, that it covers the mountains and "if the sin of Judah be looked for, it shall not be found." Hence the prophet, in a transport of holy joy and triumph in the contemplation, cries out, "Who is a God like You, who pardons iniquity and passes by the transgression of the remnant of his heritage? He retains not his anger forever, because he delights in mercy. He will turn again: he will have compassion on us: he will subdue our iniquities; and you will cast all our sins into the depths of the sea" (Micah 7:18–19). How truly blessed, then, must it be, to carry the same kind of reasoning concerning God into all the departments of thinking, in relation to himself and his dealings with us. . . . This sweet verse stands for a memorandum to inform me: "For my thoughts are not your thoughts, neither are your ways my ways, says the Lord." . . . Say, my soul, do you feel delight in such views of Jehovah? Is it blessed to you that in all your Jesus has taught you, he has brought you to see more and more your nothingness, your littleness, and the Lord's all-sufficiency? Surely it must be divine teaching alone that can create joy in the heart when such discoveries are made that tend to humble the creature and exalt the Creator. Blessed be the Lord!

1621—Robert Sanderson (1587–1663) was a professor of divinity at Oxford, chaplain to King Charles I of England, and, later in life, the Bishop of Lincoln. On this day, in St. Paul's Cathedral, London, he delivered a stirring sermon on the topic of charity, which takes 1 Corinthians 7:24 as its text: "Brethren, let every man, wherein he is called, therein abide with God."

——————— •◄ξ ξ►• ———————

Has not Christ required us to feed the hungry and to clothe the naked and to be free and charitable to the poor? Nothing surer. God forbid any man should preach against charity and almsdeeds. But remember, just as God does not approve of alms or any other work if done without charity, neither does he approve of charity itself if done without discretion. Honor widows, says St. Paul, but those that are widows indeed: so relieve the poor, but relieve those that are poor indeed. Not everyone that asks, not everyone that wants, nay more, not everyone that is poor, is poor indeed; and he that in his indiscreet and misguided charity should give meat, or clothing or alms to everyone that asks or wants or is poor would soon make himself more hungry and naked and poor than he that is most hungry or naked or poor. The poor, whom Christ commends to you as a fit object for your charity, the poor indeed, are those that want not only the things they ask, but want also means to get without asking. A man that is blind or aged and past his work; a man that is sick or weak or lame and cannot work; a man that desires it and seeks it and cannot get work; a man that has a greater charge upon him than his honest pains can maintain—such a man as one of these, he is poor indeed. Let your ears be open and your eyes open and your hands open to such a one: it is a charitable deed and a sacrifice of sweet smelling. With such sacrifices God is well pleased. Forget not to offer such sacrifices upon every good opportunity; and be well assured God will not forget in due time to reward you.

1828—Rev. *Sydney Smith (1771–1845) was a celebrated English wit and clergyman whose political influence was considerable due to his well-reasoned essays and letters. He was particularly instrumental in achieving broader rights for Catholics in England, even though he himself was ordained in the Church of England. On this day, for instance, at the Cathedral Church in Bristol, England, he preached one of his most stirring pronouncements on the subject of religious toleration, a sermon called "Rules of Christian Charity." Here is an excerpt.*

———— ❦ ————

A great deal of mischief is done by not attending to the limits of interference with each other's religious opinions—by not leaving to the power and wisdom of God that which belongs to God alone. Our holy religion consists of some doctrines which influence practice and of others which are purely speculative. If religious errors be of the former description, they may, perhaps, be fair objects of human interference; but if the opinion be merely theological and speculative, there, the right of human interference seems to end, because the necessity for such interference does not exist. Any error of this nature is between the Creator and the creature—between the Redeemer and the redeemed. If such opinions are not the best opinions which can be found, God Almighty will punish the error, if mere error seems to the Almighty a fit object of punishment. Why may not man wait if God waits? Where are we called upon in Scripture to pursue men for errors purely speculative? To assist Heaven in punishing those offenses which belong only to Heaven? In fighting, unasked, for what we deem to be the battles of God—of that patient and merciful God, who pities the frailties we do not pity—who forgives the errors we do not forgive—who sends rain upon the just and the unjust and makes his sun to shine upon the evil and the good? . . .

The object is to be at the same time pious to God and charitable to man; to render your own faith as pure and perfect as possible, not only without hatred of those who differ from you, but with a constant recollection that it is possible, in spite of thought and study, that you may have been mistaken—that other sects may be right—and that a zeal in his service that God does not want is a very bad excuse for those bad passions which his sacred Word condemns.

1657—In Boston on this day, American Puritan clergyman John Norton (1606–63) completed his biography of Puritan author and clergyman John Cotton (1584–1652), known as the "Patriarch of New England." Norton's seminal book, Abel Being Dead, Yet Speaketh, *is historically significant because it was the first biography to have been written and published in the English colonies. In the following passage from that book, Norton discusses the Christian uses and importance of Christian biography.*

------------------ ✌ ✍ ------------------

'Tis a part of the portion of the saints that (together with the benefit of the living) they may enjoy both the life and death of those who both lived and died in the Faith. . . . By faith Abel being dead many thousand years since, yet speaks, and will speak when time shall be no more. That the living speak is no wonder; but that the dead speak is more than miraculous. . . .

A considerable part of the Scripture is a divine testimony of what the faithful have done and suffered, recorded for succeeding generations, not only as a memorial of them, but as so many practical demonstrations of the faithfulness of God, as so many full and glorious triumphs over the world, sin, and Satan, obtained by persons in the like temptations and subject to like passions with ourselves. . . .

You may believe it: what God has done for the soul of the least saint of some few years continuance, were it digested into order, would make a volume full of temptations, signs, and wonders—a wonderful history, because it would be a history of such experiences that each one of them is more than a wonder. There are no greater acts than their obedience, both active and passive, to the death. The sufferings of the apostles may well be reckoned among the Acts of the Apostles. No greater monuments than their register; to live and die in the faith of Jesus, to do things worthy to be written, and to write things worthy to be done, both is good and does good.

1586—The English translation of A Work Concerning the Trueness of the Christian Religion *by French Huguenot leader Philippe de Mornay (1549–1623) was entered at the Stationer's Register in London on this day (that is, it was officially registered for publication). Translated from the French by renowned English poets Sir Philip Sidney (1554–86) and Arthur Golding (c. 1536–c. 1605), the work remains a classic of Elizabethan religious prose. In the following slightly modernized passage, the author makes use of the famous "clockmaker" metaphor as a way of proving the existence of God.*

We see the heaven—how it moves around with a continual moving. Also, we see there the planets, one under another, . . . each having a separate course and movement of its own. And shall we say that these movings happen by chance? But the same chance that made them move should also make them stand still. Again, as for chance, it is nothing else but disorder and confusion; but in all these diversities, there is one uniformity of moving which is never interrupted. How then do they move of themselves? Nay, for nothing moves itself; and where things move one another, there is no possibility of infinite holding on; but in the end men must be fain to mount up to a first beginning, and that is a rest. As for example, from the pendulum of a clock we come to a wheel, and from that wheel to another, and finally to the wit of the clockmaker who by his cunning has so ordered them that notwithstanding that he makes them all to move, yet he himself vanishes not. It remains then that of all these movings, we must imagine one unmovable; and of all these so constant diversities, one always like itself; and of all these bodies, one Spirit.

1591—On this day, Mary Magdalen's Funeral Tears, the most famous sermon by English Jesuit poet and martyr Robert Southwell (1561–95; see also December 25), was registered for publication. It is a beautifully poetic exposition of John 20, in which Mary Magdalen comes to the empty tomb of Jesus. In the closing paragraphs, the author exhorts the reader to be more like Mary.

———— ✥ ————

O Christian soul, take Mary for your mirror; . . . learn, O sinful man, from this once-sinful woman, that sinners may find Christ if their sins be amended. Learn that those who are lost to sin may be recovered by love, that those who have been chased away by faintness of faith may be recalled by firmness of hope, and that which no mortal force, favor, or policy can grasp may be obtained by the continued tears of constant love.

Learn of Mary [to] rise early in the morning. . . . Run with repentance to your sinful heart, which was meant to be a temple, but, through your own fault, was no better than a tomb for Christ, since, being unable to feel him living in you, he seems as if he were dead. Roll away the stone of your former hardness; remove all the heavy loads that oppress you in sin; and look into your soul to see if you can find the Lord. If he is not within you, then stand outside weeping. . . .

Seek him only and nothing beside him. And if at first search he does not appear, then persevere in tears and continue your seeking. Stand upon the earth, treading upon all your earthly vanities, touching them with no more than the souls of your feet, that is, with the lowest and least part of your affection. To look better into the tomb, bow down your neck with the yoke of humility and stoop from lofty and proud conceits, so that with humbled and lowly looks you may find him whom your swelling and haughty thoughts had driven away. . . .

And if he grants you the glorious sight of himself to your inward eyes, presume not to know him, but as his unworthy suppliant prostrate your petitions before him that you may truly discern him and faithfully serve him. . . . If with Mary you crave no other solace from Jesus but Jesus himself, he will answer your tears with his presence and assure you of that presence with his own words, so that having seen him for yourself you may make him known to others, saying, with Mary, "I have seen our Lord, and these things he said to me."

1662—Dr. Robert South (1634–1716), one of the most popular preachers in England in the seventeenth century, preached his most famous sermon on this day at St. Paul's Cathedral in London. It was called "Man in Paradise." Not yet thirty when he delivered this sermon, South afterward never preached another sermon that proved as popular. His text was Genesis 1:27: "So God created man in his own image . . ." After having described the perfection of our original, unfallen image, South compares it, in the following excerpt, to our present fallen condition.

——————— ⋰§ §⋱ ———————

Take the picture of a man in the greenness and vivacity of his youth and in the latter date and declensions of his drooping years, and you will scarce know it to belong to the same person. . . . The same and greater is the difference between man innocent and fallen. He is, as it were, a new kind of species; the plague of sin has even altered his nature and eaten his very essentials. The image of God is wiped out; the creatures have shook off his yoke, renounced his sovereignty, and revolted from his dominion. Distempers and diseases have shattered the excellent frame of his body, and by a new dispensation, immortality is swallowed up in mortality. . . . The light within us is become darkness, and the understanding, that should be eyes to the blind faculty of the will, is blind itself, and so brings all the inconveniences that attend a blind follower under the conduct of a blind guide. . . .

In the last place, we learn from hence the excellency of Christian religion in that it is the great and only means that God has sanctified and designed to repair the breaches of humanity, to set fallen man upon his legs again, to clarify his reason, to rectify his will, and to compose and regulate his affections. The whole business of our redemption is, in short, only to rub over the defaced copy of the creation, to reprint God's image upon the soul, and (as it were) to set forth nature in a second and fairer edition.

The recovery of which lost image, as it is God's pleasure to command and our duty to endeavor, so it is in His power only to effect—to Whom be rendered and ascribed, as is most due, all praise, might, majesty, and dominion, both now and for evermore. Amen.

1942—The primary literary production of little-known American Quaker poet William Bacon Evans is his experimental collection of poems called Seven Score Bird Songs. In these poems, he tries to imitate actual songs of birds. Although Evans is all but forgotten today, in his time his book drew highly favorable reviews from such well-known readers as botanist George Washington Carver and novelist Grace Livingston Hill. On this day, Evans wrote the following sonnet (which is not part of his songbird cycle), called "The Spider."

Ringed all about with God's eternity,
In vain the spider dips her plummet thread!
Beyond the known, the knowable is spread,
But who can touch the limits of the sky?
With patient toil she imps infinity
Which wraps her like a garment! Yet instead
She clutches remnants of her tattered shred,
And thinks that home, in her simplicity!

But thou, O soul! count not this nether sphere,
Nor yonder starry vault thy resting place,
For all shall crumble—vanish as a tale!
Beyond crude visibles of now and here,
Prefer thou Truth, which outlasts time and space,
And enters into that within the veil.

Fourth century—This day is traditionally known in Europe as Martinmas, in honor of Martin of Tours (c. 315–c. 399), an early French prelate and saint. Early in his life Martin lived as a poor soldier. Later, he became the bishop of the city of Tours and was the teacher of Patrick, the great Irish saint. Aside from being the patron saint of France, Martin is also the patron saint of innkeepers because of his great charity and hospitality, as can be seen in the following legend from his life.

———————— ✌§ ੬☙ ————————

While a soldier he won the love of everyone with whom he came in contact for his true whole-hearted benevolence. The winter of 332 was one of unusual severity in Amiens where Martin was then stationed. Marching with his company one bitter day, Martin saw a man scantily clothed, shivering with the cold. Many already had passed but none had tried to succor him. Martin's impecuniosity was proverbial in the army, not from his extravagance but from his never-failing generosity. But this day he surprised even those who knew him best. Having neither food nor money for the poor stranger, Martin took the cloak from his own shoulders and, with the sharp blade of his sword, divided it in half—laying one part over the shivering pauper and covering his own exposed person with the rest. The act was quickly done and so wholly unostentatiously that few saw it. Later he bore without a word the witty jibes of his fellows over his abbreviated garment.

This much is literally true. His legend tells us that that night he had a vision in which he saw Jesus Christ wearing the half of the divided cloak and saying to his angel host, "Martin has clothed me in his garment." . . .

Martin, at the time of his vision above spoken of, was yet unbaptized; but very soon thereafter the sacred rite was performed, and when forty years of age he left the military, taking holy vows and for many years leading a hermit's life until in 371 he was named Bishop of Tours.

—from H. Pomeroy Brewster's *Saints and Festivals of the Christian Church*

1939—In 1939, 366 English-speaking ministers from all over the world were asked to contribute short, one-page reflections for a daily devotional volume called God's Purpose: A Book of 366 Daily Sermonettes. *The following sermonette, written for November 12 by a Rev. S. Willis McKelvey of Kansas City, Missouri, takes a rather unusual Bible verse as its text, Psalm 104:26: "There go the ships."*

⋯⋯⋯

The faculty of imagination is very marked in the success of human lives. James A. Garfield, when a boy, stood on the curb and saw the President of the United States ride by receiving the acclaim of the crowds. He imagined another day when the crowds would cheer him as the President, and he put his will back of his imagination and realized that day. Ulysses S. Grant, while a cadet at West Point, stood at attention before the commanding General of the United States Army. He envisioned himself in that high command and set his will to realize that vision. [The Renaissance painter] Raphael opened the Bible to the record of Christ's transfiguration and in imagination saw a great picture. Later he spread it upon the canvas, his masterpiece. Christ appeals to the finest in our imaginations. He says, "The kingdom of heaven is like to a grain of mustard seed . . . ," "The kingdom of heaven is like unto leaven . . . in three measures of meal," "The kingdom of heaven is like unto a net, that was cast into the sea."

"There go the ships." You are one and I another. But *where* go the ships? Will they turn about with the gales of life and be cast up a wreck on the shores of time? We must bring our wills into action to make that port. "Jesus, Savior, pilot me."

c. 525—Georgius Florentius, better known as Gregory of Tours (c. 538–93), was a French bishop and historian. His most important work is his History of the Franks, one of the earliest and most reliable histories of the French people. But he is also remembered for his outstanding collection of saints lives, Vita Patrum ("The Lives of the Fathers"). What makes this work unique is that Gregory either knew personally or spoke with those who had known many of the saints he discusses. For example, the following is an anecdote he tells about St. Quintianus, who died on this date and whose feast is held on this date. Quintianus was an African man who became a French bishop.

———————— ⋘ ⋙ ————————

The blessed man was assiduous in prayer, and he loved his people so much that when [King] Theodoric came with his army to besiege the city, [Quintianus] spent the night in psalmody, going about the walls; and in order that God would quickly vouchsafe to succor the land and its people he prayed earnestly with vigils and fasting. The King Theodoric, just when he thought to throw down the city's walls, was softened by the Lord's mercy and by the prayers of His priest whom the king was thinking to send into exile. And during the night, seized with fear, he leapt from his bed and strove to flee alone by the public highway. He had lost his wits and no longer knew what he was doing. When his men saw this, they tried to restrain him and did so only with difficulty, exhorting him to fortify himself with the saving sign of the Cross. Then Hilpingus, one of his dukes, drew near to the king and said, "Listen, most glorious king, to the counsels of my littleness. See, the walls of that city are very strong and great fortifications defend it. And in order that Your Majesty recognize this more fully, I need only to speak of the churches of the saints which are about the city's walls; further, the bishop of this place is great before God. Do not do what you have in mind; do no evil to the Bishop, and do not destroy the city." The King received this counsel favorably and gave the order that no one be harmed within eight miles of the city. No one doubted that this was granted by the prayer of the holy Bishop.

—from *Vita Patrum,*
translated by Fr. Seraphim Rose and Paul Bartlett

1940—On this day German planes bombed central England and destroyed the cathedral at Coventry. In 1964 the following anonymous prayer, entitled "Father, Forgive," was inscribed on a plaque near the ruined altar.

The hatred which divides nation from nation,
    race from race, class from class,
Father, forgive.
The covetous desires of men and nations
    to possess what is not their own,
Father, forgive.
The greed which exploits the labors of men,
    and lays waste the earth,
Father, forgive.
Our indifference to the plight of the homeless
    and the refugee,
Father, forgive.
The lust which uses for ignoble ends
    the bodies of men and women,
Father, forgive.
The pride which leads to trust in ourselves
    and not in God,
Father, forgive.

1714—Solomon Stoddard (1643–1729), an American Congregational clergyman, was dubbed "the pope of western Massachusetts" in honor of his considerable prominence and influence. For more than fifty years he served as a minister in Northampton. He was the grandfather of Jonathan Edwards (see July 8). On this day, Puritan minister Increase Mather (1639–1723; see July 9 and December 11), who was an admiring but dissenting critic of Stoddard's theology, wrote the preface to Stoddard's book A Guide to Christ. That book is a manual for ministers on how to respond to those expressing an interest in Christianity. Here is some advice from Stoddard's book concerning what the new convert may expect.

————— ✺ —————

Faith is the first act of grace. If the man had a gracious principle, he would immediately entertain Christ and the gospel. After a man has received a principle of regeneration, the first way that it works in is by drawing the heart to Christ. When men's hearts are changed and a new nature put into them, it does not first work in a way of sorrow for sin or thirsting after God's glory or delighting in holiness; but always the first act of grace is to draw close to Christ. God leads him into the exercise of this that he may be justified (Romans 5:1). If he did any other gracious act before this, it could not be accepted, for the person is not accepted before faith. All sanctification is the fruit of faith (Acts 26:18)....

Warn him to depend still on the free grace of God in Christ. He must expect many dark hours and times of temptation, but his way must be to grow in the knowledge of Christ. He must not think that now he shall always live a life of joy and comfort. Satan will be busy with him and he will have many workings both of carnal confidence and unbelief, and he must get more and more convinced of his own righteousness and the fullness of Christ. If he lives many years, he must never expect anything to glory in but Christ Jesus. And he is likewise to be warned that he lives up to the mercy of God in him, that he does not fall into a languishing and pining condition, but maintain the life and power of godliness so that he may not expose himself to temptation and darkness, and that he may not dishonor the holy name of God, showing forth the virtue of Him who has called him out of darkness into His marvelous light.

1521—On this day in London, printer Henry Pepwell published seven mystical treatises, which later acquired the title The Cell of Self-Knowledge. *These essays include the work of such earlier English and Continental mystics as Catherine of Siena (see February 15), Margery Kempe (see January 23), the anonymous author of the classic mystical treatise* The Cloud of Unknowing, *and the author of the following selection, English mystic Walter Hilton (who died in 1396). The following excerpt is from Hilton's treatise "The Song of Angels."*

───────── ⋘ ⋙ ─────────

Our Lord comforts a soul with angels' song. What that song is may not be described by any physical likeness, for it is spiritual and beyond all manner of imagination and reason. It may be felt and perceived in a soul, but it may not be shown. Nevertheless, I will tell you what I think it is like. When a soul is purified by the love of God, illumined by wisdom, established by the might of God, then is the eye of the soul opened to behold spiritual things, such as virtues and angels and holy souls and heavenly things. Then is the soul able, because of cleanness, to feel the touching, the speaking of good angels. . . .

Now, then, I think no soul can truly feel angels' song nor any heavenly sound, unless that soul is in perfect charity. All who are in perfect charity have not felt it, but only that soul that is so purified in the fire of love that all earthly savor is burned out of it and all mean hindrance between the soul and the cleanness of angels is broken and put away from it. Then truly may he sing a new song, and truly may he hear a blessed heavenly sound, an angels' song without deceit or feigning. Our Lord knows where the soul is that, for abundance of burning love, is worthy to hear angels' song. Whoever would hear angels' song and not be deceived by feigning, nor by imagination, nor by the illusion of the enemy, he it is who should have perfect charity; and that is when all vain love and dread, vain joy and sorrow, are cast out of the heart, so that it loves nothing but God, nor dreads anything but God, nor joys nor sorrows in anything but in God. . . . Whoever might, by the grace of God, go this way—he should not err.

1890—Over a period of two days, November 16–17, an African-American woman named Amanda Smith (1837–1915) received a supernatural "call" to preach the gospel. Later known as the "colored evangelist," she eventually became one of the most noted preachers of the African Methodist Episcopal Church and traveled throughout the world. Here she describes the circumstances of her "call," which began while attending a church service in Brooklyn, New York. This excerpt is from her Autobiography.

————— ❧ ❧ —————

Brother Gould, then pastor of the Fleet Street Church, took his text. I was sitting with my eyes closed in silent prayer to God, and after he had been preaching about ten minutes, as I opened my eyes, just over his head I seemed to see a beautiful star, and as I looked at it, it seemed to form into the shape of a large white tulip; and I said, "Lord, is that what you want me to see? If so, what else?" And then I leaned back and closed my eyes. Just then I saw a large letter "G," and I said, "Lord, do you want me to read in Genesis, or in Galatians? Lord, what does this mean?"

Just then I saw the letter "O." I said, "Why, that means go." And I said, "What else?" And a voice distinctly said to me, "Go preach."

The voice was so audible that it frightened me for a moment, and I said, "Oh, Lord, is that what you wanted me to come here for? Why did you not tell me when I was at home or when I was on my knees praying?" But His paths are known in the mighty deep, and His ways are past finding out. On Monday morning, about four o'clock, I think, I was awakened by the presentation of a beautiful white cross—white as the driven snow.... It was as cold as marble. It was laid just on my forehead and on my breast. It seemed very heavy; to press me down. The weight and the coldness of it were what woke me; and as I woke I said: "Lord, I know what that is. It is a cross."

I arose and got on my knees, and while I was praying these words came to me: "If any man will come after Me let him deny himself and take up his cross and follow Me." And I said, "Lord; help me and I will."

1866—On this day, English church worker Katherine Hankey (1834–1911) wrote the stanzas of the popular hymn "I Love to Tell the Story," at a time when she was recovering from a serious illness. This hymn is sung to a melody written three years later by American music teacher and choral conductor William G. Fischer (1835–1912).

I love to tell the story
  Of unseen things above,
Of Jesus and his glory,
  Of Jesus and his love;
I love to tell the story
  Because I know 'tis true;
It satisfies my longings
  As nothing else can do.

CHORUS: I love to tell the story,
  'Twill be my theme in glory
To tell the old, old story
  Of Jesus and his love. . . .

I love to tell the story;
  'Tis pleasant to repeat
What seems, each time I tell it,
  More wonderfully sweet:
I love to tell the story,
  For some have never heard
The message of salvation
  From God's own Holy Word.

I love to tell the story;
  For those who know it best
Seem hungering and thirsting
  To hear it like the rest.
And when, in scenes of glory,
  I sing the new, new song,
'Twill be the old, old story
  That I have loved so long.

1640—On this day, a Reverend John Hansley wrote a prefatory note veri-fying the orthodoxy of a little book called The Nature of Truth *by Robert Greville, Lord Brook (1608–43), an English nobleman, soldier, and ama-teur theologian. In* The Nature of Truth, *Greville argues that all theological disputations ultimately pale before the fact that God, according to Scripture, is drawing all things into a magnificent unity with himself. The "nature of truth," Greville believes, is precisely this—that all truth is ultimately God's own.*

If God grants you the grace to walk by this light [that he is draw-ing all things together into unity], practical questions will be laid aside, as well as theoretical. You will not dispute whether you ought to be more holy on one day (as at a sacrament) than at other times, for you will then know that these Scriptures express fully the rule you must walk by: "Pray continually," "Rejoice evermore," "Blessed is he that fears always," "Be holy (not by fits and starts) as I am holy, serving me always, with all your heart, your might, your affections"—so that every day, every duty, is to you a holy day, an ordinance divine. . . .

For while God draws all things to a unity, we shall know that sor-row and joy may meet in the same substance at once; they must be both in the actings of faith. We must not sorrow as though we were without hope. We may not lose our faith in our tears. Our tears must be tears of joy. We may think that we have sinned—and so sigh. But at the same instant we must know we have a Savior—and so triumph. And if I were now all gore-blood, would I not now go to the surgeons? Truly the greater my sin, the sooner ought to be my return to Christ, and the higher my faith. . . .

Thus if we could lay aside foolish questions, if we could seek into our hearts, . . . then we might have a heaven here; we might see how Christ is one with God, and we one with Christ; so we in Christ, one with God.

If we cannot reach the perfection of this knowledge, yet let us come as near it as we can, for the true knowledge of God in Christ is life ever-lasting.

1576—John Woolton (1535–94) was a professor, writer, and minister in sixteenth-century England. He eventually became Bishop of Exeter. His chief work was a book called The Christian Manual, *which Woolton dedicated to a Sir William Cordell on this day. In it he attempts to outline the fundamentals of the Christian faith. Here he summarizes the Ten Commandments.*

———— ❧ ❧ ————

The Ten Commandments are the most certain and most absolute platform of good works, and so that it may more evidently appear, I will by a brief enumeration (as it were in a table) note and point out the same. To the first commandment ["Thou shalt have no other gods before me"] we may refer the fear of God, faith, love, and assured hope in adversity, together with patience and constancy. The second commandment ["Thou shalt not make graven images"] contains all true worship of God and the avoiding of all superstition and idolatry. The third commandment ["Thou shalt not take God's name in vain"] comprehends the reverence of God's name, together with invocation and confession of the same. And the fourth commandment ["Remember the Sabbath and keep it holy"] calls for the preaching of God's Word, public prayers, and for external worship and service of God; allowing also seemly and moderate ceremonies and especially those that lead to edifying the church of God. To the fifth ["Honor thy father and mother"] we may refer piety toward our parents, country, and kinfolk, lawful obedience to the magistrate and all superiors, and the offices in civil life. The sixth ["Thou shalt not kill"] commands justice and judgment, the defending of the fatherless and widows, and the deliverance of those that are oppressed, and beneficence, and innocence. The seventh ["Thou shalt not commit adultery"] comprehends faith and truth between married persons, and the duties of matrimony, honest and godly education of children, the love of chastity and sobriety. We may refer to the eighth ["Thou shalt not steal"] justice in contracts and bargains, munificence, liberality, and hospitality. To the ninth ["Thou shalt not bear false witness"] we may refer the love and study of truth throughout all our life, faith in word and deed, learned, honest, and profitable communication. And under the tenth ["Thou shalt not covet"] are contained good and godly affection, together with all holy and honest cogitations.

1876—James Cardinal Gibbons (1834–1921), a well-known Catholic priest, was noted for his many books and for being a founder of the Catholic University in Washington, D.C. On this day, he wrote the preface to his book-length defense of Catholic doctrine, The Faith of Our Fathers. *In one chapter, he attempts to clear up any misunderstanding about the use of art in church, at a time when many Protestants believed that images of Jesus and the apostles were not art but idols.*

———————— ⋅◦§ §◦⋅ ————————

First, religious paintings embellish the house of God. . . . What beauty, what variety, what charming pictures are presented to our view in this temple of nature which we inhabit! Look at the canopy of heaven. Look at the exquisite pictures painted by the Hand of the Divine Artist on this earth. "Consider the lilies of the field. . . . I say to you that not even Solomon in all his glory was arrayed as one of these." If the temple of nature is so richly adorned, should not our temples made with our hands bear some resemblance to it? . . .

Second, religious paintings are the catechism of the ignorant. . . . How many thousands would have died ignorant of the Christian faith if they had not been enlightened by paintings! When Augustine, the Apostle of England, first appeared before King Ethelbert to announce to him the Gospel, a silver crucifix and a painting of our Savior were borne before the preacher, and these images spoke more tenderly to the eyes than his words to the ears of his audience.

Third, by exhibiting religious paintings in our rooms, we make a silent, though eloquent profession of our faith. I once called on a gentleman in a distant city, some time during our late war, and, on entering his library, I noticed two portraits, one of a distinguished General, the other of an Archbishop. These portraits at once proclaimed to me the religious and patriotic sentiments of the proprietor of the house. "Behold!" he said to me, pointing to the pictures, "my religious creed and my political creed." If I see a crucifix in a man's room I am convinced at once that he is not an infidel. . . .

We cannot, therefore, overestimate the salutary effect produced upon us in a church or room adorned with sacred paintings. We feel, while in their presence, that we are in the company of the just.

1640—Today the imprimatur (the official church seal proclaiming the book free of doctrinal error) was granted to The Pious Prentice or the Prentice's Piety, a small self-help manual for Christian servants and employees, by an obscure English religious writer Abraham Jackson (1589–1646). In his book Jackson teaches Christians how to be faithful to both God and their masters. In the following selection, the author answers questions concerning those times when an employee's faith may be at odds with the employer's demands.

QUESTION: What if my master commands me to do that which is unseemly and unfitting? May I not refuse to do it?

ANSWER: Saint Paul bids servants obey their masters in all things. If therefore your master commands you to do that which in your opinion may seem to be unmeet or unfit, if he in his own judgment thinks it fit and expedient, though it seems to cross your credit, profit, ease, or liking, you may not refuse to obey.

QUESTION: What if my master commands me to do a wicked or sinful thing, must I obey?

ANSWER: 1. A thing may seem evil in your opinion, which is not so in its own nature; therefore, unless that thing required is truly sinful and wicked, either by the express Word of God or by necessary consequence, you must obey.

2. If the thing commanded is evidently wicked, then know that it is better to disobey your master than offend God; but in refusing to obey, you must take heed of harsh and insolent behavior; you must beware of provoking words; you must express your unwillingness in mild speeches and entreat him not to urge you to that which goes against your conscience to do, as being expressly forbidden by God's Word. For know this, that though God frees you from actual obedience to your master in this case, yet He frees you not from reverence in the manner of your refusal to obey.

1654—French philosopher and scientist Blaise Pascal (1623–62) was one of the greatest geniuses of the seventeenth century. Among his mathematical accomplishments was the invention of a mechanical computer. In our time, he is chiefly remembered for his sublime collection of thoughts, the Pensées. On this day, he had an ecstatic experience that marked his conversion, which, in turn, led to his entrance into a religious community the following year. For the rest of his life, Pascal carried with him, sewn into the lining of his jacket, a written reminder—his "Memorial"—of his experience on this day. It reads as follows.

———————— ⋘ ⋙ ————————

Fire.
God of Abraham, God of Isaac, God of Jacob,
not of the philosophers and the scholars.
Certainty, certainty, feeling, joy, peace.
(God of Jesus Christ). . . .
Your God will be my God.
Forgetfulness of the world and everything except God.
He is only found by the ways taught in the Gospel.
Grandeur of the human soul.
Righteous Father, the world has not known You, but I knew You.
Joy, joy, joy, tears of joy.
I separated myself from Him. . . .
My God, will you abandon me?
Let me not be eternally separated from Him.
This is life eternal, that they might know You,
the only true God, and the One that you sent, Jesus Christ.
Jesus Christ. Jesus Christ.
I separated myself from Him; I fled, renounced, crucified Him.
Let me never be separated from Him.
He can only be kept by the ways taught in the Gospel.
Total and sweet renunciation, etc.
Total submission to Jesus Christ and to my guide.
Eternal joy for one day of effort on earth. . . . Amen.

1651—Jeremy Taylor (1613–67), whom poet Samuel Taylor Coleridge dubbed "the Shakespeare of divines," was an English bishop and devotional writer. On this day, English printer and publisher Richard Royston registered for publication Taylor's most famous work: The Rule and Exercise of Holy Living. *This book, a classic of Anglican spirituality, stresses moderation and order. In the following passage, Taylor discusses the value of contentment.*

───────── ⋖⸙ ⸙⋗ ─────────

Is not all the world God's family? Are not we his creatures? Are we not as clay in the hand of the potter? Do we not live upon his meat and move by his strength and do our work by his light? Are we anything but what we are from him? And shall there be a mutiny among the flocks and herds because their Lord or their Shepherd chooses their pastures and suffers them not to wander into deserts and unknown ways? If we choose, we do it so foolishly that we cannot like it long, and most commonly not at all. But God, who can do what he pleases, is wise to choose safely for us, affectionate to comply with our needs, and powerful to execute all his wise decrees. Here therefore is the wisdom of the contented man: to let God choose for him. For when we have given up our wills to him and stand in that station of the battle where our great General has placed us, our spirits must rest while our conditions have for their security the power, the wisdom, and the charity of God.

Contentedness in all accidents brings great peace of spirit and is the great and only instrument of temporal felicity. It removes the sting from the accident and makes a man not to depend upon chance and the uncertain dispositions of men for his well-being, but only on God and his own Spirit. We ourselves make our fortunes good or bad.... The old Stoics, when you told them a sad story, would answer, "What is that to me?" Yes, for the Tyrant has sentenced you also to prison. Well? What is that? He will put a chain upon my leg, but he cannot bind my soul.... This in Gentile philosophy is the same with the discourse of St. Paul: "I have learned in whatsoever state I am therewith to be content. I know both how to be abased, and I know how to abound, everywhere and in all things I am instructed, both how to be full and to be hungry, both to abound and suffer need" (Philippians 4:11–12; 1 Timothy 6:6; Hebrews 13:5).

1675—Scotsman Robert Barclay (1648–90), the most profound of all Quaker theologians, brought many into the Society of Friends through the power of his intellect and persuasiveness. Barclay traveled to the New World, was friends with William Penn, and was eventually appointed governor of East New Jersey (1683). On this day, years before traveling to America, he addressed his theological masterwork, An Apology for the True Christian Religion, *to King Charles II and pleaded with the King to bring to an end the persecution of Quakers in England. In this impressive work, Barclay presents fifteen essential propositions of Quaker theology, including the doctrine of "inner light." In the following excerpt, Barclay defends the Quaker scorn for titles of position and honor.*

—————— ✺ ——————

All these titles and styles of honor are to be rejected by Christians because [we] are to seek the honor that comes from above and not the honor that is from below. . . . For we know well enough what industry and what pains men are at to get these things, and what part it is that seeks after them: to wit, the proud, insolent, haughty, aspiring mind. For judge, is it the meek and innocent Spirit of Christ that covets that honor? Is it that Spirit that must be of no reputation in this world, that has its conversation in heaven, that comes to have "fellowship with the sons of God" (Philippians 3:20)? Is it that Spirit, I say, that loves that honor, that seeks after that honor, that pleads for the upholding of that honor, that frets and rages and fumes when it is denied that honor? Or is it not rather the lordly insulting spirit of Lucifer, the prince of this world, he that of old affected and sought after this honor and loved not to abide in the submissive low place? And so all his children are possessed with the same ambitious proud mind, seeking and coveting titles of honor, which indeed belong not to them. For let us examine who they are that are honorable indeed. Is it not the righteous? Is it not the holy? Is it not the humble-hearted, the meek spirited? And are not such as those that ought to be honored among Christians? [And] of these, may there not be poor men, laborers, silly fishermen?

1842—On this day, English writer George Borrow (1803–81) wrote in the preface to his greatest book, "The work now offered to the public, . . . The Bible in Spain, consists of a narrative of what occurred to me during a residence in that country, to which I was sent by the Bible Society as its agent for the purpose of printing and circulating the Scriptures." The true story that follows is pure adventure. Borrow was the first to translate the Bible into Romany, the language of the gypsies. The following passage, from The Bible in Spain, *is the author's reflections at the end of the book as he departs Spain, sailing past the impressive Rock of Gibraltar.*

Mighty and threatening appeared the fortifications and doubtless, viewed in any other situation, would have alone occupied the mind and engrossed its wonder; but the hill, the wondrous hill, was everywhere about them, beneath them, or above them, overpowering their effect as a spectacle. Who, when he beholds the enormous elephant, with his brandished trunk, dashing impetuously to the war, sees the castle which he bears or fears the javelins of those whom he carries, however, skillful and warlike they may be? Never does God appear so great and powerful as when the works of his hands stand in contrast with the labors of man. . . . O what are the works of man compared with those of the Lord? Even as man is, compared with his Creator. Man builds pyramids and God builds pyramids: the pyramids of man are heaps of shingles, tiny hillocks on a sandy plain; the pyramids of the Lord are Andes and Indian hills. Man builds walls and so does his Master; but the walls of God are the black precipices of Gibraltar and Horneel, eternal, indestructible, and not to be scaled; whilst those of man can be climbed, can be broken by the wave or shattered by the lightning or the powder blast. Would man display his power and grandeur to advantage, let him flee far from the hills, for the broad pennants of God, even his clouds, float upon the tops of the hills, and the majesty of God is most manifest among the hills. Call Gibraltar the hill of Tarik or Hercules if you will, but gaze upon it for a moment and you will call it the hill of God. Tarik and the old giant may have built upon it; but not all the dark race of whom Tarik was one, nor all the giants of old renown of whom the other was one, could have built up its crags or chiseled the enormous mass to its present shape.

1858—Samuel Irenaeus Prime (1812–85) was an American Presbyterian clergyman, author, and editor of the religious weekly The New York Observer, *in which he wrote a regular column. He later became a regular writer for* Harper's Magazine. *He was the author of several books, including* The Old White Meeting House *(1845) and* Travels in Europe and the East *(1855). On this day he completed the preface to his memoirs called the* Power of Prayer, *in which he describes prayer as follows.*

Prayer is the chain that draws the soul to God and brings down promised mercies to us; or, like the hook which draws the boat to the shore, though the shore itself is immovable. Prayer is to the church what the breath of spring and the sun, the rain, the dew of summer, are to the earth. Without them, the church and the earth must remain in their wintry shrouds. And all the indications are that the church is beginning to feel, to an unwonted degree, the connection between true prayer and its true prosperity.

God is now, as in days of old, showing himself to be a God that hears prayer. The prayers of Abraham healed Abimelech; the prayers of Moses prevailed in Egypt and in the wilderness; the prayers of Daniel quelled the ferocity of lions. "Prayer," says Jeremy Taylor, "can obtain everything; can open the windows of heaven and shut the gates of hell; can put a holy constraint upon God, and detain an angel till he leave a blessing; can open the treasures of rain and soften the iron ribs of rocks till they melt into a flowing river; can arrest the sun in his course, and send the winds upon our errands." Nor is there a church, not a true Christian, who cannot from their own history record instances of the power of prayer. A spy upon Luther followed him to a hotel and slept in a room adjacent to that of the Reformer. He told his employer next day that Luther prayed nearly all night and that he could never conquer a man that prayed so earnestly.

1848—Hannah Whitall Smith (1832–1911), best known for her classic book Christian's Secret of a Happy Life, *was an American writer and religious leader. She was raised in a devout Quaker home but passed through other denominations as an adult in search of authentic Christian understanding. In her spiritual autobiography,* The Unselfishness of God, *she divides her life into four epochs, each one of which began with a unique spiritual insight. The first epoch of spiritual awakening began on this day, when she was only sixteen years old, and assured her of the existence and grandeur of God. The following entry from her diary describes her moment of realization. (See also October 25.)*

———— ⋅§ ξ⋅ ————

An eventful day! Eventful I mean in my spiritual life. Today I have felt and thought enough for a year. My friend Anna read to us in class a book called *Other Worlds*, and also "Future Existence" from the *School Boy* by Abbott. It was all intensely interesting and had an almost overpowering effect on me. As I listened to the accounts of those mighty worlds which are everywhere scattered around us, some of which are so distant that the rays of light from them which enter our eyes have left these stars six thousand years ago! As I reflected that these worlds were all moving on regularly, never disturbing each other, but all obedient to one mighty Creator, the grandeur of the thought was intense, and for a few minutes I felt as though the happiness of being born into a universe so limitless, so magnificent, so glorious, was too great. And as I heard of our future existence, of the glorious unimaginable happiness in store for us, of the perfect bliss of the good and holy, I inwardly thanked my Creator for placing me among beings whose anticipations were so happy. But then came the awful, the overwhelming thought that that eternity of endless bliss was only for the good, and the remembrance that I could have no share in it unless my heart was changed. Oh, I cannot describe the misery of that moment! It was almost too great to be borne. And these thought linger with me. Why is it?

1577—St. Teresa of Ávila (1515–82; see also June 30) was a Spanish Carmelite nun and one of Christendom's greatest mystic writers. On this day she completed the writing of what many feel is her masterwork, a book about the inner life of prayer and contemplation, called The Interior Castle. *In it she describes the soul as a castle, and to find God in our souls, we must first approach and enter this castle, as she describes here.*

Now let us turn to our beautiful and delightful castle to see how we might be able to enter it. It must seem as if I'm talking nonsense, for if this castle is the soul, it is clear that there can be no question of our entering it—for we ourselves are the castle. How absurd it would be to tell someone to enter a room when that person is already standing in it! But you must understand that there are many ways to be in a place, and many souls stand in the courtyard of the castle, which is where the guards stand, who have no interest in entering it and are not aware of the marvels of the place or even how many rooms are in it. You've probably read books on prayer that counsel the soul to enter into itself, and that is precisely what is meant.

A little while ago a very learned man said that souls that do not have prayer are like people who are paralyzed; they have feet and hands but cannot use them. In the same way, there are souls so infirm and so used to getting caught up in superficial things that nothing can be done for them; they don't seem to be able to enter into themselves at all. They are so used to living constantly with the lizards and other beasts who are in courtyard of the castle that they have almost become like them; and though nature has richly bestowed upon them the power to have conversations with none other than God, there is no remedy for them. And if these souls do not work to understand their great misery, they will be turned into pillars of salt for not looking inside themselves, just as Lot's wife was for looking back.

So, as far as I can understand, the door of entry to this castle is prayer and meditation.

1924—On this day Miguel de Unamuno (1864–1936), Spanish novelist and philosopher, underwent a spiritual crisis while assisting in services at a Greek Orthodox church in Paris. At the time, he was exiled from Spain by an often tyrannical government that had the support of many Christians. The crisis Unamuno experienced led him to write his book The Agony of Christianity, *and in the following passage he takes exception to those who equate various "isms" (nationalism, socialism, capitalism, etc.) with Christianity.*

───────── ⋖§ ⁊⋗ ─────────

What is all this talk about social Christianity? What is all this noise about the social kingdom of Christ . . . and what about the much-heralded Christian democracy?

"My kingdom is not of this world" (John 18:36), said Christ when He saw that the end of history was not at hand. And again: "Give to Caesar what is Caesar's, and to God what is God's" (Luke 20:25). But we must remember in what circumstances this sentence of cardinal importance was pronounced.

Those who persecuted Christ in order to destroy Him agreed among themselves to ask Him whether it was lawful to pay tribute to Caesar, the invader, the enemy of the Jewish fatherland, who represented political authority. If He answered in the affirmative, they would then picture Him to the people as a bad Jew, as a bad patriot; and if He answered in the negative, they would accuse Him of sedition in the face of the imperial authorities. Once the question had been posed, Jesus asked for a piece of money, and, pointing to the image depicted on the coin, He inquired, "Whose picture is this?" "Caesar's," they replied. And then He said, "Very well: give to Caesar what is Caesar's, and to God what is God's." The meaning is clear: give to Caesar, to this world, to society, the money which belongs to Caesar, to the world, to society; and to God give the soul which is destined to rise with its body. Christ thus detached Himself from every problem of social economy; the same Christ Who said that it is more difficult for a rich man to enter into the kingdom of heaven than for a camel to pass through the eye of a needle: and He showed clearly that His glad tidings have nothing to do with socio-economical or national questions, nothing to do with democracy or international demagogy, nothing to do with nationalism.

—from *The Agony of Christianity*,
translated by Kurt F. Reinhardt

December

English Puritan writer John Bunyan imagines the story of
Christian, the archetypal pilgrim (see December 15, also
February 18 and August 18). From the frontispiece to
the 1682 edition of *Pilgrim's Progress*.

1902—On this day, Henry van Dyke (1852–1933; see also February 28), an American minister and writer, completed the preface to his collection of stories The Blue Flower, *which included his most famous and beloved piece,* "The Story of the Other Wise Man." *It is the fanciful tale of Artaban, a fourth wise man, who was unable to make his way to the manger in time to find the infant Jesus. He spends the rest of his life wandering the earth, seeking the King, and doing good deeds by giving away the precious jewels he had intended to give to the child. On his deathbed, he gives his final jewel, a rare pearl, to a slave girl who has cared for him, so that she may buy her freedom.*

───────── ·❧ ❧· ─────────

[Artaban] knew that all was well, because he had done the best that he could.... He had not seen the revelation of "life everlasting, incorruptible, and immortal." But he knew that even if he could live his earthly life over again, it could never be otherwise than it had been....

He lay breathless and pale, with his gray head resting on the [slave] girl's shoulder.... As she bent over him, fearing that he was dead, there came a voice through the twilight, very small and still, like music sounding from a distance, in which the notes are clear but the words are lost. The girl turned to see if someone had spoken from the window above them, but she saw no one.

Then the old man's lips began to move, as if in answer, and she heard him say ... , "Not so, my Lord! For when saw I thee hungry and fed thee? Or thirsty and gave thee drink? When saw I thee a stranger and took thee in? Or naked and clothed thee? When saw I thee sick or in prison and came to thee? Three-and-thirty years have I looked for thee; but I have never seen thy face nor ministered to thee, my King."

He ceased and the sweet voice came again. And again the maid heard it, very faint and far away. But now it seemed as though she understood the words: "Verily I say unto thee, inasmuch as thou hast done it unto one of the least of these my brethren, thou hast done it unto me."

A calm radiance of wonder and joy lighted the pale face of Artaban like the first ray of dawn on a snowy mountain peak. A long breath of relief exhaled gently from his lips.

His journey was ended. His treasures were accepted. The Other Wise Man had found the King.

1577—St. John of the Cross (1542–91) was a Spanish poet, mystic, and religious leader. His enemies, who were very powerful, had him kidnapped on this day and imprisoned, and it was during this imprisonment that he probably wrote his beautiful poem "The Dark Night of the Soul" (see August 16). John's devotional method was to compose deeply mystical poems and then to expound them in carefully thought-out prose, as in the following excerpt from his book The Dark Night of the Soul, *in which he explains one meaning behind the title of his poem.*

O spiritual soul, when you see your desires fade, when your affections become arid and meager, when you lose your knack for interior spiritual exercises, do not grieve but consider it a great blessing. For God is freeing you from yourself. He is taking matters out of your hands. For your own hands, no matter how well they have served you in the past, have never labored so well or so perfectly or so surely (because of their impurity and clumsiness) as they do now, when God Himself takes your hand in His and leads you through the darkness, as if you were blind, along an unfamiliar path to an unfamiliar place. Nor could you ever travel that path with your own eyes and feet, no matter how good a traveler you are.

The reason that the soul not only travels more safely when it walks in this darkness, but also makes greater progress and finds greater good, is that the soul usually only finds these advantages along the path that is least understood. . . . So the soul is like the traveler who, in order to reach new and unknown countries, must seek out unfamiliar and untried paths, roads on which the traveler cannot be guided by prior knowledge, where the traveler experiences many doubts and is dependent on the directions of others. . . . And so, since God is the master and the guide for such a blind soul, the soul may truly rejoice when it understands all this, and say, "In darkness—and secure." . . .

In this way the dark night of contemplation absorbs the soul into itself and brings it so close to God that it protects and liberates the soul from everything that is not God. So, as if it were undergoing a cure, the soul is able to regain its health—for truly its health is nothing other than God Himself.

1927—In a makeshift recording studio in Dallas, Texas, on this day, a blind African-American gospel singer known as Blind Willie Johnson (c. 1902–49) made his first recordings. With his bluesy guitar playing and his thundering vocals, he became one of the most influential "guitar evangelists" of his generation, responsible for popularizing such gospel standards as "You're Gonna Need Somebody on Your Bond," "Keep Your Lamp Trimmed and Burning," "I Know His Blood Can Make Me Whole," and "Nobody's Fault But Mine." This last song, from which the following verses are taken, was recorded on this day.

It's nobody's fault but mine,
It's nobody's fault but mine,
If I don't read and my soul be lost,
It's nobody's fault but mine.

I have a Bible in my home,
I have a Bible in my home,
If I don't read and my soul be lost,
It's nobody's fault but mine.

My mother she taught me how to read,
My mother she taught me how to read,
If I don't read and my soul be lost,
It's nobody's fault but mine.

My sister she taught me how to pray,
My sister she taught me how to pray,
If I don't pray and my soul be lost,
It's nobody's fault but mine.

It's nobody's fault but mine,
It's nobody's fault but mine,
If I don't read and my soul be lost,
It's nobody's fault but mine.

1731—Gerhard Tersteegen (1697–1769) was a German Protestant devotional writer, considered one of the finest of the group known as the Pietists. While working as a humble ribbon weaver, he spent much of his spare time writing hymns, telling others about Christ, attending devotional meetings, and writing letters of deep spiritual insight. An example can be seen in his following reflections on prayer, which were written in a letter on this day to a friend.

———— ✍ ————

Prayer is to look to the omnipresent God and to allow oneself to be seen by him. What is now easier and more simple than to turn our eyes upward and to see the light that surrounds us on all sides? God is far more present to us than the light. In him we live, we move, and we are. He penetrates us, he fills us, he is nearer to us than we are to ourselves. To believe this in simplicity and to think of this simply as well as one can, that is prayer. How can it be difficult to allow oneself to be looked after by so kind a physician who knows better what is troubling us than we ourselves know? We have no need to bring this or that, to present ourselves in this way or in that way, or to look too much or to experience much if we wish to pray, but we need only simply and briefly to say how we are and how we wish to be. Indeed, it is not even necessary that we say this, but we need only allow the ever-present good God to see. We are not to let him see only the surface, but at every point we are to remain by him and before him so that he can see us correctly and heal us. We must not say anything to him or allow him to see anything other than what is in us. What will be is what he wills. If you find yourself disturbed, dark, with no spiritual experiences, simply tell God and let him see your suffering; then you have prayed properly. Is there a natural laziness or diffidence at hand? Take heart but a little and turn again with humility to God. If one can remain awake standing better than kneeling, let one fight sleep in such a way; if one can do so better by looking in a book, this is not forbidden. In short, one must help oneself at a particular time as well as one can, so long as one does not disturb one's chief goal by doing so, namely, prayer, but, rather, always turn oneself again to this task. Deny your own will and desires and you will pray properly and easily. For the Lord will work prayer in your soul through his grace.

—from *The Pietists*, edited by Peter Erb

1093—St. Anselm (1033–1109), a Benedictine theologian and monk, was made archbishop of Canterbury on this day. He was appointed to the position, in part, because of his profound and influential theological writings, of which his Proslogion ("Address") is the most famous. In this treatise he presents a fascinating proof of the existence of God, whom he defines as "that than which nothing greater can be conceived"—for if something greater could be conceived, then that too would be God. And since to exist in reality is greater than to exist in the mind alone, then the greatest conceivable thing (God) must exist in reality as well. Though many are unconvinced by his ingenious and complex proof, here is a beautiful prayer of invocation from that great work. (See also April 21.)

———————— ◦§ §◦ ————————

Come now, poor child of man, turn awhile from your business, hide yourself for a little time from restless thoughts, cast away your troublesome cares, put aside your wearisome distractions. Give yourself a little leisure to converse with God, and take your rest awhile in Him. Enter into the secret chamber of your heart; leave everything outside but God and whatever may help you to seek after Him, and when you have shut the door, then truly seek Him. Say now, O my whole heart, say now to God, "I seek Your face; Your face, O Lord, do I seek" (Psalm 27:9). Come now, then, O Lord my God, teach my heart when and how I may seek You, where and how I may find You. O Lord, if You are not here, where else shall I seek You? But if you are everywhere, why do I not behold You, since You are here present? Surely, indeed, You dwell in the light that no man can approach (1 Timothy 6:16). But where is that light unapproachable? How may I approach it? . . .

Deliver me, take away my burden, lest the pit of my wickedness shut its mouth upon me; grant that I may look upon Your light, though from afar off, though out of the deep. I will seek You by longing for You; I will long for You by seeking You. I will find You by loving You; I will love You by finding You. I confess to You, O Lord, and I give thanks to You because You have created in me Your image, so that I may remember You, think upon You, and love You.

—adapted from the translation of Clement C. J. Webb (1903)

1272—After returning from a strenuous and heated theological debate, Thomas Aquinas (c. 1225–74), the finest thinker of his age, gave up writing after Mass on this day, the feast of St. Nicholas. As he told a friend, "I can write no more. I have seen things which make all my writing like straw." And thus it was that he left unfinished his greatest work, the Summa Theologica. *What Thomas experienced is not known, but it shook his faith in pure intellect and had a profound influence on the rest of his life. He died two years later. His more humbled approach to the role of intellect in faith may be seen in the following personal letter to a friend, in which Thomas outlines a few simple principles of devotion and religious study.*

—————— ❧ ❧ ——————

Since you have asked me, John, most dear to me in Christ, how you should go about studying to obtain the treasure of knowledge, I give you this advice. Do not seek to plunge into the sea of knowledge all at once, but go there by way of the many streams that flow into it, since it is wiser to reach the more difficult things by way of the less difficult things. This, then, is my advice and instruction. I charge you to be slow to speak and slow to frequent places where men talk. Embrace cleanness of conscience. Be constant in prayer. Love to dwell in your cell if you would penetrate into the cell of your Beloved. Be courteous to everyone. Do not look too deeply into the deeds of others. Do not be overly familiar with anyone, for too great a familiarity breeds contempt and offers an occasion for being distracted from study. Do not in any way wish to pry into the words and deeds of worldly people. Flee from useless conversations. Do not forget to imitate the ways of the saints and holy people. Do not feel obliged to listen to what everyone says, but commit to memory anything good that you might hear others say. And whatever you read or hear, make an effort to understand it. Make certain of whatever is doubtful and try to remember everything you can, just as if your mind were a jar that needed filling. Do not seek things that are beyond your understanding. By these steps you will bring forth useful branches and fruits in the vineyard of the Lord of Sabaoth while life is in you. If you walk this way, you may obtain all that you desire.

1673—Matthew Henry (1662–1714) was a minister in Chester, England, and one of the world's greatest Bible commentators. His masterwork, Exposition of the Old and New Testaments, has been almost continually in print since its first publication, although it was left unfinished at his death and completed by other hands. Henry was himself the son of a Nonconformist minister. On this day, long before becoming such an influential Christian writer, Matthew Henry, as a precocious eleven-year-old, wrote in his diary about his recent conversion.

———— ⊷§ ⊱ ————

I have found several marks that I *am* a child of God. His ministers say there is true conversion:

1. Where there have been covenant transactions between God and the soul. And I found that there have been such between God and my soul, and I hope in truth and righteousness. If I never did this before, I do it now; for I take God in Christ to be mine....

2. Where there has been true repentance for sin, and grief and shame and sorrow for it as to what is past, with all the ingredients of it, as confession, aggravation, self-judging, self-condemning, etc. And I have found this in me, though not in that measure that I could desire. I have been heartily sorry for what is past....

3. Where there is true love of God. For to love the Lord our God with all our soul and with all our strength is better than whole burnt offerings and sacrifices. Now, as far as I know my own heart, I love God in sincerity. But is that love indeed sincere? As far as I can judge it is so, for (1) I love the people of God; all the Lord's people shall be my people; (2) I love the word of God. I esteem it above all. I find my heart so inclined. I desire it as the food of my soul. I greatly delight in it, both in reading and hearing of it, and my soul can witness subjection to it in some measure.

—from J. B. Williams' *Life of Matthew Henry* (1830)

1924—On this day in Oxford, England, Leonard Hodgson, who was Dean of Divinity at Magdalen College and a respected writer, completed his book The Place of Reason in Christian Apologetics. *In one portion of it he asks how Christians can claim to believe in "one faith" when people have such different experiences of the Christian life.*

⋅⊰ ⊱⋅

How can artist and moralist, philosopher and man of action all share in one precisely similar "specific Christian experience"? All may join in saying such prayers as the seventy-first psalm to the ideals of beauty, truth, goodness, or noble endeavor, which it is sin to betray, but the manner in which the God who forgives and enables is laid hold on in experience may be infinitely various.

Here we find the real value of the study of religious and Christian experience—or rather, experiences. It prevents our becoming shut up in the narrowness of believing that only in this or that way does God reveal Himself. . . .

A single Christian faith, and agreement to unite in fellowship in the common practice of that faith, seem to me to be aims for which, as being possible though yet far off, it is reasonable to strive. But when we are united in faith and worship, I think we should set no bounds to the possible variety of Christian experiences but should endeavor to learn from one another of the infinite richness of the mercies of God in Christ Jesus vouchsafed to all sorts and conditions of people. . . .

Let me end with a parable. A certain duke is said to have remarked: "The other day I dreamed that I was on my feet addressing my brother peers in the House of Lords, and when I woke up I found that I *was* addressing my brother peers in the House of Lords." Now there are those today who assure us that [all Christian experience is] a fantasy, as it were a dream projection of our unconscious selves. But perhaps to us dreamers, who in this life dream that we walk in the presence of the Blessed Trinity with the comradeship of the saints and angels, death will be the awakening to find that we are indeed walking in the company of angels and saints, in the grace of our Lord Jesus Christ and the love of God, and the fellowship of the Holy Ghost.

1767—*Englishman William Cowper (1731–1800) was a renowned early romantic poet, author of the long narrative poem* The Task. *Though he suffered from severe emotional disturbances, he was one of the most widely admired authors of his time. With English minister John Newton (see March 21) he co-wrote* The Olney Hymns *(1779), which included "Oh for a Closer Walk with God," which was originally penned on this day. As he wrote to his aunt the next day, "I began to compose [these verses] yesterday morning before daybreak, but fell asleep at the end of the two first lines; when I awaked again the third and fourth were whispered to my heart in a way which I have often experienced."*

———————— ✌ ཉ ࿇ ————————

Oh for a closer walk with God,
    A calm and heavenly frame,
A light to shine upon the road
    That leads me to the Lamb!

Where is the blessedness I knew
    When first I sought the Lord?
Where is the soul-reaching view
    Of Jesus and His Word? . . .

Return, O Holy Dove, return,
    Sweet Messenger of rest,
I hate the sins that made Thee mourn
    And drove Thee from my breast.

The dearest idol I have known,
    Whate'er that idol be,
Help me to tear it from Thy throne,
    And worship only Thee.

Then shall my walk be close with God,
    Calm and serene my frame,
Then purer light shall mark the road
    That leads me to the Lamb.

1941—One of the best-selling Christian autobiographies of modern times is The Seven Storey Mountain *by Thomas Merton (1915–68), from which the following extract is taken. The book chronicles Merton's early life, portraying him as a budding young writer, scholar, and poet, who, because of deep spiritual yearnings for a closer relationship to God, decides to enter the monastery. On this day, on the train to Kentucky, where he intends to join the Trappist monks at Gethsemane, Thomas Merton ponders his future, not knowing whether the order would accept him or whether the U.S. Army would draft him first. He was accepted by the Trappists and spent most of the rest of his life at Gethsemane.*

───────── ⋘ ⋙ ─────────

It was a strange thing. Mile after mile my desire to be in the monastery increased beyond belief. I was altogether absorbed in that one idea. And yet, paradoxically, mile after mile my indifference increased, and my interior peace. What if they did not receive me? Then I would go to the army. But surely that would be a disaster? Not at all. If, after all this, I was rejected by the monastery and had to be drafted, it would be quite clear that it was God's will. I had done everything that was in my power; the rest was in His hands. And for all the tremendous and increasing intensity of my desire to be in the cloister, the thought that I might find myself, instead, in an army camp no longer troubled me in the least.

I was free. I had recovered my liberty. I belonged to God, not to myself: and to belong to Him is to be free, free of all the anxieties and worries and sorrows that belong to this earth, and the love of the things that are in it. What was the difference between one place and another, one habit and another, if your life belonged to God, and if you placed yourself completely in His hands? The only thing that mattered was the fact of the sacrifice, the essential dedication of one's self, one's will. The rest was only accidental.

1673—Increase Mather (1639–1723) was a renowned Puritan theologian and statesman in colonial New England (see July 9). Though a stern denouncer of apostasy, he contributed to ending the infamous "witch-hunt" frenzy of his time. He found his true calling in the pulpit, and on this day in Boston he delivered a sermon, "The Day of Trouble Is Near," in which he exhorts his hearers to expect "troublous times," but in the following passage he also reminds them of their hope in Christ.

————— ⋅≫⋅ —————

So does the Apostle instruct us: "Beloved, think it not strange concerning the fiery trial which is to try you, as though some strange thing happened to you" (1 Peter 4:12). Why, this is no more than what has been in almost all ages of the church and will be to the world's end, and therefore why should we strain at it? Nor should we be dismayed thereat, but rather say as the Church does, "God is a very present help in trouble, therefore we will not fear though the earth be removed, and though the waters roar and be troubled, though the mountains shake with the swelling thereof" (Psalm 46). Truly, thus it is at this day. The multitude of many people make a noise like the noise of the seas. We have heard the rushing of the nations. Yea, we have heard the sea and the waves thereof roaring. . . . Kingdoms shake. Nations shake. Yet let us not be dismayed, for the Lord will carry on his own good work and glorious designs in the midst of these troubles. It is said that the City should be "built in troublous times" (Deuteronomy 9:25). The Lord is carrying on the building of his own House even in these troublous times. And why should we be dismayed? For all these affairs are ordered and managed by the hand of him that is our Mediator. Therefore, in Ezekiel's vision of the wheel, that is, the wheel of Providence, it is indeed said that the "rings were high and dreadful" (1:18), but it is said, "There is a Man above on the throne" (v. 26), that is to say, Jesus Christ, who is Man as well as God, even He as Mediator does order all the affairs and motions of the wheel of Providence, which is a matter of wonderful encouragement, when its revolutions are dreadful for us to behold. Christ has become head of all things to his church, as well as for his father's glory. And therefore though troubles come, why should we be dismayed? . . . A glorious issue and happy deliverance out of all these troubles shall certainly arise to the Church in due time.

*1909—Gaius Glenn Atkins (1868–1956) was an American religious writer
and minister who, for part of his career, served as pastor of the First Congregational Church in Detroit, Michigan. At that church, on this day, he delivered a beautiful sermon on the subject of "The Vision of God," based on
Matthew 5:8: "Blessed are the pure in heart, for they shall see God." An
excerpt follows.*

—✥ ✥—

There are times when God comes to us out of the kind shadow of
the night, speaks down to us from quiet spaces, looks at us out of the
eyes of holy human love, and when the majestic and engulfing tides of
the Divine presence roll on, bearing us up in their blessedness and
peace. What does it all mean? Is it a dream of the night or some aspect
of emotional exaltation? I tell you, no. It is deep speaking unto deep. It
is the spirit of God come out of His remoter dwelling places to meet
your spirit. When you have given Him room and when in serenity and
unselfishness you wait for the least word of the Lord of love and life and
sympathy, such experiences grow deeper and more intimate. The sense
of God felt in stars and flowers and grass is intensified by the suggestion
of the Divine in human life. Carlyle and Emerson went together
through the roaring streets of the East End in London. Carlyle pointed
out to Emerson depth upon depth of sin and misery and cruel fault, asking all the while in his hammering Scottish accent, "Do you believe in
the Devil now? Do you believe in the Devil now?" And Emerson as constantly answered, "I am more and more persuaded of the love and goodness of God." Neither Carlyle's sardonic despair nor Emerson's serene
complaisance are likely to have said the last word about so sad, so mas-
sive, and so complex a fact as East London, but the answer marks the
man. The deeper meaning of it is that we hear the voices to which our
spirits are attuned, and rest upon those realities which have come to be
our supreme desire. . . .

The transient is shot through and through with the permanent, as
the skies are shot through with light, and the pure in heart suspect it,
sense it, feel it, know it, glory in it. You may persuade them that there
is no sun in the skies, nor solid ground beneath their feet, but they know
whom they have believed. They walk with their Father, and in His
strength they are glad.

—from *Things That Remain* by Reverend G. G. Atkins (1910)

1550—Englishman Thomas Lever (1521–77) was a Nonconformist Puritan preacher who, for a time, was an influential administrator at Cambridge University. He was noted for his boldness in criticizing not only the vices of the time, but the greed of powerful merchants and the indifference of the nobles in particular. His boldness and prophetic zeal can be seen in this excerpt, which is from a sermon he preached on this day at Paul's Cross Church in London.

———— ⚜ ————

Take heed, you merchants of London, that you be not merchants of mischief, conveying away so much old lead, wool, leather, and such substantial wares as would set many Englishmen to work and to every good service; and bringing home silks and sables, fur and foolish feathers to fill the realm full of such baggage as will never do rich or poor good and necessary service. Be sure, if this realm be rich, you shall not need to be poor; if this realm be poor, you shall not be able to keep and enjoy your riches. Take heed then that your merchandise be not a serving of foolish men's fancies, which will destroy the realm; but let it be a providing for honest discreet men's commodities, which will be the upholding and enriching of you and of the whole realm. Take heed of your vocations, [you] prelates and preachers, magistrates and officers, landlords and tenants, craftsmen and merchants—all manner of men take heed of yourselves and of your conversation and living. . . .

Show the nobility that they have oppressed the commonalty, keeping them under in fear and ignorance by power and authority, which might and should have been lovingly learned by their obedience and duty to both God and the King by preaching of the Gospel. . . . Tell all England, high and low, rich and poor, that everyone prowling for themselves be servants of Mammon, enemies of God, disturbers of the commonwealth and destroyers of themselves. And for all this, let them know that I have no pleasure in the death of a sinner. But rather I give him respite and send him warning that he may turn and live comfortably here on earth and joyfully in Heaven forever. Therefore if any in England do turn and amend, he shall save himself.

*1509—On this day Norman printer Richard Pynson completed the printing
of* The Ship of Fools, *a lengthy satirical, moralizing poem by Scottish poet
and priest Alexander Barclay (c. 1475–1552). The work, which is partly
original and partly a translation from a German source, is a catalog in verse
of every type of folly the author could imagine. Among the "fools" discussed,
for instance, are those who willingly put themselves in peril, who are ungrateful, who are noisy in church, or, as in the following modernized and adapted
passage, who have contempt for the Bible.*

————— ⋅৭ ৡ⋅ —————

He who despises ancient Scripture,
Which has been proven of great authority,
Who finds no pleasure, joy, or cure
In reading the Prophets, true and holy—
Such a one is a fool, for he will more readily
Believe in the tales of an old wife
Than in the doctrine of eternal life.

The Holy Bible, that source of Truth and Law,
Is set at naught and rejected by many;
For whom godly Scripture is not worth a haw,
Who love tales that are full of ribaldry,
And who are so blind to their own folly
That they think Scripture is no more true nor good
Than are the foolish tales of Robin Hood. . . .

Out of your slumber, fools, I call you to rise.
Follow and embrace the Scriptures Divine
Be not so bold as such a book to despise,
But purchase it and make it thine;
Remember, great is the comfort and solace
Within the Holy Book of Life you shall have.
Whoever follows it receives special grace,
But he who does not is a wretch and a slave.

1917—On this day, while riding a train between New York City and his home in upstate New York, Episcopal musician C. Winfred Douglas (1867–1944) wrote the tune for the hymn "He Who Would Valiant Be," popularly called "To Be a Pilgrim." The verses, adapted by Percy Dreamer in 1906, are originally from a poem by John Bunyan (1628–88) in his Pilgrim's Progress *(1564).*

He who would valiant be
'Gainst all disaster,
Let him in constancy
Follow the Master.
There's no discouragement
Shall make him once relent
His first avowed intent
To be a pilgrim.

Who so beset him round
With dismal stories;
Do but themselves confound;
His strength the more is.
No foes shall stay his might,
Though he with giants fight;
He will make good his right
To be a pilgrim.

Since, Lord, thou dost defend
Us with thy Spirit,
We know we at the end
Shall life inherit.
Then, fancies, flee away!
I'll fear not what men say;
I'll labor night and day
To be a pilgrim.

Thirteenth century—During Advent services at the Cathedral Church in Salisbury, England, beginning on this day, the first of what are called the "O Antiphons" was traditionally sung. A new one was sung each day until December 23. These eight short hymns are called the "O Antiphons" because of their first lines: "O Israel's Scepter," "O Dayspring," etc. (John Mason Neale drew on them for his famous Advent hymn "O Come, O Come, Emmanuel.") This tradition, part of what is known as the Sarum Rite, is still practiced in parts of England to this day. Here, four of those Advent verses are given, as translated by English clergyman Earl Nelson in 1864.

————— ❧ ❦ —————

O Israel's Scepter! David's key!
Come and set death's captives free;
Unlock the gate that bars their road,
And lead them to the throne of God.
    Draw near, O Christ, with us to dwell,
    In mercy save thine Israel.

O Dayspring and Eternal Light!
Pierce through the gloom of error's night—
Predestined Sun of Righteousness!
Haste with thy rising beams to bless!
    Draw near, O Christ, with us to dwell,
    In mercy save thine Israel.

O King! Desire of nations, come,
Lead sons of earth to heaven's high home;
Chief and precious cornerstone,
Binding the severed into one.
    Draw near, O Christ, with us to dwell,
    In mercy save thine Israel.

O Lawgiver! Emmanuel! King!
Thy praises we would ever sing;
The gentiles' hope, the Savior blessed,
Take us to thine eternal rest.
    Draw near, O Christ, with us to dwell,
    In mercy save thine Israel.

1870—On this day, the Right Reverend Dr. Moriarity of Kilarney, Ireland, sent a letter to the Sisters of the Convent of Poor Clares in Kenmare, in which he gave his blessing to their newly published edition (one of the first in English) of The Life and Revelations of St. Gertrude. *Gertrude (1256– c. 1302) was a German mystic who was known for her many spiritual visions. Although never officially declared a saint, she is widely admired for her piety and for the beauty of her* Life and Revelations, *portions of which book were actually written by Gertrude herself. It is considered one of the finest examples of medieval mystical writing. In the following passage, Gertrude has a vision of Christ's being beaten before his execution, and she learns a lesson about the symbolic meaning of Christ's passion.*

———————— ⚜ ————————

Our Lord appeared to St. Gertrude.... [He was] tied to a pillar between two executioners, one of whom tore him with thorns, and the other bruised him with a whip full of large knots. Both struck his face, which seemed so disfigured that her very heart melted away with compassion; nor could she restrain her tears whenever she recalled that mournful spectacle during that day, since it appeared to her that none upon earth had ever been so cruelly used as her Lord Jesus. Even the very pupil of his eye was torn and inflamed, both by the thorns and the blows of the scourge. It appeared also to her that her Lord turned his face from side to side; but when he turned it from one executioner, the other struck it still more furiously; then he turned to her and exclaimed, "Have you not read what is written of me: 'We have thought him, as it were, a leper'?" (Isaiah 53:4). The Saint replied, "Alas, Lord! What remedy can we find to soothe the agonizing pains of your divine face?" Our Lord replied, "The most efficacious and the tenderest remedy which you can prepare for me is to meditate lovingly on my passion and to pray charitably for the conversion of sinners." These two executioners represent the laity who offend God openly, striking him with thorns, and the clergy who strike him still more unpitiably with the knotted cords of secret sins. But both offend him to the face and outrage the very God of heaven.

1904—East Indian Christian mystic Sundar Singh (1889–1929) suffered great persecution for his faith, but he was one of the most courageous evangelists that India, or the world, has ever known. To make the Gospel more palatable to Hindus, he dressed as a "Sadhu" (an Indian holy man) and traveled on foot to preach in remote areas of India and Tibet. He disappeared in 1929 while on a solitary journey deep into Tibet. Early in his life, however, he had a deep hatred of Christians and Christianity, and at the age of fifteen, to symbolize that hatred, he burned a copy of the Bible. That act caused him such guilt that he resolved to commit suicide. But before he could kill himself, he had an encounter on this day with the living God, which he described as follows.

———— ◈ ————

In the room where I was praying I saw a great light. I thought the place was on fire. I looked round but could find nothing. Then the thought came to me that this might be an answer that God had sent me. Then as I prayed and looked into the light, I saw the form of the Lord Jesus Christ. It had such an appearance of glory and love. If it had been some Hindu incarnation I would have prostrated myself before it. But it was the Lord Jesus Christ whom I had been insulting a few days before. I felt that a vision like this could not come out of my own imagination. I heard a voice saying in Hindustani, "How long will you persecute me? I have come to save you; you were praying to know the right way. Why do you not take it?" The thought then came to me, "Jesus Christ is not dead but living and it must be He Himself." So I fell at His feet and got this wonderful peace which I could not get anywhere else. This is the joy I was wishing to get. This was heaven itself. When I got up, the vision had all disappeared, but although the vision disappeared the peace and joy have remained with me ever since. I went off and told my father that I had become a Christian. He told me, "Go and lie down and sleep; why, only the day before yesterday you burnt the Bible; and you say you are a Christian now." I said, "Well, I have discovered now that Jesus Christ is alive and have determined to be His follower. Today I am His disciple and I am going to serve Him."

—from *The Sadhu* by B. H. Streeter and A. J. Appasamy (1926)

1852—Frederick William Robertson (1816–53) was a popular English minister who was notable for at least two reasons. First, unlike many ministers, he actively embraced the working classes in his ministry and teaching. Second, he was one of the first to incorporate motive and psychological insight into his preaching. In the following passage, from a sermon delivered on this day, he discusses grace and salvation as seen in 2 Corinthians 6:1–2: "Receive not the grace of God in vain. . . . In the day of salvation I have succored you: behold, now is the accepted time; behold, now is the day of salvation."

———— ⋅⊰ ⊱⋅ ————

That Christ died for all and that God is reconciled to all—this is the state of grace. Now the word *grace*, being exclusively a Scriptural one, seems mysterious, and is often misunderstood: it is supposed to be a mystical something infused into the soul. But grace is only God's favor, and a state of grace is the state in which all men are who have received the message of salvation which declares God's good will toward them. So speaks St. Paul in the Epistle to the Romans. The Corinthians had received this grace; they were baptized into the name of God the Father, and Christ the Son. They were told that God was their Father and their Friend. . . .

St. Paul quotes from Isaiah: "I have heard you in an accepted time and in the day of salvation have I succored you." . . . Now here was a precedent, declaring the limitation of the time during which grace is open, and St. Paul, applying it, says, "Now." . . . Every man has his day of grace: what in vulgar English we should call one's "chance." There comes to each man a crisis in his destiny, when evil influences have been removed or some strong impression made—after an illness or an escape or in some season of solitary thoughtfulness or disappointment. . . .

The power of God is not conveyed by physical contact, but by the reception of a Spirit. . . . The mind of Christ, as set forth in his apostles, acts on other minds, whether by ideas or character, and produces likeness to itself. Love begets love. Faith generates faith. Lofty lives nourish the germs of exalted life in others. There is a spiritual birth. John was the successor of the spirit of Elias. Luther was the offspring of the mind of Paul. We are children of Abraham if we share in the faith of Abraham; we are the successors of the apostles if we have a spirit similar to theirs.

1758—On this day Reverend James Hervey (1714–58; see also May 20) was visited by his doctor; the scene is described below by an anonymous biographer. Hervey died five days later. He was a popular writer, known in his time for his many volumes of meditations: Meditations among the Tombs; Reflections on a Flower Garden; Contemplations on the Night; Contemplations on the Starry Heavens; *and others.*

———— ⋅⊰ ⊱⋅ ————

He was visited by Dr. Stonehouse, who declared that in his opinion Mr. Hervey could not live above three or four days. And happening to speak of the many consolations through Christ which a good man enjoys in the prospect of death, and discoursing on the emptiness of worldly honor to an immortal, and on the unprofitableness of riches to the irreligious, Mr. Hervey replied: "True, Doctor, true. The only valuable treasures are in heaven. What would it avail me now to be Archbishop of Canterbury? Disease would show no respect to my miter. That prelate is not only very great, but I am told he has religion really at heart. Yet it is godliness and not grandeur that will avail him hereafter. The gospel is offered to me, a poor country parson, the same as to his Grace. Christ makes no difference between us. Oh! Why do the ministers thus neglect the charge of so kind a Savior, fawn upon the great, and hunt after worldly preferments with so much eagerness to the disgrace of our order? These, these are the things, Doctor, and not our poverty or obscurity which render the clergy so justly contemptible to the worldlings. No wonder the service of our Church, grieved I am to say it, is become such a formal lifeless thing, since it is, alas, too generally executed by persons dead to godliness in all their conversation, whose indifference to religion and worldly minded behavior proclaim the little regard they pay to the doctrines of the Lord who bought them."

When the doctor was going away, Mr. Hervey, with great tenderness, observed to him that as not long ago he had a dangerous fall from his horse, by which he was much bruised, and as he had been lately ill and then looked very pale, he hoped he would think on these narrow escapes so often fatal to others as a kind of warning from God to him, and remember them as such, adding, "How careful ought we to be to improve those years which remain at a time of life when but few can remain for us."

1849—*The denominational magazine* The Congregationalist, *on this day, published a hymn called "Shepherd of Tender Youth," by Henry M. Dexter (1821–90), a New England clergyman and pastor. It is a translation of a hymn by St. Clement (c. 170–220), who was an early Christian theologian and teacher in Alexandria, Egypt. Clement's original hymn has the distinction of being the earliest known hymn of Christendom. Dexter tempered his translation somewhat, for a more accurate rendering of Clement's original first line would be, "Tamer of unbridled steeds"!*

———————⋖§ §⋗———————

Shepherd of tender youth,
Guiding in love and truth,
Through devious ways;
Christ, our triumphant King,
We come thy name to sing,
And here our children bring
To shout thy praise.

Thou art the great High Priest;
Thou hast prepared the feast
Of heavenly love;
In all our mortal pain
None call on thee in vain;
Help thou did'st not disdain,
Help from above....

So now, and till we die,
Sound we thy praises high,
And joyful sing;
Let all the holy throng
Who to thy church belong,
Unite and swell the song
To Christ the King.

1850—Congregational preacher Thomas Binney (1798–1874) was a noted English Nonconformist. As such, he was critical of the established church of his time. He published many books, including works of theology and collections of sermons. The following excerpt is from a sermon he delivered on this day in King's Weigh House Chapel in London. Called "Gethsemane," it sensitively deals with the connection between Christ's suffering and our own.

———— ⋅≼ ξ≽⋅ ————

Being in agony, [Jesus] prayed "more earnestly." As his grief and sorrow increased upon him, he increased in the strength and fervor of his prayer. And yet, as he proceeded to repeat his request, the language of acquiescence became more absolute; at first he says, "if it be possible let this cup pass," but afterward he says, "if this cup may not pass, Your will be done"—as if he felt what that will was and meekly placed himself in harmony with it. We have reason to believe, however, that he did obtain, if not the thing he sought, that which was sufficient to supply its place. . . . He was not literally delivered from death; nor from those deadly mental pangs so much worse than the Cross itself. But he was saved from sinking under them. He was strengthened by an angel sent to him from the Father and was thus enabled to bear up till the darkness had passed away. . . . In the trials and conflicts of the Christian life, in every season of suffering and sorrow, let us learn to imitate the example of Jesus. However we may value or desire the sympathy of others, let us not depend on it. Let us never forget that in conflict with temptation and in wrestling with God, we must of necessity act alone. Let us pray with fervor, importunity, repetition: if the surges rise and overwhelm the spirit, if, like the Lord, we have agony and anguish, let us learn to pray "the more earnestly"—to pray, if needs be, with prostration and tears. The grace of Christ will never be denied to the sincere and sorrowful, though its manifestation may be delayed. He lives "a faithful and merciful High Priest, in that, he himself having suffered being tempted, he knows how to succor them that are tempted." Imitating his example and confiding in his mercy, succor and light will come at last. No Christian must ever expect to be without his Gethsemanes, but he that faints not, but continues to pray without ceasing, will always find that there is no Gethsemane without its angel.

1843—On this day, Scottish writer and religious leader Andrew A. Bonar (1810–92) expressed in his diary his exultation after having completed, the day before, his Memoirs and Remains of the Rev. Robert Murray M'Cheyne. *The book is one of the great classics of nineteenth-century religious biography. M'Cheyne (1813–43) was a Scottish minister who, though he died at age thirty, had a tremendous influence as an evangelist and preacher in the years before his death. In the following final passage from the book, Bonar challenges ministers in particular, and all believers in general, to emulate M'Cheyne's Christlikeness and zeal in spreading the Gospel.*

───────── ❧ ⚜ ─────────

Ministers of Christ, does not the Lord call upon us especially? . . . Oh, how seldom do we hear of fresh supplies of holiness arriving from the heavenly places (Ephesians 1:3), new grace appearing among the saints, and in the living ministers. . . .

But there has been one among us who . . . dwelt at the Mercy seat as if it were his home—preached the certainties of eternal life with an undoubting mind—and spent his nights and days in ceaseless breathings after holiness and the salvation of sinners. Hundreds of souls were his reward from the Lord ere he left us; and in him have we been taught how much one man may do who will only press farther into the presence of his God and handle more skillfully the unsearchable riches of Christ and speak more boldly for his God.

We speak much against unfaithful ministers, while we ourselves are awfully unfaithful! Are we never afraid that the cries of souls whom we have betrayed to perdition through want of personal holiness and our defective preaching of Christ crucified may ring in our ears forever? Our Lord is at the door. In the twinkling of an eye our work will be done. "Awake, awake, O arm of the Lord, awake as in the ancient day," till every one of thy pastors be willing to impart to the flock, over which the Holy Ghost has made him overseer, not the gospel of God only, but also his own soul. And oh that each one were able, as he stands in the pastures feeding thy sheep and lambs, to look up and appeal to Thee: "Lord, Thou knowest all things! Thou knowest that I love Thee!"

1818—Probably the most famous rendition of any hymn took place on this day at St. Nicholas Church in Oberndorf, Austria. Because of a broken church organ, assistant priest Joseph Mohr (1792–1848) gave his poem "Stille Nacht" to organist Franz Gruber (1787–1863) to arrange for guitar, two voices, and choir. It has come to light in recent years, however, that Gruber commonly arranged special worship music for guitar and that the story of the organ's being broken may be a myth. Whatever the truth, "Silent Night" remains one of the world's most popular Christmas songs. For interest's sake, the words are presented here in an older and less-familiar translation so that the meaning of the lines can be appreciated anew.

———— ᵕᶟ ᶝᵔ ————

Holy night! peaceful night!
Through the darkness beams a light;
Yonder, angels their sweet vigils keep
O'er the Babe, who in silent sleep
    Rests in heavenly peace,
    Rests in heavenly peace.

Silent night! holiest night!
Darkness flies and all is light!
Shepherds hear the angels sing—
"Hallelujah! hail the King!
    Jesus Christ is here!
    Jesus Christ is here!"

Silent night! holiest night!
Guiding star! oh, lend thy light!
See the eastern wise men bring
Gifts and homage to our King!
    Jesus Christ is here!
    Jesus Christ is here!

Silent night! holiest night!
Wonderous Star! oh, lend thy light!
With the angels let us sing
Hallelujah to our King!
    Jesus Christ is here!
    Jesus Christ is here!

—from J. Barnby's *Original Tunes to Popular Hymns* (1872)

Late sixteenth century—Robert Southwell (1561–95) was an English Jesuit poet during the reign of Queen Elizabeth I. He was cruelly martyred for his faith; in 1970 he was canonized. His poems, often mystical and always deeply moving, have found a wide audience among both Catholics and Protestants. The following, entitled "The Burning Babe," must be among the most unusual and startlingly original Christmas poems ever written.

As I in hoary winter's night stood shivering in the snow,
Surprised I was with sudden heat which made my heart to glow;
And lifting up a fearful eye to view what fire was near,
A pretty Babe all burning bright did in the air appear;
Who, scorched with excessive heat, such floods of tears did shed,
As though his flood should quench his flames which with his tears
    were fed.
"Alas!" quoth he, "but newly born in fiery heats I fry,
Yet none approach to warm their hearts or feel my fire but I.
My faultless breast the furnace is, the fuel wounding thorns;
Love is the fire, and sighs the smoke, the ashes shame and scorns;
The fuel justice layeth on, and mercy blows the coals;
The metal in this furnace wrought are men's defiled souls:
For which, as now on fire I am to work them to their good,
So will I melt into a bath to wash them in my blood."
With this he vanished out of sight and swiftly shrunk away,
And straight I called unto mind that it was Christmas day.

Early nineteenth century—English writer and antiquarian Davies Gilbert (1767–1839) heard the folk song "Saint Stephen" sung in the streets of Bodmin, England, and in 1822 he published it in his book A Collection of Christmas Carols. *The popular carol, commonly sung on this day, St. Stephen's Day, commemorates the first Christian martyr, whose moving story is told in the book of Acts, chapters 6 to 8.*

───────── ⋙ ⋘ ─────────

Saint Stephen was a holy man,
 Endued with heavenly might,
And many wonders he did work
 Before the people's sight;
And by the blessed Spirit of God,
 Which did his heart inflame,
He sparéd not, in every place,
 To preach God's holy name.

CHORUS: O man, do never faint nor fear
 When God the truth shall try,
But mark how Stephen, for Christ's sake,
 Was willing for to die.

... Then Stephen did put forth his voice,
 And he did first unfold
The wondrous works which God hath wrought,
 Even for their fathers of old. ...
But when they heard him so to say
 Upon him they all ran,
And then without the city gates
 They stoned this holy man.

There he most meekly on his knees
 To God did pray at large,
Desiring that he would not lay
 This sin unto their charge;
Then yielding up his soul to God,
 Who had it dearly bought,
He lost his life, whose body then
 To grave was seemly brought.

1920—Pioneering American missionary Sam Higginbottom (1874–1958) wrote, on this day, the preface to his autobiography, The Gospel and the Plow. *Higginbottom aroused suspicion among some in the missionary community for his philosophy that the poor needed first to be fed before they could be witnessed to, as he explains in the final chapter of* The Gospel and the Plow:

———————— ◆§ ♭◆ ————————

I went out to India having specialized in philosophy and hoping to be an evangelist. I end up by being a missionary farmer. I have had friends tell me they could not see why I am interested in the things in which I am interested. They ask what plows, harrows, tractors, silos, threshing machines, and better cattle have to do with evangelization in India. Bulletins upon the use of manure and silage are good, but what is their value as missionary tracts?...

After the years in India the greatest abiding impression that remains is one of "loss" in India. Appalling loss of human life and stupendous economic waste. Human life is so abundant, so cheap, so easily given up that it is depressing. No other civilized country has such a high infant death rate. Preventable disease is ever carrying off great hosts who have survived infancy....

I am always brooding over ways and means of avoiding this fearful waste of human life, of transforming it into a positive asset to enrich the world. Then there is fearful economic waste due to ignorance and superstition.... As Jesus looks over India today with its rich soil and teeming multitudes as sheep without a shepherd, so surely does He say to those who hear His voice, gather up the fragments that remain that nothing of human life or of material that builds up human life be lost. But rather that it be conserved to help to bless all men everywhere. When we save India from these incalculable losses we are helping to save one-fifth of the human race. A task great enough and worthwhile enough to stretch to the limit the best America has and cause us to pray anew: The Harvest truly is plenteous, the laborers are few. Pray ye therefore to the Lord of the Harvest that He—God Almighty Himself—will send forth laborers, men and women willing to work out His will, properly equipped with all labor-saving devices, tractors, plows, harrows, threshing machines, that India may be one of the brightest jewels that ennoble the glorious Crown of Him who once wore the Crown of Thorns.

1927—Dorothy Day (1897–1980) was an American journalist and political activist, a church worker deeply committed to social causes, and the cofounder of the Catholic Worker, *an important religious journal that espoused social causes and Christian pacifism. She spent her life working for social justice. On this day, as a thirty-year-old mother, she was baptized into the Catholic Church. In her stunning autobiography,* The Long Loneliness, *she describes the steps that led her to that decision.*

"Thou shalt love the Lord thy God with thy whole heart and with thy whole soul and with thy whole mind." This is the first Commandment.

The problem is, how to love God? We are only too conscious of the hardness of our hearts, and in spite of all that religious writers tell us about *feelings* not being necessary, we do want to feel and so know that we love God.

"You would not seek Him if you had not already found him," Pascal says, and it is true too that you love God if you want to love Him. One of the disconcerting facts about the spiritual life is that God takes you at your word. Sooner or later one is given a chance to prove his love. . . . It is all very well to love God in His works, in the beauty of His creation which was crowned for me by the birth of my child. Forster [the child's father] had made the physical world come alive for me and had awakened in my heart a flood of gratitude. The final object of this love and gratitude was God. No human creature could receive or contain so vast a flood of love and joy as I often felt after the birth of my child. With this came the need to worship, to adore. I had heard many say that they wanted to worship God in their own way and did not need a Church in which to praise Him, nor a body of people with whom to associate themselves. But I did not agree to this. My very experience as a radical, my whole make-up, led me to want to associate myself with others, with the masses in loving and praising God.

1170—Thomas Becket (1118–70) was one of the most capable religious leaders in Europe in the twelfth century. In 1162, King Henry II of England made Thomas the Archbishop of Canterbury, though they became alienated through a series of political and religious conflicts. Thinking they were acting on the King's behalf, four English barons murdered Becket on this day in Canterbury cathedral. Eight centuries later, Becket's death became the subject of a deeply moving play by famed Anglo-American poet T. S. Eliot (1888– 1965). The play is Murder in the Cathedral, and in the following sermon excerpt, the character Becket reflects on the meaning of martyrdom.

Consider also one thing of which you have probably never thought. Not only do we at the feast of Christmas celebrate at once Our Lord's Birth and His Death: but on the next day we celebrate the martyrdom of His first martyr, the blessed Stephen. Is it an accident, do you think, that the day of the first martyr follows immediately the day of the Birth of Christ? By no means. Just as we rejoice and mourn at once, in the Birth and in the Passion of Our Lord; so also, in a smaller figure, we both rejoice and mourn in the death of martyrs. . . .

We do not think of a martyr simply as a good Christian who has been killed because he is a Christian: for that would be solely to mourn. We do not think of him simply as a good Christian who has been elevated to the company of the Saints: for that would be simply to rejoice: and neither our mourning nor our rejoicing is as the world's is. A Christian martyrdom is never an accident, for Saints are not made by accident. Still less is a Christian martyrdom the effect of a man's will to become a Saint, as a man by willing and contriving may become a ruler of men. A martyrdom is always the design of God, for His love of men, to warn them and to lead them, to bring them back to His ways. It is never the design of man; for the true martyr is he who has become the instrument of God, who has lost his will in the will of God, and who no longer desires anything for himself, not even the glory of being a martyr. So thus as on earth the Church mourns and rejoices at once, in a fashion that the world cannot understand; so in Heaven the Saints are most high, having made themselves most low, and are seen, not as we see them, but in the light of the Godhead from which they draw their being.

1819—William Blake (1757–1827) was an English artist, poet, and vision-ary. He wrote, printed by hand, and hand colored his own books, which, though considered mere curiosities in his time, are now priceless works of art. (See also August 27.) On this day he sold the only known copy of his epic visionary poem Jerusalem *to his friend and patron John Linnell. In the fol-lowing extract, the narrator of* Jerusalem *relates a vision in which he sees a fiery sword-like wheel turning in the sky. He asks an angel, a "Holy One," to explain the meaning of the wheel.*

———— ᥬᥩ ᥩᥬ ————

[The angel] answered: "It is the Wheel of Religion."
I wept and said: "Is this the law of Jesus,
This terrible devouring sword turning every way?"
He answered, "Jesus died because he strove
Against the current of this Wheel; its Name
Is Caiaphas, the dark Preacher of Death,
Of sin, of sorrow and of punishment:
Opposing Nature! It is Natural Religion;
But Jesus is the bright Preacher of Life
Creating Nature from this fiery Law
By self-denial and forgiveness of Sin.
Go therefore, cast out devils in Christ's name,
Heal thou the sick of spiritual disease,
Pity the evil, for thou art not sent
To smite with terror and with punishments
Those that are sick, like to the Pharisees
Crucifying and encompassing sea and land
For proselytes to tyranny and wrath;
But to the Publicans and Harlots go,
Teach them True Happiness, but let no curse
Go forth out of thy mouth to blight their peace;
For Hell is opened to Heaven; thine eyes beheld
The dungeons burst and the Prisoners set free."

*1855—Dinah Maria Mulock Craik (1826–87), the daughter of an English
Nonconformist minister, was a popular and influential Victorian novelist and
poet, who was particularly known for her best-selling morality novel* John
Halifax, Gentleman. *In 1855 she wrote "Psalm for New Year's Eve" in
honor of this day. A portion of that beautiful poem follows.*

O New Year, teach us faith!
The road of life is hard:
When our feet bleed and scourging winds us scathe,
Point thou to him whose visage was more marred
Than any man's: who saith,
"Make straight paths for your feet," and to the oppressed,
"Come ye to me, and I will give you rest."

Yet hand some lamplike hope
Above this unknown way,
Kind year, to give our spirits freer scope
And our hands strength to work while it is day.
But if that way must slope
Tombward, oh, bring before our fading eyes
The lamp of life, the hope that never dies.

Comfort our souls with love—
Love of all human kind;
Love special, close, in which, like sheltered dove
Each weary heart its own safe nest may find;
And love that turns above
Adoringly; contented to resign
All loves, if need be, for the love divine. . . .

Books for the Soul

❦

Most of us find little joy in wading through Augustine's *City of God*, Milton's *Paradise Lost*, or Calvin's *Institutes*. Many classics are long and ponderous, and we live with the guilt of knowing we *should* read them—but we just can't get through them! The following list is for readers who believe, as we do, that spiritual reading should be fun as well as edifying. The following books are generally short, accessible, and, we think, delightful. All but one or two are still in print and may be ordered from your local bookstore.

Arnold, Duane W. H., editor. *Prayers of the Martyrs*. Grand Rapids: Zondervan, 1991. A moving collection of prayers by Christian martyrs—from St. Stephen to Oscar Romero—from all eras and all parts of the world. Inspiring and thought provoking.

Bacovcin, Helen, translator. *The Way of the Pilgrim*. New York: Doubleday, 1978. A gentle, anonymous nineteenth-century tale of a humble pilgrim who, in the process of seeking an answer to the question "How is it possible to pray constantly?" learns the mystery of "the Jesus Prayer." One of Russia's most cherished spiritual classics.

Blake, William. *Songs of Innocence* and *Songs of Experience*. New York: Dover, 1971 and 1984. Lovely, inexpensive facsimile editions of two of Blake's great illuminated books. If you don't already have them, you owe it to yourself to own, read, and cherish these gems. Blake's *Marriage of Heaven and Hell* is also available in this series.

The Book of Psalms. New York: Henry Holt, 1986. The entire book of Psalms in the King James Version is here lavishly decorated with reproductions from medieval illuminated manuscripts. A truly aesthetic devotional experience. Also in the same illustrated format are *The Epistles of Saint Paul; The Book of Common Prayer; Bible: Stories from the Old Testament*; and *Bible: New Testament—Illustrated Selections*.

Bunyan, John. *Pilgrim's Progress*. Available in more than two dozen different editions. When one grows accustomed to the archaic language, the original is easy to read, although this classic is available in numerous modernized and abridged editions that are much less daunting. One of the most popular Christian books of all time.

Canton, William. *A Child's Book of Saints*. Once available in several editions, all of which are now out of print. Still, this romantic collection of saints' lives can be found in many libraries and offers countless moments of wonder and delight.

Catherine of Siena. *The Prayers of Catherine of Siena*. Edited and translated by Suzanne Noffke. Mahwah, N.J.: Paulist Press, Classics of Western Spirituality Series, 1983. Intense, passionate prayers written by a truly remarkable fourteenth-century Italian saint. This publisher's entire series is highly recommended.

Chesterton, G. K. *The Man Who Was Thursday*. New York: Dover, 1986, and other editions. A boisterous whodunit that turns into a cosmic spiritual comedy of vast dimensions. Mystifying, zany, and fun.

_____. *Orthodoxy*. New York: Doubleday, 1973. Chesterton, in his inimitable witty, profound style, examines the basic tenets of the Christian faith. A nice counterpart to C. S. Lewis's *Mere Christianity*.

_____. *St. Francis of Assisi.* New York: Doubleday, 1974. A loving and insightful portrait of one of Christianity's most beloved and influential saints. Chesterton has a knack for capturing the man and his times.

_____. *Saint Thomas Aquinas: "The Dumb Ox."* New York: Doubleday, 1974. A loving tribute to one of Christendom's most brilliant minds by one of Christendom's most amusing minds.

Clissold, Stephen, editor. *The Wisdom of the Spanish Mystics.* New York: New Directions, 1977. An outstanding collection of short reflections by such saints as John of the Cross and Teresa of Ávila.

_____. *The Wisdom of St. Francis and His Companions.* New York: New Directions, 1979. For the general reader, this is one of the most accessible compilations of meditations and anecdotes from St. Francis and his circle.

Davie, Donald. *The New Oxford Book of Christian Verse.* Oxford and New York: Oxford University Press, 1982. An outstanding selection of the best Christian poetry in English, from Geoffrey Chaucer to Wendell Berry. The author's preface concerning what makes poetry "Christian" is particularly enlightening.

De Gasztold, Carmen Bernos. *Prayers from the Ark and the Creature's Choir.* New York: Viking/Penguin, 1976. Translated by Rumer Godden. Beautiful, whimsical, worshipful poems of praise from the point of view of the animals on Noah's ark. Always a hit with children and adults alike.

Drummond, Henry. *The Greatest Thing in the World.* Available in several different editions. A passionate and beautiful nineteenth-century reflection on the "love" passage from 1 Corinthians 13. One of the most cherished of all devotional classics.

Hildegard of Bingen. *Mystical Writings.* New York: Crossroad, 1990. An accessible introduction to the life and work of one of the great geniuses of the Middle Ages. Offers short samplings from several of her books.

Johnson, James Weldon. *God's Trombones: Seven Negro Sermons.* New York: Viking/Penguin, 1976. Johnson, a prominent figure in black literature, captures the power and drama of African-American preaching at its best. A true treasure.

Kelly, Thomas. *A Testament of Devotion.* New York: HarperCollins, 1992. Practical Quaker wisdom on living the life of the spirit. Justifiably one of the most beloved devotional books of the twentieth century.

Kempis, Thomas à. *The Imitation of Christ.* Available in several editions. Though often astringent in tone, this wise and profound volume continues to be one of the most renowned of Christian classics.

Kierkegaard, Søren. *The Parables of Kierkegaard.* Princeton, N.J.: Princeton University Press, 1989. Edited by Thomas Oden. A compilation of insightful and amusing parables from Kierkegaard's many writings. Short, accessible, and delightful. The book is usually a revelation for readers who think they don't like Kierkegaard.

Knight, William Allen. *The Song of the Syrian Guest.* Cleveland: Pilgrim Press, 1972. A lovely parable-like reflection on the meaning of the Twenty-third Psalm, originally written in the early 1900s.

Lattimore, Richard. *The Four Gospels and the Revelation* and *Acts and Letters of the Apostles.* New York: Farrar, Straus, Giroux, 1979 and 1982. The late Richard Lattimore, renowned translator and scholar, offers the entire New Testament in two volumes. His strength is his sensitivity to the tone, cadence, and music of the original texts, making this sometimes rugged version a refreshing change-of-pace from the more familiar and often overrefined translations.

Lawrence, Brother, of the Resurrection. *The Practice of the Presence of God.* New York: Doubleday, 1977, translated by John J. Delaney. Also available in other editions. One of the world's most beloved classics—from seventeenth-century France—on the subject of union and communion with God.

Lewis, C. S. *The Chronicles of Narnia*. New York: HarperCollins, 1994. Stunning new
editions of Lewis's classic series of seven fantasy novels for children—which are
probably just as popular among adults: *The Magician's Nephew*; *The Lion, the Witch
and the Wardrobe*; *A Horse and His Boy*; *Prince Caspian*; *The Voyage of the Dawn-
treader*; *The Silver Chair*; and *The Last Battle*.

_____. *Mere Christianity*. New York: Macmillan, 1986. A classic; perhaps the most
widely read introduction to the Christian life in modern times.

_____. *The Screwtape Letters*. New York: Macmillan, 1982. Deeply convicting and
hilarious fictional letters from a bureaucratic administrative demon to his nephew
on the subject of how to win souls away from God. A must read.

MacDonald, George. *The Fantasy Stories of George MacDonald*. 4 vols. Grand Rapids:
Eerdmans, 1980. This appealing set of four books contains many of MacDonald's
most charming and beautiful fantasy stories and fairy tales, including such classics
as "The Light Princess," "The Golden Key," and "The Gray Wolf."

_____. *The Heart of George MacDonald: A One-Volume Collection of His Most Impor-
tant Fiction, Essays, Sermons, Drama, Poetry, and Letters*. Edited by Rolland Hein.
Wheaton, Ill.: Shaw, 1993. For a good introduction to MacDonald's depth and originality in several genres, this compilation can't be topped.

_____. *Phantastes* and *Lilith*. Grand Rapids: Eerdmans, 1981. These two novels,
though separate volumes, are usually mentioned in one breath, being the finest
examples of MacDonald's outrageously evocative and mystifying fantasy writing.
Worth reading, especially if you are already a fan of the genre.

Macleod, John. *Some Favorite Books*. Edinburgh, Scotland: Banner of Truth, 1988. First
published as articles from 1918 to 1922, these short introductions to twenty-two
Puritan spiritual classics have achieved classic status in their own right. These readable essays explore some fascinating and little-known byways of Christian literature.

Merton, Thomas. *Raids on the Unspeakable*. New York: New Directions, 1964. Of Merton's many wonderful books, this is one of the most appealing. These essays are
short, surprising, and deeply challenging. A good introduction to his thought.

_____. *The Wisdom of the Desert*. New York: New Directions, 1960. Touching and
often funny stories and meditations of some of the world's most deeply spiritual
people: the desert fathers of Egypt in the first few centuries after Christ. A true gem.

Muggeridge, Malcolm. *Something Beautiful for God*. New York: Harper & Row, 1986.
This is Muggeridge's moving and affectionate portrait of Mother Teresa of Calcutta,
gathered from his interviews with her and from her own words.

Palmer, G. E. H., Philip Sherrard, and Kallistos Ware, translators. *Prayer of the Heart:
Writings from the Philokalia*. Boston: Shambhala, 1993. These spiritual writings from
the fourth and fifth centuries were compiled in the eighteenth century by two Greek
monks, Saints Nikodimos and Makarios. Since then, the *Philokalia* has been the most
beloved devotional book of the Eastern church. This miniature volume of selections
is an outstanding introduction to its riches.

Pascal, Blaise. *Pensées*. New York: Viking/Penguin, 1966. These short meditations from
this seventeenth-century French genius are still readable and surprisingly modern.

Phillips, J. B. *Your God Is Too Small*. New York: Macmillan, 1961. A perennial favorite,
this book confronts our unrealistic notions of who God is. A book of great wisdom.

Tolstoy, Leo. *Where Love Is, There God Is Also*. Nashville: Thomas Nelson, 1993. This
slender gift volume contains three of Tolstoy's most beloved spiritual parables:
"Where Love Is, There God Is Also," "The Three Hermits," and "What Men Live
By." Classic Russian wisdom from one of the world's great authors.

Toon, Peter. *Spiritual Companions: An Introduction to the Christian Classics*. Grand
Rapids: Baker, 1992. A book of brief character sketches of nearly a hundred impor-
tant Christian writers. A highly recommended guidebook for delving into the great
Christian classics on your own.

Toulson, Shirley. *The Celtic Year*. Longmead, England: Element, 1993. A beautiful introduction to the great saints and feasts of the Celtic church; full of legends, poems, saints' lives, and spiritual tales.

van Dyke, Henry. *The Story of the Other Wise Man*. Available in many editions, sometimes titled simply *The Other Wise Man*. A gentle and wise parable about a fourth wise man, who, because of his good deeds, was unable to accompany the other wise men to Bethlehem—but found the Savior nonetheless.

Ward, Benedicta, translator. *The Prayers and Meditations of St. Anselm*. New York: Viking/Penguin, 1979. This collection of beautiful, psalm-like prayers and meditations by a medieval English archbishop and saint makes for perfect first-thing-in-the-morning devotional reading.

Webb, J. F., translator. *The Age of Bede*. New York: Penguin, 1985. This is actually four short books in one, all medieval biographies of important saints of the Celtic church. Though all are interesting, the real treasure here is the fanciful *Voyage of St. Brendan*. As readable and fun as any modern fantasy novel.

Weil, Simone. *Gravity and Grace*. London and New York: Routledge, 1992. Translated by Emma Craufurd. Short reflections on nearly forty themes by this influential twentieth-century French philosopher and activist. Orthodox and unorthodox by turns, she is always surprising, provocative, and refreshing.

Williams, Charles. *All Hallows' Eve*. Cutchogue, N.Y.: Lightyear Press, 1993. An eerie and powerful fantasy novel from the 1940s about Redemption among the lost spirits of the dead. A haunting spiritual thriller.

Woolman, John. *Journals*. New York: Carol Publishing Group, 1972. Wise and compelling reflections from the journal of an itinerant eighteenth-century Quaker preacher and social reformer. Profound and mystical. Woolman seems to know what it means to be "fully alive" as a Christian.

Zundel, Veronica. *Eerdmans' Book of Christian Classics*. Grand Rapids: Eerdmans, 1985. This elegant coffee-table book offers the finest specimens of Christian writing. It is one of the best and most accessible introductions to the riches of the spiritual classics available. Nicely compiled. Beautifully designed and illustrated.

And Don't Forget Music for the Soul

The following compact discs, which contain music relating to readings in this book, are all currently available. If your local music store does not stock a title you are interested in, it can be ordered by providing the store with the catalog information given in parentheses.

Bach, Johann Sebastian. *The Passion According to St. Matthew*. Available in several versions. Considered by some the greatest choral work in the history of music; source of the hymn "O Sacred Head Now Wounded."

Brown, Greg. *Songs of Innocence and Experience* (Red House Records RHR CD 14). William Blake's poetry set to music and performed by a major American folk artist. It is hard to imagine a more perfect combination than Brown's rugged vocals, his sensitive musical settings, and Blake's verse. Truly outstanding.

Coulter, William, and Barry Phillips. *Simple Gifts: Instrumental Arrangements of Shaker Melodies* (Gourd Music GM 106). Beautifully arranged instrumental versions of Shaker folk hymns and dances, including "Simple Gifts." Look also for the outstanding sequel by the same artists, *The Tree of Life* (Gourd Music GM 114).

Davis, Rev. Blind Gary. *Complete Recorded Works: 1935–1949* (Document Records DOCD-5060, also on Yazoo 2011). A true original, Rev. Gary Davis displays some of folk music's finest guitar work in the course of these powerful country gospel songs.

These are the earliest recordings of some of his most familiar standards, such as "I Belong to the Band," "Twelve Gates to the City," and "I Am the True Vine."

Handel, George Frideric. *The Messiah*. Available in many versions. This classic oratorio, popular at Christmas, is a must for every household with a record or CD player. Some of the most sublimely praiseful music ever written.

Hildegard of Bingen. *Canticles of Ecstasy* (Deutsche Harmonia Mundi 05472 77320 2). Performed by the group Sequentia. Lovely, meditative renditions of Hildegard's vocal music, to which background instrumentation has been added. The sound is very close to Gregorian chant. Another excellent recording of her music is *A Feather on the Breath of God* (Hyperion CDA66039).

Johnson, Blind Willie. *The Complete Blind Willie Johnson* (Columbia/Legacy C2k 52835). 2 CDs. Although this rough-hewn African-American gospel singer of the 1920s will not appeal to all tastes, his blues-tinged guitar and powerful vocals are poignant and unforgettable. He is the source for several well-known gospel standards. Spiritual music for the lover of Delta blues.

McMeen, El. *Of Soul and Spirit: Hymns and Irish Meditations Arranged for Acoustic Guitar* (Shanachie 97012). Charming and meditative instrumental-guitar arrangements of favorite English and Irish hymns. A truly contemplative recording.

Phillips, Barry, and Shelley Phillips. *Wondrous Love* (Gourd Music GM 118). This husband-and-wife team gather a group of outstanding folk and classical musicians for seemingly flawless instrumental renderings of well-known *Sacred Harp* hymns, including "Amazing Grace" and "Wondrous Love." First rate.

Prior, Maddy, with the Carnival Band. *Sing Lustily and with Good Courage: Gallery Hymns of the 18th and Early 19th Centuries* (Saydisc CD-SDL 383). Maddy Prior, a major figure in the folk revival, performs rollicking, authentic vocal renditions of English hymns. Wesley and Watts were not nearly as tame as you might think. Look also for these artists' two highly enjoyable Christmas albums: *Carols and Capers* (Park Records PRK CD9) and *A Tapestry of Carols* (Saydisc CD-SDL 366).

Robertson, Kim. *Celtic Christmas* (Invincible INVCD110). Instrumental Celtic harp renditions of familiar and unfamiliar Christmas songs and hymns. Quiet and appropriate for the Advent season. Of the dozens of Christmas albums we've heard, this and its sequel, *Celtic Christmas II* (Invincible INVCD119), are by far our favorites.

Simpson, Martin. *A Closer Walk with Thee: Instrumental Arrangements of American Gospel Songs* (Gourd Music GM 117). Emotionally charged instrumental-guitar versions of well-known American folk hymns, from both Anglo- and African-American traditions. Simpson, a major figure in the English folk revival, is a wonderfully expressive guitarist.

The Singers of Lower Shaker Village, Enfield, New Hampshire. *O Hear Their Music Ring* (Impact Media CD5001). Historically authentic choral renditions of nineteenth-century Shaker songs, recreating the sound of an original Shaker worship service. Includes "Simple Gifts" and thirty-two other short, gem-like hymns.

Various artists. *The Steeple on the Common* (North Star Records SS0007). New England folk musicians perform charming instrumental versions of twenty-five familiar hymns on a vast array of traditional instruments. Includes "Amazing Grace," "Gloria Patri," and "Old Rugged Cross." Also look for the sequel, *The Steeple on the Common 2* (North Star Records NS0017) and their two Christmas albums: *New England Christmastide 1 & 2* (North Star Records CS0002 and CS0006). All four CDs provide excellent settings for singing along.

Word of Mouth Chorus. *Rivers of Delight: American Folk Hymns from the Sacred Harp Tradition* (Elektra/Nonesuch 9 71360-2). Unlike most professional choirs who attempt to sing shape-note hymns, this choir manages to retain the rugged harmonies and boisterous expressiveness of traditional *Sacred Harp* hymns. Probably the best collection of traditional shape-note singing on CD.

Acknowledgments

❦ ❧

We wish to thank Zondervan editor Lyn Cryderman and publisher Scott Bolinder for championing this project. Thanks too to graphic designer John Lucas, designer/compositor Sherri Hoffman, and the staff of Calvin College Library, where most of the research was done. We would also like to express our gratitude to John Topliff, Mark Mixter, Christine Anderson, and Chris Grant of the Marketing Department of Zondervan Publishing House for their encouragement and enthusiasm. Thank you to those who offered special advice and encouragement: Mary McCormick, Stan Gundry, Ken Gire, Walter Wangerin, Jr., Dave Lambert, Jack Kuhatschek, Ann Spangler, Ed van der Maas, Sue Koppenol, Verne and Nancy Becker, Mike Steenstra, Tracy Danz, and Sue Fox. Last—and most importantly—a special thank you goes to Lori Walburg, who is simply one of the best editors in the whole world, if not the universe!

The compilers and publisher of *Companions for the Soul* wish to thank the following publishers for permission to use materials from these books:

Barth, Karl. *Deliverance to the Captives.* Translated by Marguerite Wieser. Copyright © 1978 by Harper & Row. Reprinted by permission of HarperCollins Publishers, Inc.

Boehme, Jacob. *A Way to Christ.* Translated by John Joseph Stoudt. English translation copyright 1947 by John Joseph Stoudt, renewed © 1975 by John Joseph Stoudt. Reprinted by permission of HarperCollins Publishers, Inc.

Bonaventure, St. *Collation on the Six Days,* from *The Works of Bonaventure,* Vol. 5, translated by José de Vinck. Copyright © 1970 by St. Anthony's Guild. Reprinted by permission of St. Anthony's Guild Press.

"Brigid's Feast," from *Celtic Fire* by Robert Van de Weyer. Copyright © 1990 by Robert Van de Weyer. Used by permission of Doubleday, a division of Bantam Doubleday Dell Publishing Group, Inc., U.S., and Darton, Longman & Todd, Ltd., UK.

Catherine of Siena. *The Prayers of Catherine of Siena.* Edited and translated by Suzanne Noffke for the Classics of Western Spirituality Series. Copyright © 1983 by Suzanne Noffke. Used by permission of Paulist Press.

Chambers, Oswald. *My Utmost for His Highest.* Copyright © 1935 by Dodd Mead and Co., renewed © 1963 by the Oswald Chambers Publications Assn., Ltd., and used by permission of Discovery House Publishers, Box 3566, Grand Rapids MI 49501. All rights reserved.

Day, Dorothy. *The Long Loneliness.* Copyright 1952 by Harper & Row, Publishers, Inc. Copyright renewed © 1980 by Tamar Teresa Hennessy. Reprinted by permission of HarperCollins Publishers, Inc.

Index

❧ ❧

NOTE: Dates in parentheses indicate secondary references.

Hilton, Walter: Nov. 16
Hodgson, Leonard: Dec. 8
Hooper, Wynnard: (July 31)
Hopkins, Gerard Manley: March 17
Hügel, Baron Friedrich von: May 5
Huysmans, Joris-Karl: Feb. 23
Hyde, Rev. Dr.: (Feb. 25)

Ignatius of Antioch: Aug. 23
Ignatius of Loyola: (April 7)
Ingram, Arthur F. W.: April 25

Jackson, Abraham: Nov. 22
Jacobs, Joseph: Oct. 26
Jay, William: Feb. 26, Sept. 10
James, William: (Sept. 9)
Jebb, Dr.: May 30
Jerome: April 8
John of Hildesheim: June 11
John of the Cross: Aug. 16, Dec. 2
Johnson, "Blind" Willie: Dec. 3
Johnson, James Weldon: Oct. 23
Johnson, Dr. Samuel: March 28, Sept. 18
Joly, Henri: May 7
Jones, Eli Stanley: July 7
Joseph of the Studium: March 19
Jowett, John Henry: May 31
Julian of Norwich: May 14

Keble, John: Aug. 4
Kellogg, Samuel Henry: June 19
Kelly, Thomas R.: Jan. 17, Sept. 9
Kempe, Margery: Jan. 23, (Nov. 16)
Ken, Thomas: Feb. 17
Kenach: March 13
Kennedy, Annie Richardson: July 15
Kennedy, G. A. Studdert: June 15
Kieran of Saighir: March 5
Kierkegaard, Søren: July 29
Kinane, Dean: Aug. 5
King James Bible: Jan. 16, (April 8), (May 6)
Kingsley, Charles: June 22
Kipling, Rudyard: July 16
Kittredge, A. E.: Feb. 27
Knight, William Allen: Sept. 1
Knox, John: Aug. 19
Kuyper, Abraham: Oct. 29

Latimer, Hugh: Jan. 18
Law, William: (Jan. 1), June 16
Lawrence, Brother: (Jan. 17), (July 7), Aug. 3
Leo, Brother: May 11, Aug. 11
Leo XIII: June 20
Lever, Thomas: Dec. 13
Lewis, C. S.: Feb. 7, (July 20), (July 28), Sept. 20, (Oct. 9)
Liguori, Alfonso de: March 7, April 28
Livingstone, W. P.: Aug. 2
Locke, John: Sept. 27
Longfellow, Henry Wadsworth: (Sept. 5), Sept. 14
Longfellow, Marian: Sept. 5

Luther, Martin: April 18, (Aug. 22)
Lydgate, John: June 8
Lyte, Henry Francis: Sept. 4

MacDonald, George: July 20
MacDonald, Robert: April 29
MacInnes, Rennie: (Oct. 15)
MacLaren, Alexander: Jan. 28
Maedoc of Ferns: Jan. 31
March, Daniel: Oct. 18
Martin of Tours: Nov. 11
Martyn, Henry: Aug. 28
Mather, Cotton: May 27
Mather, Increase: (May 27), July 9, (Aug. 7), (Nov. 15), Dec. 11
Mather, Richard: (Aug. 7)
M'Cheyne, Robert Murray: Dec. 23
McClure, J. B.: (Jan. 30)
McKelvey, S. Willis: Nov. 12
Merton, Thomas: March 24, Dec. 10
Miller, James Russell: May 13, Aug. 6
Mills, Abbie: July 2
Milton, John: (Jan. 1), April 27, (Oct. 20)
Misyn, Richard: July 4
Mohr, Joseph: Dec. 24
Montgomery, James: Aug. 13, Oct. 14
Moody, Dwight L.: Jan. 30, (Feb. 5), (March 9), (April 24), (May 10), (July 24), Oct. 8
More, Sir Thomas: April 17, Sept. 3
Moriarity, Reverend, of Kilarney: (Dec. 17)
Moule, Handley C. G.: April 22
Murray, Andrew: Oct. 28

Neale, John Mason: March 19, (Nov. 1), (Dec. 16)
Nelson, Earl: Dec. 16
Newton, John: March 21, (Dec. 9)
"Nicene Creed": (May 22)
Nicholson, Isaac: (Aug. 10)
Norton, John: Nov. 9
Nowel, Dr. Alexander: Feb. 13
Nowell, Samuel: June 3

Oengus the Culdee: March 11
Osler, Sir William: April 20
Ovington, Irene H.: Aug. 9

Palmer, Phoebe: July 26, Oct. 30
Parker, Theodore: March 4, Oct. 17
Pascal, Blaise: Nov. 23
Pastoris, Heinrich: Feb. 15
Patrick: (Feb. 1), (March 5), March 29, (June 9), Aug. 5
Paul: Jan. 25, (Feb. 10)
Paul, Kegan: Oct. 24
Payne, Daniel A.: May 16
Penn-Lewis, Jesse: April 11
Pepwell, Henry: (Nov. 16)
Perpetua: March 7
Phelps, Elizabeth Stuart: Oct. 22
Phelps, Samuel: March 30
Phelps, William Lyon: Feb. 3
Pierce, Samuel Eyles: Aug. 10